Human Resource Management in Government

Human Resource Management in Government

Hitting the Ground Running

JONATHAN TOMPKINS

University of Montana

HarperCollins*College*Publishers

Acquisitions Editor: Leo A. W. Wiegman
Project Coordination and Electronic Page Makeup: Ruttle, Shaw & Wetherill, Inc.
Design Manager and Cover Design: Nancy Sabato
Text Design: Tomasina Webb/TWINC
Art Studio: FineLine, Inc.
Electronic Production Manager: Valerie A. Sawyer
Manufacturing Manager: Helene G. Landers
Printer and Binder: R. R. Donnelley & Sons Company
Cover Printer: R. R. Donnelley & Sons Company

For permission to use copyrighted material, grateful acknowledgment is made to the copyright holders on pp. 361–362, which are hereby made part of this copyright page.

Human Resource Management in Government: Hitting the Ground Running

Library of Congress Cataloging-in-Publication Data

Tompkins, Jonathan.
    Human resource management in government : hitting the ground
    running / Jonathan Tompkins.—1st ed.
        p.   cm.
    Includes bibliographical references and index.
    ISBN 0-06-501807-9
    1. Civil service—United States—Personnel management. I. Title.
JK765.T596 1995
353.001—dc20   94-15318
                                                         CIP

94 95 96 97 9 8 7 6 5 4 3 2 1

To Debra

Contents

Preface

The idea to write a textbook must come from somewhere. Mine was born the day a top-ranking personnel officer in state government told me that prospective managers and personnel officers must be prepared to "hit the ground running." He argued that they must possess a broader working knowledge of labor law, a clearer understanding of how human resource policies and practices contribute to the attainment of organizational objectives, and better problem-solving skills than are typically acquired from current textbooks. After giving this much thought, I concluded that more can and should be done in the classroom to prepare students interested in public service careers, and that this could be accomplished without overwhelming those students who simply wish to be introduced to the subject. Accordingly, this textbook combines a skills-based approach designed to help prepare students interested in public service to "hit the ground running" with an academic approach that introduces all students to the essentials of human resource management and the competing values and larger purposes that shape it.

This integrated approach is pursued in three ways. First, chapters attend to the practical aspects of human resource management. Although there is certainly no "one right way" to manage human resources, each chapter stops occasionally to discuss strategies that might be pursued to advantage. Second, considerable effort is made to clarify key concepts early in each chapter so that students can learn about the structures, processes, and tools of human resource management from the perspective of what they are intended to accomplish. Learning objectives are also presented at the beginning of each chapter to guide the learning process and provide benchmarks for assessing mastery of the material. Finally, classroom exercises and cases provide students with opportunities to apply key concepts and develop problem-solving skills. They are purposefully designed to encourage students to struggle with the competing values, contradictions, and compromises that human resource management often entails.

The primary concern of this textbook is how to enhance government's performance through the full development and use of its human resources. This concern is premised on the belief that an organization's success is determined above all else by how well it recruits, develops, uses, and supports its human resources. Accordingly, otherwise routine practices, such as how to appraise performance, test job applicants, or classify positions, are discussed in the context of what they are intended to achieve. This orientation is reflected in the arrangement of chapters. Each Part deals with a key task that must be performed well by the human resource function if agencies are to fulfill their stated missions in a superior manner. These include strategic planning and policy making, position management, staffing, performance management, and maintenance of supportive workplace relations.

Finally, the instrumental purposes of human resource management are discussed in the context of the political environment in which it is practiced. Public human resource management is a dynamic process shaped by politics and characterized by the clash of such competing values as merit, efficiency, social equity, political account-ability, and due process. Openly acknowledging that it is shaped by political consid-erations helps us to understand, for example, the reasons for reform movements, the gulf between theory and practice, and the persistence of patronage and partisanship. It may also help managers and personnel officers to choose appropriate courses of action from among competing alternatives.

There are several individuals I wish to thank for their professional assistance in writing this book. Foremost among these is my wife, Debra, who edited the manu-script and assisted with research. I also wish to thank Jim Nys of Personnel Plus, Inc., for his technical assistance. Lastly, I would like to thank those individuals who reviewed the manuscript and provided me with many valuable comments and sug-gestions.

Jonathan Tompkins

CHAPTER I

An Introduction to the Human Resource Function

Learning Objectives

After mastering the material contained in this chapter, you will be able to:

1. Define human resource management and its essential task.
2. Define the role of the human resource function in terms of five key tasks.
3. Use what you have learned about the line–staff relationship to evaluate conflicts you may have observed in organizational settings.
4. Describe five institutional roles performed by personnel officers and evaluate how each affects the line–staff partnership.
5. Identify the central tenets of four theoretical perspectives on human resource management and use them to develop your own perspective.

Introductory chapters serve important purposes. They introduce basic concepts, key definitions, and dominant themes so that the reader can gain the fullest value from subsequent chapters. Accordingly, this chapter defines human resource management, analyzes the respective roles of managers and personnel officers, reviews theoretical perspectives relating to human resource management, and offers a performance model designed to help students visualize the connections between human resource policies and practices and desired organizational outcomes.

The Essential Task of Human Resource Management (HRM)

The quality of our lives depends in no small measure on the services that governments provide. From safeguarding the national defense to maintaining local libraries, government programs serve the public interest in countless ways. In the final analysis, however, these services are not provided by government programs but by the people who work within them. People, not programs, clean streets, arrest lawbreakers, issue driver's licenses, and send men and women into space. Fully 17 percent of the national civilian work force, representing more than 17.2 million individuals, are engaged in public service at one level of government or another.[1] They hold jobs in a broad range of occupations and possess diverse kinds of expertise. In short, it is no exaggeration to say that our civil servants represent highly valuable human resources.

The importance of managing these resources wisely has never been greater. In these times of declining confidence in public institutions, tax revolts, and slow economic growth, governments are under mounting pressure to accomplish more with less. As will be seen in the chapters that follow, decisions regarding human resources are pivotal to their success. With so much at stake, it is crucial for governments at all levels to establish and maintain highly qualified, motivated, and productive workforces. This is the essential task of human resource management—a task that is as difficult and complex as it is important.

Defining Human Resource Management

The subject of this book is human resource management. Perhaps it can be explained best by describing what it is not. It is not simply the administration of personnel systems by personnel officers, although this is a part of it. In the early 1900s personnel administration began to develop as an area of professional practice and a field of study. The term *personnel* first appeared in a government report in 1909[2] and the first textbook on "personnel administration" was published in 1920.[3] During this period personnel administration came to be recognized as a set of administrative duties performed by trained personnel specialists. The range of these duties in the public sector quickly expanded beyond employment testing and screening to include the administration of position classification, compensation, and employee benefits systems.

The problem with focusing narrowly on personnel administration is that it tends to reinforce the separation of personnel administration from general management. The pressures confronting governments today demand a broader and more strategic perspective. The term human resource management is used in this book because it encompasses the management of people as well as the administration of personnel systems. It refers to a broader set of activities performed jointly by personnel officers and managers and with the strategic objectives of the organization clearly in mind. Megginson defines it as "the performance of all managerial functions involved in planning for, recruiting, selecting, developing, utilizing, rewarding, and maximizing the potential of the human resources of an organization."[4] Megginson's definition reflects a continuing evolution in the meaning of human resource management. Today, for example, it often refers to a specific theoretical perspective, one that views employees as assets to be invested in wisely and assumes that satisfying each employee's need for job security, personal growth, career advancement, and fair treatment is the key to enhanced organizational performance.

The term *human resource function* provides a shorthand way of referring to the activities that managers and personnel officers are jointly engaged in. A *function* is simply a specialized activity necessary to effective organizational performance. The managerial functions to which Megginson refers collectively constitute the human resource function. As will be discussed shortly, the human resource function is best viewed as a set of activities performed jointly by managers and personnel officers, rather than as a specialized staff function separate and distinct from general management. In contrast to the legal, budgeting, and auditing functions, the human resource function deals primarily with the people-related aspects of management. Among its primary tasks are the following:

Strategic Planning and Policy Making This task involves establishing organizational objectives and developing strategies and policies for achieving them. It allows agencies to anticipate future human resource needs, adjust to environmental constraints, and focus their efforts on accomplishing organizational objectives.

Position Management Performed primarily by personnel specialists, this task involves specifying job duties, identifying the knowledge and skills required to perform them, grouping similar positions into classes, and evaluating their relative worth. These efforts facilitate employee selection, budget preparation, and pay determination.

Staffing This task involves recruiting qualified job applicants and selecting those whose qualifications best match the requirements of open positions.

Performance Management This task is performed by those who directly supervise other workers. It involves training and developing employees, establishing performance standards, providing feedback, and rewarding superior performance.

Supportive Workplace Relations The purpose of this task is to create and maintain a work environment in which the expectations of employees and management are met simultaneously. It is accomplished through flexible personnel policies and employee benefits, employee assistance programs, maintenance of workplace discipline, and mechanisms for addressing the mutual concerns of labor and management.

How well these tasks are performed has a direct bearing on organizational performance. Because it is important for students of human resource management to understand how these tasks contribute to (and sometimes impede) the attainment of organizational objectives, this book examines each of them in turn.

The Human Resource Function as a Line-Staff Partnership

The advent of independent merit agencies in the late 1800s and central personnel offices in the early 1900s hastened the development of personnel administration as a profession and contributed to the growing separation of personnel administration from general management. Activities previously performed by managers were gradually transferred to personnel specialists. Applicant testing and screening duties were often given to an independent merit agency, while payroll and records keeping duties were turned over to the personnel office. Additional activities, such as classifying positions, administering benefit plans, and negotiating labor contracts were later assigned to the personnel office in response to newly emerging institutional needs. Even policy making responsibilities tended to gravitate to the personnel office over time. Although the centralization of personnel activities increased administrative efficiency, the resulting separation of personnel administration from general management meant that the linkage between personnel decisions and the attainment of agency goals could no longer be taken for granted. As later chapters will show, personnel systems can promote political neutrality, administrative efficiency, and equal employment opportunity without improving the ability of managers to fulfill their mandated obligations. Today there is growing awareness of the importance of reestablishing strategic linkages between personnel policies and practices and the attainment of organizational objectives. Success in this regard will require a *line-staff partnership* in which managers, supervisors, and personnel officers work together strategically and proactively to accomplish the central purposes of government.

To understand what is meant by a line-staff partnership we must begin with a distinction between line and staff personnel. *Line personnel* are directly involved in accomplishing organizational purposes by providing benefits and services to the public. The chief of police, as well as the rookie patrol officer, are examples of line personnel. *Staff personnel,* by contrast, assist, advise, and otherwise support line personnel in accomplishing organizational goals. Thus, personnel officers, whether situated in a central personnel office or in a particular department such as the police department, are considered staff officers. They provide assistance to line managers in developing and maintaining a productive workforce.

The line-staff distinction helps to underscore the point that the human resource function is not a set of specialized activities performed solely by the personnel staff. It refers instead to a set of personnel related responsibilities shared jointly by line managers and personnel officers. When line managers select, train, appraise, and motivate employees, they are involved by definition in human resource management. And when personnel officers assist them with daily personnel decisions and administer personnel systems designed to help them achieve unit goals, they too are involved in human resource management. Although line officers are directly responsible for accomplishing organizational goals, the efforts of the personnel staff can greatly influence whether goals are achieved. For example, without the assistance of the personnel staff in building employee morale, anticipating changes in human resource needs, and recruiting the best available talents, line managers are unlikely to accomplish their goals effectively.

Exhibit 1.1 illustrates how personnel-related responsibilities may be shared between line and staff officers. In actual practice no two organizations divide and share responsibilities in exactly the same way.

The effectiveness of the human resource function depends on the agency's degree of success in forging a partnership between line and staff officers. Together they must achieve positive results without violating merit principles or the law. Benton G. Moeller, an administrator with the U.S. Department of the Army, describes his view of the "ideal" partnership by drawing an analogy between human resource management and a jungle safari:

> *Whenever I think of the ideal staff advisor-to-manager relationship in today's Federal context, I visualize the safari movies I used to love as a child and adolescent. The great hunter could never get through the jungle without people who were cutting their way through the thicket with machetes. The wise guide's job was making sure that the hunter did not step on a poisonous snake or blunder into a lion's den. The hunter decided in advance what was to be hunted, in what vicinity and, of course, once the guide had led the party to the place where there was game, it was the responsibility of the hunter to take the risks associated with bagging it.*
>
> *I see the staff advisor functioning much as the guide and the bearers did in the jungle romance. The manager must make the major decisions. The staff advisor must understand what the manager wants to do. The advisor must use his exper-*

EXHIBIT 1.1

DIVISION OF PERSONNEL-RELATED RESPONSIBILITIES BETWEEN LINE AND STAFF

Line Executives:
- establish the goals of the human resource function
- organize the human resource function (as allowed by law)
- formulate merit system rules and personnel policies

Line Managers/Supervisors:
- establish job qualifications
- select and orient new employees
- interpret personnel policies to employees
- supervise and direct the work of subordinates
- train and develop employees
- reward, promote, and otherwise motivate employees
- initiate disciplinary actions
- appraise job performance
- initiate classification appeals
- maintain unit morale

Staff Personnel Officers:
- advise executives in the formulation of personnel policies
- develop and maintain recruitment sources and applicant pools
- conduct initial screening of job applicants
- develop and administer selection tests
- classify positions and review classification appeals
- administer employee benefit and compensation programs
- advise line officers of EEO and other legal requirements
- monitor compliance with EEO and merit system rules
- supervise EEO and merit system complaint procedures
- develop training programs and assist with individualized training
- assist in negotiating labor contracts
- provide technical assistance (e.g., job analysis)
- advise and assist line officers with supervisory duties on request
- maintain employee records

---

tise *to discuss the merits and demerits of various ways of trying to accomplish what the manager wishes to accomplish (and this may and often will involve warning the manager that one cannot shoot elephants in a game preserve or willfully violate the law or public policy if he wants to stay out of the funny papers).*[5]

A line-staff partnership of this kind is difficult to achieve because of the inevitable conflicts that arise between line and staff officers and the inherent contradictions in the roles personnel officers are asked to play in the public sector. It nonetheless represents an ideal toward which to strive.

Sources of Conflict in the Line-Staff Relationship

Because line and staff officers share responsibility for human resource management, it is important that their relationship be characterized by mutual trust and cooperation. Unfortunately, it is often characterized more by suspicion and conflict. Public agencies, as a result, face the never-ending task of creating and maintaining a constructive relationship between line and staff. Understanding the historical and institutional sources of line-staff conflict is important to building a constructive working relationship.

An underlying source of conflict is the loss of autonomy suffered by supervisors as personnel offices and formal merit systems were established around the turn of the twentieth century. Before this time supervisors handled nearly all aspects of human resource management. They hired employees after superficial checks of their credentials and put them to work with only modest instructions. They disciplined and discharged employees as they saw fit, with employees enjoying few protections from arbitrary and capricious treatment. Gradually, however, as legislative bodies and agency heads began to appreciate the importance of high morale, low turnover, and competent employees, they established central and departmental personnel offices staffed by trained professionals.

The advent of trained personnel staffs fundamentally and permanently altered the role of line supervisors. Whereas they had previously enjoyed almost complete autonomy, they now became subject to the functional authority of personnel officers. Increasingly, for example, supervisors were required to obtain approval from the personnel staff before taking certain personnel actions, such as discharging employees. In addition, supervisors now had to act within a framework of rules and procedures enforced by the personnel office (or civil service commission). From the supervisor's perspective such constraints further reduced their freedom of action and denied them the flexibility needed to achieve organizational goals. This continues to be a source of resentment and potential conflict.

A second source of conflict is lack of clarity regarding who has authority over what. The potential for conflict exists whenever two authorities operate in the same sphere and the division of that authority is not clear. As Eilbirt notes,

> *Cooperation between two authorities is never likely to be easy. The question of where the responsibility of one begins and the other ends is not subject, as a rule, to precise definition. If conflict arises, one or the other must lose face, and ultimately be subordinated or reduced in effectiveness.*[6]

Differences of opinion regarding who has responsibility for what, or who should have the final say, naturally arise in the course of pursuing organizational goals. This is especially true when line and staff officers must make decisions jointly. If one or the other party feels consistently "subordinated or reduced in effectiveness," resentments may build, further undermining line-staff relations.

A third source of conflict is differences in institutional roles and values. Charged with accomplishing operational goals, line managers focus on the immediate needs of the unit. The values of efficiency and economy are uppermost in their minds. The institutional role of the personnel officer, by contrast, embraces concerns that go beyond the immediate needs of the unit. Although responsible for assisting line managers in accomplishing agency goals, personnel officers are also responsible for ensuring compliance with personnel policies and procedures and safeguarding employee rights. In addition, statute law and professional ethics require them to protect and promote the values of equity and equal opportunity. In doing so, personnel officers may find themselves caught between legal and professional requirements and the more immediate desires of line managers. A manager, for example, may attempt to tailor a job announcement to match the qualifications of a personal acquaintance who he or she believes will be a valuable asset to the agency. The personnel officer may then feel obliged to intervene by insisting that equal employment opportunity not be denied to other applicants. The potential for conflict in this kind of situation is high, and the personnel officer may risk much in resisting an influential line manager.

The historical and institutional causes of conflict between line managers and personnel staff are not easily addressed. Nonetheless, constructive relations can be established and maintained if everyone concerned is willing to commit time and effort to the task. As discussed below, the institutional roles assigned to the personnel staff, and the degree of clarity achieved in defining who has what authority, are important factors determining the character of line-staff relations.

The Institutional Roles of Personnel Staffs

Personnel staffs exist to perform two basic organizational functions: *service* to line management and *control* of organizational behavior. Among the roles that flow from these two functions are the following:

Policy Development/Planning Role This role involves drafting personnel policies for consideration by upper management or a personnel board, providing information to assist in policy deliberations, and, ideally, participating in strategic planning. The latter involves working closely with upper management to ensure that the human resource management system is contributing effectively to the attainment of organizational goals.

Consultative Role This role involves consulting with line officers about how to comply with the law and organizational policies, how best to motivate employees, and how to handle special problems as they arise.

Routine Support Role This role involves providing routine services to line units to assist them in accomplishing their missions. Routine services may include testing and screening job applicants, classifying positions, negotiating collective bargaining agreements, and administering pay and benefit programs. They may also include routine record keeping, data gathering, and auditing.

Innovator Role This role involves constantly evaluating the effectiveness of current policies and procedures, experimenting with new ways of improving human resource management, and exerting leadership in giving human resource management a strong sense of purpose and direction. It is a role that receives little emphasis in most public agencies.

Watchdog Role This role involves monitoring the activities of line units to ensure compliance with the law, organizational policies, and merit system rules. It also involves investigating and adjudicating charges that employee rights have been violated.

The policy development/planning, consultative, routine support, and innovator roles are different aspects of the service function. Their performance promotes managerial effectiveness and goal attainment. The watchdog role, by contrast, is related to the control function. By monitoring and enforcing personnel policies, vital organizational objectives may be achieved. These include predictability of performance, consistency of behavior, coordination of effort, and protection of key values such as due process and equal opportunity.

Although both service and control roles are important to organizational success, they are seldom accorded equal weight. The priorities established between them hold important implications for line-staff relations. If a high priority is placed on control, personnel officers will emphasize their role as watchdogs. This in turn increases the potential for conflict. For example, in carrying out their responsibility for safeguarding the integrity of merit principles, personnel officers often find themselves directly at odds with supervisors. In such instances supervisors are likely to perceive personnel officers more as police than as partners in a joint enterprise.

Because control and service functions are both important to organizational success, governments must seek an appropriate balance between them, establishing enough control to achieve coordination, predictability, and protection of merit values, while placing a strong emphasis on providing personnel services to line units. There is, after all, more than one way to accomplish control objectives. Micromanagement and usurpation of managerial authority lie at one end of this continuum, whereas setting general policies to guide operational decisions and monitoring results lie at the other. The latter approach is less likely to generate conflict. In addition, the wise personnel officer seeks results through persuasion rather than through the formal exercise of authority. The development of political and interpersonal skills is particularly important in this regard.

Moeller's ideal line-staff partnership is difficult to achieve because conflicts continue to occur between line and staff officers as the former pursue their immediate operating goals and the latter intervene to safeguard merit, due process, and equal opportunity. At times personnel officers have to enforce rules, and how to do so without alienating their partners remains a central dilemma of human resource management.

Four Theoretical Perspectives

The cross-fertilization of ideas between practitioners and academics has produced several theoretical perspectives relating to human resource management. These perspectives offer distinct ideas about how the human resource function should be organized and the values, roles, and purposes it should serve. Together they have had a cumulative effect, building on each other, and continuously influencing the theory and practice of human resource management. A brief review of four of these perspectives will help introduce the key themes around which this book is organized.

The Administrative Management Perspective

This perspective emerged during the 1920s and 1930s from efforts by academicians and practitioners to identify fundamental principles of administration that would promote government efficiency and effectiveness.[7] Among its many themes, the following are particularly relevant to public human resource management:

1. Human resource management is a vital management function over which the chief executive should have full authority.
2. It is the responsibility of the chief executive to provide energy, direction, and leadership in human resource management.
3. The primary role of the personnel staff is to assist line managers in attaining their goals efficiently and effectively.

These themes received their fullest expression in the final report of the President's Committee on Administrative Management, better known as the Brownlow Committee. President Franklin Roosevelt charged the Committee with studying the organization of the executive branch and submitting recommendations regarding administrative improvements. Luther Gulick, an administrative management theorist, helped draft the final report. The influence of the administrative management perspective is readily apparent:

> Stated in simple terms these canons of efficiency require the establishment of a responsible and effective chief executive as the center of energy, direction, and administrative management; the systematic organization of all activities in the hands of a qualified personnel under the direction of the chief executive; and to aid him in this, the establishment of appropriate managerial and staff agencies.[8]

The Committee's recommendation to establish a set of staff agencies to assist the president in managing the work of government became a reality with the creation of the Executive Office of the President in 1939. Similarly, the recommendation that personnel staffs should emphasize service roles was reflected in Executive Order 7916, which mandated the establishment of personnel offices in each cabinet-level department. Another 40 years would pass, however, before the Committee's recommendation to replace the semi-independent Civil Service Commission with an agency directly accountable to the president became a reality with the establishment of the Office of Personnel Management in 1978.

The themes of the administrative management perspective continue to influence the theory and practice of human resource management today. Perhaps its most important contribution lies in its shift in emphasis, from how to administer a politically neutral civil service to how to promote efficient and effective management.

The Positive Personnel Management Perspective

The civil service reforms of the late 1800s and early 1900s were barely in place when complaints about the "negative" character of personnel management in the public sector began to surface. Such complaints eventually gave rise to what has been called positive personnel management.[9] Traditional personnel management, according to its critics, betrays a "negative" bias in at least three respects.

First, most civil service reforms have focused narrowly on the elimination of politics from personnel management rather than on the promotion of governmental effectiveness. By the 1920s civil service reformers readily acknowledged that the idea of a merit system as a "negative, formal, mechanical system of competitive examinations designed to keep the rascals out" should be replaced by "a positive, constructive plan of employment management designed to make the public service a career for trained and competent persons."[10] Mosher and Kingsley, authors of the first public personnel textbook, expressed a similar view in 1936. The concept of the personnel office as a "politics eliminator," they wrote, belongs to "the horse-and-buggy age."[11]

Second, personnel practitioners, according to critics, demonstrate more interest in utilizing the latest scientific techniques than in achieving results. This emphasis on techniques has its roots in the scientific management philosophy developed by Frederick Taylor in the early 1900s. According to Taylor, increased organizational efficiency can be achieved by using scientific methods to discover the "one best way" to perform a task, design a job, or train an employee. Not surprisingly, the newly emerging field of personnel administration focused its attention on the means for achieving technical efficiency and rationality. Job analysis techniques were developed to identify work tasks and the qualifications needed to perform them, position classification systems were developed to rationalize compensation systems, and performance rating systems were developed so that each worker's performance could be evaluated with greater accuracy.

Wallace Sayre wrote perhaps the best-known critique of the overreliance on scientific techniques in 1948. When asked to review a newly published textbook in public administration, Sayre seized the opportunity to blast what he described as "the triumph of techniques over purpose."[12] Simply put, Sayre believed that personnel administrators had so focused their attentions on the tools of the trade that they had completely lost sight of the purposes for which those tools existed. The techniques to which he referred included methods of scientific management that promoted efficiency and rationality but displayed little regard for the needs of employees; quantitative techniques that created a false sense of scientific objectivity; and the traditional methods of employee testing, position classification, and performance appraisal, which were implemented too often without determining their adequacy for achieving intended purposes.

A third "negative bias" is the tendency of merit system rules and regulations to interfere with administrative efficiency and managerial effectiveness. According to Jay M. Shafritz, abuses of authority in the nineteenth century led reformers to place accountability in procedures rather than in individuals.[13] This situation seems to have changed little. Writing in 1992, Osborne and Gaebler noted that "the control mentality lives on, creating a gridlock that turns public management into the art of the impossible."[14]

Reversing these negative biases, according to critics, will require personnel practitioners to shed their image as low-level technicians and to become actively involved in human resource management. Major themes of the positive personnel management perspective include the following:

1. Personnel administration should no longer be divorced from general management. Personnel officers and managers must work together to enhance employee morale and improve organizational performance.
2. Rules, regulations, and procedures that reduce administrative efficiency or discourage innovation should be identified and eliminated or modified.
3. Line managers should be allowed to manage. They should be held accountable for their actions through policy guidelines rather than systems of detailed rules, and through routine audits rather than close supervision.

The Strategic Planning Perspective

Strategic planning is a process in which organizations define their missions (what they exist to do), establish goals that are consistent with their missions and environmental realities, and pursue their goals strategically and proactively.[15] The logic behind strategic planning is that the members of an organization, and of each unit within it, must know where they want to go before they can focus their efforts in required directions.

The strategic planning perspective holds important implications for human resource management. Two key themes may be stated as follows:

1. Human resource managers should be fully involved in the strategic planning process as an important first step toward integrating personnel administration with general management.
2. Line managers and personnel officers at all levels of the organization should jointly establish human resource goals, strategies, and action plans that are consistent with and supportive of the organization's mission.

According to this perspective, the strategic planning process should begin with high-ranking officials, including human resource managers, establishing organizational goals and strategies for achieving them. If implemented correctly, alternative courses of action will be assessed in terms of their implications for human resource management. A decision to upgrade the kinds of services delivered, for example, may be found to be too ambitious in light of available human resources. Once organizational goals and strategies are established, the strategic planning process moves to lower levels of the organization. Line managers and personnel officers in each agency, for example, may meet to forecast human resource needs and plan how to obtain or develop them, evaluate the level of employee morale and how to raise it, and assess work performance and how to improve it. This strategic approach stands in contrast to traditional approaches that focus on individual outcomes, such as lower turnover, better job performance, and improved job satisfaction in response to specific problems as they arise.

The strategic planning process includes conscious adoption of a human resource strategy. This refers to a shared vision of what is to be achieved in the area of human resource management and how. Its primary goal is to ensure that human resource philosophies, policies, programs, and practices are systematically linked to the strategic needs of the organization.[16] Different strategies may be adopted for different purposes. Inducement strategies, for example, rely on economic rewards to increase employee productivity, investment strategies seek to increase employee competence and commitment by developing their skills and satisfying their needs, and involvement strategies aim at increasing employee commitment by providing employees with greater work autonomy and decision making authority.[17]

Despite the apparent benefits of linking human resource management with the strategic needs of the organization, strategic planning has enjoyed rather limited use in government. It requires considerable time, energy, and commitment, and is often derailed by political pressures. If it is allowed to deteriorate into meaningless exercises, it can create additional barriers to organizational effectiveness.[18] Nonetheless, for reasons that will be discussed in Chapter 2, strategic planning is likely to become increasingly more important to effective human resource management in the years ahead.

The Human Resource Management Perspective

The goals of the human resource management perspective, according to David E. Guest, are to maximize organizational integration, employee commitment, organizational flexibility, and work quality.[19] It shares with human resources theory the assumptions that employees want to contribute to organizational goals, are capable of self-direction, and respond positively to work that is personally meaningful. At the same time, it shares with scientific management theory an emphasis on individual goal setting and careful selection and training of employees.

The human resource management perspective advocates an approach that is different in important ways from what might be labeled traditional personnel management. Although there is no agreement regarding how to define the human resource management perspective, recent works generally share the following themes:

1. Human resources are an organization's most valuable asset.
2. Human resources must be managed strategically, taking into account the individual needs and expectations of employees and the strategic needs of the organization.
3. The primary role of the human resource function is to proceed in a proactive fashion to improve organizational performance through the full use and development of employees, careful management of human performance, increased employee commitment, and greater organizational flexibility.

The first theme suggests that employees should be viewed in a new light: as valuable reservoirs of untapped resources rather than as labor commodities. Although organizational performance has always depended on how well human resources are developed and utilized, this is especially true in today's postindustrial society. A significant proportion of government employees are now engaged in complex, knowledge-intensive jobs.[20] Because they possess specialized knowledge and create value through the use of their intellects, they represent particularly valuable "human capital." For this reason government agencies must be prepared to invest more funds in training and development programs and in reward systems that will allow them to successfully recruit and retain highly qualified employees.

The second theme underscores the importance of integrating routine personnel operations with overall strategic planning and management. Organizational goals, according to this perspective, are not achieved automatically by performing routine duties such as classifying, recruiting, testing, and selecting, nor by offering advice to line managers after problems have arisen. Organizational success requires personnel policies and programs to be internally consistent and to bear directly on goal accomplishment. It is not enough simply to integrate personnel operations into a strategic management process, however. Human resources must be strategically managed so that their capabilities are fully developed and utilized to the benefit of employee and employer alike.

The final theme addresses what it means to manage human resources strategically. One line of attack is to expand traditional personnel policies and programs to increase employee motivation and commitment. This process may include establishment of flexible benefits programs that recognize the diversity of employee needs; job enrichment programs that invest greater challenge, responsibility, and autonomy in each job; efforts to establish a positive work environment by enhancing the quality of work life; participative management programs that allow employees to use and develop their unique talents; and programs that use management-by-objectives to reinforce the connection between employee performance and reward. A second line of attack involves liberating human capabilities by altering operating systems. Examples include simplifying position classification standards, developing flexible compensation systems, eliminating counterproductive rules and regulations, and authorizing team-based work arrangements that lie outside of traditional job descriptions.

A few words of caution are warranted regarding the human resource management perspective. First, many ideas regarding how best to strategically manage human resources remain highly prescriptive and untested by empirical research. It would certainly be unwise to assume that these prescriptions will produce positive results in all situations. Second, many of these ideas may prove cost-prohibitive in practice. Employee development programs, for example, may not be within the means of many agencies despite their apparent benefits. Finally, many of these ideas may prove unrealistic in view of the political realities and bureaucratic structures that characterize work life in the public sector.

These four perspectives, taken in combination, lay the groundwork for several themes that are explored more fully in subsequent chapters. These include, among others, how to increase executive leadership without sacrificing political neutrality, how to retain the benefits of traditional personnel systems without allowing techniques to triumph over purpose, how to pursue human resource management goals in a truly strategic fashion, and how to invest wisely in human resources.

Linking HRM Tasks and Outcomes

Citizens expect their public institutions to perform well. Although there is considerable disagreement about what it means to perform well, citizens generally expect government agencies to achieve their mandated purposes in an efficient, cost-effective, and responsible manner. If managers and personnel officers are to think and act strategically, they must have a clear understanding of how their efforts contribute to desired results. The model presented in Exhibit 1.2 illustrates the connections between the tasks performed by the human resource function (identified earlier in this chapter), the policies and practices that flow from those tasks, and the human resource

EXHIBIT 1.2

Linking HRM Tasks and Outcomes: A Performance Model

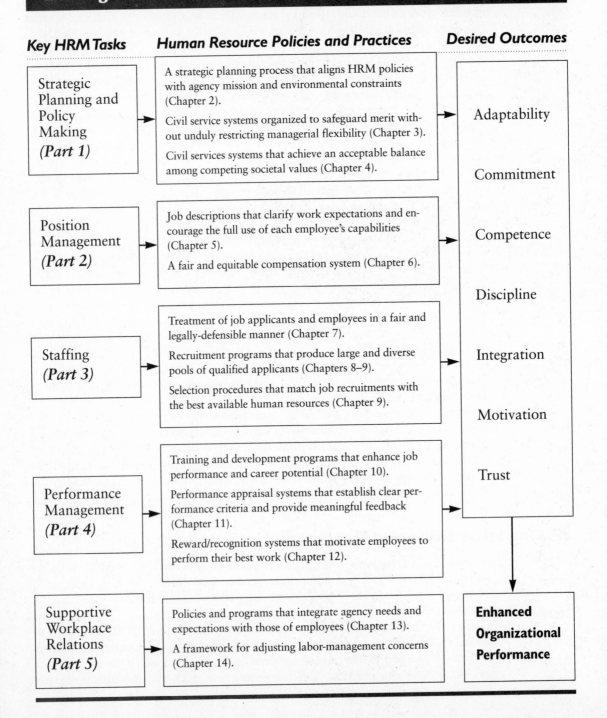

Key HRM Tasks

Strategic Planning and Policy Making *(Part 1)*

Position Management *(Part 2)*

Staffing *(Part 3)*

Performance Management *(Part 4)*

Supportive Workplace Relations *(Part 5)*

Human Resource Policies and Practices

A strategic planning process that aligns HRM policies with agency mission and environmental constraints (Chapter 2).

Civil service systems organized to safeguard merit without unduly restricting managerial flexibility (Chapter 3).

Civil services systems that achieve an acceptable balance among competing societal values (Chapter 4).

Job descriptions that clarify work expectations and encourage the full use of each employee's capabilities (Chapter 5).

A fair and equitable compensation system (Chapter 6).

Treatment of job applicants and employees in a fair and legally-defensible manner (Chapter 7).

Recruitment programs that produce large and diverse pools of qualified applicants (Chapters 8–9).

Selection procedures that match job recruitments with the best available human resources (Chapter 9).

Training and development programs that enhance job performance and career potential (Chapter 10).

Performance appraisal systems that establish clear performance criteria and provide meaningful feedback (Chapter 11).

Reward/recognition systems that motivate employees to perform their best work (Chapter 12).

Policies and programs that integrate agency needs and expectations with those of employees (Chapter 13).

A framework for adjusting labor-management concerns (Chapter 14).

Desired Outcomes

Adaptability

Commitment

Competence

Discipline

Integration

Motivation

Trust

Enhanced Organizational Performance

outcomes that are at stake. The model is intended to encourage students to view human resource management strategically. It does not claim to have identified all pertinent linkages.

The outcomes identified in the model are representative of the immediate goals or products of human resource policies and practices. They must be viewed as variables to the extent that each government or government agency chooses, either implicitly or explicitly, which outcomes to pursue and to what degree. These outcomes may be defined as follows:

Adaptability The capacity of the organization to adjust effectively to changing circumstances by reducing structural rigidities, planning strategically, and encouraging employees to develop a wide array of skills and abilities.

Commitment The degree to which employees identify with the organization and its goals; it holds important implications for turnover and potentially job performance.

Competence The extent to which employees, individually and collectively, possess the knowledge, skills, and abilities needed to perform job tasks well.

Discipline A quality that exists when workplace relations are well-ordered and governed by rules of personal conduct that are fairly and consistently enforced; it holds important implications for morale, trust, and workplace efficiency.

Integration The extent to which human resource policies and practices mesh with all other organizational policies and practices to ensure the efficient and cost-effective use of human resources.

Motivation The willingness of employees to perform their duties in a superior manner; along with competence, motivation is a key contributor to job performance.

Trust Confidence by employees that they will be treated fairly and that communications will be open and honest; it holds important implications for morale and motivation.

The model's underlying assumption is that organizations that succeed in achieving these outcomes will perform better than those that do not. The outcomes identified in the model are not, however, the only ones with which the human resource function must be concerned. As will be seen in Chapter 4, the human resource function is often asked to promote other values as well, including political neutrality, merit, equal employment opportunity, and political responsiveness.

Notes

1. U. S. Department of Commerce, *Public Employment: Compendium of Public Employment, Volume 3* (Washington, D.C.: U.S. Government Printing Office, 1991), v.

2. See James G. Stockard, *Rethinking People Management: A New Look at the Human Resources Function* (New York: AMACOM, 1980), 42.

3. The first textbook was Ordway Tead and Henry C. Metcalf, *Personnel Administration* (New York: McGraw-Hill Book Company, 1920). The first public personnel administration textbook was William E. Mosher and J. Donald Kingsley, *Public Personnel Administration* (New York: Harper & Brothers, 1936).

4. Leon C. Megginson, *Personnel Management: A Human Resources Approach* (Homewood, Illinois: Richard D. Irwin, 1981), 6.

5. Benton G. Moeller, "What Ever Happened to the Federal Personnel System?", *Public Personnel Management* 11 (Spring, 1982), 6.

6. Henry Eilbirt, "The Development of Personnel Management,"*Business History Review* 33 (Autumn 1959), 362.

7. See, as examples, Henri Fayol, *General and Industrial Management,* trans. Constance Storrs (London: Pitman Publishing, 1949); F. W. Willoughby, *Principles of Public Administration* (Washington, D.C.: Brookings Institution, 1927); and Luther Gulick and Lyndall Urwick, eds., *Papers on the Science of Administration* (New York: Institute of Public Administration, 1937).

8. Louis Brownlow, Charles E. Merriam and Luther Gulick, *Report of the President's Committee on Administrative Management* (Washington, D.C.: U.S. Government Printing Office, 1937), 2.

9. See, as examples, William Seal Carpenter, *The Unfinished Business of Civil Service Reform* (Princeton, New Jersey: Princeton University Press, 1952); and Jay M. Shafritz, *Public Personnel Management: The Heritage of Civil Service Reform* (New York: Praeger, 1975).

10. Frank Mann Stewart, *The National Civil Service Reform League* (Austin, Texas: University of Texas Press, 1929), 260.

11. Mosher and Kingsley, *Public Personnel Administration,* 84.

12. Wallace S. Sayre, "The Triumph of Techniques Over Purpose," *Public Administration Review* 8 (Spring 1948):134–137.

13. Shafritz, *Public Personnel Management.*

14. David Osborne and Ted Gaebler, *Reinventing Government: How the Entrepreneurial Spirit is Transforming the Public Sector* (Reading, MA: Addison-Wesley, 1992), 125.

15. A good discussion of strategic planning may be found in John M. Bryson, *Strategic Planning for Public and Nonprofit Organizations* (San Francisco: Jossey-Bass, 1988).

16. Randall S. Schuler, "Strategic Human Resource Management: Linking the People with the Strategic Needs of the Business," *Organizational Dynamics* 21 (Summer 1992):18–32.

17. Lee Dyer and Gerald W. Holder, "A Strategic Perspective of Human Resource Management," in Lee Dyer, ed., *Human Resource Management: Evolving Roles and Responsibilities* (Washington, D.C.: Bureau of National Affairs, 1988).

18. Osborne and Gaebler, *Reinventing Government,* 234.

19. David E. Guest, "Human Resource Management and Industrial Relations," *Journal of Management Studies* 24 (September 1987):503–521.

20. Eugene B. McGregor, Jr., "The Public Sector Human Resource Puzzle: Strategic Management of a Strategic Resource," *Public Administration Review* 48 (November/December 1988):941–950.

Part 1

Strategic Planning and Policy Making

Human resource management does not occur in a vacuum. It is shaped by the nature and purposes of government, organizational structures, social values, stakeholder interests, and changes taking place in the external environment. These contextual factors—the subjects of Part 1—sometimes constrain the attainment of organizational objectives. For this reason strategic planning and policy making is potentially the most important task that the human resource function can perform. One of its primary purposes is to adjust to contextual factors in ways that enhance organizational performance. Where human resource management is practiced strategically, agency heads and human resource managers work together, within boundaries set by political executives and legislative bodies, to draft policies and plan for the future. Together they seek to integrate the means and ends of human resource management by developing policies with the agency's mission, stakeholders, and internal and external constraints in mind.

Linking HRM Tasks and Outcomes: A Performance Model

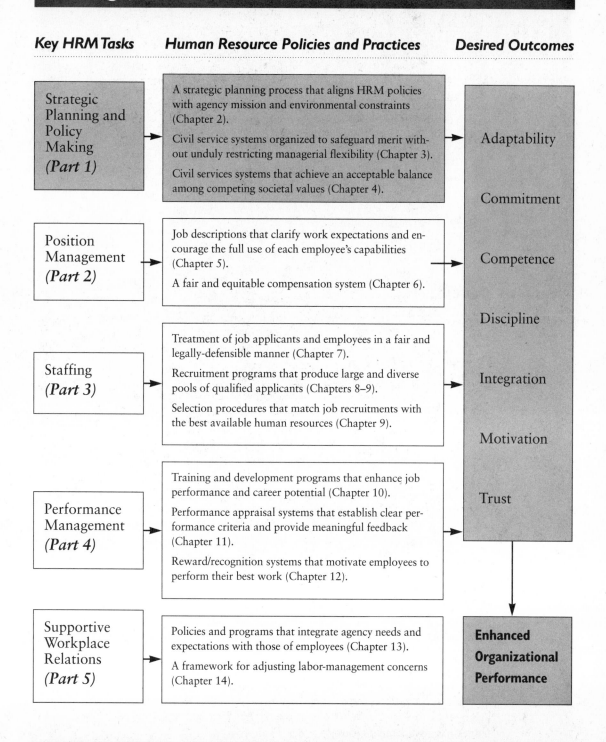

Key HRM Tasks | **Human Resource Policies and Practices** | **Desired Outcomes**

Strategic Planning and Policy Making (Part 1)

A strategic planning process that aligns HRM policies with agency mission and environmental constraints (Chapter 2).

Civil service systems organized to safeguard merit without unduly restricting managerial flexibility (Chapter 3).

Civil services systems that achieve an acceptable balance among competing societal values (Chapter 4).

Position Management (Part 2)

Job descriptions that clarify work expectations and encourage the full use of each employee's capabilities (Chapter 5).

A fair and equitable compensation system (Chapter 6).

Staffing (Part 3)

Treatment of job applicants and employees in a fair and legally-defensible manner (Chapter 7).

Recruitment programs that produce large and diverse pools of qualified applicants (Chapters 8–9).

Selection procedures that match job recruitments with the best available human resources (Chapter 9).

Performance Management (Part 4)

Training and development programs that enhance job performance and career potential (Chapter 10).

Performance appraisal systems that establish clear performance criteria and provide meaningful feedback (Chapter 11).

Reward/recognition systems that motivate employees to perform their best work (Chapter 12).

Supportive Workplace Relations (Part 5)

Policies and programs that integrate agency needs and expectations with those of employees (Chapter 13).

A framework for adjusting labor-management concerns (Chapter 14).

Adaptability

Commitment

Competence

Discipline

Integration

Motivation

Trust

Enhanced Organizational Performance

CHAPTER 2

The Political and Social Environment

Learning Objectives

After mastering the material contained in this chapter, you will be able to:

1. Explain how and why human resource management in the public sector differs from that in the private sector.
2. Provide examples of how elected officials have manipulated personnel systems to achieve greater political control over government agencies.
3. Provide examples of how managers have bent or violated merit rules to obtain the flexibility they believed they needed to achieve agency goals.
4. Describe the challenges that changing technologies, legal requirements, workforce characteristics, and public attitudes are posing for human resource management.
5. Suggest several ways personnel staffs can assist government agencies in responding to challenges posed by their external environments.

Human resource management in the public sector is shaped not only by the structure of personnel systems but also by the nature and purposes of government and the many changes occurring in government's external environment. Exhibit 2.1 presents five factors that affect various aspects of human resource management, including the skills required to perform work tasks, the availability of skilled workers, the means by which they are attracted to the organization and motivated to do their best work, and the way personnel decisions are made. An understanding of these factors is important if managers and personnel officers are to assist governments in responding appropriately to the many challenges facing them. This chapter examines the unique characteristics of human resource management in the public sector, describes how politics permeates the policies and practices of human resource management, and reviews factors in the external environment that pose special challenges for governments today.

EXHIBIT 2.1

ENVIRONMENTAL FACTORS AFFECTING THE PRACTICE OF
HUMAN RESOURCE MANAGEMENT

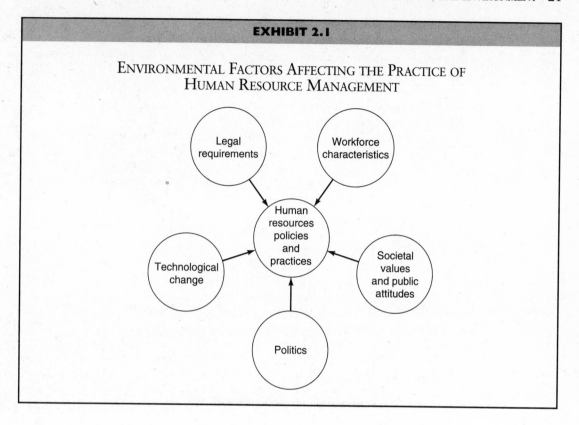

Characteristics of Human Resource Management in the Public Sector

All organizations must recruit, select, and motivate employees if they are to remain viable. But despite basic similarities in how these ends are achieved, human resource management in the public and private sectors differ in several important respects. First, although government agencies are charged with providing public services in an efficient manner, their actions are not driven by the profit motive. Nor are they subject to the same competitive pressures because their services are often of a monopolistic character. As a result, although budgetary constraints may create a heightened concern for productivity, there is not quite the same pressure to promote efficiency, select the most highly qualified applicants, or keep labor costs low. Agency goals also tend to be vague, and without profit to serve as a yardstick it is more difficult to measure the effectiveness of human resource management.

Second, personnel policies in the public sector are established through a relatively open process in which outcomes are influenced by the demands and expectations of many actors, including members of the legislative and judicial branches of government, other executive branch agencies, interest groups, political parties, and the media. As a result, even where there is a high commitment to the wise use and development of human resources, personnel policies may be responsive to other values, including merit, equal opportunity, political neutrality, and veterans' preference. Economy is another competing value. Under pressure from taxpayers, legislative bodies may refuse to authorize or adequately fund salary increases and the kinds of employee benefits that are important to government's ability to attract and retain the best available job applicants. State personnel directors reported in a recent survey that their greatest frustrations resulted from inadequate resources and political meddling by legislatures and appointed department heads.[1]

Third, as a result of how power is divided in American government, managers and personnel officers often find themselves caught in a struggle between the legislature and chief executive for control of the bureaucracy. Political appointees, for example, may pressure civil servants to act in ways contrary to legislative intent, professional ethics, or the public interest as defined by their professional expertise. Legislative committees and interest groups may exert similar pressures. Subject to more than one boss, and working in a climate characterized by political conflict, agency personnel may find it extremely difficult to pursue program goals with consistency and singleness of purpose.

Finally, civil servants in democratic systems are held accountable for their actions through controls exercised by other political actors and through systems of law that establish their authority and limit their range of options. As a result, civil servants generally work within more highly centralized personnel systems, are constrained by more rules and regulations, and are subject to greater public scrutiny than their private sector counterparts. Constraints are particularly apparent in the area of employee discipline. Because public managers must be prepared to defend the decisions they make, disciplinary systems are characterized by formal procedures for protecting each employee's due process rights and paper trails for showing that all infractions have been documented and procedural requirements faithfully observed.

The Political Environment of Human Resource Management

It should be clear from the foregoing analysis that public human resource management takes place in an environment permeated by politics. Personnel decisions are affected by the interplay of many values, and efficiency and effectiveness may or may not be foremost among them. As a result, students entering or returning to the agency environment who view their jobs in terms of the rational application of professional expertise untainted by political considerations soon become frustrated and disillusioned. Successful job performance for managers and personnel officers alike often requires a high degree of tolerance for ambiguity, a full understanding of politics, an ability to deal with political conflict, and an ability to distinguish legitimate political demands from potentially illegitimate ones.

Frank J. Thompson draws a useful distinction between *elective* and *generic* personnel politics.[2] The former refers to the involvement by elected officials and their appointees in specific personnel decisions, such as whom to hire, and the latter refers to efforts by various individuals—elected officials, political appointees, career civil servants, legislators, and interest group representatives—to influence the substance of personnel policies.

Elective Personnel Politics

One type of elective personnel politics is evident in the patronage systems that prevailed in the 1800s and that still exist to a certain extent in state and local jurisdictions. Under patronage systems, politicians maintained the strength of the party apparatus by providing government jobs to individuals in exchange for their efforts on the party's behalf. Political considerations, not job-related qualifications, determined who was selected and retained in government employment. In the late 1800s and early 1900s, as more and more government employees were selected through the use of competitive examinations, this kind of politics came to influence personnel decisions to a much smaller degree.

This does not mean, however, that patronage no longer influences personnel decisions. A case that reached the Supreme Court in 1990 provides an interesting example of the resilience of patronage politics.[3] On November 12, 1980, Governor James Thompson of Illinois instituted a hiring freeze covering 60,000 positions in state government. No position could be filled by initial hire, promotion, or transfer without first obtaining approval from the Governor's Office of Personnel. In deciding which exceptions to grant, the Office of Personnel allegedly used political criteria, including whether the person to be hired, promoted, or transferred had voted in Republican primaries, provided financial or other support to the Republican Party, promised to join and work for the Party in the future, or had the support of Republican officials at the state or local levels. Cynthia B. Rutan, a state employee since 1974, brought suit along with several other employees claiming that she had been repeatedly denied promotions to supervisory positions because she had not supported the Republican party. Governor Thompson, the plaintiffs argued, had replaced the merit system with a patronage system under the guise of a hiring freeze. In remanding the case to the District Court, the Supreme Court ruled that while the use of political criteria may be permissible for upper-level, policy-determining positions, applying them to all other civil servants constitutes a violation of their First Amendment rights.

A second type of elective personnel politics Thompson labels *leadership politics*. This is the use of the personnel system by elected officials and their appointees to ensure the bureaucracy's responsiveness to their political agendas. The process begins with the appointment of politically loyal individuals to strategically important positions at or near the top of the bureaucratic hierarchy. These individuals in turn attempt to direct the activities of career civil servants so that they are consistent with the leadership's policy agenda. Within certain limits leadership politics is necessary to and consistent with principles of democratic governance. Because elected executives are responsible for the faithful execution of the law, they must possess adequate means for holding the bureaucracy accountable. They may also claim to have a mandate from the voters to determine the policy directions the bureaucracy will take. But elected officials often find that the power of appointment is not sufficient to guarantee their political control over the career civil service. In practice, elected officials and their appointees sometimes encounter civil servants who are unsympathetic to their policy goals, and they may be tempted to overstep legitimate boundaries in their efforts to secure bureaucratic compliance.

A classic example of this kind of elective politics came to light during the Watergate hearings. The *Malek Manual*, written by a White House personnel officer named Frederick Malek, warned President Nixon that his conservative social agenda might be sabotaged by an unsympathetic bureaucracy and identified several ways to get around merit system rules.[4] Such actions were warranted, according to Malek, because policy, program, or management control cannot be achieved without political control. And because "Political disloyalty and insimpatico relationships with the Administration, unfortunately, are not grounds for the removal or suspension of an employee,"[5] extraordinary measures must be used, he argued, to get rid of troublesome employees or to create an environment sufficiently threatening to ensure their cooperation. Exhibit 2.2 provides excerpts from the *Malek Manual*. Regardless of whether they are technically illegal, strategies of this kind clearly violate the spirit of the law.

Merit system rules may also be circumvented by appointed or career managers in an effort to increase their administrative flexibility. This occurs when managers believe that personnel rules and procedures are interfering with their ability to hire the most qualified job applicants, discipline unproductive employees, or reward and retain their best workers. A common example occurs when, despite vacancy announcements and equal opportunity procedures that give the appearance of an open, competitive recruitment process, a job is "wired" for a particular individual. Often this is accomplished through the use of "creative job descriptions." Individuals are informally recruited for a position, and the job requirements are then tailored to fit that person's job qualifications so that he or she will appear to be the most "meritorious" applicant. A second technique is to hire the desired candidate as a temporary employee, which usually can be done quickly and without an open competition, and moving him or her into a permanent position after the new employee has established the necessary qualifications. A third technique, which is more clearly illegal but occasionally done nonetheless, is to actively discourage those highest on the list of eligible applicants from accepting the open position so that an individual farther down the list may be reached. Applicants may be told, for example, that the work is unpleasant or allows few opportunities for advancement.[6]

Hiring authorities occasionally resort to these kinds of maneuvers to achieve predictability and control over the hiring process. Unconvinced that merit procedures produce the best candidates, or wishing to avoid the surprises that sometimes occur when hiring an unknown person, they may feel justified in informally recruiting personal acquaintances whose qualifications are known to them. Although such practices may serve immediate managerial purposes, they nonetheless threaten merit principles. Ironically, pressures placed on managers and personnel officers to bend the rules may become greater as reformers push for more executive control over career civil servants. As will be seen in Chapter 4, some critics believe that the 1978 civil service reforms have politicized human resource management in the federal sector to an unacceptable degree.

Governments at all levels continue to search for an acceptable balance between the values of political control, managerial flexibility, and operational effectiveness on the one hand, and other important values such as merit and equal employment opportunity on the other. In the meantime, situations often arise in which personnel officers are asked to choose between their responsibility for safeguarding merit and equal opportunity and their duty to assist managers in achieving their operational objectives. For example, with a greater number of married couples pursuing professional

EXHIBIT 2.2

EXCERPTS FROM THE MALEK MANUAL

Techniques for Removal Through Organizational or Management Procedures

The Civil Service system creates many hardships in trying to remove undesirable employees from their positions. . . . Even if you follow the time consuming process of documenting a case to proceed with an adverse action, the administrative and legal process is slow and lengthy and great damage can accrue to the Department prior to your successful conclusion of your case. However, there are several techniques which can be designed, carefully, to skirt around the adverse action proceedings.

a. Individual Techniques

(a-1) Frontal Assault: You simply call an individual in and tell him he is no longer wanted, that you'll assist him in finding another job and will keep him around until such time as he finds other employment. . . . You, naturally, point out that should he not accept such an offer, and he later is forced to resign or retire through regular process or on his own volition, that his employment references from the Department and his permanent record may not look the same as if he accepted your offer. There should be no witnesses in the room at the time.

(a-2) Transfer Technique: By carefully researching the background of the proposed employee-victim, one can always establish that geographical part of the country and/or organizational unit to which the employee would rather resign than obey and accept transfer orders. . . . It is always suggested that a transfer be accompanied with a promotion, if possible. Since a promotion is *per se* beneficial to the employee, it immediately forecloses any claim that the transfer is an adverse action.

(a-3) Special Assistant Technique (The Traveling Salesman): This technique is especially useful for the family man and those who do not enjoy traveling. What you do is to suddenly recognize the outstanding abilities of your employee-victim and immediately seize upon his competence and talent to assign him to a special research and evaluation project. . . . Along with his promotion and assignment your expert is given extensive travel orders criss-crossing him across the country to towns (hopefully with the worst accommodations possible) of a population of 20,000 or under. Until his wife threatens him with divorce unless he quits, you have him out of town and out of the way. When he finally asks for relief you tearfully reiterate the importance of the project and state that he must continue to obey travel orders or resign. Failure to obey travel orders is a grounds for immediate separation.

b. The Layering Technique

The layering technique . . . is an organizational technique to "layer" over insubordinate subordinates, managers who are loyal and faithful. This technique, however, requires at least the temporary need for additional slots. . . . You have thus layered into the organization into key positions your own people, still isolating your road-blocks into powerless make-shift positions. In all likelihood the [employee-victims] will probably end up resigning out of disgust and boredom.

EXHIBIT 2.2 *(continued)*

c. Shifting Responsibilities and Isolation Technique

This is a classic organizational technique first introduced by Franklin D. Roosevelt.... Its purpose is to isolate and bypass an entire organization which is so hopeless that there is an immediate desire to deal with nobody in the organization at all. This shifting responsibilities and isolation technique entails the setting up of a parallel organization to one already in existence, and giving that new organization most of the real authorities previously vested in the old organization it parallels.

d. New Activity Technique

Another organizational technique for the wholesale isolation and disposition of undesirable employee-victims is the creation of an apparently meaningful, but essentially meaningless, new activity to which they are all transferred. This technique, unlike the shifting responsibilities and isolation technique designed to immobilize a group of people in a single organizational entity, is designed to provide a single barrel into which you can dump a large number of widely located bad apples.

Source: U.S. Congress, Senate, Select Committee on Presidential Campaign Activities, *Executive Session Hearings Before the Select Committee on Presidential Campaign Activities, Watergate and Related Activities,* Book 19 (Washington, D.C.: Government Printing Office, 1974):9006–9010.

careers simultaneously, managers sometimes pressure personnel officers to find a position for the spouse of a desired job candidate even if it means bending or violating merit rules to do so. In such instances personnel officers may comply with pressures to subvert merit principles either because it represents the course of least resistance or because they lack sufficient professional training. Although internalizing professional values does not eliminate politics from personnel decisions, as more personnel officers receive professional training they will become more adept at resisting pressures from their superiors that they know overstep legitimate boundaries.

Generic Personnel Politics

Generic personnel politics refers to efforts by various individuals and groups to influence the substance of personnel policies. Although elective politics has received more attention in the personnel literature than generic politics, understanding the influence of the latter on human resource management is also important. Generic politics are most apparent when political coalitions form to influence policy decisions made within an agency or external to it. Personnel policies involving such issues as employee rights, affirmative action, sexual harassment, and veterans' preference are often the vehicles through which social change is accomplished. Jobs, after all, are valuable societal resources. They represent important opportunities for social mobility and financial security for those who can obtain them. With so much at stake, many individuals and organized groups compete to influence the substance of personnel policies. Political battles are often waged over routine decisions as well. Performance appraisal systems, for example, have diverse objectives, including employee development, performance improvement, risk management, and rationalization of the distribution of organizational rewards. Much political maneuvering may take place as individuals with different points of view seek to define system objectives and appraisal formats. Such policy decisions are shaped by the mobilization of political values as well as by the technical application of professional expertise, and it is important for students of human resource management to understand that the influence of politics is not inherently irrational or pernicious.

Challenges Posed by a Changing Environment

The human resource management system may be viewed as an open system in which human resource policies and practices are constantly being shaped and reshaped by changes taking place in the external environment. Technological advances, demographic shifts, new laws and judicial decisions, and changing public attitudes all pose special challenges for government agencies. Effective attainment of agency goals depends in part on how well the human resource function assists government in responding to these challenges.

A Changing Workforce

Release of the Hudson Institute's *Workforce 2000* report in 1987 and *Civil Service 2000* report in 1988 sent shock waves through the public and private sectors.[7] It described trends taking place in the nation's social and economic environment that will pose serious challenges for organizations of all kinds well into the future. Among its projections are the following:

- The workforce will grow more slowly than at any time since the 1930s because of declining birth rates.
- The average age of the workforce will rise with the aging of the baby boom generation and the shrinking pool of young workers entering the labor market.
- Most of the new entrants into the labor force will be women, minorities, and immigrants.
- Jobs will demand increasingly higher levels of knowledge and technical skills.

These trends threaten to adversely affect government in several ways. First, as growth in the labor force slows, governments are likely to experience increased competition from other employers in recruiting skilled workers. The predicted gap between the skill levels of new workers and skill requirements of jobs is particularly troubling to government agencies because they depend heavily on jobs requiring high levels of knowledge and skills. Concerned about the prospect of increasingly competitive labor markets, governments at all levels are taking steps to prevent further deteriorations in the quality of their workforces.[8] These include upgrading their human resources planning capabilities; initiating aggressive recruitment programs; improving salaries, benefits, and working conditions; and committing additional resources to training and developing current employees. Although more resources are being invested in various innovative activities, progress has been described as "spotty."[9]

Second, the increasing number of working couples, working mothers, and single parents in the workforce is creating a greater diversity of employee needs and expectations. Today's workers have a wide range of personal obligations to fulfill, including raising families, commuting, continuing their education, caring for elders, and running important errands during work hours. As a result, government's ability to recruit and retain competent employees, and the degree of commitment it can expect from them, may depend on its willingness to help workers fulfill their personal obligations as well as achieve their career goals. Cognizant of this fact, many governments are now experimenting with innovative kinds of personnel policies and programs, including flexible work schedules, cafeteria benefit plans, child care assistance, expanded leave policies, and enhanced opportunities for personal growth and development (See Chapters 10 and 13).

Finally, as demographic changes produce workforces that are more diverse in their racial, ethnic, and gender composition, governments will be challenged to manage the resulting diversity effectively. An increasing number of new recruits, for example, may be burdened with lower levels of language competence, poorer educational preparation, culture-based behaviors that may be easily misunderstood, and difficulties associated with reconciling the demands of work and family. Greater diversity may also heighten interpersonal conflict within the organization. Concerned about the potentially negative effects of these factors on organizational performance, many governments have established diversity management training programs in recent years. The goals of these programs are to assist women and minorities in ways that will help them advance successfully within the organization and to provide managers and employees alike with the interpersonal skills and cross-cultural awareness necessary for working together effectively.

Factors cited in the *Workforce 2000* report—tight labor markets, mismatches between job requirements and employee skills, and dramatic demographic changes—indicate a pressing need to transform traditional human resource policies and practices. Nonetheless, it is important for agencies to investigate the extent to which these predictions are valid for them before attempting to define appropriate responses. Research conducted by the U.S. General Accounting Office (GAO) indicates that some of its predictions may be overstated.[10] Labor economists consulted by the GAO concluded that widespread labor shortages are unlikely to occur, and those shortages that do occur are likely to be limited to certain occupations, agencies, and geographic areas. Evidence collected by the GAO did, however, support other projections contained in the *Workforce 2000* report. For example, workforces will certainly become more diverse as the result of demographic trends, although their affects may be felt more slowly than implied in the report. The GAO concluded that the trends were serious enough to justify taking immediate steps to ensure that governments are competitive in attracting and retaining the best available workers.

There is yet another change occurring in the labor force that is not encompassed by these demographic trends. Values regarding work are also changing.[11] Klare describes this change as follows,

Where once work was seen as a religious duty, a fate to be endured, or a mere means to the end of acquiring income, it is now increasingly understood as one of

the central opportunities in life to grow, to experience autonomy from and connectedness with others, and to acquire respect.[12]

If autonomy and opportunities for personal growth are becoming more important to workers, then governments may have to invest more in career development, job enrichment, and participative management if they are to maintain highly motivated and productive workforces. Not all workers, however, will insist on opportunities for personal growth at work. As values change, some workers may focus instead on leisure and recreational opportunities outside of the workplace. Motivating these employees may prove to be especially difficult.

The challenges represented by a changing workforce are causing governments to rethink the role of the personnel office and to consider expanding its activities beyond the traditional categories of personnel administration. With tighter labor markets and more diverse workforces, employees can no longer be recruited, motivated, and managed through traditional "one-size-fits-all" personnel policies and practices. Appropriate, strategically determined changes in policies and practices are required if the human resource function is to assist government agencies in coping with a changing environment. These changes are explored in greater detail in the chapters that follow.

Changes in Technology

The rapid rate of technological change is altering the organization and character of work, as well as the work experience itself. The organization of work, for example, is being dramatically altered by the extensive use of automated, computer-based technologies. The implications of these changes are several. Desktop computers are now available to most white collar workers, creating extensive training needs in word processing, electronic spreadsheets, and data-based management. Those who use these technologies and those who maintain the systems require higher-level knowledge and skills, thereby intensifying recruitment and retention problems. Technical and professional workers in particular are highly mobile and are harder to recruit and retain. Computers are also changing traditional communications patterns by allowing workers to communicate with other employees across institutional boundaries and allowing them greater access to information. This in turn may hasten the movement toward decentralized organizational structures and create a need for managers to be trained in how to manage effectively in more open, less hierarchical work environments.

A second aspect of technological change is reflected in the growing number of government jobs that require specialized knowledge and skills. Most government employees now hold knowledge-intensive jobs.[13] The specialized training and cumulative insights that they invest in their work are the ultimate determinants of the quality of government services. The diagnostic skill of health professionals, the subject-matter competence of teachers, and the knowledge of community networks possessed by social workers are examples of the "human capital" represented by government workers today.[14] Knowledge-intensive work increases the strategic value of employees. It also increases the importance of managing human resources strategically. It is now more important than ever to invest organizational resources in employee training and development programs and to take steps to ensure that human capital does not depreciate through lack of use. All of this requires planning of a kind that is practiced only rarely today—planning designed to determine what human resources are needed to achieve strategic objectives, how to attract and retain individuals with the required knowledge and skills, how to invest wisely in their continued training and development, and how to alter management styles and organizational structures so that human resources may be used to best advantage.

A Changing Legal Climate

Changes in employment law have placed increasingly stricter boundaries on personnel decisions. Among the many laws, judicial decisions, and executive orders regulating the conduct of human resource management, none have had a greater impact than those dealing with the protection of civil rights. Where once government employers were relatively free to select, promote, and discipline workers as they pleased (as long as they stayed within existing merit rules), they now cannot, without running the risk of lawsuit, exclude job applicants or discharge employees who are pregnant or thought likely to become pregnant. They cannot reject job applicants with disabilities unless it can be demonstrated that they are unable to perform job requirements adequately or that they pose serious risk of injury to others. Employers cannot treat employees differently on the basis of race, gender, or national origin; nor can they maintain selection procedures that adversely affect the employment opportunities of women and minorities unless the validity of those procedures can be established. To fulfill their legal obligations, agencies have also had to establish information systems for tracking the fate of job applicants and determining the racial and gender balance of their workforces at each organizational level.

By asking managers and personnel officers to be foot soldiers in the battle to eliminate discriminatory biases, society has placed additional burdens on them. First, personnel officers must obtain the knowledge and skills necessary to validate examinations and develop affirmative action plans and information systems. Second, both managers and personnel officers must possess a broad understanding of employment law if they are to safeguard the civil rights of employees and protect the organization from legal risk. Finally, personnel officers are expected to act as the organization's conscience by insisting on fair and unbiased treatment of employees—a role that may bring them into more frequent conflict with line managers.

Since the 1970s, an employee rights movement has emerged that is likely to rival the civil rights movement in terms of its impact on human resource management. It can be seen in the greater willingness of employees to assert their right to be treated fairly. Second, it can be seen in the rise of collective bargaining in the public sector and the resulting establishment of contractual rights. Third, it can be seen in the enactment of laws that safeguard each worker's right to a healthy and safe work environment and in demands by nonsmokers for a smoke-free work environment. Finally, evidence that employee rights are expanding can be seen in the growing willingness of courts to recognize exceptions to the at-will employment doctrine that allows employees with no fixed term of employment to be terminated at the discretion of the employer. More courts are now willing to view a job as a property right and to allow employees to sue for wrongful discharge. Legislatures are also demonstrating a greater willingness to redefine the balance between managerial prerogatives and employee rights. In 1988, for example, Montana became the first state to enact a wrongful discharge law prohibiting employers from discharging employees without a showing of good cause.[15]

The employee rights movement, like the civil rights movement, has created special challenges for human resource management. New legal requirements, the willingness of the courts to allow wrongful discharge suits, and an increasingly litigious workforce, have caused personnel staffs to work harder at maintaining positive employee relations. They are more likely today to rely on grievance procedures, progressive discipline systems, employee assistance programs, and improved performance appraisals to safeguard rights and settle disputes. At other times, however, agencies seem more interested in avoiding litigation than in promoting effective management practices. They may, for example, fail to discipline employees whose work histories clearly warrant sanctions because they fear losing a court challenge. Or they may stop issuing employee handbooks for fear that they may contain implied contractual obligations. In such instances risk management takes priority over effective human resource management, to the great frustration of managers, personnel officers, and employees alike. Achieving simultaneous success in avoiding legal risks, protecting employee rights, and improving organizational performance remains a challenging task.

Changing Public Attitudes

Surveys and opinion polls provide evidence that public confidence in government and those who do the work of government has declined significantly since the mid-1960s.[16] Public attitudes are vitally important to governmental effectiveness. Without the public's trust and confidence, the morale of public employees soon deteriorates and the ability of governments at all levels to recruit the nation's best and brightest talents is severely undermined. Without a competent and committed public service, government loses its capacity to govern.[17]

Government's negative public image, reinforced by vigorous political attacks on civil bureaucracies, has led to a reduced willingness to invest in employee pay and benefits and administrative capacity generally. Cutbacks in resources, according to Lane and Wolf, tend to occur most heavily in the area of human resources:

> Employees are released, positions are reduced, and surviving employees are forced to contend with diminishing material resources and uncertain career prospects. The generally restrictive and negative personnel actions that are required during program cutbacks undermine the human resources in public organizations. In many cases, the simple threat of severe personnel actions diminishes administrative capacity.[18]

Coping with such negative impacts will also prove challenging.

The kind of "bureaucrat bashing" that often takes place during electoral campaigns further encourages the public to blame the ills of the country on its civil servants. Government agencies have responded to the challenges posed by negative public attitudes by placing a higher emphasis on productivity. However, there is little they can do to improve employee morale and the success of their recruitment efforts as long as political leaders are unwilling to do their part. As the following quotations indicate, perhaps the first steps are being taken by political leaders, at least at the federal level, to restore public confidence in their civil servants:[19]

For all the glories of Adam Smith, somebody has to set the rules and adjudicate disputes. Somebody has to defend the country and explore space. Somebody has to keep the air clean and the environment safe for the next generation. Somebody has to respond to those more mundane, but nonetheless sometimes quite challenging, assignments of keeping government working effectively and efficiently if self government is to work at all. (Paul A. Volcker, 1986)

How well the tasks of government are done affects the quality of the lives of all our people. Moreover, the success of any political leadership in implementing its policies and objectives depends heavily upon the expertise, quality, and commitment of the professional career employees of government. (President George Bush, 1989)

Our bedrock premise is that ineffective government is not the fault of people in it. Our government is full of well-intentioned, hard-working, intelligent people— managers and staff. We intend to let our workers pursue excellence. (Vice President Al Gore, 1993)

Safeguarding the capacity to govern requires civil service systems that are supported by a public that demands high standards of competence and integrity from civil servants, values and respects the work they do, and compensates them well. One of the greatest challenges governments will face in the decades ahead lies in restoring public confidence and nurturing public support.

The Emergence of Strategic Human Resource Management

The primary focus of personnel as a field of study has evolved from performing routine personnel operations efficiently *(personnel administration)*, to improving organizational effectiveness through a line-staff partnership *(personnel management)*, to managing vital human resources in ways that are strategically linked to organizational objectives *(strategic human resource management)*.[20] In theoretical terms, strategic human resource management combines the strategic planning and human resource management perspectives defined in Chapter 1. Its emergence in the 1980s, in the realms of both theory and practice, is largely attributable to the impacts of technological and demographic change. Turbulent environments naturally give rise to the realization that organizations must reexamine their basic missions and deliberately shape their structures, operating procedures, and personnel decisions to achieve their missions.[21]

Exhibit 2.3 illustrates a strategic approach to human resource management. It involves establishing a strategic planning process, making strategic-level decisions regarding the organization's mission and general strategies for achieving it, and making tactical-level decisions regarding the design of operating systems and the deployment of resources. The latter involves linking the kinds of workforce characteristics that are needed to achieve strategic goals with the knowledge, skills, and abilities of the available workforce. Routine day-to-day personnel operations such as staffing and employment are then conducted in such a way as to achieve those linkages.

According to Eugene B. McGregor Jr., the strategic management of strategic resources requires all managers to "learn to think systematically about the many connections between strategy and people."[22] But practicing strategic human resource management as depicted in Exhibit 2.3 may not be possible in the public sector for

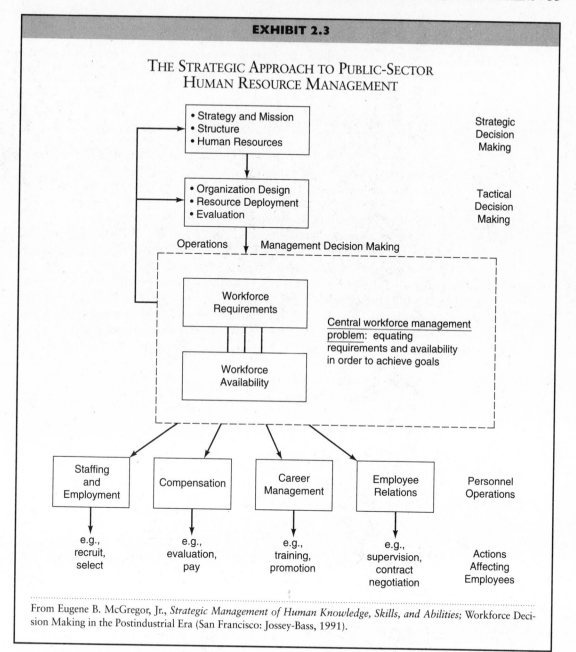

EXHIBIT 2.3

THE STRATEGIC APPROACH TO PUBLIC-SECTOR HUMAN RESOURCE MANAGEMENT

- Strategy and Mission
- Structure
- Human Resources

Strategic Decision Making

- Organization Design
- Resource Deployment
- Evaluation

Tactical Decision Making

Operations   Management Decision Making

Workforce Requirements

Central workforce management problem: equating requirements and availability in order to achieve goals

Workforce Availability

Staffing and Employment	Compensation	Career Management	Employee Relations	Personnel Operations
e.g., recruit, select	e.g., evaluation, pay	e.g., training, promotion	e.g., supervision, contract negotiation	Actions Affecting Employees

From Eugene B. McGregor, Jr., *Strategic Management of Human Knowledge, Skills, and Abilities; Workforce Decision Making in the Postindustrial Era* (San Francisco: Jossey-Bass, 1991).

two reasons. First, personnel departments are not strategically placed. For the most part, they remain staff agencies that enjoy relatively low status in the organization. They continue to perform essentially policing and routine administrative duties, and they are rarely involved in strategic planning. Second, the fragmented character of governmental systems and the resulting political interference from outside the agency make it virtually impossible to follow through on strategic plans with any degree of consistency. As McGregor notes, "Indeed, in the minds of many a case-hardened practitioner, the idea of strategic public-sector human resource management may well be an oxymoron."[23] But the obstacles confronting strategic human resource management in the public sector does not make it any less important. The concept itself represents a goal toward which to strive.

■ **CASE 2.1**   Merit, Agency Needs, and the Dual-Career Couple[24]

Tom and Susan Westin are a dual-career couple. Susan supported Tom while he completed his degree in urban planning and Tom supported Susan as she completed joint degrees in public administration and law. Now for the first time they are free to pursue their professional careers simultaneously. Tom has just interviewed for the position of Assistant City Planner in River Grove, a rapidly growing city of approximately 120,000 inhabitants. During the interview Tom explained that, although he liked the area of River Grove very much, his ability to accept an offer of employment would depend on Susan's success in finding a position with the City as well.

Members of the selection committee view Tom as a "superstar," possessing precisely the qualifications they have been looking for. The Director of the Planning Office, Bill Johnson, calls the Director of Personnel, Christine Abrams, and asks her to make every effort to find employment for Susan. This places the Personnel Office in a serious bind. Although there is no nepotism policy forbidding the employment of spouses, and although there is a vacant position for which Susan appears to be qualified, extending an offer of employment to her will create the perception that officials have purposefully circumvented the merit process simply to hire Tom. Conversely, if the Personnel Office does not recommend hiring Susan, the Planning Office may lose the opportunity to secure the services of a person who can do much to improve River Grove's planning efforts.

1. What values are brought into conflict in this situation? How do situations of this kind pose a threat to the line-staff partnership?
2. What can or should Abrams do? In what ways, if any, can the needs of dual-career couples be accommodated without unduly sacrificing merit principles?

■ **CASE 2.2**   The Public Manager from the Private Sector

In August 1992 the Administrator of the Data Processing Division in the Department of Revenue resigned. The vacant position, which required strong supervisory skills as well as extensive knowledge of data processing, was advertised both internally and externally. Two employees of the division competed for the job. Both possessed outstanding records as bureau chiefs. The job was nonetheless offered to George Bancroft, an applicant from the private sector who possessed several years of supervisory experience managing a local business and who demonstrated impressive verbal and leadership abilities during the interview.

Bancroft's first act as Administrator was to call a meeting with all division employees to explain his ideas for improving unit efficiency and effectiveness. Everyone, including the bureau chiefs who had applied for the position, was impressed. Not long after the meeting, however, his congeniality began to disappear. He called on each member of his division individually and enquired as to whom he could or could not trust. He then initiated a series of personnel changes.

Bancroft's first attempt at change was to ask a well-liked secretary to find another job. He explained he wanted someone in her position to be able to handle minor data processing duties along with normal secretarial responsibilities. He gave her 30 days to find another job. The secretary, aware of her rights as a classified state employee, as well as her rights under the collective bargaining agreement, refused to resign or look for another job. She knew she could not be dismissed without just cause. Nor could her job description be changed without the Department Head's approval.

His second attempt at change was to discharge David Wilson. Wilson was one of the bureau chiefs who had competed for the position of Administrator. Although it was never clear why Bancroft wanted to get rid of Wilson, it is possible that he felt threatened by the highly respected bureau chief. Bancroft first tried to build a disciplinary case against Wilson, hoping to force a resignation or succeed in discharging him. On one occasion he issued a written reprimand to Wilson for failing to type one of the forms used to make corrections to computer programs. In fact, he had removed the form from the secretary's desk before it could be typed. Bancroft next adopted a deep freeze strategy. During the following months he assigned Wilson no new duties, invited him to no division meetings, and instructed the division staff not to interact with him. Wilson contacted the division personnel officer, but the latter seemed more interested in pleasing the Administrator than in assisting Wilson with his complaints. When Wilson apprised the Department Head of the matter, Bancroft responded that it had all been a misunderstanding.

Finally, Bancroft attempted to eliminate Wilson's position by reorganizing the division. At this point Wilson had had enough. He arranged a meeting with the Department Head, explained that the division's morale and productivity had declined significantly since Bancroft had been hired, and asked that the reorganization plan be placed on hold until an investigation of his charges could be completed. The subsequent investigation confirmed Wilson's charges. Bancroft was asked to resign.

1. Bancroft apparently was unfamiliar with merit system requirements, was inexperienced in dealing with organized employees, and did not understand fundamental concepts such as just cause. Do you believe the Selection Committee erred in finding someone without government experience to be the best qualified applicant?
2. Does it seem that Bancroft's failure was attributable to his lack of government experience, personal characteristics unrelated to his employment record, or a combination of the two?
3. What are the relative advantages and disadvantages of hiring external job candidates versus promoting from within?

Notes

1. Steven W. Hays and Richard C. Kearney, "State Personnel Directors and the Dilemmas of Workforce 2000: A Survey," *Public Administration Review* 52 (July/August 1992), 386.

2. Frank J. Thompson, "The Politics of Public Personnel Administration," in Steven W. Hays and Richard C. Kearney, eds., *Public Personnel Administration: Problems and Prospects* (Englewood Cliffs, New Jersey: Prentice-Hall, 1990), 3–19.

3. *Rutan v. Republican Party of Illinois* (497 U.S. 62, 1990). See also, David K. Hamilton, "The Staffing Function in Illinois State Government after *Rutan*," *Public Administration Review* 53 (July/August 1993):381–386.

4. U. S. Congress, Senate, Select Committee on Presidential Campaign Activities, *Executive Session Hearings Before the Select Committee on Presidential Campaign Activities, Watergate and Related Activities*, Book 19 (Washington, D.C.: Government Printing Office, 1974).

5. Ibid., 9006.

6. Carolyn Ban, "The Realities of the Merit System," in Carolyn Ban and Norma M. Riccucci, eds., *Public Personnel Management: Current Concerns—Future Challenges* (New York: Longman, 1991), 23.

7. William B. Johnston, *Workforce 2000: Work and Workers for the 21st Century* (Indianapolis: Hudson Institute, June 1987); William B. Johnston and others, *Civil Service 2000* (Washington, D.C.: Office of Personnel Management, June 1988).

8. See Hays and Kearney, "State Personnel Directors"; and Blue Woolridge and Jennifer Wester, "The Turbulent Environment of Public Personnel Administration: Responding to the Challenge of the Changing Workplace of the Twenty-first Century," *Public Personnel Management* 20 (Summer 1991):207–224.

9. Steven W. Hays, "Environmental Change and the Personnel Function: A Review of the Research," *Public Personnel Management* 18 (Summer 1989), 115–116.

10. U.S. General Accounting Office, *The Changing Workforce: Demographic Issues Facing the Federal Government* (GAO\GGD-92-38, March 1992).

11. Daniel Yankelovich, *New Rules: Searching for Self-Fulfillment in a World Turned Upside Down* (New York: Random House, 1981).

12. Karl E. Klare, "The Labor-Management Cooperation Debate: A Workplace Democracy Perspective," *Harvard Civil Rights—Civil Liberties Law Review* 23 (Winter 1988), 44.

13. Eugene B. McGregor Jr., *Strategic Management of Human Knowledge, Skills, and Abilities: Workforce Decision-Making in the Postindustrial Age* (San Francisco: Jossey-Bass, 1991), 33.

14. Ibid., 41.

15. Jonathan R. Tompkins, "Legislating the Employment Relationship: Montana's Wrongful-Discharge Law," *Employee Relations Law Journal* 14 (Winter, 1988):387-398.

16. Seymour Martin Lipset and William Schneider, *The Confidence Gap: Business, Labor and Government in the Public Mind* (New York, Free Press, 1983).

17. Larry M. Lane and James F. Wolf, *The Human Resource Crisis in the Public Sector: Rebuilding the Capacity to Govern* (New York: Quorum Books, 1990).

18. Ibid., 4.

19. As quoted in the Volcker Commission Report, *Leadership for America: Rebuilding the Public Service* (Lexington, Massachusetts: D.C. Heath, Lexington Books, 1989), 2–4; and Al Gore, *Creating a Government That Works Better and Costs Less: Report of the National Performance Review* (New York: Times Books, 1993), 68.

20. For a discussion of this evolution, see Thomas A. Mahoney and John R. Deckop, "Evolution of Concept and Practice in Personnel Administration/Human Resource Management (PA/HRM)," *1986 Yearly Review of Management* of the *Journal of Management* 12 (No. 2):225.

21. McGregor, *Strategic Management,* 37.

22. Ibid., 49.

23. Ibid., 50.

24. The dilemma posed in this case was suggested in part by Christine M. Reed, "Anti-Nepotism Rules and Dual Career Couples: Policy Questions for Public Personnel Administrators," *Public Personnel Management* 17 (Summer 1988):223–230.

CHAPTER 3

Civil Service Systems and How They Are Organized

Learning Objectives

After mastering the material contained in this chapter, you will be able to:

1. Explain the problems that rank-in-position career systems pose for the effective use of human resources.
2. Define four merit principles and explain how they have influenced the organization and operation of civil service systems in the United States.
3. Use the commission and executive personnel office models to assess the organizational format of a state or local government with which you are familiar.
4. Evaluate the relative advantages of centralized and decentralized personnel systems.

Human resource management in the public sector usually takes place in the context of merit-based civil service systems. How these systems are organized holds important implications for government's ability to manage its human resources effectively. Consider the following examples. Placing personnel policy-making authority in the hands of an independent commission may rob the chief executive of all opportunity to exercise leadership over the human resource function. Limiting the scope of the personnel office's authority, thereby preventing it from responding to demands for child care programs, alternative work schedules, or flexible benefit plans, may reduce government's ability to attract and retain highly qualified employees. And centralizing control over personnel matters in the central personnel office may result in decisions that are inconsistent with the operational needs of line agencies. As these examples suggest, structural factors may play critical roles in determining how efficiently personnel systems are operated, how well their various components are coordinated, and the extent to which human capabilities are liberated or constrained.

Unfortunately, exploring these matters is difficult because of the infinite variety that characterizes civil service systems. Their authority and organizational structures are derived from constitutions, state and federal laws, executive orders, and municipal charters. As a result, no two civil service systems are organized or operated in quite the same way. Nonetheless, general organizational patterns can be identified and described. This chapter examines these patterns, focusing specifically on how merit-based civil service systems and personnel offices are organized, and the division of responsibilities between central and departmental personnel offices.

Merit-Based Civil Service Systems

A useful way to begin our discussion of human resource management's organizational context is to sort out the sometimes confusing terminology used to refer to government personnel systems. A *civil service system* is a personnel system covering the civilian employees of a government. It is defined largely by the laws and regulations that govern employee selection, promotion, and treatment. Governments often maintain more than one civil service system. For example, although reference is often made to "the American civil service system," the federal government maintains separate systems for the Federal Bureau of Investigation, Tennessee Valley Authority, and Foreign Service. The latter systems are established under different pieces of legislation, and their employees are organized and managed differently from those in the primary civil service system operated by the Office of Personnel Management.

Civil service systems can be organized on either a merit or a patronage basis. As will be seen shortly, merit-based civil service systems are now the norm in the United States.

Career and Non-Career Systems

Civil service systems are composed of political appointees and career civil servants. Although the system as a whole is staffed primarily on the basis of merit, top-level administrators are appointed on the basis of patronage. This means that their political or personal connections determine their appointment more than do their formal qualifications. These politically appointed civil servants constitute the *noncareer* system. Their role is to ensure that the policies of elected officials are carried out. Patronage continues to flourish at the upper reaches of government in the United States, more so than in most European countries, because in our highly fragmented political systems it is one of the few means elected officials have of ensuring the loyalty of those they depend on most to achieve their political agendas. Political appointees serve at the pleasure of the appointing authority and may be dismissed at any time. However, the Supreme Court has restricted the use of patronage in recent years by ruling that only those holding (or desiring) upper-level, policy-determining positions may be selected, promoted, transferred, or dismissed on the basis of political beliefs or party affiliation.[1] Even in these situations there must be a convincing connection between partisanship and successful job performance.

Members of the *career service,* in contrast to political appointees, constitute the bulk of the civil service. They generally enter government by competing for available positions and with the idea of making it their career. Although they cannot be removed from office for political or partisan reasons, they are supervised directly or indirectly by political appointees who are charged with ensuring that they carry out the policies of elected officials.

Two Types of Career Systems

One way that civil service systems may differ is in the type of career system they use. Most civilian government employees in the United States work within *rank-in-position career systems.* This means that they are hired to fill a particular position and their status and pay is determined by the nature of the position that they hold. Some employees, by contrast, work within *rank-in-person career systems.* This means that their status and pay is determined primarily by the rank they have achieved within the organization. Their rank, in turn, is determined by their accumulated work experience and qualifications rather than the demands of the particular position they hold. At the national level, for example, members of the armed services, foreign service, and senior executive service work within rank-in-person systems. At the local level, police and fire departments also share many of the characteristics of rank-in-person systems. These systems are often called *closed* systems because individuals normally enter at the lower ranks and work their way up through the promotions process. Rank-in-position systems, by contrast, are called *open* systems because individuals are usually allowed to enter laterally at any level of the organization as long as they possess the necessary job qualifications.

Most governments in the United States adopted rank-in-position systems both to avoid the elitism associated with the closed European systems and to obtain the benefits promised by the scientific management movement. The logic of scientific management seems unassailable at first glance: fairness and efficiency is maximized by determining the tasks that need to be performed, combining tasks into identifiable positions, establishing the qualifications needed to perform required tasks, filling vacant positions with persons who possess the established qualifications, and paying employees according to the demands of the job.

This logic coincides well with the nation's faith in science and commitment to hiring on the basis of demonstrated competence. Nonetheless, from the human resource management perspective, rank-in-position systems are seriously flawed in two respects. First, they make it difficult for managers to motivate and retain their best workers. This is because in the absence of a pay-for-performance system each employee's pay is set according to the position he or she holds. This tends to have a demotivating effect on superior performers who, if they are not rewarded in other ways, may choose to look for work elsewhere. Similarly, in the absence of a series of ranks through which to advance (of the kind that usually exist in rank-in-person systems), workers often find that they cannot advance in their careers except by leaving their current jobs. This also tends to have a demotivating effect because workers cannot anticipate any long-term reward for superior performance. Second, job duties tend to be limited to those found in the job description regardless of the employee's abilities or actual qualifications. From the human resource management perspective, this results in a serious waste of human potential.

Overcoming the inherent limitations of rank-in-position systems is one of the greatest challenges facing human resource management today. An increased willingness to experiment with alternative systems can be seen in the use of rank-in-person systems in the federal government's senior executive service and the executive personnel systems in a few states. The Civil Service Reform Act of 1978 also authorized demonstration projects designed to add flexibility to position-based civil service systems, but only a few experiments have been conducted.[2]

Merit Systems and Merit Principles

A *merit system* is any civil service system (or part of one) governed by a set of procedures specifically designed to protect and promote merit principles. As defined below, these principles include open competition, selection based on personal qualifications, political neutrality, and protection from arbitrary treatment. The typical merit system covers most employees in the career service but does not cover political appointees. Career employees are normally selected by competitive examination and are protected from politically motivated dismissals.

In 1883, for example, part of the federal civil service system began to operate as a merit system. Although it initially referred to little more than an examination system for selecting qualified job applicants, it quickly evolved into a complex system of rules and regulations designed to reduce the influence of politics and partisanship in many areas of human resource management. Today, more than 90 percent of federal civil servants are covered by merit regulations. Comparable levels of coverage are found in most states and large municipalities, and in some counties.

Because merit principles defined in the late 1800s continue to influence the organization of merit systems today, they deserve a closer look:

Open Competition   This principle states that the competition for government jobs should be open to everyone. As often interpreted today, open competition means that available positions must be widely publicized; all interested persons must have a reasonable opportunity to apply for available positions regardless of their politics, religious beliefs, race, national origin, or gender; valid standards of competence and fitness must be applied impartially to all persons who apply; each applicant should be able to learn what consideration was given to his or her application; and, finally, each applicant should be provided on request an administrative review of how his or her application was treated.

Selection Based on Personal Qualifications   This principle states that civil servants should be selected on the basis of merit as determined through an assessment of each candidate's knowledge, skills, and abilities. It rejects the view that selection should be based on political beliefs, party service, nepotism, or heredity.

Political Neutrality   This principle holds that civil servants should serve the public interest in an impartial manner without being pressured to serve the interests of a particular political party or becoming involved in electoral politics. To safeguard this principle, supervisors are typically prohibited from soliciting campaign contributions from employees or coercing them to participate in campaign activities. Limitations are also placed on the right of employees to participate in political campaigns.

Protection from Arbitrary Treatment   According to this principle, civil servants should be guaranteed certain due process rights when adversely affected by management decisions. Procedural guarantees typically include notifying employees in writing of the reasons for any adverse action, and providing them with opportunities to respond in writing, request a formal hearing, and appeal adverse decisions beyond the agency level. Originally established to protect employees from politically motivated dismissals, these procedural guarantees were gradually extended to other situations where employees are disciplined or otherwise adversely affected.

Continuing Evolution of the Merit Concept

Far from remaining static, merit principles have evolved in character and expanded in number. This can be seen most dramatically at the national level. Exhibit 3.1 presents the nine merit principles contained in the Civil Service Reform Act of 1978. In contrast to the strong emphasis placed on political neutrality by the nineteenth century reforms, the Civil Service Reform Act stresses the importance of equal employment opportunity (principles 1 and 2), professional ethics (principle 4), and employee productivity and administrative efficiency (principles 3, 5, 6, 7, and 9). The reasons for

---

EXHIBIT 3.1

NINE MERIT PRINCIPLES

1. Recruitment should be from qualified individuals from appropriate sources in an endeavor to achieve a work force from all segments of society, and selection and advancement should be determined solely on the basis of relative ability, knowledge, and skills, after fair and open competition which assures that all receive equal opportunity.

2. All employees and applicants for employment should receive fair and equitable treatment in all aspects of personnel management without regard to political affiliation, race, color, religion, national origin, sex, marital status, age, or handicapping condition, and with proper regard for their privacy and constitutional rights.

3. Equal pay should be provided for work of equal value with appropriate consideration of both national and local rates paid by employers in the private sector, and appropriate incentives and recognition should be provided for excellence in performance.

4. All employees should maintain high standards of integrity, conduct, and concern for the public interest.

5. The Federal work force should be used efficiently and effectively.

6. Employees should be retained on the basis of the adequacy of their performance, inadequate performance should be corrected, and employees should be separated who cannot or will not improve their performance to meet required standards.

7. Employees should be provided effective education and training in cases in which such education and training would result in better organizational and individual performance.

8. Employees should be a) protected against arbitrary action, personal favoritism, or coercion for partisan political purposes, and b) prohibited from using their official authority or influence for the purpose of interfering with or affecting the result of an election or a nomination for election.

9. Employees should be protected against reprisal for the lawful disclosure of information which the employees reasonably believe evidences a) a violation of law, rule, or regulation, or b) mismanagement, a gross waste of funds, an abuse of authority, or a substantial and specific danger to public health or safety.

Source: Civil Service Reform Act of 1978 (5 U.S.C 2301).

the continuing evolution in the meaning of merit are described in Chapter 4. These reasons aside, as merit principles have evolved, so too have the ways that merit systems are organized and operated.

Identifying Merit Systems in Practice

Merit principles have been adopted so extensively in the United States that the terms *civil service system* and *merit system* are often used interchangeably. In practice, however, whether a particular civil service system may rightly be called a merit system is a matter of definition as well as degree. To fully appreciate this point, consider two different definitions. First, a merit system may be defined as a system in which positions are filled through open competition on the basis of personal qualifications and employees are protected against removal for partisan reasons. By this definition, the vast majority of civil service systems qualify as merit systems. As we have already seen, more than 90 percent of federal civil servants are covered under such merit requirements. More than two-thirds of state governments have statewide merit systems, and most of the remainder continue to maintain merit systems covering employees in agencies receiving federal funds even though the requirement that they do so was lifted in the early 1980s. Finally, most large and medium-sized municipalities also maintain jurisdiction-wide merit systems.

Now consider a second definition. Based on the federal model established by the Pendleton Act of 1883, a formal merit system is one that possesses the following characteristics:

1. A semi-independent commission authorized to establish merit system rules and regulations
2. Centralized development of qualification standards considered necessary for effective performance of various job categories
3. Centralized administration of examinations to determine each applicant's job qualifications
4. Use of the rule of three, by which the names of those passing a particular test are entered on a "register" according to their scores and the top three names are forwarded to a particular agency each time a job vacancy occurs
5. Extensive rules designed to protect employee rights, and formal mechanisms for appealing certain personnel decisions above the agency level.

Relatively few jurisdictions today could claim to be organized as a merit system under this stricter definition. Many governments never adopted the federal model. In other instances, semi-independent commissions have been abandoned to achieve greater executive control, the rule of three has been abandoned because it denied managers the flexibility they needed to make good hiring decisions, and responsibility for examining and selecting candidates has been decentralized to the agency level as part of a larger decentralizing trend. Although fewer merit systems today possess the formal characteristics required by the second definition, most civil service systems nonetheless meet the requirements of the first definition. Reviewing these two definitions simply helps to clarify some of the ambiguities surrounding the use of the term.

In the final analysis, merit systems are distinguished from nonmerit-based systems not so much by their legal mandates or formal characteristics as by their commitment to merit principles in daily practice. Some civil service systems are structured as merit systems by law but violate merit principles routinely in practice. Others are governed by general personnel policies rather than a system of detailed rules and regulations but are fully committed to protecting and promoting merit principles nonetheless. In short, a true merit system in practice is one that is characterized by adequate funding, a competent personnel staff, a supportive political culture, and demonstrated commitment from the administration to preserving the integrity of merit principles.

The Inevitable Clash of Values

Merit is only one of several values that personnel policies are designed to promote. These values inevitably conflict with each other, and there may be times when managers feel justified in compromising merit to secure other benefits. Consider, for example, this seemingly straightforward situation. A selection committee composed of the immediate supervisor and two other managers is asked to select the best candidate for a vacant position from among a pool of six finalists. Each finalist gained entry to the pool after a scored review of their qualifications. The first candidate appears to be the logical choice because he received the highest number of points for education and work experience and is thus arguably the "best qualified." But one member of the selection committee argues in favor of a second candidate on the grounds that women are significantly underrepresented in the agency and hiring her would help the agency meet its affirmative action goals. This prompts another committee member to point out that an argument could be made in favor of the remaining candidates as well. A case could be made for the third candidate on the basis of seniority (this candidate has worked for the agency longer than any of the others), for the fourth on the basis of veterans' status (the agency has a veterans' preference policy in place), and for the fifth because the candidate has political supporters who dislike being disappointed. Managers often face situations involving competing values, and adhering to a narrow definition of merit may not represent the best course of action in every instance.

Similarly, there is a danger of incorporating merit principles into personnel policies at the expense of other important values. Rules designed to guarantee due process and protect employees from partisan pressures, for example, can create a level of job security beyond that which reformers had intended. Lacking sufficient documentation, or wishing to avoid lengthy appeals, supervisors sometimes tolerate marginal employees rather than attempt to discipline or discharge them. Another of the many challenges facing human resource management today is how to retain the integrity of merit principles without unduly tying the hands of managers.

The Organization of Personnel Systems

Although personnel systems may be organized in any number of ways, they tend to follow either the commission or the executive personnel office model. An examination of these models will help to illustrate the variety of ways that personnel systems are organized in practice.

The Commission Model

Civil service reformers adopted the commission model in 1883 for purposes of governing the new federal merit system. Policy making and administrative powers were given to a semi-independent commission rather than to the president. Reformers

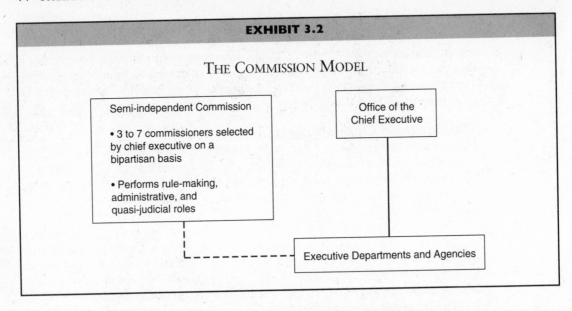

EXHIBIT 3.2

THE COMMISSION MODEL

Semi-independent Commission

• 3 to 7 commissioners selected by chief executive on a bipartisan basis

• Performs rule-making, administrative, and quasi-judicial roles

Office of the Chief Executive

Executive Departments and Agencies

hoped that a commission located outside of the president's chain of command would ensure that civil servants were henceforth selected on the basis of merit rather than patronage and that the career service would operate in a politically neutral fashion. The commission model was quickly adopted by many state and local governments. Other states adopted the commission model in the 1940s because the Social Security Act of 1939 required state agencies whose employees were paid with federal funds to be governed under a merit system. Key characteristics of the commission model are illustrated in Exhibit 3.2.

Commissions typically comprise three to seven individuals appointed by the chief executive on a bipartisan basis and for staggered terms. Although their powers and responsibilities can vary greatly from one jurisdiction to the next, strong commissions of the kind adopted by the federal government in 1883 are responsible for direct administration of the personnel system, including rule-making authority, administration of merit examinations, and enforcement of merit rules. They also perform a quasi-judicial role by adjudicating appeals by employees of personnel decisions made at the agency level.

The Executive Personnel Office Model

The commission's chief asset—its considerable independence from the chief executive—proved to be its biggest liability. Proponents of positive personnel management had argued for years that completing the reforms begun in 1883 would require "the reconciliation of recruitment for the public service on a basis of merit and fitness with the requirement that the chief executive shall at all times be able to control the amount and quality of the administration for which he is by law responsible."[3] Agreeing with the substance of this argument, the same National Civil Service League that advocated the commission model in 1883 decided in 1970 to repudiate it in favor of the executive personnel office model. Critics argued that change was desirable for sev-

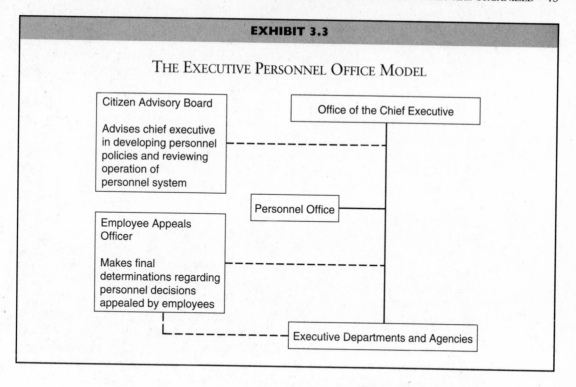

EXHIBIT 3.3

THE EXECUTIVE PERSONNEL OFFICE MODEL

Citizen Advisory Board

Advises chief executive
in developing personnel
policies and reviewing
operation of
personnel system

Office of the Chief Executive

Personnel Office

Employee Appeals
Officer

Makes final
determinations regarding
personnel decisions
appealed by employees

Executive Departments and Agencies

eral reasons. First, placing policy-making and administrative powers in the hands of a semi-independent commission, although done for reasons deemed important at the time, divorced personnel administration from other areas of management and prevented chief executives from exercising positive leadership in human resource management. Second, commissioners tended to be amateurs in personnel administration, ill-equipped to perform the leadership role that had been denied to chief executives. Third, strong commission formats combined legislative, executive, and judicial functions in a single agency, leading critics to question whether commissions could objectively and effectively perform all three functions at once. Finally, critics argued that commissions often lacked the necessary funds to perform their tasks well or were too remote from the operating problems of line agencies to provide the positive assistance they required. Members of the National Civil Service League hoped that by restoring control over the human resource function to the chief executive, and by building in safeguards to protect the political neutrality of the merit system, each of these concerns could be alleviated.

Key characteristics of the executive personnel office model are presented in Exhibit 3.3. These characteristics are derived from the National Civil Service League's *A Model Public Personnel Administration Law*, published in 1970.[4] They include a personnel agency headed by a single administrator appointed by the chief executive; a citizens advisory board to advise the chief executive on all aspects of human resource management; and a hearings officer whose duty it is to investigate employee grievances and to offer recommendations to the chief executive regarding their resolution.

Governments that abandoned the commission model did not necessarily adopt all of the structural features recommended by the National Civil Service League. Citizens advisory boards, for example, were seldom created, although some type of independent board was normally established to approve policies formulated in the central personnel office or to hear employee appeals.

Several state and local governments had created executive personnel offices earlier in the century in response to the Progressive Party's advocacy of stronger executive leadership. Others responded to the National Civil Service League's call for reforms in the 1970s, and the federal government eventually made the switch in 1978. Although the strong commission format is rarely found today, current personnel systems are nonetheless designed to serve many of the same goals espoused in 1883. They typically include formal mechanisms that allow employees to appeal adverse personnel decisions to a board outside of the administrative chain of command, as well as boards that must approve policies formulated by the executive personnel office staff.

The Location of the Central Personnel Office

Consistent with the executive personnel office model, the organizational structure of most governments includes a central personnel office headed by a personnel director who is appointed directly or indirectly by the chief executive. Its location, however, tends to vary from one jurisdiction to the next. Small governments seldom have any personnel office at all; routine personnel matters are handled by the operating agencies and perhaps by an administrative assistant to the chief executive. Among larger jurisdictions, the central personnel office may be situated as a staff agency attached to the office of the chief executive, as a separate cabinet-level department, or as a division within a cabinet-level department. These variations are illustrated in Exhibit 3.4. Beginning in the 1950s it became fashionable, particularly among state governments, to establish a Department of Administration that combined the housekeeping functions of government, including human resource management, purchasing, and budgeting. As shown in Exhibit 3.4, the central personnel office in this instance is usually called the personnel division. Among state governments, more than half of the personnel offices are now part of a larger agency.[5] Only Texas has no central personnel office at all.

The Relationship Between Central and Departmental Personnel Offices

Although personnel responsibilities can be handled by each agency individually, establishment of a central personnel office holds several advantages. Central offices can coordinate personnel activities on a governmentwide basis so that strategic objectives are achieved, ensure that personnel policies are implemented consistently, and administer applicant screening, pay, and classification systems so that duplications of effort can be avoided at the departmental level. By maintaining staffs of personnel specialists, they can also provide agencies with various kinds of technical assistance that would not otherwise be available to them.

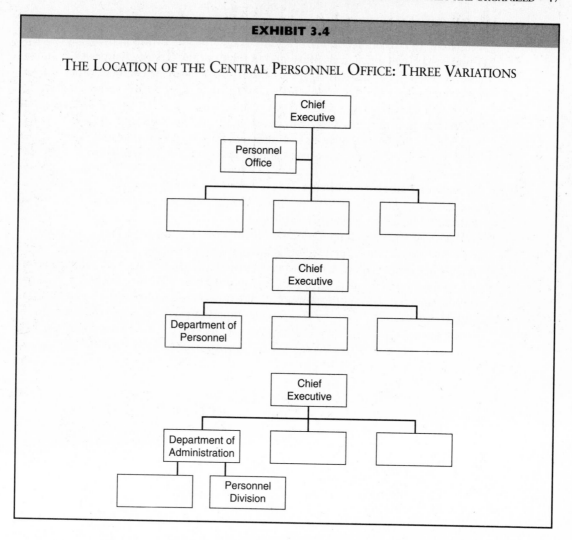

EXHIBIT 3.4

THE LOCATION OF THE CENTRAL PERSONNEL OFFICE: THREE VARIATIONS

As governments grew in size, and as the practice of personnel administration became more specialized, personnel offices were also established in the major departments and agencies of government. At the federal level, for example, offices had already been established in the departments of Agriculture, Treasury, and Interior when President Roosevelt issued Executive Order 7916 in 1938.[6] This order required each cabinet department to establish a personnel office staffed with individuals trained in personnel administration. Roosevelt believed that the central office was too far removed from operating decisions at the department level and that agency effectiveness could be improved by making trained professionals more readily available to assist line managers.

A similar trend took place at state and local levels. Today central personnel offices are found in conjunction with separate departmental offices in every state except Texas (which has no central office) and in many of the largest counties and municipalities. The relationship between the central and departmental offices varies according to how responsibilities are divided and the degree of authority delegated to the departmental level. The character of their relationship is not determined by the central office alone. It is influenced by many actors in the internal and external political environment, including executive branch officials, citizens groups, civil service commissions or advisory boards, legislative committees, and the line agencies themselves.

Division of Responsibilities

In one way or another central and departmental offices must divide responsibilities and coordinate their respective efforts. To a certain extent responsibilities divide themselves along natural lines. Central offices seem naturally suited to providing governmentwide personnel services, developing and coordinating personnel policies, and monitoring agency compliance with merit system rules. To protect selection decisions from political interference, or to simply reduce the administrative burdens on the operating agencies, central offices are often asked to recruit and screen job applicants as well. Departmental offices, by contrast, seem naturally suited to making routine personnel decisions and assisting managers at the operating level. Exhibit 3.5 illustrates how responsibilities might be divided in a large government. In practice, of course, each jurisdiction divides responsibilities differently and in ways that defy easy explanation.

As noted in Chapter 1, the division of responsibilities between central and departmental offices holds important consequences for line-staff relations. In terms of the organizational hierarchy, departmental personnel officers are positioned between agency managers and the central personnel staff. The greater the emphasis department personnel officers are asked to place on monitoring agency operations, the more they will experience divided loyalties between securing compliance with merit system rules and providing technical assistance to managers.

The Degree of Centralization

How best to divide responsibilities between central and departmental offices depends largely on the degree of centralization desired. In a centralized system, authority to formulate policies, as well as to make many routine personnel decisions, is retained by the central office. In a decentralized system, by contrast, a significant amount of authority is delegated to the departmental level. Departmental offices, for example, may be allowed to classify positions, establish performance appraisal systems, and screen and test applicants for vacant positions. The primary role of the central office in a decentralized system is to maintain accountability and achieve consistency of purpose by establishing standards that agencies are to follow in exercising their delegated authority. The range of activities that can be decentralized is often constrained by the size of departmental offices. Staffs are generally small, sometimes consisting of only a single personnel officer. In such instances it may not be practical to delegate a broad range of responsibilities or to expect staff members to be anything but personnel generalists because of the broad range of functions they must handle.

EXHIBIT 3.5

DIVISION OF RESPONSIBILITIES BETWEEN CENTRAL AND DEPARTMENTAL PERSONNEL OFFICES

Central Personnel Office
- formulates personnel policies and merit rules (sometimes in conjunction with a separate board)
- adjudicates employee appeals (if no separate appeals board exists)
- administers employee benefit programs
- administers pay and classification systems
- coordinates and assists agencies with labor negotiations
- provides governmentwide training and development programs
- provides technical assistance to line agencies
- establishes recruitment programs
- tests, screens, and refers job applicants
- monitors agency compliance with relevant laws and personnel policies (if no separate board exists)

Departmental Personnel Office
- determines agency's human resources needs
- assists with selecting and orienting new employees
- explains personnel policies and merit system rules to agency personnel
- advises line officers regarding EEO/Affirmative Action requirements
- assists line officers with supervisory responsibilities
- assists in resolving employee complaints or grievances
- classifies positions according to established standards
- negotiates (or assists in negotiating) labor contracts

A key advantage of a centralized system lies in its ability to safeguard political neutrality by establishing the framework of rules and regulations within which agency decisions are made and by removing some decisions from the agency level altogether. Centralized control over screening and testing, for example, reduces opportunities for personal favoritism and other biases to affect selection decisions. Centralized control also allows consistent administration of special employment programs for veterans, women, minorities, and disabled persons. A second advantage of centralized systems is that staff specialists in the central office can provide services to all agencies in such areas as position classification, testing, and training. This reduces the duplication of effort that results when these responsibilities are handled by individual departmental offices. Employee recruitment and testing provides a good example. For jobs common to several agencies, such as clerical or data processing jobs, it is far more cost-effective for a single agency to recruit, examine, and rate job applicants. This may also benefit applicants because they can file a single application rather than having to contact several agencies individually.

The primary disadvantage of centralized systems is that they may become bureaucratized in ways that interfere with effective human resource management. Complex systems of rules and regulations imposed from above may dictate courses of action not fully appropriate to situations at the agency level. This occurs either because the central office does not understand the operational needs of individual agencies or because the rules do not allow enough flexibility to cover diverse situations. A centralized system of rules also tends to reduce managerial discretion, thereby denying to managers the flexibility they need to hire and retain competent employees. In addition, the administration of centralized classification, screening, and testing systems is often slow and inefficient. Several recent studies have concluded, for example, that the federal government is failing to obtain the best available talent for vacant positions because centralized screening and testing procedures are too complex and lengthy.[7] Evidence indicates that many job seekers are discouraged from applying because of procedural complexities, whereas others lose interest and accept jobs elsewhere during the several months it often takes for them to get placed on a register and be referred to an agency. Yet another problem is that the examination and rating of candidates may be done by members of a central office staff who are unfamiliar with the technical requirements of the position to be filled and the special work-related needs of the agency. As a result, applicants may be referred who are not well suited to available positions.

In light of these problems, the rationale behind decentralizing decision-making authority becomes more apparent. The primary advantage of a decentralized system is that authority to make basic personnel decisions is delegated to the departmental level where personnel officers and line managers can work together to promote unit effectiveness. Being closer to the situation at hand, they are better positioned to decide how to appraise, discipline, counsel, and motivate employees. In the area of selection they may be able to screen applicants more quickly, identify individuals who show an interest in specific positions, and do a better job of matching applicants to positions with special skill requirements. Finally, decentralized systems may help facilitate cooperative line-staff relations by reducing the perception that personnel decisions are dictated by faceless individuals in the central office.

As the work of government has become more complex and the field of human resource management more specialized, some governments have felt compelled to centralize personnel activities and place them in the hands of staff specialists. This pressure toward greater centralization aside, the stronger trend now seems to be in the direction of decentralization. This can be seen in some of the changes taking place at the federal level. Concerned with the negative effects of centralized control on managerial effectiveness, the authors of the 1978 Civil Service Reform Act included provisions in the law allowing the delegation of previously centralized activities to the agency level. Agencies may now develop their own testing and selection procedures for many job classes (not including those whose job requirements are common to other agencies). They may also develop their own performance appraisal systems within guidelines set by law. Through these reforms the federal government is attempting to find a balance between centralization and decentralization that captures the advantages of both while minimizing the disadvantages of each. Similar trends may be seen at the state level. The degree of change will be less dramatic, however, because personnel systems in state government have been less centralized historically than in the federal government.

In practice, the choice faced by governments is not whether to establish a centralized or decentralized system, but what to centralize and to what degree. Although the choice is affected by factors such as size of government, availability of resources, external pressures, and historical precedents, it is also determined by each government's perception of the proper balance between the values of merit system protection and consistent application of personnel policies on the one hand, and managerial autonomy and flexibility on the other.

The Evolving Roles of the Central Personnel Office

The nature and division of personnel-related responsibilities will change as the roles of the central office continue to evolve. A changing workforce, for example, is causing personnel offices to perform the innovator role more than in the past. Personnel policies and programs are being designed to improve government's ability to recruit and retain employees. Policy innovations may be seen in such areas as child care assistance, work scheduling, leave policies, flexible benefits, and employee development (see Chapter 13).

Performing the innovator role effectively will require broadening the scope of the personnel office's responsibilities to include an expanded concern for human resource management generally. In practice this may mean reducing the traditional emphasis on its watchdog role and placing a greater emphasis on system responsiveness and flexibility. The results of a survey of state personnel directors published in 1992 provides some clues regarding the evolving roles of the central personnel office. State personnel directors believed that their systems were doing particularly well in protecting employee rights, ensuring political neutrality, and promoting equal employment opportunity, but relatively poorly in recruiting, rewarding, and retaining the best available talents.[8] The inefficiencies of the merit system, including cumbersome recruitment practices, outdated testing procedures, and poorly designed classification and pay systems, remain major sources of complaint. Although they believed they were most successful in performing their traditional control functions, state directors reported that they were nonetheless moving ahead aggressively to introduce innovations such as those just listed. With so much at stake, the central personnel office's efforts to move beyond its traditional staffing and control functions deserves to be watched closely.

Conclusion: The Impact of Organizational Structure

We have seen in this chapter how organizational structure can affect the practice of human resource management in important ways. Whether a particular personnel system is organized on a merit or patronage basis, adopts a rank-in-person or a rank-in-position career system, or is highly centralized or relatively decentralized can greatly affect organizational performance. Structured in one way, the personnel system can successfully attract and retain highly qualified employees, empower employees and managers to pursue organizational objectives together, and adapt appropriately to an ever-changing environment. Structured another way, the personnel system may become overregulated and characterized by cumbersome and inflexible procedures that protect marginal employees, reduce managerial flexibility, and rob the organization of the ability to adapt appropriately to changing circumstances. The challenge for the future lies in finding a proper balance between merit values and the legitimate operational needs of managers.

Notes

1. *Elrod v. Burns* (427 U.S. 347, 1976); *Branti v. Finkel* (445 U.S. 507, 1980); and *Rutan v. Republican Party of Illinois* (497 U.S. 62, 1990).

2. Eugene B. McGregor, "The Public Sector Human Resource Management Puzzle: Strategic Management of a Strategic Resource," *Public Administration Review* 48 (November/December 1988), 947.

3. William Seal Carpenter, *The Unfinished Business of Civil Service Reform* (Princeton, New Jersey: Princeton University Press, 1952), preface.

4. National Civil Service League, *A Model Public Personnel Administration Law* (Washington, D.C.: National Civil Service League, 1970).

5. *State Personnel Office: Roles and Functions* (Lexington, Kentucky: The Council of State Governments, 2nd ed., 1992), 2.

6. Paul P. Van Riper, *History of the United States Civil Service* (Evanston, Illinois: Row, Peterson, 1958), 311.

7. See, for example, the Volcker Commission Report, *Leadership for America: Rebuilding the Public Service* (Lexington, Massachusetts: D.C. Heath, Lexington Books, 1989).

8. Steven W. Hays and Richard C. Kearney, "State Personnel Directors and the Dilemmas of Workforce 2000: A Survey," *Public Administration Review* 52 (July/August 1992):380–388.

CHAPTER 4

Societal Values and Civil Service Reform

Learning Objectives

After mastering the material contained in this chapter, you will be able to:

1. Explain the impact of societal values on federal civil service reforms in each of five historical periods.
2. Identify and describe four reforms instituted by the Civil Service Reform Act of 1978.
3. Assess how well the 1978 reforms have succeeded in balancing the values of efficiency, responsiveness, political neutrality, and protection of employee rights.

Civil service systems periodically undergo institutional reforms that alter their design and operation. Because of the importance of the public service in a democratic society and the benefits derived by those who control the distribution of jobs, the stakes involved in reform are often high and the debates often intense. In addition, the resulting reforms often hold important implications for human resource management and the attainment of organizational objectives. The efficient use of human resources, for example, may or may not be among the values that civil service systems are designed to promote. This chapter focuses on changes that have occurred in the federal civil service system since 1789. Its purpose is to illustrate how the design and operation of civil service systems are influenced by competing societal values and how the resulting reforms can affect the practice of human resource management.

Societal Values and Historical Change

Generally speaking, social change occurs as the result of shifting forces in society and the values that such forces reflect. These values are often translated into political demands that, if conditions are right, may emerge from the political system in the form of legislation, executive orders, or judicial decisions. To illustrate the dynamic nature

---

EXHIBIT 4.1

ASCENDANT VALUES DURING FOUR PERIODS OF REFORM

Reform Period	Initial Source of Change	Ascendant Values
1789–1829	Precedents set by George Washington	Merit (fitness of character) Political neutrality
1829–1883	Patronage system introduced by Andrew Jackson	Representativeness Political responsiveness
1883–1923	Pendleton Act of 1883	Merit Political neutrality Employee rights
1923–1978	Classification Act of 1923	Efficiency Executive leadership
1978–Present	Civil Service Reform Act of 1978	Efficiency Political responsiveness Merit Employee Rights

---

of civil service reform, this chapter focuses on changes that have occurred at the federal level. Exhibit 4.1 identifies five historical periods of civil service reform, as well as the initial source of change and the ascendant values in each period. Although these periods are rather arbitrarily defined, they nonetheless help to illustrate the impact of societal values on the design and operation of civil service systems.

Dominant values in society often recede in importance as others emerge to take their place. Although they continue to exist side by side, their relative influence rises and falls over time. Although many values have shaped the nature and direction of civil service reform, those identified in Exhibit 4.1 have been particularly influential. Their meanings in the context of human resource management may be defined as follows:

Efficiency. Personal systems should be designed to maximize productivity and minimize waste.

Executive Leadership. The chief executive should possess full authority over the human resource function so that he or she, assisted by a well qualified personnel staff, can provide energy, direction, and leadership in human resource management.

Merit. Career civil servants should be appointed and promoted on the basis of their job-related knowledge, skills, and abilities.

Political Neutrality. Civil servants should serve the public and the current administration in an impartial and detached manner, without being pressured to serve the interests of a particular party or becoming involved in electoral politics.

Political Responsiveness. As unelected officials, civil servants should be accountable to the chief executive, respectful of his or her electoral mandate, and responsive to his or her political directives.

Representativeness. To ensure equal employment opportunity and the representation of diverse viewpoints in the bureaucracy, the civil service should reflect the heterogenous character of the American population, both geographically and socially.

Protection of Employee Rights. Civil servants should be protected from arbitrary and capricious treatment, and "due process" should be observed in situations where adverse personnel actions are contemplated.

These values reflect conflicting ideas about how civil servants should be appointed (merit, patronage, or social representation), how responsive they should be to executive direction, how protected they should be from partisan intrusions, whether political considerations should outweigh norms of efficiency, and whether protection of employee rights is more important than managerial effectiveness. These value conflicts are never fully resolved. Civil service reforms in the United States have moved back and forth from one set of values to another in search of a proper balance.

Early Precedents, 1789–1829

The years after 1789 must be viewed more as a period of new beginnings than as a period of reform. The small number of government officials appointed under the Articles of Confederation had been discharged by the time the new Constitution went into effect. This left President Washington in the enviable position of being able to establish an entirely new civil service. By skillfully pursuing his own understanding of merit and political neutrality, Washington fashioned a civil service widely admired for its integrity and competence.

Washington's commitment to *merit* and *political neutrality* can be seen in his use of "fitness of character" as the primary criterion for selecting civil servants. Although it would seem odd today to measure competence in terms of such things as family background, personal reputation, and general level of educational attainment, Washington used such measures to establish a civil service remarkably free of corruption and inefficiency.[1] Washington believed that safeguarding the integrity of the civil service by insisting on fitness of character was essential to the success of the new government. Integrity and competence came, however, at the expense of *representativeness.* Although Washington worked with members of Congress to establish a bureaucracy that was geographically representative of the new nation, the criterion of fitness of character produced a civil service that was decidedly white, male, and upper class.

Washington also believed that his administration must avoid strongly biased political views if it was to maintain its credibility with the people. For this reason Washington sought to establish a civil service that was, relatively speaking, politically neutral and impartial in its conduct. This is not to say that political considerations never entered into his appointment decisions. Washington routinely conferred with members of Congress about appointments, occasionally extended employment preferences to military officers who had served in the Revolutionary War, and generally avoided appointing individuals who were known to be openly hostile to his political views.

Nonetheless, fitness of character, not political orientation or party affiliation, remained the primary selection criterion. And although Washington did not define political neutrality in the same way as it would be defined after 1883, he did seek to establish an administration relatively balanced in its political views and impartial in its conduct.

The birth of political parties during Washington's first term placed Washington and Adams under greater pressure to appoint individuals on the basis of party affiliation. As a result, when Thomas Jefferson took office in 1801 he found that most government positions were held by Federalists. Believing that presidents must have the capacity to control and direct government officials consistent with the will of the electorate, Jefferson replaced approximately 15 percent of the civil service with members of his own Democratic Republican party. In so doing, he acted in accordance with the value of *political responsiveness*. Once in office, these high-ranking appointees helped ensure that the civil service as a whole was responsive to Jefferson's political agenda.

By continuing to embrace Washington's concept of fitness of character, and by refusing to bow to partisan pressures that might undermine the integrity of the service, Jefferson succeeded in maintaining an effective balance between the values of merit, political neutrality, and political responsiveness. Although Madison, Monroe, and John Quincy Adams also followed Washington's lead in applying the criterion of fitness of character, they found it increasingly difficult to resist pressures from Congress to make appointments on the basis of party affiliation and personal connections.

The Rise and Fall of the Patronage System, 1829–1883

Admission of nine western states to the Union during the 1820s, and the elimination of property qualifications that had previously disenfranchised members of the lower classes, simultaneously shifted electoral power westward and away from the upper classes. Taking full advantage of these changes, Andrew Jackson campaigned for the presidency in 1828 as the champion of the "common man." Once in office, Jackson wasted no time in adopting patronage as the basis for appointing government employees. The patronage system involved selecting civil servants on the basis of their party service or political backing, regardless of their class background, with the understanding that appointees should not expect to serve beyond the current administration's tenure in office. By means of the patronage system, Jackson hoped to reduce corruption and complacency, democratize the civil service, increase executive control over the bureaucracy, and strengthen the party organization all at the same time. As will be seen shortly, the values behind these goals provided strong justification for Jackson's reforms.

By the 1820s the elitist, upper-class character of the civil service had become a significant source of resentment for many Americans. By declaring that jobs in government should be made accessible to all citizens on an equal basis, Jackson reinforced the value of egalitarianism then being expressed by many western frontiersmen and members of the lower classes generally. Once the patronage system was firmly in place, the "common man" gained an important source of social mobility and the civil service became more representative of society as a whole. To Jackson, this was a reform fully consistent with the basic tenets of democracy.

In his first inaugural address Jackson sought to reassure Americans that greater *representativeness* would not be achieved at the expense of *efficiency*. Rotation in office, he said, would reduce the corruption and lackluster performance of employees who had been granted unlimited tenure in office. To those who feared that rotation in office would actually reduce government efficiency by undermining the continuity that is so vital to administrative decisions, Jackson responded that this need not occur as long as patronage was applied judiciously and personal competence remained a primary criterion for appointment to office. Acting on this principle, Jackson replaced less than twenty percent of the civil service during his two terms in office.[2] Unfortunately, Jackson's commitment to administrative efficiency would not survive the actions of later presidents who paid little attention to the personal competence of those they appointed and who practiced nearly clean sweeps of office among those higher-level positions requiring Senate confirmation.

Basing appointments on party service also promoted *political responsiveness* by increasing the president's influence over civil servants. Because patronage represented a test of political loyalty, individuals appointed in this way were more likely to act on the president's understanding of the public interest. The president's ability to dismiss government officials at will would also help ensure their "faithful cooperation." And although the civil service system's *political neutrality* would be greatly reduced, Jackson believed that increased executive control would not necessarily come at the expense of individual competence. A central element of Jackson's philosophy was that the average citizen was fully capable of performing the duties of public office. In his first annual message to Congress Jackson argued that the duties of public office are "so plain and simple that men of intelligence may readily qualify themselves for their performance. . . "[3] There was much truth in this statement because most positions then filled by patronage were relatively unskilled positions in agencies such as the Postal Service, Treasury, and Customs. Only later, as the nature of government work increased in complexity, and as the civil service became increasingly politicized, would the value of political neutrality regain its former importance.

From Patronage to Spoils

Ironically, the changes conceived by Jackson as reforms soon came to be known collectively as the "spoils system"—a reference to Senator Marcy's remark that "to the victor belong the spoils." Because he appointed individuals to office on the basis of fitness as well as patronage and replaced only slightly more incumbents than Jefferson, Jackson probably does not deserve to be called the father of the spoils system. Nonetheless, it is true that Jackson established the philosophical basis for a system that was highly susceptible to abuse. As these abuses became increasingly apparent, several criticisms of the patronage system emerged. First, critics emphasized the loss in administrative efficiency resulting from high turnover in office. To enhance their control over the bureaucracy and to gain favor with important congressmen, Jackson's successors replaced increasingly greater numbers of civil servants. Although many midmanagers and clerks succeeded in retaining their positions during the patronage period, most of those civil servants appointed by an outgoing president were subsequently replaced by the incoming president, even when they belonged to the same political party. The numbers replaced by Buchanan and Lincoln, for example, far exceeded the twenty percent replaced by Jackson.[4] High turnover among civil servants had the effect of limiting career development among employees and reducing continuity in the administration of government programs. As government jobs became more specialized, losses in efficiency also resulted from the practice of hiring party supporters who did not possess the skills required to perform their jobs effectively.

Second, critics voiced concern over the loss of political neutrality resulting from the twin practices of requiring employees to campaign for the reelection of politicians and assessing a portion of their paychecks to help support the party in power. The latter practice was finally outlawed by Congress in 1876 but was not consistently enforced until much later. Political neutrality was perhaps the greatest casualty of the spoils period. As a result of political coercion, and the underlying threat of losing their jobs, civil servants were much less free than previously to act impartially in accordance with public policy and their professional view of the public's interest.

A third criticism of the patronage system was its tendency to encourage corruption. Despite Jackson's assurances that rotation in office would reduce corruption, it inevitably increased as patronage degenerated into the politics of greed. Scandals became commonplace as civil servants were caught awarding lucrative government contracts to politically favored individuals or businesses. Outright looting of the public treasury occurred as well, including theft of property and embezzlement of funds by government employees.

Birth of a Reform Movement

The excesses of the patronage system hastened the growth of a civil service reform movement in the post–Civil War period. Reformers tended to be a mixture of businessmen, professionals, and intellectuals who were shocked by government corruption and ineptness and concerned that the needs of modern society, particularly those of business enterprises, could not be met without significant reforms. The idea of a career civil service protected from partisan pressures provided the basis for their discussions. Although early reform proposals were largely ignored by Congress, by 1871 the reform movement had gathered sufficient strength to secure an amendment to an appropriations bill authorizing President Grant to establish a career civil service in which appointments were based on the "fitness of each candidate." To nearly everyone's surprise, Grant appointed a Civil Service Commission that proceeded to design a system of competitive examinations for selecting government employees. This initial effort at reform ended two years later, however, when Congress, fearing loss of its patronage powers, refused to continue its funding.

Despite this setback, the reform movement continued to build steam. The New York Civil Service Reform Association was established in 1877, and by the early 1880s many other cities had organized similar associations. Reform legislation known as the Pendleton bill was introduced into Congress in 1881, and with popular sentiment building in favor of reform, its enactment seemed only a matter of time. An event that would help ensure its enactment was not long in coming. When President Garfield was shot on July 2, 1881, by Charles Guiteau, an obviously insane individual driven by his disappointment that Garfield had not appointed him general consul to Paris, the public had little difficulty in connecting the excesses of the spoils system with the murder of the president. But despite the intense public outcry that followed Garfield's assassination, it took more than a year for Congress to act. Only when the Republican-dominated Congress realized that the next president was likely to be a Democrat did it enact the Pendleton bill. The Republicans hoped in this way to appear to the public as reformers and to protect civil servants appointed by Republican presidents from dismissal by an incoming Democratic president.[5]

Institutionalizing the Merit System, 1883–1923

The Pendleton Act represented the first significant effort by Congress to reform the civil service system since it was established in 1789. It addressed simultaneously how civil servants were to be selected, how the human resource function was to be organized, and what rules and regulations were to govern the conduct of human resource management. The four major reforms contained in the Pendleton Act may be summarized as follows:

1. It established an open system of competitive examinations to facilitate the selection of civil servants on the basis of personal competence (merit) rather than patronage.
2. It prohibited the dismissal of civil servants for political reasons, the assessment of financial contributions to support party activities, and the practice of coercing civil servants into participating in political campaigns.
3. It authorized the president to establish a bipartisan Civil Service Commission to oversee the examination of applicants to the civil service and to protect those appointed to office from political coercion.
4. It authorized future presidents to increase (or to decrease) the number of positions covered by the merit system beyond the ten percent of government positions initially covered by the Act.

Born as a reaction to the excesses of the spoils system, these reforms were designed to facilitate the gradual development of a professional, career civil service. The ten percent of government positions initially covered by the Act comprised 13,780 mostly clerical positions in Washington and in the larger post offices and customs houses outside of Washington. By limiting the number of positions originally covered, the authors of the Pendleton Act hoped to achieve a gradual expansion of the merit system without threatening its chances of success by attempting to cover too many positions at once. The Act authorized future presidents to "blanket in" additional positions. As a result of subsequent presidential and congressional actions, more than 90 percent of federal civilian employees are covered by merit protections today.

A Continuing Commitment to Representativeness

The excesses of the spoils system had produced a much-needed reassessment of the values on which a democratic civil service system should be based. The reforms of 1883 were designed to retain Jackson's commitment to the value of representativeness, reestablish the value of political neutrality, and place a new emphasis on the value of protecting employee rights. Continued commitment to the value of *representativeness* (in regards to social class) is reflected in the open character of the competitive examination system. The original Pendleton bill had proposed the creation of a "closed" personnel system based on the British model, in which prospective applicants were recruited from the universities and appointed to the civil service only at its lowest levels. Fearing that these provisions might result in an elite-dominated civil service, Congress amended the Pendleton bill to establish an "open" personnel system in which individuals could enter the civil service at any level as long as they possessed the required qualifications. Congress also rejected the essay form of examination, fearing that it might unduly advantage university-educated applicants. It substituted a requirement that examinations be "practical in nature" and relevant to the positions under consideration.

Commitment to this value may also be seen in efforts by the new Civil Service Commission to make government positions accessible to as many people as possible. Examining boards were established throughout the United States, and special provisions were made for ensuring that available jobs were publicized widely and standards of fitness applied equally to all applicants. The merit principle, in the view of reformers, was closely associated with the principles of equal opportunity and equal treatment. Although these principles were never fully realized during this period, the commitment to egalitarianism helped prevent the reemergence of an elite-dominated civil service.

A Restored Commitment to Political Neutrality

The reforms of 1883 were intended, above all else, to achieve the value of *political neutrality*. This value rests on two beliefs: first, that civil servants should be fully competent to perform their duties effectively, and, second, that they should be insulated from partisan pressures so that they might serve the public interest impartially and professionally. The primary means by which the Pendleton Act sought to ensure the competence of civil servants was by selecting them on the basis of *merit* through a system of competitive examinations. As noted above, these examinations tested applicants on the basis of their general knowledge as it related to the jobs for which they were applying. One of the primary tasks of the Civil Service Commission was to oversee the impartial administration of the examination and selection process. The names of individuals passing the examination were placed on a list of "eligibles" in rank order according to their scores. When a job vacancy arose, the Civil Service Commission provided the top three names on the list to the hiring authority. This "rule of three" allowed hiring authorities a choice among candidates while greatly restricting their ability to make decisions on the basis of partisan considerations. Even if partisan considerations did influence the final choice, the examination process increased the probability that the individual selected was competent to perform job duties.

The authors of the Pendleton Act understood that the public interest and the interests of the party in power are not always identical. Believing that the public interest should come first, they hoped to create a work environment in which civil servants could perform their duties in a manner unbiased by partisan considerations. Accordingly, the Pendleton Act sought to protect civil servants from political coercion and to limit their involvement in partisan politics. It prohibited managers from dismissing employees for refusing to participate in political campaigns and it authorized substantial fines on officials who tried to collect party contributions from employees or to otherwise "coerce the political action of any person." The Act also authorized the Commission to develop rules for implementing the law and to investigate violations of the rules. To protect the merit system as a whole from partisan interference, Congress established the Civil Service Commission as a three-member, bipartisan board and granted it the authority to fulfill its responsibilities largely independent of the president. Although the president was given the power to appoint new commissioners as their terms expired (subject to Senate confirmation) and to remove them at will, the Commission nonetheless functioned as a separate agency outside of the president's chain of command. By placing the Commission on a bipartisan basis, the authors of the Pendleton Act hoped that at least one of the three commissioners would work to prevent attempts by other commissioners to evade provisions of the law for partisan purposes.

The value of political neutrality took on a new meaning with passage of the Hatch Act in 1939. To ensure their neutrality, federal employees were forbidden from contributing to or participating in political campaigns, even on a voluntary basis. Although critics continue to maintain that this constitutes an unwarranted infringement on the political rights of federal employees, the Supreme Court has upheld the law's constitutionality. As a result of the 1993 Hatch Act reforms, most federal employees may now work on political campaigns in their spare time and hold offices within the party. However, they still may not run for elected office themselves.

The value of political neutrality ultimately rests on the questionable assumption that administration involves technical skills that may be exercised in a neutral fashion regardless of which president or party is in power. In reality, political considerations inevitably influence the administration of government programs. This reality aside, political neutrality continues to serve as a powerful ideal supporting the use of merit examinations, prohibitions against the worst forms of political coercion, and semi-independent agencies to safeguard merit principles.

A New Concern for Employee Rights

Concern for the *protection of employee rights* originated with the desire to shield employees from the kinds of political coercion prevalent during the spoils period. Although the Commission devoted most of its attention during its early years to administering the system of competitive examinations, it gradually began to identify a broad range of employee rights and to police the personnel decisions of agency officials more aggressively.

Arbitrary and capricious treatment of government employees by supervisors had been common during the spoils period. The Commission's initial efforts to expand employee protections centered on the problem of arbitrary dismissals. The Pendleton Act had not addressed the executive's removal powers except to prohibit dismissals for political reasons. Unfortunately, this prohibition was easily circumvented. Employees identified with one party were often discharged for offenses that went unpunished if committed by individuals identified with another party. To prevent abuses of this kind, President McKinley issued an executive order in 1897 (amended in 1899) stating that

> *No removal shall be made from the competitive classified service except for just cause and for reasons given in writing; and the person sought to be removed shall have notice and be furnished a copy of such reasons, and shall be allowed a reasonable time for personally answering the same in writing.*[6]

These procedural rights were later incorporated into the Lloyd-LaFollette Act of 1912.

Originally intended to curb abuses of managerial discretion in the area of dismissal, procedural rights were gradually extended to other areas in which employee interests might be adversely affected, such as demotions, suspensions, and reassignments. The processes established for appealing adverse actions usually did not extend beyond the department heads who were the final authorities over personnel decisions. In the 1940s, however, the Commission began acting as an appeals court in cases involving dismissals and other adverse actions. According to advocates of the positive personnel management perspective, the Commission's expanded role in protecting employee rights proved to be a mixed blessing. As managers found their personnel decisions being second-guessed, they became increasingly more reluctant to discharge and discipline employees. This provided civil servants with a degree of job security beyond that intended by civil service reformers.

Rationalizing Personnel Administration, 1923–1978

In every historical period, according to Herbert Kaufman, society has expected the public service to pursue multiple values.[7] What distinguishes one period from another is the particular emphasis placed on one value relative to others. Although *efficiency* was clearly a subject of much concern to reformers, it tended to be overshadowed, even constrained, by the greater emphasis placed on political neutrality. As noted in Chapter 1, the reforms of 1883 were essentially negative in character, designed more to prevent the politicization of the civil service than to promote positive personnel management. Reformers tended to assume that eliminating corruption and partisan abuses of power, and selecting individuals on the basis of merit, would necessarily result in greater efficiency. No doubt this was partially true, but the reforms also constrained administrative efficiency by removing personnel-related authority from the chief executive's chain of command and placing it with the semi-independent Commission. In the early 1900s the scientific management and administrative management movements helped shift attention to the values of efficiency and executive leadership.

The Scientific Management Movement

Efficiency might have received greater attention in 1883 except that the technical means for improving the practice of human resource management did not then exist. Not until the emergence of the scientific management movement around the turn of the century was systematic study given to developing and refining techniques for improving organizational efficiency. Frederick Taylor, the "Father of Scientific Management," believed that there was "one best way" to perform a task and that it was management's responsibility to discover it through scientific study. Scientific management involved the application of industrial engineering principles to the analysis and organization of work. These principles included dividing work narrowly so that tasks might be mastered easily, analyzing jobs to determine how to perform them most efficiently, standardizing work by drafting job descriptions and standard operating procedures, selecting workers on the basis of their task-related skills, and training them in "the one best way" to perform their tasks.

Scientific management's preoccupation with efficiency meshed well with the moralistic concerns of the reform movement. Efficiency not only reduced waste but also encouraged adoption of formal systems that reduced opportunities for political favoritism. In the early 1900s private research institutes, such as the New York Bureau of Municipal Research, took the lead in applying principles of scientific management to public personnel administration. The influence of scientific management at the federal level is most apparent in the Classification Act of 1923. This Act established the first comprehensive classification and pay system for jobs in the federal government. The new system promoted equity in employee compensation by linking the pay of each position to the particular class and pay grade to which it had been assigned according to the nature of its duties. Efforts to rationalize the practice of personnel administration also included the use of newly developed techniques in job analysis, testing, performance appraisal, and training.

It is worth noting that personnel administration emerged as a recognized field of practice during the scientific management era. Largely because of the influence of scientific management personnel officers made the transition from clerical workers to semiprofessionals trained in the use of the latest scientific techniques. The development of personnel administration as a profession, although positive in most regards, produced two negative consequences. First, it contributed to the growing separation of personnel administration from the daily management of human resources. This occurred as activities once performed by managers, such as applicant screening and pay-setting, were turned over to personnel specialists. Second, the technical orientation of personnel officers tended to block their further development as professionals. According to Robert H. Elliott, scientific management's "one best way" philosophy

> placed such a heavy emphasis on technique and scientific objectivity that the field of personnel came to be viewed as the application of a series of routine procedures related to the recruitment, selection, evaluation, promotion or dismissal of employees.[8]

Often perceived as low-level technicians even today, personnel officers continue to struggle to be accepted as equal partners with line managers in securing effective human resource management.

The Administrative Management Movement

Creation of the Civil Service Commission represented the first serious effort by Congress to organize the federal human resource function in a systematic way. In fact, personnel administration before 1883 was characterized by the absence of any formal system at all. No centralized personnel office existed to coordinate personnel activities. Nor did any coherent body of personnel policies exist for keeping the behavior of employees and their supervisors within desired boundaries. The president and his department heads acted as their own personnel officers in making appointments, and in most agencies the "chief clerk" possessed relatively unchecked power to supervise and discipline employees. The chief clerk's duties also included routine aspects of personnel administration such as keeping payroll and attendance records.

Although personnel administration became more structured with the creation of the Civil Service Commission, an integrated system of human resource management was slow in coming. Initially, the Commission exerted influence over only that part of the human resource function dealing with recruiting and examining job applicants. Most aspects of human resource management remained in the hands of the line manager, whose authority was constrained only by the relatively few rules and regulations adopted by the Commission. Although the reforms of 1883 established mechanisms for selecting competent, well-qualified civil servants, they were silent about how to attract and retain the best employees, and silent as well about how to train, compensate, and motivate employees to achieve their fullest potential as workers.

By the 1930s, however, the Commission had begun to evolve into a central personnel agency responsible for managing a full range of employment matters, from pay and classification to retirement and health benefits. In short, it had begun to evolve from a policing agency for the merit system to a central staff agency responsible for overall administration of the human resource function. But despite the evolution in its roles and responsibilities, the Commission continued to function as a board of amateur commissioners acting independently of the president. This independence, a product of the earlier commitment to political neutrality, ran counter to the newly emerging principles of administrative management. According to the latter, chief executives must have full authority over the human resource function so that they can exert *executive leadership* in managing human rsources. In 1937 President Roosevelt's Committee on Administrative Management, better known as the Brownlow Committee, recommended replacing the Commission with an agency directly accountable to the president. When Congress failed to act the continuing incongruity between the Commission's political isolation and the president's need to exert leadership in managing human resources led inevitably to the reforms of 1978.

The Search for Balance, 1978–Present

The Civil Service Reform Act (CSRA) of 1978 and Reorganization Plan #2 initiated the most comprehensive set of civil service reforms since 1883. Foremost among them were the following:

1. Reorganization Plan #2 abolished the Civil Service Commission, replacing it with two agencies: the Office of Personnel Management (OPM), and the Merit Systems Protection Board (MSPB). (Because presidents possess authority to reorganize the executive branch, Reorganization Plan #2 went into effect automatically when Congress failed to object to it in the allotted 60 days.)

2. The CSRA created the Senior Executive Service, an elite corp of top-level administrators comprising both political appointees and career civil servants.
3. The CSRA required executive agencies to develop and utilize performance appraisal systems specifying performance standards and critical elements for each position, and it stipulated that the results were to be used as a basis for training, rewarding, reassigning, promoting, retaining, and removing employees.
4. The CSRA established a merit pay system for upper level civil servants that linked salary increases to job performance rather than to years of service.

Each of these reforms, and the values each was intended to achieve, are discussed in the following sections.

Adoption of the Executive Personnel Office Model

The commission model was abandoned by the federal government, as well as by many state and local governments, for reasons discussed in Chapter 3. Two characteristics of the Civil Service Commission made it particularly vulnerable to criticism. First, by establishing a semi-independent commission, the Pendleton Act divorced important aspects of human resource management from the overall management function for which the president is responsible. This placed the president in the awkward position of being dependent on the cooperation of the Commission when pursuing personnel-related initiatives. In addition, because the commissioners were typically amateurs in personnel administration, they were ill-equipped, according to critics, to provide the required leadership themselves.

Second, the strong commission model adopted in 1883 violated the principle of separation of powers by placing legislative, executive, and judicial powers in the hands of a single body. The Commission simultaneously established personnel policies and procedures, administered them, and adjudicated appeals from employees who alleged violations of their rights. This led some critics to argue that employees could not hope to obtain fair and impartial adjudication of their grievances from the same agency that formulated and enforced the rules. It seemed to them that placing the Commission in charge of protecting employee rights was equivalent to putting the fox in charge of guarding the henhouse. The apparent inability of the Commission to prevent routine violations of merit principles during the Nixon administration seemed to confirm this point of view. It must be remembered, however, that other critics had attacked the Commission for being overly zealous in protecting employee rights at the expense of managerial effectiveness. Regardless of the merits of these conflicting criticisms, the Commission's responsibility for performing all three sets of governmental functions raised legitimate questions about its ability to perform any of them well and contributed to the confusion over what its proper role should be in the federal personnel system.

Reorganization Plan #2 abolished the Civil Service Commission, replacing it with two agencies: the Office of Personnel Management (OPM) and the Merit Systems Protection Board (MSPB). The first of these is a central personnel office directly accountable to the president, and the latter, like the Commission it replaced, operates as

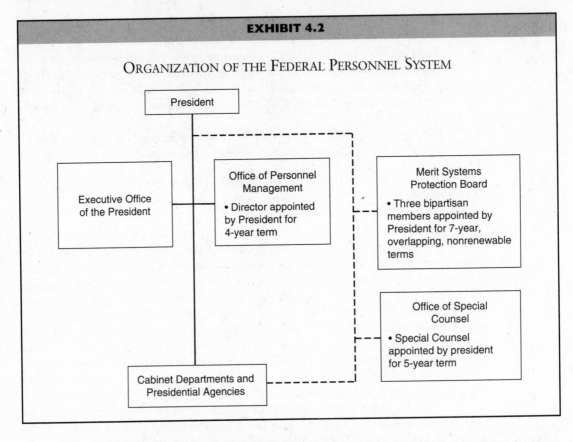

EXHIBIT 4.2

ORGANIZATION OF THE FEDERAL PERSONNEL SYSTEM

a semi-independent agency responsible for protecting merit system principles and employee rights. The executive personnel office system established by the 1978 reforms is illustrated in Exhibit 4.2.

As shown in Exhibit 4.2, the Office of Personnel Management is situated clearly within the president's chain of command. Its director is appointed by the president and confirmed by the Senate for a four-year term. OPM administers and enforces civil service rules and regulations, aids the president in developing new personnel policies, facilitates research intended to improve human resource management, and provides technical assistance to agencies in carrying out personnel-related duties and responsibilities. Although OPM is responsible for the overall efficiency and integrity of the federal personnel system, it delegates many operational decisions to the line agencies, seeking to guide the decisions of agency personnel officers and managers by establishing rules and standards for them to follow. OPM is empowered to take corrective action if its delegated authority is abused or misused.

The Merit Systems Protection Board consists of three members appointed by the president for seven-year, overlapping terms. To encourage bipartisanship, no more than two board members may belong to the same political party, and to protect the Board from partisan pressures, board members may be removed only for "inefficiency, neglect of duty, or malfeasance in office." The MSPB is charged with safeguarding the merit system by hearing and deciding charges of wrong doing, as well as appeals by employees of adverse personnel actions. It also reviews rules promulgated by OPM to ensure they are consistent with civil service laws.

The Civil Service Reform Act identifies 11 prohibited personnel practices, including such things as discriminating for or against individual job applicants and retaliating against employees for whistleblowing or filing grievances. If the Reform Act is violated in any of these regards, the MSPB is authorized to order corrective and disciplinary actions. Disciplinary actions are ordered to punish the person who committed a prohibited personnel practice, such as ordering the demotion of a supervisor who retaliated against a whistleblower. Corrective actions, by contrast, are aimed at helping the victim of a prohibited personnel practice by, for example, ordering the reinstatement of a discharged employee, or requiring the agency to alter its policies or practices. Closely associated with the MSPB is the now independent Office of Special Counsel. The Special Counsel, appointed by the president for a five-year term, is charged with investigating employee complaints involving prohibited personnel practices and bringing charges against violators to the MSPB when the evidence supports doing so.

By placing the Civil Service Commission with two separate agencies, reformers hoped to promote the values of executive leadership and political responsiveness without sacrificing political neutrality or employee rights. They believed that placing OPM under the president's control would promote executive leadership and political responsiveness in several ways. First, it would consolidate authority over personnel policies and procedures in the hands of the president, consistent with the management principle of unity of command. Second, it would allow the president to integrate actions taken in the area of human resource management with those taken in other areas of management consistent with the principle of unity of direction. Finally, it would help ensure that those individuals responsible for formulating personnel policies would be responsive to presidential leadership, thus empowering the president to eliminate unjustified constraints on managerial flexibility. Reformers argued that increased managerial flexibility would also eliminate the perceived necessity of circumventing merit system rules.

These benefits notwithstanding, critics warned that greater executive control would increase the potential for abuses of power, including renewed efforts to manipulate the behavior of civil servants for political purposes. Proponents of reform, by contrast, were willing to put their faith in a strengthened MSPB to protect employees from prohibited personnel practices. In the final analysis, the Reform Act called on OPM to promote the values of executive leadership and political responsiveness, required the MSPB to protect and promote employee rights and political neutrality, and established checks and balances between the two agencies so that all four values might be achieved simultaneously. How well the reforms succeeded in these regards will be assessed later in this chapter.

Creation of the Senior Executive Service

In 1953 Congress established the Second Hoover Commission to investigate the organization and operation of the executive branch and to offer recommendations about how to promote efficiency and economy in government. Among its 314 recommendations was one calling for establishment of a "senior civil service." By creating a separate personnel system for top administrators, allowing agency heads greater flexibility in assigning personnel to specific positions, and by offering higher pay and better benefits, the federal government could, according to the Hoover Commission, greatly increase its ability to attract and retain the best executive and managerial talent available. Although Congress failed to act on the Commission's recommendation, the idea of a senior civil service resurfaced as the Senior Executive Service (SES) in 1978.

The SES is an elite corp of political appointees and career civil servants just below the level of those political appointees requiring Senate confirmation. It comprises approximately eight thousand positions previously assigned to Executive Schedule grades IV and V (for political appointees) and General Schedule "supergrades" 16, 17, and 18 (for top-level career civil servants). These pay grade distinctions, characteristic of a rank-in-position personnel system, are irrelevant in the SES because it is organized on a rank-in-person basis. SES members are assigned a rank and corresponding salary based on their qualifications rather than on the particular positions they may hold. According to CSRA requirements, up to ten percent of SES members may be political appointees. The remainder are career civil servants. Although the largest job category in the SES is general administration, more than one-third of SES members are engineers, scientists, and lawyers. New members gain entry into the SES in one of three ways: by political appointment, promotion from the non-SES career service, or lateral entry into a career SES position. Each agency is responsible for establishing qualification standards for particular openings, and a qualifications review board must certify that new recruits are fully qualified before they may assume office. The total number of SES positions allotted to each agency is determined by OPM based on agency requests and consultations with the Office of Management and Budget.

The purpose of the SES, according to the Reform Act, is "to provide the flexibility needed by agencies to recruit and retain the highly competent and qualified executives needed to provide more effective management of agencies and their functions, and the more expeditious administration of the public business."[9] Supporters of the CSRA believed this would be achieved in three ways. First, membership in the SES would confer an elite status on top-level administrators in recognition of their important roles and valuable contributions to the public service. This in turn would create a special sense of identity and esprit de corp among SES members and help maintain morale at high levels. Removing rigid distinctions between career and noncareer positions would also allow competent careerists to move to higher-level positions and promote a greater sense of professional community. Second, career executives may earn salary bonuses based on superior performance, which allows them to increase their earnings significantly. The Act's supporters believed that these pay bonuses would motivate career executives to achieve higher performance levels and that the increased compensation would enhance their morale and job satisfaction. Finally, the Reform Act authorizes agency heads to reassign career executives as needed. In theory this not only allows agency heads to utilize human resources more efficiently, but also offers SES members greater opportunities for professional growth. Under the system prevailing before 1978, by contrast, incoming agency heads were forced to accept career incumbents regardless of how capable or willing they were to perform job duties as directed. The CSRA allows career executives to be reassigned within their own agencies, but prohibits transferring them to other agencies without their consent.

Creation of the SES also promoted political responsiveness by increasing the president's ability to place trusted appointees in positions believed to be particularly vital to achieving the president's political agenda. Congress limited this power, however, by designating approximately 45 percent of SES positions as "reserved" for career civil servants.

Adoption of New Performance Appraisal and Merit Pay Systems

The 1978 reforms also included new performance appraisal and merit pay systems designed to obtain greater productivity from civil servants. Perhaps because of Watergate, and perhaps because of alarm over the size of government in a period of slow economic growth and high inflation, public perceptions of the civil service became increasingly negative during the 1970s. President Carter took full advantage of popular perceptions of bureaucratic inefficiency to sell his reforms to Congress. "The system," he said, "has serious defects. It has become a bureaucratic maze which neglects merit, tolerates poor performance, permits abuse of legitimate employee rights, and mires every personnel action in red tape, delay, and confusion."[10] Such rhetoric helped convince Congress that new performance appraisal and merit pay systems were needed.

The CSRA requires federal agencies to develop and implement performance-based methods of appraisal. The system in place before 1978 offered little meaningful feedback to employees regarding their performance and failed to tie ratings to pay and other personnel decisions. The new system, by contrast, requires identification of the "critical elements" of each job and the development of performance standards for each element through a process involving employee participation. Employees must be appraised at least once annually, and the results are to be used as a basis for training, rewarding, reassigning, promoting, reducing in grade, and removing employees. Employees whose performance fails to meet established performance standards in one or more area, for example, may be reassigned, reduced in grade, or discharged.

The attempt to link rewards and sanctions to the results of performance appraisals may be seen in the system mandated for use in the SES. The CSRA requires the SES to be administered so as to "ensure that compensation, retention, and tenure are contingent on executive success which is measured on the basis of individual and organizational performance (including such factors as improvements in efficiency, productivity, quality of work or service, cost efficiency, and timeliness of performance and success in meeting equal employment goals). . . "[11] This is accomplished in several ways. First, career executives must receive "fully successful" ratings to be eligible for merit awards. Second, career executives entering the SES must serve a one-year probationary period during which they may be discharged at any time for unsatisfactory performance without right of appeal to the MSPB. Finally, successful completion of the probationary period does not guarantee continued membership in the SES. Career executives receiving "unsatisfactory" ratings must be either reassigned or transferred within the SES or discharged from the Service. In addition, anyone receiving two unsatisfactory ratings in any period of five consecutive years, or anyone who twice in any period of three consecutive years receives "less than fully successful" ratings (minimally satisfactory or unsatisfactory), must be discharged. Career executives discharged from the SES in this way may return to non-SES positions in the career service.

SES merit awards are of two kinds. First, career executives who receive "fully successful" ratings may be recommended for a "performance award" by an agency's performance review board. The performance award is a lump-sum cash bonus in an amount up to 20 percent of an executive's current base pay. The actual amount of the award is determined by the agency head. Although the Act originally specified that up to 50 percent of SES career executives may receive an award during each fiscal year, this figure was later reduced to 20 percent for budgetary reasons. Second, career executives may receive special awards from the president for outstanding performance. The Meritorious Executive award carries a $10,000 lump-sum bonus and the Distinguished Executive award carries a $20,000 lump-sum bonus. No more that 5 percent of SES executives may receive Meritorious Executive awards in any given year, and no more than 1 percent may receive Distinguished Executive awards.

Assessing the 1978 Reforms

Although a full assessment of the 1978 reforms is beyond the scope of this chapter, a few general observations are offered here. First, the wisdom of separating OPM from the MSPB is now widely accepted. Although this change contributed to greater fragmentation of government institutions, it also eliminated the conflict of interest inherent in having a single agency serve as both rulemaker and adjudicator. It also allowed OPM to concentrate more on employee development, employee incentives, and other elements of constructive human resource management. This does not necessarily mean that OPM has succeeded in fulfilling the expectations of reformers. According to Lane and Wolf, "OPM has not become the primary management office for the president, as envisioned by its first director, Alan Campbell. It has not succeeded in transforming public personnel management at the federal level into a modern system of human resource management."[12]

Second, the Office of Special Counsel (OSC) has been a disappointment to those who hoped it would be a strong advocate for employee rights. In 1989 Congress enacted the Whistleblower Protection Act in an effort to strengthen the OSC. It separated the OSC from the MSPB and charged it with protecting federal employees, especially whistleblowers, from prohibited personnel practices. It also eased the burden of proof required to show retaliation for whistleblowing, and it allowed employees to appeal to the MSPB if they did not obtain relief through the OSC's efforts. Despite these changes, a study conducted by the General Accounting Office in 1992 found that it remains extremely difficult for whistleblowers to prove that they have been victims of reprisal.[13]

Third, although the concept of a mobile corp of top administrators is generally considered a good one, the Senior Executive Service has been plagued by inadequate salaries, high attrition rates, and low morale.[14] Only 27 percent of SES members surveyed in 1989 said they would recommend federal employment to others.[15] Although inadequate pay has been a matter of considerable concern, other problems have emerged as well. For example, the hope that increased mobility would allow the most competent careerists to move from agency to agency in pursuit of challenging, high-level positions in the government has not been realized.

Finally, the performance appraisal and merit pay systems have failed to justify the high hopes of their designers. Morale plummeted in the SES during the first year of implementation when Congress reduced the number of SES members who could receive merit awards annually from 50 percent to 25 percent and OPM reduced it further to 20 percent. Problems also became apparent in the Merit Pay System when managers found themselves receiving lower salary increases than their nonmanagerial counterparts at grades 13 through 15 who were still being paid under the old system. Despite efforts by OPM and Congress to correct such problems, attitudes toward the new compensation system have not improved significantly. According to the results of a study conducted among senior executives in the IRS, 78 percent said that the SES bonus system did not provide an effective incentive for them to meet their job objectives, 69 percent said the SES bonus is not administered fairly, and 76 percent said there is not a direct link between their performance and their likelihood of receiving an SES bonus.[16] The available evidence seems to indicate that the goals of the new compensation system cannot be achieved until annual merit awards are made widely available to all who are rated fully successful, awards are large enough to truly encourage higher levels of performance, agencies can guarantee a fair and equitable distribution of merit awards, and employees can trust that their supervisors can and will evaluate their performance accurately.

The Civil Service Reform Act represented an ambitious effort to achieve a workable balance among several, potentially conflicting values. The four major reforms just discussed were designed to promote the values of administrative efficiency, responsiveness, political neutrality, and protection of employee rights—all at the same time. Because achieving potentially conflicting values is never easy, it is not surprising to discover that the Reform Act contained several internal contradictions. Is it possible, for example, to increase responsiveness to the chief executive without sacrificing political neutrality? Can managerial authority be increased without also increasing the number of prohibited personnel practices? Lastly, can SES executives compete for scarce merit awards without sacrificing their sense of common purpose and esprit de corp?

Among these contradictions, greatest attention has focused on the trade-offs between increased executive control and lost political neutrality. With political appointees possessing greater powers to reassign career executives and new opportunities to influence performance ratings and the distribution of merit awards, opponents of the CSRA feared that career executives would be forced into "professional prostitution."[17] To receive desired job assignments and merit awards, they would have to demonstrate their loyalty by conforming to the policy wishes of their political superiors. Under this scenario, performance appraisals would be less likely to measure performance than to act as control mechanisms ensuring conformity of behavior and political compliance. In short, critics feared the impartiality required of public servants would be lost, leaving them to confront daily the ethical dilemmas posed when the commands of their superiors appeared to conflict with the public interest.

Certainly the 1978 reforms increased the "politicization" of the civil service. Extending the president's control over the bureaucracy was a major goal of the Reform Act. Despite claims that partisan-motivated personal actions were rampant during the Reagan years, it is difficult to judge the extent to which political appointees have abused their enhanced powers. When asked in 1989 to assess how well the government had succeeded in "maintaining a merit personnel system free from prohibited personnel practices," only 47 percent of SES members responded "completely or somewhat successful."[18] Comments offered on the survey included the following:

> *The great harm of the SES has been the muffling of independent views through the power to award bonuses. When the head of the agency's staff controls your pay, he is in a much better position to control what you say.*

> *Many SES personnel are subject to arbitrary political pressure to leave, transfer, or make improper decisions. Some political executives have little understanding of career executives' roles, and do not want the advice or assistance of careerists.*

Although it is difficult to determine whether reported violations of prohibited personnel practices represent an increase over the pre-1978 period, it does not appear that partisan-motivated personnel actions are as systematic or widespread as they were during the Nixon administration.

Overall, the CSRA represented a long overdue effort to achieve a workable balance among important but competing values. That it is often described as a "well-intended failure" is not surprising in view of what it attempted. Congress will find it necessary to reform the federal civil service system from time to time precisely because the balance among competing values is so precarious. Future reform efforts are likely to build on what was begun in 1978 by finding ways for improving cooperation between political appointees and career civil servants, increasing compensation levels, developing a merit pay system that is perceived as fair and truly performance-based, and experimenting with how to decentralize operational decisions to the agency level without sacrificing merit system integrity. The nature and extent of future reforms will ultimately depend on emerging problems, changing values, and shifting political forces.

Notes

1. Paul P. Van Riper, *History of the United States Civil Service* (Evanston, Illinois: Row, Peterson and Company, 1958), 18; Herbert Kaufman, "The Growth of the Federal Personnel System," in The American Assembly, *The Federal Government Service* (Englewood Cliffs, New Jersey: Prentice Hall, 1965), 12.

2. Van Riper, *History of the United States Civil Service*, 35.

3. Andrew Jackson, as quoted in Van Riper, *History of the United States Civil Service*, 36.

4. Van Riper, *History of United States Civil Service*, 42–43.

5. Ari Hoogenboom, *Outlawing the Spoils: A History of the Civil Service Reform Movement 1865–1883* (Urbana, Illinois: University of Illinois Press, 1961), 236–237.

6. U.S. House of Representatives, 94th Congress, 2nd Session, Subcommittee on Manpower and Civil Service, Committee on Post Office and Civil Service, *History of Civil Service Merit Systems of the United States and Selected Foreign Countries* (December 31, 1976):202.

7. Herbert Kaufman, "Emerging Conflicts in the Doctrines of Public Administration," *American Political Science Review* 50 (December 1956):1057–1073.

8. Robert H. Elliott, *Public Personnel Administration: A Values Perspective* (Reston, Virginia: Reston Publishing Company, 1985):2.

9. 5 U.S.C. 1101, note.

10. Jimmy Carter, *Message from the President of the United States: Civil Service Reform*, 95th Congress, 2nd Session, H. Doc. 95-299 (Washington, D.C.: Government Printing Office, 1978), 1.

11. 5 U.S.C. 3131(2).

12. Larry M. Lane and James F. Wolf, *The Human Resource Crisis in the Public Sector: Rebuilding the Capacity to Govern* (New York: Quorum Books, 1990):20.

13. U.S. General Accounting Office, *Whistleblower Protection: Determining Whether Reprisal Occurred Remains Difficult* (GAO\GGD-93-3, October 1992).

14. Frank D. Ferris, "Is the Senior Executive Service Viable?" *Public Personnel Management* 18 (Fall 1989):355–373; Volcker Commission Report, *Leadership for America: Rebuilding the Public Service* (Lexington, Massachusetts: D.C. Heath, Lexington Books, 1990).

15. Cited in U.S. Merit Systems Protection Board, *Working for America: A Federal Employee Survey* (Washington, D.C.: Government Printing Office, 1990), 25.

16. Cited in the Volcker Commission Report, *Leadership for America,* 143.

17. See Bernard Rosen, "Merit and the President's Plan for Changing the Civil Service System," *Public Administration Review* (July/August 1978):301–304; Frederick Thayer, "The President's Management "Reforms": Theory X Triumphant," *Public Administration Review* (July/August 1978):309–314; Norton Long, "The SES and the Public Interest," *Public Administration Review* (May/June 1981):305–312.

18. U.S. Merit Systems Protection Board, *Working for America,* 23–25.

Part 2

Position Management

Human resource management entails not only the management of people but also the management of positions. Positions are the core building blocks of organizational life. How they are defined and managed affects the attainment of organizational goals in important ways. Once job duties and the qualifications needed to perform them are determined through job analysis, people with appropriate skills and abilities can be selected to fill them, compensation systems can be designed so that employees are paid fairly, and agency budgets can be constructed to ensure a measure of accountability.

But although job analysis and evaluation can contribute to a rational, well-ordered, and effective organization, they can also adversely affect organizational performance. This occurs when techniques are allowed to triumph over purpose. One of the great challenges in the field of human resource management today, as we will see in the chapters that follow, is discovering how to retain the benefits of job analysis and evaluation without unduly constraining managerial autonomy or the full utilization of the talents of each and every employee.

Linking HRM Tasks and Outcomes: A Performance Model

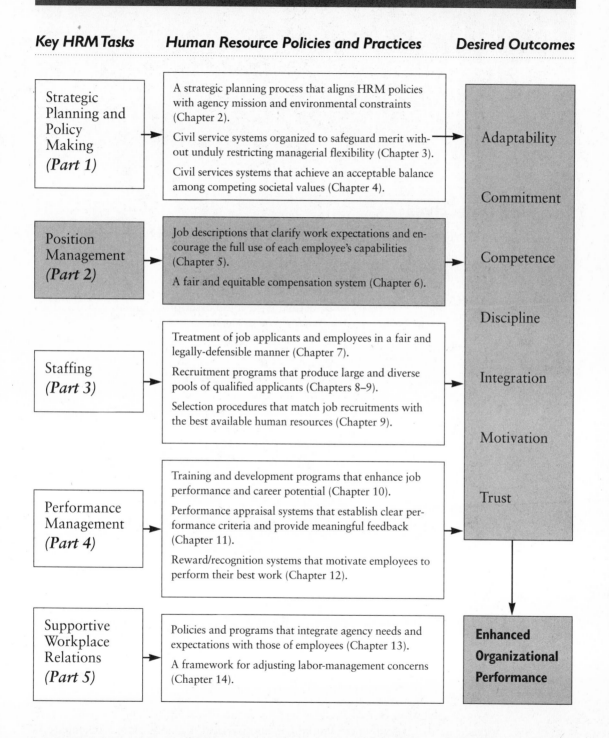

Key HRM Tasks	Human Resource Policies and Practices	Desired Outcomes

Strategic Planning and Policy Making (Part 1)

A strategic planning process that aligns HRM policies with agency mission and environmental constraints (Chapter 2).

Civil service systems organized to safeguard merit without unduly restricting managerial flexibility (Chapter 3).

Civil services systems that achieve an acceptable balance among competing societal values (Chapter 4).

Position Management (Part 2)

Job descriptions that clarify work expectations and encourage the full use of each employee's capabilities (Chapter 5).

A fair and equitable compensation system (Chapter 6).

Staffing (Part 3)

Treatment of job applicants and employees in a fair and legally-defensible manner (Chapter 7).

Recruitment programs that produce large and diverse pools of qualified applicants (Chapters 8–9).

Selection procedures that match job recruitments with the best available human resources (Chapter 9).

Performance Management (Part 4)

Training and development programs that enhance job performance and career potential (Chapter 10).

Performance appraisal systems that establish clear performance criteria and provide meaningful feedback (Chapter 11).

Reward/recognition systems that motivate employees to perform their best work (Chapter 12).

Supportive Workplace Relations (Part 5)

Policies and programs that integrate agency needs and expectations with those of employees (Chapter 13).

A framework for adjusting labor-management concerns (Chapter 14).

Desired Outcomes:

Adaptability

Commitment

Competence

Discipline

Integration

Motivation

Trust

Enhanced Organizational Performance

CHAPTER 5

Job Analysis

Learning Objectives

After mastering the material contained in this chapter, you will be able to:

1. Describe the uses and limitations of job analysis.
2. Identify five methods of collecting job information.
3. Identify five formal methods of job analysis.
4. Given the necessary information, write a job description containing clear and accurate task and job requirement statements.
5. Describe the challenges that must be overcome if job analysis is to promote effective human resource management.

Organizations divide work into discrete sets of activities called jobs. Employees are recruited and selected according to job requirements, evaluated based on job performance, and compensated largely in relation to job demands. To perform these fundamental personnel activities successfully, each job must be defined in terms of its duties and responsibilities and the skills and abilities needed for effective job performance. This is the essential task of job analysis.

Job analysis is the process of systematically gathering, documenting, and analyzing information about a job. Although this process is not nearly as precise and scientific as proponents sometimes claim, accurate and reliable job information is nonetheless an important prerequisite for effective human resource management and the realization of such values as merit and equal employment opportunity. This chapter assesses the many uses and limits of job analysis, describes methods of collecting job information, identifies five formal methods of job analysis, and explains the development and purposes of job descriptions.

The Many Uses of Job Analysis

Job analysis produces five kinds of information: information about the *nature of the work* (e.g., duties and responsibilities), the *level of the work* (e.g., degree of responsibility or complexity), *job requirements* (e.g., the knowledge, skills, abilities and other characteristics [KSAOs] needed to perform work effectively), *job qualifications* (e.g., years of education or experience that provide needed KSAOs), and *working conditions* (e.g., the psychological, emotional, and physical demands placed on employees

---

EXHIBIT 5.1

THE USES OF INFORMATION DERIVED FROM JOB ANALYSIS

Recruitment and Selection

- writing job announcements
- designing application forms
- developing recruitment strategies
- determining selection criteria

Equal Employment Opportunity

- validating tests
- determining how to accommodate disabled applicants/employees
- establishing the job relatedness of job qualifications

Performance Appraisals

- defining performance standards
- identifying evaluation criteria

Compensation

- classifying jobs
- evaluating job worth
- assessing pay equity

Job Design

- improving productivity
- accommodating disabled employees
- enlarging/enriching jobs

Training and Development

- identifying training needs
- designing a training curriculum
- identifying career tracks

---

by the work environment). This information contributes to organizational effectiveness in many ways. It is used to prepare and update job descriptions, identify job qualifications, develop criteria for appraising employee performance, define compensable factors for evaluating the relative worth of jobs, and redesign jobs to enhance job satisfaction and employee productivity. These examples only begin to indicate the importance of job analysis to effective human resource management. A more comprehensive picture is presented in Exhibit 5.1.

The Many Limitations of Job Analysis

Techniques for managing positions, as distinct from managing people, are products of the scientific management era. The goal of early twentieth century industrial engineers was to rationalize the entire work process through the application of scientific methods. They seized on positions as the fundamental building blocks of organizational design and developed methods for defining, standardizing, and managing them. The internal logic of position management may be summarized as follows:

1. Scientifically determine the most efficient ways to perform work through *task analysis*.
2. Scientifically determine the duties that must be performed and the skills and abilities needed to perform them through *job analysis*.

3. Scientifically determine the relative value of jobs and the pay that each should receive through *position classification* and *job evaluation* (see Chapter 6).
4. Scientifically determine selection criteria through *job analysis* and match the "right" applicant to each position through *employment testing* (see Chapter 9).
5. Scientifically determine the skills needed to perform work effectively through *job analysis* and ensure that employees possess them through *job training* (see Chapter 12).

Unfortunately, these techniques proved to be much less objective and precise in practice than their proponents had claimed. As Wallace Sayre noted in 1948, techniques were often allowed to triumph over purpose. And because the tools of the trade seemed to be more concerned with controlling organizational behavior than with enhancing human performance, personnel officers came to be viewed as interfering, low-level technicians. The tools themselves were often ridiculed as pseudoscience and dismissed as irrelevant.

It was not until enactment of civil rights legislation in the 1960s and 1970s that job analysis experienced a rebirth. This occurred as courts and civil rights agencies spotlighted systematic job analysis as the key to validating employment tests, verifying the job-relatedness of selection criteria, and accommodating the needs of disabled persons. Faced with the prospect of expensive lawsuits, employers quickly came to the realization that the tools of position management, despite their pseudoscientific pretentions, are an important component of human resource management. In the case of job analysis, for example, many essential management tasks cannot be accomplished effectively without complete and accurate knowledge of what a job demands of employees and what behaviors lead to superior levels of performance. If not a science, job analysis remains an important art—and one requiring considerable skill.

The challenge for human resource professionals today lies in discovering ways of overcoming the limitations of job analysis. These limitations are many. First, the dynamic character of the work environment causes the job description to become obsolete nearly as soon as it is written. Position management is based on the convenient fiction that positions have a reality apart from their environment and the individuals that hold them. This fiction suggests that positions are relatively fixed and that they can be studied and captured on paper. In reality, the environment in which work takes place is highly dynamic. Positions are constantly evolving in response to changes in technology, changes in organizational realities, and the individual impacts made by each new employee. Although this limitation is inherent in position-based systems, its negative effects can be reduced by updating the job description each time a turnover occurs to ensure that the qualification statements and selection criteria remain valid.

A second limitation is that traditional job analysis contributes to organizational rigidities at a time when greater flexibility is needed. The newly hired employee typically arrives the first day to find his or her position fixed in stone. For the sake of predictability and administrative convenience, the personnel department has already recorded its dimensions, assigned it to a grade level, and placed it in a salary range. The manager is trained to orient the new employee by instructing him or her to perform the duties stated in the job description. Not only does the position management system restrict the ability of managers to redesign the position as circumstances warrant, but it also prevents the full utilization of human resources. Employees are selected with strict reference to the duties and responsibilities to be performed, and the latter are rarely altered to take advantage of any special competencies that the new employee may possess. To overcome these rigidities, some organizations are now experimenting with job descriptions that are purposefully broad, emphasizing the goals to be achieved rather than the duties to be performed. Narrow, standardized job descriptions make little sense where employees are no longer performing specialized repetitive tasks. Building greater flexibility into job descriptions becomes increasingly important as work becomes more knowledge intensive and as governments attempt to move toward more adaptive, team-based work systems. To achieve greater flexibility, positions have to be viewed as variables, defined more by the skills and desires of employees than by rigid organizational specifications.

A third limitation is that job descriptions are rarely mission oriented or performance based. Although they provide guidance to employees about the duties to be performed, they do not typically orient employees to how their roles relate to the organization's mission. Nor do they generally describe the performance standards employees will be expected to meet. Large administrative systems such as governments will no doubt remain essentially position based. Even rank-in-person systems are based on the performance of discrete sets of duties and responsibilities. Nonetheless, job descriptions can do more to emphasize work outputs (e.g., products, services, and program goals) rather than narrowly defined duties, and job analysis techniques can be used to determine performance goals and the individual capabilities needed to achieve them.

A fourth limitation is that job analysis is not as scientifically rigorous as is sometimes claimed. Information collected through job analysis does not lead automatically to the identification of job requirements, job qualifications, test questions, performance appraisal criteria, and the like. As is discussed later in this chapter, their development requires inferences based on available information, inferences that are often difficult to defend if one's judgment is challenged. As a result, the reliability and validity of scored procedures, such as employment tests, performance appraisals, and point-factor job evaluation systems, are often low. To treat scores as precise, scientifically determined products only serves to undermine the credibility of otherwise valuable techniques. It is therefore important that the limitations on scientific rationality be understood and openly acknowledged.

A final limitation is insufficient resources to conduct professional job analysis. Legal requirements, professional standards, and good sense all point to the importance of thorough and systematic job analysis, and yet job descriptions are not routinely updated. Nor are selection criteria and employment tests routinely validated. The reality is that although textbooks often leave the unfortunate impression that "any fool can do it,"[1] professional job analysis is enormously complex and therefore time consuming and costly. Ideally, each agency would have its own separate staff of professionally trained job analysts. This is rarely the case, however, because of inadequate resources. As a result, job analysis often involves little more than asking enough questions of employees and their supervisors to be able to prepare job descriptions. These are subsequently dusted off as needed to serve various organizational purposes.

The technical information presented in this and the following chapters should be read with these limitations in mind. It may be useful as well to think about how these limitations might be overcome. The terms defined in Exhibit 5.2 are offered with the hope that they will assist in this exploration.

Methods of Collecting Job Information

Job analysis sometimes involves little more than asking employees and their supervisors to draft new job descriptions or update old ones. Ideally, however, job analysis is a rigorous fact-finding exercise performed by trained job analysts using one or more of the methods described below. To ensure collection of complete and accurate information, the use of a combination of data collection methods is desirable. The particular combination chosen depends on the number of jobs to be analyzed (some methods are not cost-effective when large numbers of jobs are involved), the type of work to be analyzed (work that is analytical in nature, for example, cannot be analyzed effectively through observation), and the type of information required (obtaining informa-

---

EXHIBIT 5.2

KEY TERMS IN JOB ANALYSIS

Hierarchy of Terms Describing Work:

Task Element The smallest division into which it is practical to divide work without analyzing separate movements or mental processes.

Task A discrete work activity necessary to the performance of an employee's job; smallest unit of work that produces an outcome usable to others.

Duty A major area of work activity comprising a group of related tasks.

Position A standardized set of tasks, duties, and responsibilities assigned to an individual employee.

Job Two or more positions within the organization having the same basic duties and responsibilities.

Job Family Jobs that have the same basic nature of work, but different levels of skill, effort, responsibility or working conditions.

Occupation A job or job family commonly found in the nation's workforce.

Terms Describing Job Requirements (KSAOs):

Knowledge Acquired information or concepts (e.g., knowledge of principles of accounting).

Skills Acquired measurable behaviors (e.g., typing skills).

Abilities Natural talents, aptitudes, or acquired proficiencies (e.g., dexterity, ability to get along with others).

Other Characteristics Characteristics of the individual (e.g., tact) or circumstances related to the work environment (e.g., availability for night work or frequent travel).

tion for evaluating the relative worth of jobs, for example, may require a different method than for determining job qualifications). Five methods are reviewed below.

Direct Observation

This method involves observing individuals performing their job duties to determine what tasks are involved and what KSAOs are required to perform them effectively. It is often used for analyzing blue-collar jobs where discrete work activities can be observed, but less often for white-collar jobs where the work is analytical in nature. Direct observation is used frequently in conjunction with the interview method. After the work is observed, or during observation, questions are asked of one or more job incumbents to clarify the analyst's understanding of the work. This combination observation-interview procedure is called a desk audit.

Individual Interview

In this method the analyst asks a set of semi-structured questions of the job incumbent designed to elicit information about job content and requirements. The same questions may be asked of the immediate supervisor in a subsequent interview to verify the information's accuracy. This method is particularly effective in analyzing administrative, managerial, professional, and technical jobs. Its major drawback is its cost. Because of the time required to conduct individual interviews, it may not be cost-effective when large numbers of jobs must be analyzed.

Group Interview

This method is essentially the same as the one just described except that the interview is conducted simultaneously with all, or a sample of, incumbents in a particular job. Although it is less time consuming than conducting individual interviews, it is not appropriate for use if an organization wishes to develop individual position descriptions rather than composite job descriptions.

Open-Ended Questionnaire

This method involves distributing a questionnaire to incumbents or supervisors that allows them considerable latitude in answering questions regarding job content and job requirements. Its purpose is usually to provide the job analyst with a first draft of a job description. It is less expensive and faster to administer than interview methods but often requires follow-up questions because of inadequacies in the information supplied. In addition, the reliability of job information may vary greatly with the writing abilities of incumbents or their willingness to report information without embellishment.

Structured Questionnaire

Rather than soliciting open-ended responses, this method limits responses to a predetermined set of answers. Incumbents, for example, may be given an inventory of diverse tasks and asked to identify those that are relevant to their jobs. Responses can be analyzed and job descriptions generated through the use of computers. The structured questionnaire is a useful method where organizations desire highly detailed information about job tasks or worker behaviors, but these questionnaires are costly to produce or purchase, and analysis of results requires trained staffs and computer capabilities.

The Importance of Obtaining Reliable Job Information

A primary consideration in selecting a data collection method is its reliability. Reliability refers to the amount of consistency in the information obtained by different job analysts or by the same analyst at different times. A method may be judged reliable, for example, if several job analysts independently obtain essentially the same information for the same set of jobs. Reliable job information is necessary for ensuring the validity of desired end products, such as employment examinations or performance appraisal criteria. For this reason organizations must make special efforts to obtain complete, accurate, and unbiased job information.

Unfortunately, data collection methods possess limitations that threaten their reliability. All methods, for example, are subject to an availability bias. This is a bias toward those pieces of information that are most readily available or come most easily to mind. There is a natural tendency to recall those activities done most frequently, done most recently, or that are most perceptually salient. An example of the latter occurs when supervisors identify typing as the primary activity of secretaries because the noise of typing is what is most salient to them.

Each method is subject to particular types of bias. The amount and quality of data provided from an open-ended questionnaire, for example, may vary more with the thoroughness and writing skills of the person completing the questionnaire than with the content of the job itself. Conversely, where questions are highly structured, the information may be accurate but the kind and amount of information may not be sufficient for its intended purposes.

The reliability of job information is also dependent on who is asked to supply job information. Personal biases or inconsistencies in judgment may be related to the institutional position of those supplying job information, the amount of their training or job knowledge, culturally engendered attitudes, or some other set of personal characteristics. Biases may also enter as a result of how data is recorded and summarized. Even when data are provided in standardized formats, significant variations may exist in the descriptive language used. Because job descriptions are not all written by the same person, and because it is difficult to standardize the language used, introduction of bias is possible. Remick notes, for example, that linguists have found patterns in the wording used in men's and women's job descriptions.[2] Those written by women tend to use "weaker" verbs. For example, men may "manage" and women "supervise;" men may "interpret" and women "use."

Although much more research is needed, some tentative suggestions may be offered regarding how to improve the reliability of job information. First, educating job analysts about potential biases may help them avoid biases. Second, using a combination of methods, such as a questionnaire followed by interview/observation audits, may help overcome the inherent shortcomings of any particular method. Third, analysts should be selected who possess good analytical abilities and interviewing and writing skills. Finally, analysis should be conducted independently by more than one person, including job incumbents and their supervisors as well as trained analysts.

Three Types of Formal Job Analysis

There is more to job analysis than collecting information to prepare a job description. For specialized purposes, such as constructing an employment test, developing a job evaluation system, or designing a performance appraisal instrument, more formal methods of job analysis are usually required. As shown in Exhibit 5.3, these formal methods may be categorized according to whether they focus on job tasks, employee behaviors, or worker attributes.[3] *Task-based methods* provide information about specific job tasks, including their nature, how often they are performed, and how critical they are to effective job performance. *Behavior-based methods* supply information about actual behaviors of job incumbents to identify those that contribute most to work effectiveness. *Attribute-based methods* ask directly about the KSAOs that job incumbents must have to perform their jobs effectively.

Consider, for example, how information about the job of a personnel officer can be expressed in three different ways, depending on which type of method is used:

Task-based Method: monitors agency personnel decisions to assure compliance with EEO/Affirmative Action requirements.

Behavior-based Method: explains rationale behind EEO/Affirmative Action requirements so that supervisors and managers understand their importance.

Attribute-based Method: knowledge of EEO law and professional personnel practices.

These differences are subtle but important. The first provides task statements, the second describes behaviors associated with effective work performance, and the third lists worker traits believed to contribute to effective work performance. As explained

---

EXHIBIT 5.3

MAJOR METHODS OF JOB ANALYSIS CLASSIFIED BY THE TYPE OF INFORMATION OBTAINED

Task-Based	Behavior-Based	Attribute-Based
Functional job analysis	Critical incident technique	Functional job analysis
Task inventory/comprehensive occupational data analysis programs	Position analysis questionnaire	Position analysis questionnaire
Dept. of Labor task analysis		Job element method
		Ability requirements scales

Source: Ronald A. Ash, "Job Elements for Task Clusters: Arguments for Using Multi-Methodological Approaches to Job Analysis and a Demonstration of Their Utility," *Public Personnel Management* 11 (Spring 1982): 82.

below, if your goal is to design examination questions for a new employment test, for example, the method you choose may determine how well your examination stands up in court.

Because each method is designed to obtain a particular kind of information, the method selected for use depends on the immediate purposes at hand. Generally speaking, task-based methods help define the nature and level of work and are useful for developing job descriptions and classifying jobs. Behavior-based and attribute-based methods, by contrast, are useful for recruitment and selection purposes because they provide information needed to determine minimum qualifications, construct employment tests, and distinguish acceptable candidates from superior candidates. They also provide information necessary for developing valid performance appraisal criteria.

The Problem of Inference

The desired end products of job analysis include written job requirements (e.g., knowledge of EEO law), job qualifications (e.g., graduate level coursework in human resource management), interview questions (e.g., what steps would you take if confronted with evidence of sexual harassment?), and performance appraisal criteria (e.g., demonstrates careful attention to detail when handling EEO complaints). Unfortunately, these products cannot be derived directly from lists of job tasks or through observation of work activities. The latter simply provide valuable pieces of information on which inferences may be based.

In conventional task-based methods, analysts infer job requirements from general knowledge of the tasks performed. The inferential leap required is sometimes a large one. For example, a task-based method may indicate that one of the tasks of a personnel officer is to ensure compliance with EEO regulations. But this information does not tell us which KSAOs are essential to successful task performance. Nor does it indicate which attributes may be used to distinguish adequate job candidates from superior ones. Identifying valid job requirements and constructing valid selection tests require analysts to make inferences that are supported by systematic study.

Behavior-based methods can claim greater validity than task-based methods because they ask about the actual behaviors of employees. Similarly, attribute-based methods can claim greater validity because they ask directly about the attributes required of employees to perform tasks successfully. Nonetheless, convincing a court that job requirements or test questions are developed in accordance with professional standards and EEOC guidelines can be extremely difficult. The following example illustrates how frustrating such efforts can be. In 1979 a federal court barred the New York State Police from using an examination for state troopers that had been professionally developed using Primoff's Job Element Method (described later in this chapter).[4] Recognizing that women and minorities were severely underrepresented among state troopers, the New York State Police contracted with a team of analysts from the U.S. Civil Service Commission, headed by Ernest Primoff, to develop a valid examination for entry-level troopers. After months of work, and at a cost of $1,245,000, the test was administered to a new group of job applicants in 1975. When only 8 percent of blacks and 10 percent of Hispanics, compared with 21 percent of whites, received passing scores, the validity of the examination was challenged in court.

In barring use of the examination for selection purposes, Judge Foley argued that the examination attempted to measure abstract traits such as "common sense" and "dependability" without relating them to specific tasks that require these qualifications. The issue of inference was central to his decision. According to Judge Foley, the Job Element Method, except when used to analyze blue-collar jobs, requires too great of an inferential leap:

> *Jobs may be placed on a continuum. On one end of the continuum are jobs involving processes that are directly observable. At the other end of the continuum are jobs involving processes that are abstract or unobservable. In a worker-oriented [attribute- or behavior-based] job analysis, the workers are making inferences about the individual differences of characteristics that are associated with superior performance. The lower the job on the continuum, i.e., a job consisting primarily of observables, the less of an inference is made between what is done on the job and the personal characteristics necessary to do the job. For instance, in a typing job the task is typing and the inference about individual characteristics, the ability to type, is not speculative. When one leaves this end of the continuum, the inference as to what personal characteristics are associated with performance of the job becomes highly speculative. Likewise, in a task-oriented analysis, the closer one is to the abstract or unobservable end of the continuum, the inference as to what psychomotor activities are associated with performance of the job becomes highly speculative. The more speculative the inference is from observable, the greater the "inferential leap."[5]*

The implication for agencies developing employment tests is that they must identify the tasks actually performed by job incumbents, identify essential job requirements, and, finally, link identified job requirements to the specific tasks that demand them. In short, organizations wishing to satisfy stringent professional and legal standards may need to use a combination of task-based and behavior/attribute-based methods to enhance the validity of their selection procedures.

Formal Methods of Job Analysis

Although it is not within the scope of this chapter to describe all formal methods of job analysis, five methods are briefly described here for illustrative purposes.[6] The Department of Labor and Functional Job Analysis methods are primarily task-based methods, the Position Analysis Questionnaire and Critical Incident Technique are behavior-based methods, and the Job Element Method is an attribute-based method.

The Department of Labor (DOL) Method

Developed in the early 1950s for inclusion in the U. S. Department of Labor's *Dictionary of Occupational Titles,*[7] the DOL method relies on written materials, observations, and interviews with workers and supervisors to obtain five kinds of job information:

1. What the worker does in relation to data, people, and things
2. The methodologies and techniques employed
3. The machines, tools, equipment, and work aids used
4. The materials, products, subject matter, or services that result
5. The traits required of the worker

The first of these lies at the heart of the method. Each job is described in terms of the worker's relationship to data, people, and things. As shown in Exhibit 5.4, these relationships are expressed by 24 functions arranged in hierarchies according to distinct levels. The higher the level, the lower the identifying number. The job of program manager, for example, might be assigned scores of 1 (coordinating data), 6 (speaking-signaling people), and 7 (handling things). The overall rating, 1-6-7, is sometimes used as an indicator of the total level of complexity of the job-worker situation.

Another major feature of the DOL method is the description of worker traits. These are the demands placed on job incumbents in terms of required aptitudes, general educational development, vocational preparation, physical demands, and personal traits. The DOL method includes a rating scale for each of these components. Information regarding aptitudes, for example, is useful for job counseling and employee training, but less useful for selection purposes because it does not establish a

---

EXHIBIT 5.4

STRUCTURE OF WORKER FUNCTIONS

Data	People	Things
0 Synthesizing	0 Mentoring	0 Setting up
1 Coordinating	1 Negotiating	1 Precision working
2 Analyzing	2 Instructing	2 Operating-controlling
3 Compiling	3 Supervising	3 Driving-operating
4 Computing	4 Diverting	4 Manipulating
5 Copying	5 Persuading	5 Tending
6 Comparing	6 Speaking-signaling	6 Feeding-offbearing
	7 Serving	7 Handling
	8 Taking instructions-helping	

Source: U.S. Department of Labor, *Handbook for Analyzing Jobs* (Washington, D.C.: Government Printing Office, 1972), 5.

clear relationship between actual job tasks and the aptitudes needed to perform them.

Functional Job Analysis (FJA)

Although the DOL method provides useful information, it is generally not complete or precise enough for developing selection criteria, defining performance standards, or determining the relative worth of jobs. It was developed primarily for collecting and recording occupational information and was not intended to meet the technical needs of other personnel functions. Because of its limitations, Sidney A. Fine subsequently refined the DOL method to create Functional Job Analysis (FJA), a more comprehensive, and hence more useful, method of job analysis.

FJA provides five kinds of information: statements of organizational objectives, descriptions of each task, analysis of each task using scales similar to those in the DOL method, identification of performance standards, and identification of the skills toward which training should be directed. The task analysis portion of FJA relies on scales that are more sophisticated and extensive than those found in the DOL method. Taken together, these pieces of information describe the tasks to be performed, the standards against which the worker's performance is to be evaluated, and the training needs of the worker. FJA represents a significant advancement over the DOL method because it addresses the technical needs of human resource management in a more comprehensive fashion.

Position Analysis Questionnaire (PAQ)

The PAQ, developed by Ernest McCormick at Purdue University, is a structured job analysis questionnaire used to analyze and describe jobs as they are currently being performed. The questionnaire comprises 187 elements relating to work activities, working conditions, and other job characteristics. A basic assumption of this method is that all jobs and levels of performance can be described in terms of these 187 elements.

PAQ elements tend to focus on human behaviors involved in the job, rather than on job tasks. They are organized into six categories: information input (where and how the worker gets information used in performing the job); mental processes (the reasoning, decision-making, planning, and information-processing activities involved in performing the job); work output (what physical activities are performed and with what tools); relationships with other persons (e.g., interviewing); job context (the physical and social contexts in which the work is performed); and other job characteristics.[8] As examples, six job elements and corresponding categories are presented below:

PAQ Category	Example of Job Element
1. Information input	5. Visual displays
2. Mental processes	40. Analyzing information/data
3. Work output	65. Use of keyboard devices
4. Relationships with other persons	100. Negotiating
5. Job context	136. Working in high temperature
6. Other job characteristics	165. Working irregular hours

EXHIBIT 5.5

RATING SCALE FOR PAQ ELEMENT 37

37 <u>S</u> Reasoning in problem solving (indicate, using the code below, the level of reasoning that is required of the worker in applying knowledge, experience, and judgment to problems)

1 Very limited (use of common sense to carry out simple, or relatively uninvolved instructions; for example, hand assembler, mixing machine operator, etc.)

2 Limited (use of some training and/or experience to select from a limited number of solutions the most appropriate action or procedure in performing the job; for example, salesperson, electrician apprentice, library assistant, etc.)

3 Intermediate (use of relevant principles to solve practical problems and to deal with a variety of concrete variables in situations where only limited standardization exists; for example, many supervisors, technicians, etc.)

4 Substantial (use of logic or scientific thinking to define problems, collect information, establish facts, and draw valid conclusions; for example, petroleum engineer, personnel director, manager of a "chain" store, etc.)

5 Very substantial (use of principles of logical or scientific thinking to solve a wide range of intellectual and practical problems; for example, research chemist, nuclear physicist, corporate president, or manager of a large branch or plant, etc.)

Source: E. J. McCormick, P. R. Jeanneret, and R. C. Mecham, *Position Analysis Questionnaire* (West Lafayette, Ind.: Occupational Research Center, Purdue University, 1969).

Each PAQ element is scored on a separate rating scale. As an example, Exhibit 5.5 presents the rating scale for element 37: reasoning in problem solving. Responses obtained from the PAQ are analyzed by computer, resulting in computer-generated job profiles or job evaluation ratings. McCormick and his associates have also developed a questionnaire specifically for use in analyzing professional and managerial jobs.

McCormick believes the PAQ is more systematic and subject to fewer biases than conventional methods that produce narrative job descriptions based on observation and interview.[9] It is simpler and quicker to use than conventional methods, and the accuracy of job information can be maintained by conducting analysis more frequently. However, structured job analysis techniques, such as the PAQ, are not intended to replace conventional methods in every instance. It is well suited for job evaluation purposes, for example, but may be less appropriate for other organizational purposes.

Critical Incident Technique (CIT)

John C. Flanagan developed this technique in the 1940s and 1950s as a means of defining jobs in terms of concrete, specific behaviors.[10] Its primary advantage is that it allows development of job requirements (KSAOs) directly from knowledge of actual job behaviors. Although implemented in a variety of ways, the essence of this technique is captured in the three steps described below.

The first step is to identify what are called critical incidents. Job analysts survey or interview employees and their supervisors about specific incidents they have observed that they believe contribute to effective (or ineffective) job performance. (Sometimes supervisors first record relevant observations in a log for a specified period). A supervisor may be asked, for example,

> *I note that you supervise three classification specialists. One of the employees is undoubtedly in your opinion more effective than the other two. I would like you to describe some incidents that you have observed during the past 6 to 12 months that made you consider his or her performance especially effective.*[11]

The supervisor is asked to report five effective and five ineffective incidents. He or she is encouraged to describe exactly what the employee did and how it contributed to effective job performance. A job analyst then writes up each "critical incident" in one or two brief sentences:

EFFECTIVE BEHAVIOR

Employee assisted co-workers with their work after her own job responsibilities were met.

INEFFECTIVE BEHAVIOR

Employee criticized co-workers who worked more rapidly than others.

The second step is to classify critical incidents so that KSAOs can be identified. After a large number of incidents are collected (sometimes several hundred), they are combined into appropriate categories, each representing a group of similar behaviors. A descriptive statement is then written for each behavioral dimension. Several related incidents, for example, may lead to identification of a dimension labeled "technical writing skills," or "ability to record job information precisely and accurately." These dimensions help identify essential KSAOs. Because they are derived from behaviors that have been identified as contributing to job success, they are more defensible than those derived from knowledge of job tasks alone.

The final step is to use critical behaviors and KSAOs for a variety of personnel-related purposes. CIT does not produce a full description of a job. It does not, for example, provide a list of job tasks and duties. What it does do is provide a defensible means of identifying critical behaviors and job requirements. For the job of classification specialist, for example, CIT may identify "technical writing skills" as a job requirement, and "writes class specifications that are clear, precise, and grammatically correct" as a critical behavior. These in turn may be used for several personnel-related purposes:

> **Job Qualification:** *Coursework in technical writing or one year of experience as a technical writer.*

Interview Question: Describe the educational and work-related experiences you have had that demonstrate your technical writing skills and abilities.

Reference Check Question: The position for which the applicant is being considered requires that he or she writes class specifications that are clear, precise, and grammatically correct. Based on your observation of the applicant's work as a former employee, how would you rate the applicant's technical writing skills.

Performance Appraisal Criterion: Writes classification specifications that are clear, precise and grammatically correct.

Always   4   3   2   1   0   *Never*

In addition to its versatility, a major advantage of this method is that KSAOs are derived from critical behaviors established through observation. In many other methods, by contrast, KSAOs are developed without a factual definition of what constitutes effective on-the-job performance. The job analyst may know *what* is to be done on the job but not *how well* it must be done to ensure effective performance. Although much subjectivity is involved in aggregating critical incidents into appropriate categories, inferences are nonetheless supported by direct observation of actual behaviors.

Job Element Method

This method was developed by Ernest Primoff of the U.S. Office of Personnel Management. The term *job element* simply refers to any KSAO that contributes to successful job performance. The goal of this method is to identify the characteristics of superior workers. Once these elements are identified, job applicants may be evaluated according to how well they meet them and selection examinations may be constructed around them. The basic steps involved are described below.[12]

The first step is to identify job elements and subelements. A panel is established comprised of job incumbents, supervisors, and personnel specialists, all of whom possess considerable knowledge of the job to be analyzed. The panel meets for three or four brainstorming sessions during which members are asked to suggest as many elements (KSAOs) as possible that they consider important to job success. After an extensive set of elements are listed, panel members are asked to identify subelements. Examples of subelements for writing skills might include accuracy of grammar, appropriateness of syntax, and clarity of expression.

The second step is to rate the job elements. Using the Job Element Blank shown in Exhibit 5.6, panelists rate elements individually in terms of the following four categories:

B—Barely Acceptable—What relative portion of even barely acceptable workers is good in the element?

S—Superior—How important is the element in picking out the superior worker?

T—Trouble—How much trouble is likely if the element is ignored when choosing among applicants?

P—Practical—Is the element practical? To what extent can we fill our openings if we demand it?

EXHIBIT 5.6

JOB ELEMENT BLANK

Job:
Grade:

Date:

Rater Name and Grade:
Title and Location:

Rater No.   Job No.

Page No. __ __
(col. 1 2)

(col. 3 4 5   6 7 8)

Element No. (Do not Punch)	Barely acceptable workers (B) + all have ✓ some have 0 almost none have	To pick out superior workers (S) + very important ✓ valuable 0 does not differentiate	Trouble likely if not considered (T) + much trouble ✓ some trouble 0 safe to ignore	Practical. Demanding this element, we can fill (P) + all openings ✓ some openings 0 also no openings	Columns	(These columns for use in hand calculation of values)						
						S × P	T	Item Index (IT) SP + T	Total Value (TV) IT + S − B − P	P' (+ = 0 ✓ = 1 0 = 2)	SP'	Training Value (TR) S + T + SP − B
					9–12							
					13–16							
					17–20							
					21–24							
					25–28							
					29–32							
					33–36							
					37–40							
					41–44							
					45–48							
					49–52							
					53–56							
					57–60							
					61–64							
					65–68							
					69–72							
					73–76							
					77–80							

Note: For all categories except P', + counts 2, ✓ counts counts 1, 0 counts 0. For category P', + counts 0, ✓ counts 1, 0 counts 2.

Source: From U.S. Civil Service Commission, Personnel Research and Development Center, Washington, D.C. as printed in Ernest S. Primoff, *How to Prepare and Conduct Job Element Examinations* (Washington, D.C.: Government Printing Office, 1975), 12.

After ratings are completed, a mathematical formula is used to determine which elements will best help distinguish superior from merely acceptable job applicants. The formula reflects a predetermined logic. For example, if even barely acceptable workers possess a particular element (the first category), then it will not be of much use in identifying potentially superior workers from among the many applicants. Similarly, if it is not practical to expect applicants to possess a particular element (the fourth category), then it will not be useful in distinguishing among applicants.

The final step is to develop selection checklists and examinations. Once the important elements and subelements are identified, they may be put to specific uses. One such use is development of a Self-Report Checklist. This is simply a form listing important job elements and asking applicants to describe their qualifications in terms of them. Completed checklists can then be used as screening devices to identify those applicants worthy of further consideration. A second use is test construction. In Primoff's words, when "every aspect of superiority is included in the list of elements, an examination that is developed to include all the elements will measure what it is supposed to measure — the extent to which applicants have the qualities that will lead to superiority on the job."[13]

The job element method is similar to the critical incident method except that it asks directly about elements (KSAOs) that contribute to job success rather than observed behaviors. The strength of this method is that KSAOs are developed systematically by persons knowledgeable about the job. But as Judge Foley ruled in *U.S. v. State of New York*, analysts must nonetheless make sizable inferential leaps when analyzing jobs requiring attributes that are not immediately observable. Subsequent to Judge Foley's ruling, Primoff modified his method to include techniques drawn from task-based and behavior-based methods. The result, according to Primoff, is a fuller description of a job, including operational definitions for KSAOs that may be used for test construction.[14]

Is Formal Job Analysis Practical?

Ideally, every government agency would develop and use an integrated system for gathering and documenting job facts. This system would simultaneously provide information on the purposes of the job, the tasks to be carried out, contextual factors related to the job (e.g., scope and effect), the KSAOs needed for minimally acceptable performance, and the special worker competencies necessary to perform the job in a superior manner. KSAOs would also be linked explicitly to the tasks requiring them. Realistically, however, this is beyond the capabilities of most organizations. Each method described above is relatively time-consuming and costly. A comprehensive system combining several of these methods would be even more time-consuming and costly. It simply would not be feasible to routinely analyze every job in the organization in this way. The best use of formal methods of job analysis probably lies in developing employment tests or performance appraisal instruments for a limited number of commonly found jobs, such as police officer or firefighter.

Job and Position Descriptions

A job description is a summary of the most important features of a job, including job tasks and the KSAOs required to perform them. It helps to define the job within larger networks of activities and roles, and it serves as the primary management tool for assigning work, communicating work expectations to employees, and monitoring individual performance. In many organizations, job descriptions also serve as the basis for determining minimum qualifications, selection criteria, and performance standards, although the information contained in them is seldom complete and accurate enough to serve these purposes effectively.

Because tasks may vary considerably among employees performing the same job, organizations sometimes choose to maintain individual position descriptions. These describe the duties assigned to a single individual. As a result, they can provide information that is more precise than that provided by a generic job description. Although developing individual position descriptions requires more time and expense, they are very useful in communicating specific task expectations.

Traditional position descriptions typically contain the kinds of information shown in Exhibit 5.7. Information about the kinds and amount of supervision exercised and received, for example, helps clarify how a position is situated relative to others in the chain of command and provides information regarding the degree of autonomy involved. Other information not shown in Exhibit 7.7 may include pertinent working conditions, the effective date of the description, the job's status (exempt or nonexempt), its location, and its pay grade or classification code.

Recent court decisions relating to EEO suggest the importance of modifying traditional position descriptions to include 20 to 40 job requirements (attributes or behaviors) that have been validated through systematic job analysis. These requirements may be subdivided according to those that are essential minimum qualifications and those that are desirable for superior performance. Once these are identified, positions may be filled as needed without conducting additional job analysis. Of course, the descriptions themselves must be updated periodically as technologies change and incumbents come and go.

To overcome limitations identified earlier in the chapter, traditional job descriptions can be modified to indicate how duties relate to the agency's mission and to allow greater flexibility in the assignment of duties and the use of employee talents. Some critics of traditional job descriptions also believe that they are appropriate places to indicate desired work outputs and performance standards. In this way new employees can be oriented not only to the duties expected of them but also to the performance standards against which they will be evaluated. Such modifications are intended to ensure that the job description is a useful tool for managing human resources as well as for managing positions.

Who Writes the Description

Who writes the job description depends on the uses to which it will be put. If its primary purpose is to clarify work expectations, then the job incumbent may be asked to write the description and the supervisor may be asked to review its accuracy. However, if the job description is to serve as a comprehensive management tool, it should be written by a trained job analyst based on the results of systematic analysis. Selection and job evaluation decisions, for example, require subtle distinctions that can only be made on the basis of complete and reliable information. Professional job analysts are trained to recognize such distinctions, to draft job descriptions using a standardized language, and to avoid personal biases.

EXHIBIT 5.7

SAMPLE POSITION DESCRIPTION

Position Title: Human Resource Specialist

Organizational Unit: Human Resources Office, Dept. of Commerce

Position Summary

Provides personnel and equal employment opportunity services to the Dept. of Commerce. Under general supervision this position is responsible for recruitment, monitoring EEO/Affirmative Action policies, employee training and development, and classification actions.

Supervision Exercised

Directly supervises one human resource technician and one office assistant. Responsible for evaluating, training, hiring, and disciplining persons in these positions.

Supervision Received

The position is mostly self-directing with general supervision by the Director of Human Resources. The human resource specialist decides priorities and develops procedures with assistance from the Director when needed.

Duties/Tasks

1. Responds to requests for reclassification by conducting desk audits, determining whether the position is correctly classified, and preparing necessary documentation to record action with the State Classification Bureau.

2. Provides advice/assistance to supervisory personnel in classifying new or existing positions as a result of reorganizations or changes in staffing patterns.

3. Develops and conducts training workshops and seminars to improve the knowledge, skills, and abilities of Department employees.

4. Monitors agency personnel decisions to assure compliance with EEO/Affirmative Action requirements.

5. Supervises collection of workforce data for EEO/Affirmative Action reports.

6. Provides technical assistance for individual hiring, including developing appropriate selection devices, developing position announcements, and determining suitability of experience and educational qualifications of applicants.

7. Other related duties as assigned.

Job Requirements and Qualifications

Working knowledge of the principles, practices, and techniques of public human resource management. Must be familiar with state and federal regulations pertaining to classification, wage and hour, nondiscrimination and affirmative action, and other law as it relates to this area of personnel. Must have excellent interpersonal relations skills. Must have ability to interpret policy and defend decisions.

These knowledges and abilities are typically acquired through a B.A. in a related field and three years of progressively more responsible experience in human resource management.

Duty/Task Statements

Part of job analysis involves dividing a job into its principal duties and subdividing each duty into its principal tasks. A job normally has three to seven major duties and each duty involves at least two tasks.[15] As a general rule of thumb, work activities accounting for five percent or more of the work should be described. For purposes of implementing the Americans with Disabilities Act, only essential, as distinct from peripheral, duties should be included. It does not matter whether these are labeled as duties or tasks as long as the desired amount of descriptive information is contained in each statement.

Task and duty statements typically begin with a verb and are written in the present tense. They are also written in a terse, direct style in which unnecessary articles, verbs, and pronouns have been omitted. The following format is often used to ensure that all important elements of a task or duty are identified and communicated to the reader:

verb/object of verb/explanatory phrase (to produce what by what means).

Example: Types letters, reports, forms, tables, and other materials into finished copies using a word processor, handwritten drafts, or shorthand notes of materials, and knowledge of grammar, punctuation, and appropriate formats.

Job Requirement Statements

Job requirements are the KSAOs needed to perform job duties effectively. Job requirement statements are typically written in much the same way as duty/task statements, except that they begin with terms such as "ability to" or "knowledge of," rather than verbs. Statements also indicate the level of competency required by using such language as "sufficient to" or "as demonstrated by." For example,

Knowledge of English grammar and punctuation sufficient to identify and correct errors in drafts of letters and reports.

Traditional job descriptions often include the qualifications that job applicants are expected to possess. These are usually defined as "minimum qualifications" and are often stated in terms of years of experience and educational degrees. However, having the stated qualifications does not guarantee that a job applicant actually possesses the KSAOs that the degree or years of experience are assumed to provide. For this reason, qualifications should be described only as indicators of how needed KSAOs are typically acquired. For example,

These knowledge, skills, and abilities are typically acquired through a B.A. in a related field and three years of progressively more responsible experience in human resource management.

To ensure that selection decisions are consistent with the principles of merit and equal employment opportunity, it is important that applicants be evaluated on the basis of their skills and abilities rather than arbitrarily defined credentials.

A Final Comment: Theory Versus Practice

Having described professional job analysis as a complex set of procedures requiring specialized expertise, this chapter may have created the impression that practice conforms with theory—that job analysis is conducted systematically by trained staffs using techniques of the kind described in this chapter. In fact, this is seldom the case. In most organizations even today, job analysis is conducted by individuals in different organizational units according to the informational needs of the moment and without particular concern for their level of professional training or the methods used. Although Ghorpade and Atchison,[16] as well as Ash and Levine,[17] suggest that each organization should have its own "Job Analysis Section" comprised of professional job analysts, this entails costs that are probably beyond the means of most governmental jurisdictions. One challenge, therefore, is to provide human resource professionals with enough training in job analysis that they can assist in establishing the validity of selection procedures and developing performance standards for the effective management of human performance. A second challenge is to achieve these institutional purposes while allowing jobs to be defined with greater flexibility. Only in this way can organizations move successfully to implement team-based work systems and to utilize the full potential of each and every employee.

▲ **EXERCISE 5.1** Job Analysis and the Duty of Reasonable Accommodation

You are members of a Selection Committee charged with recommending which candidate among three job finalists is best qualified for the vacant position of Human Resource Specialist. Although it was readily apparent during the interview that one of the three candidates is blind, all three were routinely given an opportunity to describe work-related impairments so that the Agency can fulfill its duty of reasonable accommodation. Two candidates reported no impairments. The third listed blindness.

As the first step in fulfilling your duty of reasonable accommodation, write a workplan detailing the steps you will take and the tools you will use to perform the necessary job analysis. The Americans with Disabilities Act requires you to distinguish essential from nonessential job functions (duties and tasks), and next to determine whether an otherwise qualified applicant can perform the essential functions with reasonable accommodation. The description for the vacant position is found at Exhibit 5.7, but you cannot necessarily assume that it is accurate (it may be very old). Nor does it necessarily provide the full range of information that you will need. You may also wish to refer to Exhibit 7.5 for guidance.

▲ **EXERCISE 5.2** Preparing a Position Description

This exercise requires students to interview a position incumbent using a structured questionnaire and to write a position description based on the results. Its objectives are to build skills in interviewing, writing duty/task statements, and developing minimum qualifications from knowledge of job duties.

EXHIBIT 5.8

POSITION INFORMATION QUESTIONNAIRE (PIQ)

To the Job Analyst: The completed PIQ is the official statement of the duties and responsibilities assigned to a position for use in classification, pay, recruitment, selection, performance evaluation, training, and related management functions. Complete and accurate information is essential.

I. General Information
    A. Position Title:
    B. Organizational Unit:
    C. Position Summary:

II. Supervision Exercised and Received
    A. Supervision Exercised (list names and job titles of those directly supervised):
    B. Supervision Received (identify the position's supervisor by title and describe the nature of supervision received):

III. Duties/Tasks (list and describe three to five job duties, and important tasks related to each duty where appropriate, using the verb/object/explanatory phrase format).
IV. Job Qualifications (list and describe all essential minimum qualifications—KSAOs)

Step 1: Divide into small groups of three to five students. Groups must be arranged so that there is one member who is currently or recently employed. This individual is the position incumbent, and the remaining members are the job analysts.

Step 2: Job analysts complete the position information questionnaire (See Exhibit 5.8 above) by interviewing the position incumbent. (In practice, an incumbent or supervisor will have filled out the PIQ in advance, and an analyst will have reviewed it for accuracy before drafting a position description.) This step requires taking extensive notes during the interview and drafting a final version of the PIQ based on the notes. Remember, qualifications must be demonstrably related to identified duties/tasks.

Step 3: Members of the group collectively (or individually, at the discretion of the instructor) submit a completed position description. This is essentially a final draft of the PIQ. See Exhibit 5.7 for an example.

Step 4: (optional) Groups may be reconvened during a subsequent class period to evaluate the descriptions developed by other groups, or to discuss the following questions:

1. What else might you have done as a job analyst to ensure complete and accurate job information?

2. How confident are you in the job-relatedness of the qualifications you developed? Does the PIQ/interview approach alone provide enough information to withstand a court challenge?

3. What important managerial purposes are served by developing and utilizing position descriptions? Can these purposes be achieved without sacrificing managerial flexibility in the way human resources are used and developed?

Notes

1. Erich P. Prien, "The Function of Job Analysis in Content Validation," *Personnel Psychology* 30 (Summer 1977):167.

2. Helen Remick, "Strategies for Creating Sound Bias-Free Job Evaluation Plans," in *Job Evaluation and EEO: The Emerging Issues* (New York: Industrial Relations Counsellors, Inc., 1979).

3. Ronald A. Ash, "Job Elements for Task Clusters: Arguments for Using Multi-Methodological Approaches to Job Analysis and a Demonstration of Their Utility," *Public Personnel Management* 11 (Spring 1982).

4. *U.S. v. State of New York,* 21 EPD 30,314 (1979).

5. Ibid., 2,684.

6. For a more extensive discussion of job analysis methods, see Stephen F. Bemis, Ann Holt Belenky, and Dee Ann Soder, *Job Analysis: An Effective Management Tool* (Washington, D.C.: Bureau of National Affairs, 1983); and Jai B. Ghorpade, *Job Analysis: A Handbook for the Human Resource Director* (Englewood Cliffs, New Jersey: Prentice-Hall, 1988).

7. U.S. Department of Labor, *Dictionary of Occupational Titles,* 4th ed., (Washington, D.C.: U.S. Government Printing Office, 1977).

8. Ernest J. McCormick, P. R. Jeanneret, and Robert C. Mecham, *Position Analysis Questionnaire* (West Lafayette, Indiana: Occupational Research Center, Purdue University, 1969).

9. Ernest J. McCormick, *Job Analysis: Methods and Applications* (New York: AMACOM, 1979).

10. John C. Flanagan, "The Critical Incident Technique," *Psychological Bulletin* 51 (July 1954):327–358.

11. Adapted from an example provided by Charles E. Wager and Milton I. Sharon, "Defining Job Requirements in Terms of Behavior," *Personnel Administration* 14 (March 1951): 19.

12. Ernest S. Primoff, *How to Prepare and Conduct Job Element Examinations* (Washington, D.C.: U.S. Government Printing Office, 1975).

13. Ibid., 3.

14. Ernest S. Primoff, C. L. Clark, and J. R. Caplan, *How to Prepare and Conduct Job Element Examinations: Supplement* (Washington, D.C.: U.S. Government Printing Office, 1982).

15. Bemis, Belenky, and Soder, *Job Analysis,* 65–66.

16. Jai Ghorpade and Thomas J. Atchison, "The Concept of Job Analysis: A Review and Some Suggestions," *Public Personnel Management* 9 (#3, 1980):134–143.

17. Ronald A. Ash and Edward L. Levine, "A Framework for Evaluating Job Analysis Methods," *Personnel* 57 (November/December 1980):53–59.

CHAPTER 6

Job Evaluation and Pay Systems

Learning Objectives

After mastering the material contained in this chapter, you will be able to:

1. Define job evaluation and explain how it contributes to the maintenance of fair and equitable compensation systems.
2. Describe the constraints job evaluation systems place on organizations as they seek to increase managerial flexibility and adapt to changing environments.
3. Explain how to evaluate a job using the position classification, point-factor, and Federal Evaluation System methods.
4. Describe the difficulties involved in maintaining internal and external pay equity simultaneously.
5. Identify possible explanations for the "wage gap" and propose ways of reducing pay inequities in government agencies.
6. Describe arguments for and against adopting comparable worth policies as means of correcting pay inequities.

As noted in Chapter 5, several management tools were developed during the scientific management era to make production systems more rational and efficient. Job evaluation is one of these tools. It is a formal procedure for determining the relative value of jobs based on analysis of their content. The end product is a hierarchical ranking of all jobs according to their relative worth to the organization. A job requiring a greater level of mental effort and specialized knowledge than another is placed higher on the job hierarchy, and the person performing its duties receives a commensurately higher salary. As this example suggests, the primary purpose of job evaluation is to establish the foundation for a fair and equitable compensation system. Job evaluation provides a systematic means of establishing differences in pay by linking pay to the demands of each job. With such a system in place, there is less opportunity for internal pay relationships to be upset by such factors as favoritism, discrimination, or inattention to issues of fairness.

Job evaluation is part of a larger process by which compensation levels are determined. This process involves three basic steps: collecting relevant job information (as described in Chapter 5), determining the relative worth of jobs, and developing a pay plan that sets wages and salaries. The second and third steps are the subjects of this chapter. Methods of job evaluation and pay setting are described, as well as issues relating to pay equity and comparable worth. As will soon become apparent, evaluating jobs and setting pay is more complex and controversial than indicated by this brief introduction.

The Concept of Internal Pay Equity

The primary purpose of job evaluation is to establish and maintain internal pay equity. Internal pay equity exists when employees feel their pay is fair relative to the pay received by their co-workers. If internal equity is not maintained, morale tends to plummet. This is because employees are often satisfied with their pay until they learn that fellow workers are receiving higher pay for performing similar duties. By linking pay received to duties performed, a well-designed and administered job evaluation system can help ensure that morale problems of this kind do not arise.

Conversely, if compensation systems are not based on formal job evaluation, wages and salaries may be unduly influenced by factors other than the demands of the job. These may include political favoritism, race or gender discrimination, an employee's ability to command a higher rate of pay than other employees at the time of hire, and a supervisor's aggressiveness in obtaining pay increases for favored subordinates. If such factors are not constrained by an equitable system for relating pay to job content, employees performing similar tasks may receive widely varying wages or salaries. The resulting dissatisfaction with pay is likely to undermine morale, reduce motivation, and increase turnover.

To illustrate the connection between job evaluation and equitable compensation, Exhibit 6.1 provides an example of a job hierarchy established by using one of the evaluation methods described later in the chapter. The jobs shown in Exhibit 6.1 are those of a small agency that provides technical assistance relating to energy conservation. Once the hierarchy of jobs has been established, corresponding pay grades and salary ranges can be set. The resulting system promotes administrative efficiency because each new employee is easily assigned a position in the existing hierarchy and a corresponding salary. It also promotes internal pay equity by linking each person's pay to the demands of the job.

The Limitations of Job Evaluation

Ironically, job evaluation systems can constrain managerial effectiveness at the same time that they facilitate administrative efficiency and pay equity. They can, for example, deny managers the flexibility they need to redefine job duties, reward the best performers, and utilize each employee's special talents. Such constraints on managerial flexibility impose costs on government agencies that they can ill afford in the current context of limited resources and demands for greater productivity. For this reason it is essential that the limitations of job evaluation systems be addressed. Four of these limitations are explored below.

First, the values or rankings assigned to jobs quickly lose their integrity. This occurs because job evaluation rests on the questionable assumption that jobs can be defined and evaluated apart from the employees that hold them. In practice, jobs contin-

EXHIBIT 6.1

SAMPLE JOB HIERARCHY, PAY GRADES, AND SALARY RANGES

Director	Grade 5
Deputy Director	Salary Range $43–50,000
Information Services Manager	
Accounting Manager	Grade 4
Technical Specialist III	Salary Range $36–42,000
Information Specialist III	
Resource Center Manager	
Technical Specialist II	
Information Specialist II	Grade 3
Accountant II	
Computer Specialist II	Salary Range $29–35,000
Personnel Specialist	
Administrative Assistant III	
Technical Specialist I	
Information Specialist I	Grade 2
Accountant I	
Computer Specialist I	Salary Range $22–28,000
Administrative Assistant II	
Administrative Assistant I	Grade 1
Maintenance Worker	Salary Range $18–21,000

uously change as employees come and go. This causes job descriptions and assessments of job worth to become increasingly inaccurate. As a result, job incumbents may be overcompensated or undercompensated relative to the actual demands of the job. To address this limitation, job descriptions must be updated and job worth reassessed on a regular basis.

Second, rigid job evaluation systems constrain the ability of managers to match the aptitudes and skills of employees with the work that needs to be accomplished. This is because employees are hired and paid to perform only those duties contained in the job description. Allowing them to work outside the job description, from the traditional point of view, undermines the relationship between job demands and pay. As a result, the rules of the game require jobs to be redefined and possibly reclassified before a manager can redistribute work responsibilities. A reclassification request often involves considerable time and paperwork with no guarantee of success. Not surprisingly, managers often conclude that attempting to adapt organizational resources to changing needs is not worth the effort. It is also not surprising that they tend to view job evaluation systems as constraints rather than as positive management tools and classification specialists as their adversaries. Fixed, narrowly defined job descriptions also prevent the full use and development of employee capabilities. Capabilities not required by the immediate job are likely to remain untapped, and opportunities for job enrichment or development of new skills are seldom made available. The unfortunate reality is that the tools of position management, including job evaluation, were designed to encourage workers to develop and use only a narrow range of specialized skills.

Third, traditional job evaluation and pay systems constrain the ability of managers to reward their best workers. This occurs because individuals performing similar duties are paid essentially the same salary regardless of their performance. Pay is set according to what the job demands of them rather than the level at which they are actually performing. Although this helps keep labor costs down, it also undermines the morale of the best workers and makes it difficult for managers to retain them. As a result, managers may be tempted to obtain pay increases for their best workers by requesting that their jobs be reclassified to higher pay grades. In some instances they may dishonestly report job duties and responsibilities to ensure that the jobs in question are scored more highly when they are reevaluated. If classifiers do not diligently review such requests and reject those that cannot be justified, grade creep often occurs. *Grade creep* is the process by which the integrity of the entire system is lost as more and more positions are overclassified. As the number of overclassified positions increases, other employees recognize an opportunity to appeal their classifications as well, thereby further undermining the integrity of the system.

Fourth, job evaluation systems may send the wrong message to employees and constrain the ability of organizations to adapt successfully to their changing environments. According to Lawler, job evaluation assumes that employees have prescribed duties to perform and should be held accountable for them.[1] This encourages employees to do only what the organization tells them to do rather than what rightfully needs to be done. Lawler suggests that this is the wrong message to send at a time when organizations are attempting to establish more flexible, less hierarchical work structures. The effective use of human resources, the pursuit of excellence, and the ability to adapt successfully to change requires a different message. In short, employees should be encouraged to use and develop their talents unconstrained by artificial, narrowly defined job boundaries.

Lawler concludes that job evaluation systems are neither necessary nor desirable in modern organizations. It is difficult to imagine, however, how pay equity can be maintained in any but the smallest government jurisdictions without some kind of system for classifying jobs and evaluating their worth. Solutions lie not in abandoning job evaluation systems but in overcoming their limitations. Ways must be found to maintain internal pay equity without unduly restricting a manager's ability to motivate, develop, and reward employees. This will require designing new systems that are tailored to the needs of specific organizations and are less dependent on narrowly defined job descriptions and salary ranges.[2]

Organizations, particularly in the private sector, are beginning to experiment with *broad-banding*. This involves identifying broad occupational groups (e.g., technical workers) and establishing broad salary bands for each group (e.g., $22,000–38,000) that extend across several traditional pay grades.[3] Managers exercise considerable discretion in placing individuals at various points along the salary band consistent with such factors as job demands, accumulated expertise, and performance levels. Broad-banding has several advantages. First, it shifts the emphasis from performing predetermined job duties to doing the work that needs to be accomplished, thereby allowing managers to match work requirements to human resource capabilities. Second, it facilitates the recruitment of individuals for hard-to-fill positions by allowing managers to offer higher starting salaries to persons with outstanding qualifications. Third, it allows pay to be determined on the basis of performance and the acquisition of new skills, as well as the demands of the job. Fourth, it allows employees to advance in their careers and to earn as much as or more than managers without having to take on supervisory duties. In traditional systems, by contrast, employees soon reach the top of their salary range and have no further opportunity for advancement unless they are willing to compete for a management position. The use of broad salary bands not only allows employees to earn higher salaries without leaving their current positions but also allows them to move laterally within the organization without risking a cut in pay. Finally, broad-banding encourages managers to view job evaluation and pay systems as management tools rather than devices for controlling budgets and restricting their autonomy. This is because they can readily see the connection between broad-banding and the growing concern for flexibility, employee empowerment, and capacity building.[4] Although experimentation with broad-banding is still in its early stages, the concept holds considerable promise. The Department of the Navy, for example, has reported success with broad-banding at its laboratories in San Diego and China Lake, California.[5]

Methods of Job Evaluation

The centerpiece of the job evaluation and pay-setting process is the method by which job worth is determined. Despite growing awareness of their limitations, public employers continue to use methods of evaluation that have changed very little since they were developed in the early 1900s. The purpose of these methods is to determine the relative worth of each job to the organization by measuring its content. *Job content* refers to the duties that must be performed by a job incumbent, their relative levels of difficulty and complexity, and the conditions under which they are performed. Traditional job evaluation methods rest on the assumption that the primary determinant of worth (and thus pay) should be the content of the job. Stated differently, although variables such as employee productivity, seniority, and supply and demand may play a role in determining final compensation levels, job content should be the primary determinant. This is said to be necessary to protect and promote the principle of equal pay for equal work.

Methods for evaluating job content were developed in the early 1900s to address the glaring wage inequities then existing in many public and private organizations. Methods in use today are modern variations of four methods that were developed by

1926: the ranking, position classification, factor comparison, and point factor methods. The position classification and point factor methods, along with the relatively new Federal Evaluation System, are described below. The ranking and factor comparison methods are not described because they are rarely used in the public sector.

Methods of job evaluation may be distinguished according to whether jobs are evaluated on a "whole job" or "factor" basis. In whole job methods, one job is compared with another and a decision is made regarding which deserves to be placed higher on the hierarchy of worth. In factor-based methods, by contrast, jobs are evaluated using one factor at a time. A *job factor* is simply a dimension of job content, such as complexity, responsibility, or amount of knowledge and skills required to perform job duties. The advantage of factor-based methods is that they allow greater precision in defining why one job should be placed higher on the job worth hierarchy than another.

Methods may also be distinguished according to whether the results of evaluation are quantified. No effort is usually made in whole job methods to quantify the results. A conclusion is simply reached that one job is worth more or less than another. In factor-based methods, by contrast, a numerical score for each job is usually the outcome of the evaluation process. Assuming they are properly designed and administered, factor-based, quantitative methods hold the greatest potential for producing reliable and valid results. This remains true even though numerical scores are seldom as precise or scientifically objective as their proponents claim.

Position Classification Method

The position classification method is a whole job, nonquantitative method. It involves establishing a series of pay grades defined in terms of increasingly higher levels of skills and responsibilities, and assigning classes of jobs to them according to which grade description most closely matches the level of work performed. Each grade carries with it a wage or salary range appropriate to its level, and jobs in each class are paid according to the grade to which the class is assigned.

The federal government adopted the position classification method in 1923 to achieve greater consistency in pay. As early as 1836, employees began petitioning Congress to address the serious inequalities in pay then existing in the federal service. A petition forwarded to Congress in 1838 demanded legislation "apportioning and fixing salaries to duties, so that all clerks performing like duties shall receive like salaries."[6] Recognizing the importance of standardizing pay schedules among departments, Congress responded in 1853 by establishing four job classes with one salary rate for jobs in each class. However, not until enactment of the Classification Act of 1923 was a system of classification established that could achieve the goals of the earlier legislation. Because male employees were receiving higher wages than female employees performing similar jobs, the Classification Act specifically mandated "equal compensation for equal work, irrespective of sex."[7]

Position classification systems of the kind developed for use in the federal government involve two distinct steps: the grouping of similar positions into job classes, and the assigning of classes to pay grades. In the first of these steps, positions with similar duties and responsibilities are combined into classes. For example, all personnel specialists with relatively routine duties and responsibilities may be assigned to a class labeled Personnel Specialist I. Personnel specialists with more demanding duties may be assigned to a class labeled Personnel Specialist II or Personnel Specialist III. Personnel

Specialist I, II, and III constitute a *class series,* representing a natural line of progression for individuals seeking advancement opportunities in this area of specialization. Combining jobs into classes greatly increases administrative efficiency in large organizations by allowing positions in a particular class to be treated similarly for purposes of recruitment, testing, selection, and compensation. It is important to note that this step by itself is referred to as position classification and is practiced by most large organizations regardless of whether they proceed to step 2 of the evaluation process.

The second step involves assigning job classes to appropriate pay grades by comparing class specifications with predetermined pay grade descriptions. A *class specification* describes the characteristics that all jobs in the class share in common. As shown in Exhibit 6.2, it is similar to a job description except that it is written at a more general level so that an entire class of jobs may be described.

The task of evaluating jobs does not begin until a hierarchically arranged series of pay grades has been developed. Each grade is described in narrative form according to increasingly higher levels of duties and responsibilities. These are called *pay grade descriptions.* As explained above, the process of evaluation involves selecting the pay grade description that best characterizes the work performed by positions in a particular class. The Classification Act of 1949 established a system of 18 pay grades for white-collar positions called the General Schedule (GS). Each job class is assigned to one of its 18 grades. The pay grade to which a class is assigned determines the salary range for all jobs in that class. For illustrative purposes, the pay grade description for grade GS-12 is presented in Exhibit 6.3.

Once a position classification system has been established, personnel specialists review positions to ensure that they are correctly classified. They also review classes and class series to ensure that they continue to define the nature of work being performed. Reviews are often initiated at the request of employees or their supervisors. The personnel specialist responds by determining whether current duties and responsibilities are accurately reflected in the job description, and by comparing the job description with several class specifications to determine whether the job is correctly classified.

The position classification method is relatively easy to understand and administer. It also can offer an element of scientific objectivity because pay grade descriptions represent at least a crude measurement scale against which classes of jobs can be compared. However, because no detailed, factor-by-factor analysis is conducted, blanket judgments about the whole job often produce incorrect classification decisions. In addition, the integrity of the system is difficult to protect because managers can easily draft job descriptions to match class specifications for classes in higher pay grades. Despite these disadvantages, many state and local governments followed the federal government's lead. Although the federal government adopted a new system for evaluating jobs in the early 1980s, the position classification method is still widely used in the public sector.

Point Factor Method

The point factor method is a factor-based, quantitative method of job evaluation. Jobs are evaluated several times, once for each job factor. This is done by comparing the job's content on one factor (e.g., its complexity) with a descriptive measurement scale (e.g., a task complexity scale) and repeating the process for all other factors. As illustrated in Exhibit 6.4, each scale contains degree levels describing increasingly higher levels of the relevant factor. Each degree level carries with it a specific number

---

EXHIBIT 6.2

SAMPLE CLASS SPECIFICATION

Class Title
Personnel Specialist I

Summary of Work
Performs professional work in the development and maintenance of specialized personnel systems under close to general supervision. The analytical work performed by positions in this class is conducted on routine problems or involves assisting senior professionals in more complex, nonroutine work.

Illustrative Examples of Work
Performs a number of tasks in one or two major personnel areas. Examples:

Selection
Selects appropriate selection devices from prepared inventory for individual position hirings; constructs, analyzes, and revises employment tests; participates in validity and other statistical analysis studies; participates in test item analysis; scores structured oral tests; determines suitability of experience and educational qualifications of applicants; develops position announcements; interviews job applicants; prepares lists of eligibles.

Classification
Assists in the maintenance of a classification system; reviews requests for modification and addition of positions and recommends action; participates in reviews of positions and classes and writes specifications; recommends establishment, modification, or deletion of classes or series; performs analysis based on fundamental classification factors; disseminates information on classification policies and procedures.

EEO
Reviews agency workforce data to determine deficiencies in parity employment; analyzes deficiencies to identify potential sources of discrimination and defines corrective measures; provides training to managers, department directors, and others on EEO selection guidelines, the principles of affirmative action, and other related topics; reviews agency affirmative action plans to determine compliance with legal guidelines.

Knowledge and Abilities
Working knowledge of the principles, practices, and techniques of public human resource management with emphasis in one or more of the above activities.

Ability to apply theory and principles to real situations; to perform in-depth analysis; to establish and maintain effective working relationships with employees, other agencies, and the public; to communicate effectively.

The above knowledges and abilities are typically acquired through education and experience equivalent to a B.A. degree in personnel, business, or public administration and one year of experience in personnel management.

EXHIBIT 6.3

PAY GRADE DESCRIPTION FOR GS-12

Grade GS-12 includes those classes of positions the duties of which are:

A. to perform, under general administrative supervision, with wide latitude for the exercise of independent judgment, work of a very high order of difficulty and responsibility along special technical, supervisory, or administrative lines in office, business, or fiscal administration, requiring

   i. extended specialized, supervisory, or administrative training and experience which has demonstrated leadership and attainments of a high order in specialized or administrative work; and

   ii. intimate grasp of a specialized and complex subject matter or of the profession, art, or science involved;

B. under general administrative supervision, and with wide latitude for the exercise of independent judgment, to perform professional, scientific, or technical work of marked difficulty and responsibility requiring extended professional, scientific, or technical training and experience which has demonstrated leadership and attainments of a high order in professional, scientific, or technical research, practice, or administration; or

C. to perform other work of equal importance, difficulty, and responsibility, and requiring comparable qualifications.

Source: 5 U.S.C. Sec. 5104.

---

of points. An evaluator determines which degree level definition best describes the content of the job. Points awarded on each factor scale are then added together to determine the job's overall point score. The total score determines the pay grade to which a job will be assigned.

Selecting a set of job factors requires value judgments about the dimensions of job content that should form the basis of employee compensation. Most point factor systems use similar sets of factors because they tend to measure the same underlying dimensions of job content. Factors typically include the *knowledge and skills* required to perform job duties; the physical and mental *effort* involved; work *complexity; responsibility* for such things as equipment, budgets, and clients; and *working conditions,* such as workplace hazards and hardships. Point factor systems generally use between 3 and 12 factors. Although 3 or 4 factors can differentiate between jobs nearly as well as 8 or 12, factors are sometimes added to an evaluation system to ensure its acceptance by various groups within the organization. Employees in a particular line of work, for example, may think some aspect of their job should be measured by the job evaluation plan without realizing that its contribution to the total score will be negligible.[8]

Factors are usually weighted according to their relative importance in determining job worth. For example, the complexity factor described in Exhibit 6.4 has been assigned a weight of 10 percent. This means that no more than 10 percent of a job's

---

EXHIBIT 6.4

SAMPLE FACTOR SCALE FOR TASK COMPLEXITY

Task Complexity

This factor covers the nature, number, and variety, and intricacy of tasks, steps, processes, or methods in the work performed; the difficulty in identifying what needs to be done; and the difficulty and originality involved in performing the work.

Level 1   25 points

The work consists of tasks that are clear-cut and directly related. There is little or no choice to be made in deciding what needs to be done. Actions to be taken or responses to be made are readily discernible. The work is quickly mastered.

Level 2   75 points

The work consists of duties that involve related steps, processes, or methods. The decision regarding what needs to be done involves various choices requiring the employee to recognize the existence of and differences among a few easily recognizable situations. Actions to be taken or responses to be made differ in such things as the source of information, the kind of transactions or entries, or other differences of a factual nature.

Level 3   150 points

The work includes various duties involving different and unrelated processes and methods. The decision regarding what needs to be done depends on the analysis of the subject, phase, or issues involved in each assignment, and the chosen course of action may have to be selected from many alternatives. The work involves conditions and elements that must be identified and analyzed to discern interrelationships.

---

total points can be awarded on the basis of its complexity. Factor weights are established because organizations generally do not want every factor to influence compensation levels equally. It would not make sense, for example, to treat physical effort in the same way as knowledge and skills for purposes of determining the worth of white-collar jobs. Careful thought must be given to the respective weights assigned to factors, because differences in weights will influence the pay grade to which jobs are assigned.[9] Factor weights are usually determined in one of two ways: the committee charged with developing a new system may determine weights subjectively after discussing the relative importance of the various factors, or they may be established through a statistical procedure designed to ensure that the final job hierarchy corresponds as closely as possible to the salary levels jobs are receiving in the relevant labor markets.

Despite their pseudoscientific pretentions, the measurement scales employed by the point factor method allows jobs to be evaluated with a relatively high degree of precision. However, ensuring the validity of results requires carefully written degree level descriptions and well-trained evaluators. One disadvantage of the point factor

EXHIBIT 6.4 *(continued)*

Level 4   225 points

The work typically includes varied duties requiring many different and unrelated processes and methods such as those relating to well-established aspects of an administrative or professional field. Decisions regarding what needs to be done include the assessment of unusual circumstances, variations in approach, and incomplete or conflicting data. The work requires making many decisions concerning such things as the interpreting of considerable data, planning of work, or refining the methods and techniques to be used.

Level 5   325 points

The work includes varied duties requiring many different and unrelated processes and methods applied to a broad range of activities or substantial depth of analysis, typically for an administrative or professional field. Decisions regarding what needs to be done include major areas of uncertainty in approach, methodology, or interpretation and evaluation processes resulting from such elements as continuing changes in program, technological developments, unknown phenomena, or conflicting requirements. The work requires originating new techniques, establishing criteria, or developing new information.

Level 6   450 points

The work consists of broad functions and processes of an administrative or professional field. Assignments are characterized by breadth and intensity of effort and involve several phases being pursued concurrently or sequentially with the support of others within or outside of the organization.

Source: U.S. Civil Service Commission, *Instructions for the Factor Evaluation System* (Washington, D.C.: U.S. Government Printing Office, 1977).

method is that it is relatively time-consuming. In addition, although the method is easily understood, the actual choice of factors and factor weights remains somewhat arbitrary and therefore difficult to justify to employees. Despite these disadvantages, the greater degree of precision promised by the point factor method has contributed to its increasing popularity. According to a recent GAO report, 21 state governments now use at least one point factor system to evaluate state positions, whereas only 13 states use at least one position classification system.[10]

Federal Evaluation System (FES)

The federal government's position classification system came under fire during the 1960s for its complexity, the ambiguity of its grade descriptions, and the number of positions thought to be misclassified. Congress responded by passing the Job Evaluation Policy Act of 1970, which authorized development of a new system of job evaluation. The Federal Evaluation System (FES) was subsequently developed and implemented for nonsupervisory positions in grades GS-1 through GS-15. Although it combines elements of several evaluation methods, the FES is essentially a point factor method.

The system of 18 pay grades and the administrative procedures for making grade assignments did not change with the introduction of the new evaluation system. The FES simply standardized the assignment of jobs to pay grades through the use of the point factor method. Factors, factor levels, and points for each level were chosen to retain the existing job hierarchy as much as possible. The nine factors and factor weights are listed below:

Factor	Maximum Points	Approximate Weights (%)
Knowledge Required	1850	41.0
Supervisory Controls	650	14.5
Guidelines	650	14.5
Complexity	450	10.0
Scope and Effect	450	10.0
Personal Contacts	110	2.5
Purpose of Contacts	220	5.0
Physical Demands	50	1.2
Work Environment	50	1.2

As can be seen from this list, job worth is determined principally by the knowledge factor. This is generally the case among point factor systems designed to evaluate white-collar jobs.

The FES uses both primary and occupation-specific classification standards so that positions in various occupations can be evaluated using a single system. The primary standards are the nine factor scales written in very broad terms so that they are applicable to all occupational groups. One of these scales (or standards) is shown in Exhibit 6.4. Consistent with these primary standards, factor scales have been developed for many of the more than 400 occupations in the federal service using language appropriate to each occupation. With these occupation-specific classification standards in place, the evaluation process can begin. To determine a new position's grade level, for example, a position description is prepared containing information relevant to the nine factors and a classifier compares the position description with the degree level descriptions found in the appropriate occupational standards. The position is then assigned the number of points specified for the levels of each factor that matches the position's duties and responsibilities. To increase the reliability of classification decisions, new positions are also compared with *benchmarks*. These are positions that have already been evaluated and are intended to be used as a basis for comparison in making classification decisions. This job-to-job comparison is part of what makes the FES unique among point factor systems.

Exhibit 6.5 presents a benchmark position description for a Housing Management Specialist. It provides a good illustration of how position descriptions can be written in a format that facilitates job evaluation. The assigned degree levels and point scores are shown for each factor. New positions with similar levels of job content may then be scored the same or similarly.

EXHIBIT 6.5

SAMPLE BENCHMARK POSITION DESCRIPTION

Housing Management Specialist, GS-9

The position is located in the Housing Programs Management Branch of an area office. The incumbent specializes in matters related to occupancy requirements for the projects assigned.

Duties

- Reviews occupancy policies of local agencies and housing sponsors and recommends actions for improvement or correction of deficiencies
- Reviews rent schedules for compliance with agency requirements.
- Advises and assists local agencies and housing sponsors on occupancy matters including admissions, income limits, rent ranges, family income certification, resident grievance procedures, and other related matters.
- Participates and conducts training programs to assist local agencies in implementing requirements related to occupancy matters.
- Performs independent field audits or reviews, or participates as a member of a survey team to evaluate local project activities concerning occupancy, maintenance, modernization, or other assigned activity areas.
- Develops survey reports, coordinates findings with other housing specialists, and prepares recommendations for improvement or correction of deficient project activities.

Factor 1, Knowledge Required by the Position—Level 1–6—950 Points

- Knowledge of agency management procedures and general practices for the planning, management, and occupancy of the projects assigned.
- Knowledge of agency funding requirements and skill in evaluating local funding proposals, determining their adequacy, and recommending action by appropriate budgetary approval authority.
- Knowledge of agency audit procedures and skill in performing regular or special audits or surveys of local housing operations and providing guidance or instructions for local housing personnel.

Factor 2, Supervisory Control—Level 2–3—275 Points

The incumbent receives assignments from the housing supervisor in the form of objectives, priorities, and deadlines. On complex work assignments, the incumbent receives guidance or assistance from the housing supervisor or a senior staff member.

The incumbent performs all assigned duties on a timely basis in accordance with central, regional, and area office procedures and policies.

Completed work is usually evaluated for technical soundness of conclusions or recommendations and for conformity to existing policies and requirements.

Factor 3, Guidelines—Level 3–2—125 Points

The housing specialist is provided a variety of central, regional, or area office procedures, instructions, or standards that are usually applicable to the work assignment. In addition, guides relating to occupancy, maintenance, modernization, and other survey areas are also available for reference purposes.

The incumbent uses judgment in selecting the appropriate procedures or references for the assignment. However, the established procedures must be used. Situations where significant deviations are required will be referred to the housing supervisor or senior staff member.

EXHIBIT 6.5 *(continued)*

Factor 4, Complexity—Level 4–3—150 Points

The work involves the performance of a variety of standard housing management functions related to the review and evaluation of local project occupancy, maintenance, modernization, and utilization practices within the areas assigned. The incumbent participates in team audits or reviews, inspects project facilities, and develops recommendations for maintenance or improvement actions.

The housing specialist must review case histories, examine management records and practices, interview local project personnel or tenants, and perform physical inspections to ascertain what needs to be done or evaluate conformance with established parameters.

Assignments frequently involve elements such as the type, age, size, or location of housing facilities; or the nature and frequency of expenditures for such activities as maintenance, repairs, or modernization that must be analyzed to determine the extent of management action required. However, the incumbent is not expected to resolve unusually complex problems or conditions.

Factor 5, Scope and Effect—Level 5–3—150 Points

The purpose of the work is to coordinate and monitor the operational management and utilization of local housing projects, assist local program participants in conforming with agency requirements, evaluate the adequacy of local activities, and recommend or initiate corrective actions as required.

The work involves treating a variety of conventional occupancy-related problems and affects the efficiency of housing program operations and the habitability conditions by the families housed.

Factor 6, Personal Contacts—Level 6–3—60 Points

Contacts include local project management officials or representatives; project residents; and civic, welfare, or other service organizations. The contacts are usually related to problem-solving efforts, and thus, are not established on a routine basis.

Factor 7, Purpose of Contacts—Level 7–3—120 Points

The purpose of contacts is to obtain compliance with agency housing requirements and settle issues of conflict among the persons or groups contacted. This often requires efforts to influence or persuade local project representatives that are skeptical and residents or their group leaders with special interest objectives.

Factor 8, Physical Demands—Level 8–2—20 Points

The work involves frequent onsite visits to project locations. This often requires long periods of standing and walking over uneven surfaces, and bending, reaching, or similar activities.

Factor 9, Work Environment—Level 9–1—5 Points

The work involves normal risks or discomforts associated with offices, meeting rooms, residences, or motor vehicles. The work area is usually adequately lighted, heated, and ventilated.

TOTAL POINTS—1855

The final step in the evaluation process is to assign jobs to pay grades according to their total point scores. Point scores are converted to an appropriate pay grade according to the conversion table on page 113.[11]

GS Grade	Point Range
1	190– 250
2	255– 450
3	455– 650
4	655– 850
5	855–1100
6	1105–1350
8	1355–1600
9	1605–1805
10	1855–2100
11	2105–2350
12	2355–2750
13	2755–3150
14	3155–3600
15	4055–up

The FES system was developed to bring greater precision to an otherwise traditional process of job evaluation. For this reason, it has done little to overcome the limitations of job evaluation identified earlier in the chapter. Aware of the remaining challenges, the Office of Personnel Management is now exploring ways of introducing greater flexibility into its classification, evaluation, and pay systems.

The Use of Multiple Job Evaluation Systems

Governments can ensure that all jobs of comparable value receive similar pay by using a single job evaluation and pay system. For a variety of reasons, however, governments often maintain multiple systems. One reason is that the nature of the work performed in different occupations may be fundamentally different. Accurate evaluation of jobs in such instances may require the use of different factors and factor weights for each occupational group. Categories for which separate evaluation systems often exist include clerical, administrative and professional; trade, craft and labor; police; firefighters; managerial and executive; and special occupational categories such as teachers, doctors, and scientists. A second reason for using multiple plans is to avoid the difficulties involved in writing degree levels that are descriptive of very different kinds of work. Efforts to write comprehensive degree level descriptions generally result in narrative statements that are long, complex, and difficult to use. As noted above, the developers of the Federal Evaluation System sought to avoid this problem by drafting different sets of degree level descriptions for each occupation, all of which must conform to a set of primary standards. A third reason for using multiple plans is to increase flexibility in pay setting. Single job evaluation and pay plans cannot respond as well to collective bargaining pressures or to the forces of supply and demand because all jobs are subject to the same pay schedules.

The disadvantage of multiple systems is that it is harder to maintain pay comparability across occupational lines. This is a matter of concern, for example, where pay scales in male-dominated occupations (e.g. in police, fire, or blue-collar pay systems) are able to increase at faster rates than in female-dominated occupations (e.g., in the clerical pay system).

The Validity of Job Evaluation Ratings

Establishing the validity of job ratings is difficult because there is no universal or absolute criterion of job worth against which ratings can be validated. Each job evaluation system necessarily provides its own criteria of worth in its choices of factors, factor weights, and factor descriptions. One way to enhance the validity of job ratings is to make every effort to obtain reliable job information and to take steps to ensure that the system is relatively free of bias. The recent literature on pay equity provides examples of how job evaluation systems can contain systematic biases.[12] Because most job evaluation systems were originally developed for use in factory settings, the choice of factors and factor descriptions may have greater relevance for male-dominated jobs than for female-dominated jobs. For example, a factor such as responsibility may be measured in terms of budgets and equipment, but not in terms of responsibility for the health and welfare of other human beings. Where this is the case, persons working in female-dominated, nurturing occupations, such as public nurse or social worker, may find their work undervalued by traditional job evaluation systems.

Improving the reliability of evaluation systems also improves their validity. As a practical matter, however, the validity of job ratings rests on their acceptability to both management and labor.[13] Because the perceived validity of job ratings depends in part on their acceptability to employees, it is wise to involve employees in the development of the evaluation system. This can be accomplished by establishing a development committee composed of employees who are representative of various occupations and levels within the organization. The advantages of encouraging employee involvement include increased trust as employees realize that there are no hidden agendas, increased sense of ownership as employees begin to identify with a plan they helped to develop, and increased acceptance as they learn more about the theory and practice of job evaluation.

Establishing Pay Ranges

Job evaluation systems establish a hierarchy of job worth but they do not set the corresponding pay levels. This requires separate pay-setting processes. Before establishing pay ranges for each grade, or before adjusting existing pay ranges, organizations often determine the current *pay line*. This is accomplished by plotting the points at which each job's current rate of pay intersects with its job evaluation score. A line can then be drawn, either by "eyeballing" the results or by employing statistical techniques, that best represents the existing relationship between pay and job content.

A *pay range* identifies the minimum and maximum wage or salary that can be received by employees in jobs assigned to a particular pay grade. Pay ranges are often built around the pay line. Minimum pay for jobs in each grade, for example, may be

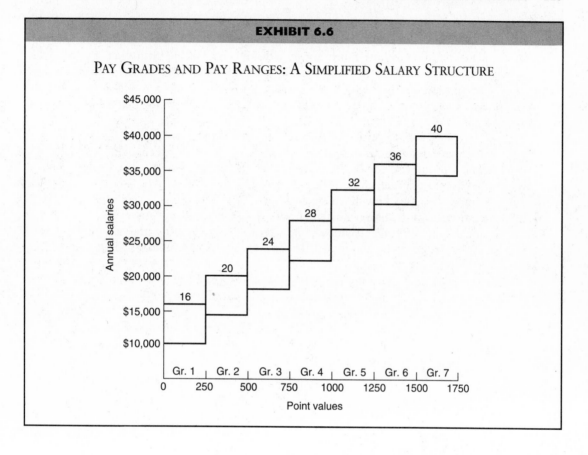

EXHIBIT 6.6

PAY GRADES AND PAY RANGES: A SIMPLIFIED SALARY STRUCTURE

set at 15 percent below the pay line and the maximum set at 15 percent above the pay line. Each pay range is typically divided into several pay steps. Depending on the organization's compensation policies, an employee's progression through these steps may reflect qualifications at time of hire, years of service, level of productivity, or other similar factors. Although traditional practices are beginning to change, it is still common in the public sector for employees to receive step increases automatically based on years of service. As illustrated in Exhibit 6.6, pay ranges for adjoining pay grades often overlap. Usually, however, they are not as uniform as shown in Exhibit 6.6. Pay ranges are typically narrower at the lower levels of the job hierarchy than at the higher levels.

If organizations are to be successful in attracting, retaining, and motivating employees, pay ranges must be set so that salaries are more or less consistent with prevailing labor market rates. This means, for example, that jobs of the kind assigned to pay grade 1 must be receiving salaries in the $10 to 16,000 range from other employers as well. If other employers are paying considerably more for comparable jobs, serious recruitment, retention, and performance problems can occur. *Salary surveys* are the primary means of determining how salaries within the organization compare with those paid by other organizations. A set of representative, well-understood jobs are chosen for the survey. Once these jobs are priced, they help anchor the entire pay plan according to how much above or below comparable institutions the organization believes it can pay. Compensation managers in the public sector may not have the authority to adjust the pay plan without legislative approval, but survey results are often useful in making arguments to the legislative body that adjustments are needed.

The typical survey asks employers a series of questions regarding the number of employees, the number of hours normally worked, salary policies, and employee benefits. This information is used to determine the relevance of the data to the organization conducting the survey. The survey also provides brief job descriptions, and the employer is asked how much it pays for similar jobs. Because surveys are expensive to develop, many public sector employers rely instead on the survey data for professional, administrative, technical, and clerical jobs routinely gathered by the U.S. Bureau of Labor Statistics or associations such as the International City/County Management Association (ICMA).

Wages and salaries in the public sector are based primarily on job content, with some adjustments for marketplace realities (variations in supply and demand, costs of living, and union negotiations). They are also set in the context of budgetary constraints and political pressures that may affect government's ability or willingness to pay. Within this general framework, compensation systems may incorporate additional factors that allow for individual variations in pay. These include the following:

Market factors: paying more based on how much an individual can command for his or her knowledge and skills in the relevant labor market; usually achieved by bringing new employees in at higher salary steps.

Work assignment hardships: paying more for such things as extensive travel or shiftwork.

Skill/educational attainment: paying more for acquiring additional skills or achieving higher levels of education.

Volume of work: paying more to employees who are doing essentially the same work as others but more of it.

Longevity/seniority adjustments: paying employees more according to how long they have worked for the organization.

Merit/performance: awarding employees an addition to base salary or a pay bonus for superior work performance.

As noted earlier, some organizations are now experimenting with alternative evaluation and pay-setting systems. As more and more governments adopt broad-banding techniques, for example, pay systems will contain fewer pay grades and broader pay ranges. It is also likely that more governments will replace automatic step increases with various forms of pay-for-performance systems and skill-based pay incentives that reward employees for learning new skills on the job. Grounded in a desire for greater employee motivation and productivity, these alternative forms of compensation represent an emerging shift in emphasis from the demands of the job in the abstract to the skills and performance levels of individual employees.

Balancing Internal and External Pay Equity

Compensation policies are necessarily shaped by considerations of equity. For example, employee morale and motivation are adversely affected when employees perceive their pay as unfair relative to their co-workers (a matter of internal pay equity) and when their pay is unfair relative to what other employers are paying for similar jobs (a matter of external pay equity). One of the compensation manager's most difficult tasks is to secure both internal and external pay equity while holding the line on labor costs. Internal pay equity, as explained earlier, is maintained by arranging jobs in a hierarchy of job worth and compensating employees accordingly. External pay equity is achieved by conducting salary surveys to determine the "going rates" for various jobs and adjusting the pay plan as a whole. External pay equity is important not only because morale will suffer if salaries are allowed to fall below market levels, but the ability of the employer to successfully recruit and retain workers will be seriously undermined as well.

Balancing internal and external pay equity can be an enormously difficult task. Because of the dynamics of supply and demand, the salaries that jobs can command on the labor market at any particular time will seldom correspond exactly to the scores or rankings established through job evaluation. As a result, the goals of internal and external equity are potentially in conflict. If, for example, the supply of computer programmers is low, the salaries they can obtain on the labor market will tend to be high. To attract and retain qualified computer programmers, an organization may need to pay higher salaries than those provided for in the pay plan. Doing so, however, will alter the job worth hierarchy and undermine internal pay equity. The resulting dilemma is an inescapable part of a system in which compensation is determined by both job content and market comparisons. Because compensation managers cannot adjust the entire pay structure to accommodate changes in market rates for specific jobs, their options are severely limited. In some instances, individuals may be recruited successfully by hiring them at a higher pay step. In other instances, managers may be allowed to make pay exceptions until supply and demand problems correct themselves.

Two other aspects of pay equity are currently receiving well-deserved attention. The first involves the level of pay received in relation to employee performance. Traditional compensation systems are designed to provide equal pay for equal work—not equal pay for equal work performance. It is easy to imagine the dissatisfaction that can form in the mind of a superior performer who is reminded on a daily basis that the poor performer at the next desk is receiving essentially the same pay. The superior performer has little incentive to remain a superior performer and may choose to look for work elsewhere. The problem is reinforced by traditional longevity-based pay increases and automatic cost-of-living adjustments that do little to encourage greater productivity. As a result, many public employers are adopting pay-for-performance systems that allow managers to award superior workers with pay bonuses or additions to their base pay. Pay incentives of this kind are particularly important as organizations strive to increase productivity and achieve organizational excellence. The federal government and 23 states now have some form of pay-for-performance systems in place.[14] The philosophy behind pay-for-performance systems is described more fully in Chapter 12.

A second issue that has received considerable attention in recent years involves inequities in the pay received by men and women for performing job duties that are of comparable value. There is evidence suggesting that women are not always paid in relation to job demands, are adversely affected by systematic biases in job evaluation and market pricing systems, and are restricted in their access to higher-level jobs where salaries are proportionately higher. These issues are explored later in this chapter.

Compensation Policies in the Public Sector

Compensation managers, whether situated in a central budget or personnel office, are responsible for formulating and proposing compensation policies. Policy issues include what range of benefits to provide, how to administer benefit programs cost-effectively, and whether to establish a pay policy that is more or less than other public and private employers. Policy decisions in the public sector are made within constraints set by legislative bodies, economic realities, political pressures, union pressures (see Chapter 14), and legal requirements. Pay and benefit packages, for example, are generally established as the result of legislative action. Legislators may understand the importance of investing in human resources but feel unable to make the necessary investments because of budgetary constraints, declining tax revenues, or an electorate that does not understand its importance or simply does not care. Policy decisions are also made within the boundaries of legal requirements. The Fair Labor Standards Act, for example, regulates minimum pay, hours of work, and overtime for most state and local employees. The Equal Pay Act of 1963 requires equal pay for equal work for men and women, and the civil rights laws described in Chapter 7 require employees to be compensated without regard to their race, gender, religion, national origin, age, or disability. Finally, compensation decisions are often subject to collective bargaining. Although federal employees may not negotiate over wages, the right to collectively bargain over pay and benefits is common in other public jurisdictions.

A key issue for compensation managers is pay comparability with the private sector. Recognizing that external pay equity is essential to an organization's ability to attract, motivate, and retain qualified employees, Congress enacted the Federal Salary Reform Act of 1962 and the Federal Pay Comparability Act of 1970 to maintain pay comparability with the private sector. Because of politics, budgetary constraints, and economic realities, the goals of these acts have never been achieved. By the late 1980s, the Civil Service 2000 and the Volcker Commission reports warned that the large and growing gap between federal and private sector pay was seriously jeopardizing government's ability to recruit and retain qualified individuals in many occupations.[15] A subsequent U.S. General Accounting Office study found that the average private sector pay advantage ranged from 6 percent in San Antonio to 39 percent in San Francisco.[16] Congress responded by enacting the Federal Pay Reform Act of 1990. It authorized pay increases for all employees in an effort to achieve salaries comparable to those in the private sector and deviations from the pay plan to provide "locality pay" for workers in high cost-of-living localities. Whether this legislation will succeed in easing recruitment and retention difficulties remains to be seen. The issue of pay comparability is also a matter of concern at the state and local levels. As their fiscal situations worsened in the late 1980s, many state and local governments began to experience greater difficulty in recruiting and retaining skilled workers. Pay comparability remains one of the most urgent policy issues with which compensation managers must cope.

When attempting to compare total compensation packages it is important to include an assessment of the value of employee benefits. Total employee compensation encompasses financial and nonfinancial benefits as well as wages and salaries. Benefits that employees are entitled to receive by law include social security, worker's compensation, and unemployment insurance. Discretionary benefits include retirement plans, health insurance, vacation and leave benefits, employee assistance and wellness programs, child care assistance, and tuition reimbursement. Discretionary benefits are currently receiving considerable attention for two reasons. First, benefit costs have grown at an alarming rate. It is not uncommon today for benefit costs to represent 30 to 40 percent of total compensation. Health insurance costs in particular have skyrocketed. As a result, more and more employers are exploring strategies for containing health-related costs, including self-insurance programs, wellness programs, and managed care plans that emphasize preventive medicine and health maintenance.[17] Greater attention is also focusing on discretionary benefits because of their growing relevance for employee motivation, commitment, and retention. As the competition for individuals with special skills increases, and with the entry of single parents, working mothers, and dual-income couples into the workforce in larger numbers, more employers are viewing flexible, expanded benefit packages as the key to recruiting and retaining employees. Benefits such as cafeteria plans, employee assistance and wellness programs, child care assistance, and flexible leave policies are discussed in Chapter 13.

Pay Equity and Comparable Worth

Comparable worth emerged as a civil rights issue in the 1980s as the result of mounting concern over the large disparities in pay received by men and women. (Although racial and ethnic minorities are also subject to a wage gap, most attention has focused on gender disparities). Today women earn an average of 65 cents for every dollar earned by men (for year round, full-time employees). Research indicates that only one-fifth to one-half of the wage gap can be explained by factors such as years of experience, union bargaining power, or the forces of supply and demand.[18] Evidence of this kind led many pay equity advocates to conclude that much of the unexplained portion of the wage gap is the result of job segregation, promotional barriers, and the systematic undervaluing of jobs performed by women.

Many pay equity advocates support comparable worth as a means of closing the wage gap. *Comparable worth* refers to a wage policy requiring equal pay for jobs of comparable value. Under such a policy, for example, a state government that finds through its job evaluation process that a librarian position in the Department of Justice (a female-dominated position) is of comparable value to an engineering position in the Department of Transportation (a male-dominated position) would be obligated to pay the two positions essentially the same salary.

Job Segregation

Job segregation is often cited as the single most important cause of the wage gap.[19] It refers to the fact that women tend to be concentrated in a narrow range of low-paying, sex-segregated occupations. An estimated 80 percent of all working women are found in female-dominated jobs (defined as being 70 percent or more female), including those shown in Exhibit 6.7. Because these jobs pay less on average than male-dominated jobs, job segregation is generally viewed as a major cause of the wage gap.

Whether job segregation is a product of purposeful discrimination is a matter of much dispute. According to "human capital" theorists, women often delay entry into or drop out of the labor market to raise families. As a result, many women gravitate toward low-paying, dead-end jobs where entry and exit are easy, or are disadvantaged in their careers because of lost seniority and work experience.

The "sex role socialization" explanation, by contrast, holds that society defines the kinds of work that are "appropriate for women," nurtures the kinds of traits that will prepare them for such work (e.g., to be pleasing, nurturing, deferential), and socializes them to believe that they are best suited for such work because of their gender. Parents and school counselors, according to this explanation, often encourage women to pursue jobs in the nurturing and helping professions, where 73 percent of all workers are female.[20] Women may make career choices that contribute to job segregation, as the human capital theorists suggest, but the sex role socialization explanation emphasizes that such choices cannot be considered freely determined. Sex role socialization, according to this view, represents a form of societal discrimination.

Research continues to be conducted on the causes of job segregation and its effects on pay. Such efforts are likely to find that career choices by women, sex role stereotypes, and overt discrimination all contribute to the complex phenomenon of job segregation.

EXHIBIT 6.7

FEMALE-DOMINATED OCCUPATIONS

Occupation	Percent Female
Dental Hygienist	99.8
Secretary	99.0
Child Care Worker	96.0
Cleaners & Servants	95.8
Registered Nurse	94.5
Bookkeeper	91.5
Speech Therapist	88.2
Elementary School Teacher	85.9
Librarian	83.0
Waiter/Waitress	81.6

Source: U.S. Bureau of Census, *Statistical Abstract of the United States: 1992* (Washington D.C., 1992), Table 629.

The Undervaluation of Female-Dominated Jobs

That women tend to work in different occupations than men is less troubling than the possibility that the work performed by women is systematically undervalued. The available evidence indicates that the greater the concentration of women in a particular occupation, the lower its pay relative to the demands of the job. Stated differently, women are often paid less for performing work that is judged to be of comparable value to work performed largely by men. Pay equity studies conducted in the public sector during the 1980s demonstrated with surprising consistency that jobs performed by women are undervalued by as much as 20 percent. These studies involved evaluating a sample of jobs using the point factor evaluation method and comparing point scores with the average wages of their incumbents. Exhibit 6.8 presents results from a pay equity study conducted by the State of Washington. The warehouse worker (a male-dominated position), for example, received a salary that was 109 percent of the rate predicted by its point score, whereas the laundry worker (a female-dominated position) received a salary that was 73 percent of its predicted rate. Results such as these indicate that pay-setting practices often contain systematic biases that cause women to be paid less than men for performing work of comparable value. The marketplace undervalues work performed by women and the resulting biases are apparently incorporated into government pay structures through reliance on wage and salary surveys.

The Legal Status of Comparable Worth

Efforts to remedy pay inequities through the courts have met with little success. The Equal Pay Act of 1963 requires employers to pay equal wages to men and women performing jobs requiring equal skill, effort, and responsibility, and that are performed under similar working conditions. Exceptions are allowed for pay differentials related to a seniority system, merit system, piecework system, or any other factor other than sex. The Equal Pay Act, however, provides a remedy for wage discrimination only where the jobs in question are substantially the same. Because men and women tend to work in dissimilar jobs, the Equal Pay Act cannot address the kinds of inequities that contribute most to the wage gap.

Title VII of the Civil Rights Act of 1964 also provides a potential remedy for wage discrimination. The type of situation in which women may prevail was demonstrated in 1981 in *County of Washington v. Gunther*.[21] Four female jail matrons at Washington County Jail in Oregon alleged Title VII violations on the grounds that male guards were being paid significantly higher wages for performing very similar duties. Evidence produced in court showed that the County purposefully paid women 70 percent of prevailing market rates while paying men 100 percent. The Supreme Court ruled that Title VII, unlike the Equal Pay Act, does not restrict its protections only to "equal jobs." Although the jobs were somewhat different, male and female employees had been treated unequally in violation of Title VII.

The situation found in *Gunther* is not the kind women typically confront, because men and women tend to work in different occupations. Although cases have been brought to court on the theory that Title VII prohibits employers from paying different wages for jobs of comparable value, the Supreme Court in *Gunther* largely rejected such a theory. Intentional discrimination must be demonstrated to establish a case of wage discrimination involving dissimilar jobs.

EXHIBIT 6.8

COMPARISON OF SALARIES AND POINTS FOR SELECTED SEX-SEGREGATED POSITIONS STATE OF WASHINGTON

Benchmark Title	Evaluation Points	Monthly Prevailing[1] Rates	Prevailing Rate as % of Predicted[2]	% Female Incumbents
Warehouse Worker	97	1286	109.1	15.4
Truck Driver	97	1493	126.6	13.6
Laundry Worker	105	884	73.2	80.3
Telephone Operator	118	887	71.6	95.7
Retail Sales Clerk	121	921	74.3	100.0
Data Entry Operator	125	1017	82.1	96.5
Intermediate Clerk Typist	129	968	76.3	96.7
Highway Engineering Tech.	133	1401	110.4	11.1
Word Process. Equip. Operator	138	1082	83.2	98.3
Correctional Officer	173	1436	105.0	9.3
Licensed Practical Nurse	173	1030	75.3	89.5
Automotive Mechanic	175	1646	120.4	0.0
Maintenance Carpenter	197	1707	118.9	2.3
Secretary	197	1122	78.1	98.5
Administrative Assistant	226	1334	90.6	95.1
Chemist	277	1885	116.0	20.0
Civil Engineer	287	1885	116.0	0.0
Highway Engineer 3	345	1980	110.4	3.0
Registered Nurse	348	1368	76.3	92.2
Librarian 3	353	1625	90.6	84.6
Senior Architect	362	2240	121.8	16.7
Sr. Computer System Analyst	384	2080	113.1	17.8
Personnel Representative	410	1956	101.2	45.6
Physician	861	3857	128.0	13.6

[1]Prevailing rates of July 1, 1980. Adopted State rates for midpoint of ranges, October 1981.
[2]Predicted salary from line of best fit = ($2.43)(points) + $936.19, $r = 0.8$.

Source: Helen Remick, "The Comparable Worth Controversy," *Public Personnel Management* 10 (Winter 1981): 378.

The ineffectiveness of Title VII as a means of closing the wage gap is seen most clearly in *AFSCME v. State of Washington*.[22] Two unions filed a class action suit in 1982 against the State of Washington on behalf of 15,500 workers in jobs held principally by women. The suit alleged that the state's system of compensation violated Title VII by providing unequal pay for work of comparable value, and that the state was guilty of intentional wage discrimination when it failed to take corrective action. To the surprise of many, a federal district court agreed, and ordered wage adjustments for current and past employees in designated job classifications. A short time later, however, a federal court of appeals reversed the district court's decision. It ruled that "absent a showing of discriminatory motive, which has not been made here, the law does not permit the federal courts to interfere in a market-based system for the compensation of Washington's employees."[23] Although Washington State's compensation system had adversely affected women, the court was unwilling to use Title VII to address wage inequities it believed were caused by the market.

Organizational Strategies for Closing the Wage Gap

Employers can ill afford to ignore pay inequities because they undermine morale and create barriers to equal employment opportunity. One strategy for addressing pay inequities is to take an aggressive affirmative action approach. This involves actively recruiting female applicants for positions traditionally held by men and facilitating their promotion to higher levels of the organization, where salaries are commensurately higher. Employers can also take steps to reduce the impact of sex role stereotyping and to discourage organizational members from thinking in terms of what work is "appropriate" for men and women. The affirmative action approach directly attacks the phenomenon of job segregation. There is now considerable evidence that as women enter careers traditionally held by men their wages become more comparable to those received by men. Affirmative action, however, is slow to produce results and does not offer an immediate remedy for the undervaluation of female-dominated jobs. For this reason, many public employers are under pressure to adopt strategies that promise results more quickly.

A second strategy is to adopt a comparable worth wage policy requiring all jobs to be compensated primarily on the basis of job content. Providing equal pay for jobs of comparable value is typically accomplished by conducting a pay equity study, establishing a trend line defining the relationship between point scores and average salaries of incumbents in male-dominated positions, and adjusting the pay upward for positions that fall significantly below the trend line. Male-dominated jobs are used to define the trend line because it is presumed that their salaries are not contaminated by gender-related biases.

This strategy has brought renewed attention to the practice of job evaluation. Point-factor evaluation systems provide a relatively objective means of determining job worth and can help eliminate systematic sources of undervaluation. A U.S. General Accounting Office study conducted in 1986 found that ten states had established written pay equity or comparable worth wage policies and 20 had conducted pay equity studies of the kind described above.[24] According to Evans and Nelson, 20 states have also made wage adjustments where inequities were found.[25] Many local governments have implemented pay adjustments as well, often under intense pressure from labor unions. The state of Minnesota has gone the farthest in pursuing a comparable worth strategy by enacting laws requiring local governments, as well as state government, to adopt comparable worth policies.

Adopting comparable worth policies need not involve fundamental changes. It may require little more than removing systematic biases from pay-setting practices and adjusting pay accordingly. A comprehensive comparable worth strategy may involve the following:

1. Adopting a formal pay equity or comparable worth policy.
2. Adopting a new job evaluation method, or adjusting the current method, to allow greater precision in evaluating jobs, and scrutinizing it for gender-related biases in the choices of factors, factor weights, and degree level descriptions.
3. Basing external pay comparisons on jobs believed to be unaffected by gender-related marketplace biases.
4. Conducting pay equity studies periodically and adjusting wages if significant pay inequities are found.
5. Eliminating job classifications that reflect artificial distinctions between similar jobs held by women and men. The distinction between jail guard and jail matron, for example, may be found to be artificial and unnecessary.
6. Incorporating pay equity concerns into the agency's affirmative action program. This may involve identifying and breaking down gender-segregated classifications through such means as aggressive training programs, careful use of promotions and transfers, and targeted hiring practices.
7. Searching for ways to achieve pay comparability across multiple job evaluation and pay plans.

Although most of these actions are consistent with well-established personnel practices, the issue of comparable worth will continue to be controversial for a number of reasons. One reason is that pay adjustments are expensive. Many critics will expect to see stronger evidence that the apparent undervaluation of female-dominated jobs is the result of discrimination rather than factors such as supply and demand, personal characteristics of employees, or differences in the ability of collective bargaining units to secure pay increases.

Perhaps the greatest reason for the controversy is that the concept of comparable worth rests on values that strongly challenge traditional marketplace values. According to classical economic theory, it is the marketplace, guided by Adam Smith's invisible hand, that should determine wage rates. Forces of supply and demand, and an individual's ability to negotiate an advantageous salary, play large roles in the traditional view of wage-setting. The comparable worth perspective, by contrast, takes a technical approach to wage-setting that sounds like unwarranted social engineering to its critics. It rests on the nontraditional value assumptions that jobs of comparable value are deserving of equal pay, and that wages should be set rationally according to an evaluation of job content. Although it may not be possible to finally reconcile these competing values, it may be possible for them to coexist. According to most advocates, comparable worth does not require setting pay according to job content alone. Factors such as seniority, personal qualifications, individual productivity, and supply and demand may still determine an individual's pay in important ways. The main thrust of comparable worth policies is to remove systematic biases from job evaluation plans, salary surveys, and other pay-setting practices.

Conclusion

Compensation issues hold enormous implications for employee recruitment, retention, motivation, and performance. Because these factors affect organizational productivity and effectiveness in important ways, compensation managers must constantly struggle to maintain an acceptable balance among the potentially competing goals of internal, external, performance-related, and gender-related pay equity. They must also give careful consideration to the public's interest in controlling labor costs. Because compensation decisions are inevitably made in a highly political and conflict-laden environment, their task is enormously difficult.

■ **CASE 6.1**   **The Case of the Troublesome Pay Exception**

You are the manager of a data processing unit in state government that is finding it very difficult to recruit qualified computer programmers. One person who appears to be qualified for the position is willing to accept an offer of employment, but only at a salary equivalent to what she had received in her previous job with a private firm. This would place her at step 7 in the current pay grade. A pay exception must be granted before she can be hired at step 7. You are inclined to ask for a pay exception, but another computer programmer who has worked for you for several years is still at step 5.

The applicant also asks you to pay relocation expenses. Such expenses have not been paid in the past. Hiring her will involve other costs as well. Lacking previous experience with government, she will also require training in the state's software systems at a cost of more than $5,000.

1. What human resource management issues are raised in this case?
2. Will you request a pay exception? Will you pay the relocation costs? Why or why not?

Notes

1. Edward E. Lawler III, "What's Wrong with Point-Factor Job Evaluation," *Compensation and Benefits Review* 18 (March/April 1986).

2. Alfred J. Candrilli and Ronald D. Armagast, "The Case for Effective Point-Factor Job Evaluation, Viewpoint 2," *Personnel* 64 (April 1987):33–36.

3. National Academy of Public Administration, *Modernizing Federal Classification: An Opportunity for Excellence* (Washington, D.C.: National Academy of Public Administration, 1991).

4. N. Joseph Cayer, "Classification in the Federal Service: New Looks at Alternative Approaches," *Public Administration Review* 52 (March/April 1992):217–220.

5. Carolyn Ban, "The Navy Demonstration Project: An 'Experiment in Experimentation'," in Carolyn Ban and Norma M. Riccucci, eds., *Public Personnel Management: Current Concerns—Future Challenges* (New York: Longman, 1991):31–41.

6. Committee on Position Classification and Pay Plans in the Public Service (Ismar Baruch, Chairman), *Position Classification in the Public Service,* (Chicago: Civil Service Assembly of the United States and Canada, 1941), 14.

7. Ibid., 18.

8. Donald J. Treiman, *Job Evaluation: An Analytic Review* (Washington, D.C.: National Academy of Sciences, 1979).

9. Kermit R. Davis, Jr., and William I. Sauser, Jr., "A Comparison of Factor Weighting Methods in Job Evaluation: Implications for Compensation Systems," *Public Personnel Management* 22 (Spring 1993):91–106.

10. U. S. General Accounting Office, *Pay Equity: Status of State Activities* (GAO-GGD-86-141BR, September 1986).

11. U.S. Civil Service Commission, *Instructions for the Factor Evaluation System* (Washington, D.C.: U.S. Government Printing Office, 1977).

12. See, for example, Jonathan Tompkins, "Sources of Measurement Error and Gender Bias in Job Evaluation, *"Review of Public Personnel Administration* 9 (Fall 1988):1–16.

13. Jonathan Tompkins, "Comparable Worth and Job Evaluation Validity," *Public Administration Review* 47 (May/June 1987):254–258.

14. U.S. General Accounting Office, *Pay for Performance: State and International Public Sector Pay-For-Performance Systems* (GAO/GGD-91-1, October 1991).

15. William B. Johnston et al., *Civil Service 2000* (Washington, D.C.: Office of Personnel Management, 1988); Volcker Commission Report, *Leadership in America: Rebuilding the Public Service* (Lexington, MA: D. C. Heath, Lexington Books, 1989).

16. U.S. Government Accounting Office, *Federal Pay: Private Sector Salary Differences by Locality,* (GAO-GGD-91-63FS, April 1991).

17. Perry Moore, "Health Care Cost Containment in Large American Cities," *Public Personnel Management* 18 (Spring 1989):87–100.

18. Donald J. Treiman and Heidi I. Hartmann, eds., *Women, Work, and Wages: Equal Pay for Equal Value* (Washington, D.C.: National Academy Press, 1981), 42.

19. See, for example, Paula England, "Socioeconomic Explanations of Job Segregation," in Helen Remick, ed., *Comparable Worth and Wage Discrimination: Technical Possibilities and Political Realities* (Philadelphia: Temple University Press, 1984):28–46.

20. Ibid., 30.

21. 452 U.S. 161 (1981).

22. 578 F. Supp. 846 (1983).

23. Ibid., 1408.

24. U.S. General Accounting Office, *Pay Equity.*

25. Sara M. Evans and Barbara J. Nelson, *Wage Justice: Comparable Worth and the Paradox of Technocratic Reform* (Chicago: University of Chicago Press, 1989).

Part 3

Staffing

Staffing, *the task of securing a highly qualified and dedicated workforce, lies at the heart of successful human resource management. The agency that fails to recruit the best available talent, distinguish superior applicants from adequate ones, and obtain the services of those it selects will lack the capacity to achieve mandated objectives and maintain credibility with the public.*

Staffing decisions today are made within the context of equal employment opportunity requirements and affirmative action policies. These create both obligations and constraints for managers and personnel officers. Obligations include a duty to comply with the law, protect employee rights, handle complaints of discrimination, and safeguard the organization from legal risk. Constraints arise because traditional personnel activities must now be conducted differently—conducted so that daily personnel decisions do not create barriers to equal employment opportunity. Affirmative action policies also create constraints. Decisions involving recruitment, selection, and promotion often must be made with a view to achieving and sustaining a workforce that is representative of the diversity of society as a whole. Debates over the merits of these policies aside, the resulting obligations and constraints are very much a part of the daily work life of both managers and personnel officers. For this reason, Part 3 establishes the legal context in which staffing decisions are made before examining the more technical issues of recruitment and selection in Chapter 9.

Linking HRM Tasks and Outcomes: A Performance Model

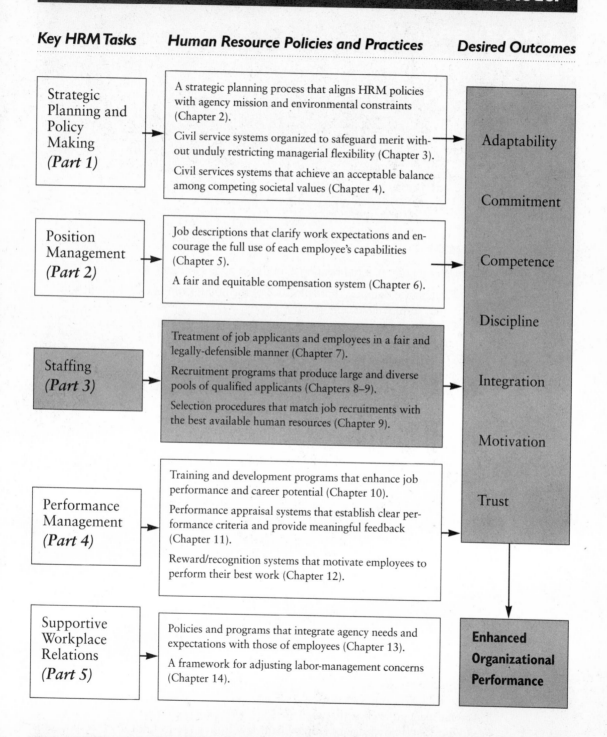

Key HRM Tasks	Human Resource Policies and Practices	Desired Outcomes

Strategic Planning and Policy Making *(Part 1)*

A strategic planning process that aligns HRM policies with agency mission and environmental constraints (Chapter 2).

Civil service systems organized to safeguard merit without unduly restricting managerial flexibility (Chapter 3).

Civil services systems that achieve an acceptable balance among competing societal values (Chapter 4).

Position Management *(Part 2)*

Job descriptions that clarify work expectations and encourage the full use of each employee's capabilities (Chapter 5).

A fair and equitable compensation system (Chapter 6).

Staffing *(Part 3)*

Treatment of job applicants and employees in a fair and legally-defensible manner (Chapter 7).

Recruitment programs that produce large and diverse pools of qualified applicants (Chapters 8–9).

Selection procedures that match job recruitments with the best available human resources (Chapter 9).

Performance Management *(Part 4)*

Training and development programs that enhance job performance and career potential (Chapter 10).

Performance appraisal systems that establish clear performance criteria and provide meaningful feedback (Chapter 11).

Reward/recognition systems that motivate employees to perform their best work (Chapter 12).

Supportive Workplace Relations *(Part 5)*

Policies and programs that integrate agency needs and expectations with those of employees (Chapter 13).

A framework for adjusting labor-management concerns (Chapter 14).

Adaptability

Commitment

Competence

Discipline

Integration

Motivation

Trust

Enhanced Organizational Performance

CHAPTER 7

The Nondiscrimination Approach to EEO

Learning Objectives

After mastering the material contained in this chapter, you will be able to:

1. Explain the defining characteristics of the nondiscrimination approach to equal employment opportunity.
2. Describe the basic steps involved in pursuing a complaint of discrimination under the federal Civil Rights Act.
3. Distinguish disparate treatment discrimination from disparate impact discrimination and provide examples of each.
4. Identify key legal issues relating to discrimination on the basis of race, religion, sex, national origin, and disability.
5. Develop a list of actions managers and personnel officers can take to avoid unlawful employment discrimination.

The civil rights movement of the 1950s and 1960s sought to end discriminatory practices that prevented blacks, other minorities, and women from obtaining the benefits of society on an equal footing with all other citizens. Demands for social change resulted in legislation, executive orders, and administrative regulations aimed at eliminating discrimination in many areas, including employment. The impact of the civil rights movement on human resource management has been dramatic. Not since the scientific management movement of the early 1900s has anything altered the practice of human resource management so fundamentally. Today managers and personnel officers are jointly responsible for investigating complaints of discrimination, ensuring that all personnel decisions and techniques are free of discriminatory biases, and protecting the organization from legal risk. The design and application of personnel techniques has changed as well. Today, for example, steps must be taken to ensure that employment tests are predictive of subsequent job performance and that interview questions treat all job applicants equally.

Perhaps it would have been better if these developments had occurred earlier — as the result of changes in professional practice rather than government regulation. This issue aside, it is clear that managers and personnel officers today must possess a broad working knowledge of employment law if they are to fulfill their responsibilities effectively. Accordingly, this chapter defines the concept of equal employment opportunity (EEO), distinguishes between two legal theories of discrimination, reviews basic legal requirements pertaining to EEO, and assesses their relevance to the design of personnel techniques and the practice of human resource management.

The Concept of Equal Employment Opportunity

Work is important to members of society because it provides income needed to support self and family, gives purpose and discipline to life, integrates individuals into a network of social relationships, and enhances individual self-esteem. It is because work is so central to personal identity and collective well-being that we as a nation have come to recognize the importance of pursuing equal employment opportunity as a matter of government policy. *Equal employment opportunity* (EEO) refers to the right of every individual to compete for employment opportunities on an equal footing with all other members of society without being restrained by arbitrary or irrelevant barriers. This does not mean that everyone must have an equal chance of success. Rather, EEO is a guarantee of being able to obtain the benefits of employment consistent with each person's abilities, talents, and desires. As a policy goal, EEO represents society's commitment to removing arbitrary or irrelevant employment barriers so that individual qualifications and the operation of the marketplace can determine the actual distribution of employment benefits. Among these barriers are laws that treat individuals differently because of their race, ethnicity, gender, or disability, and institutional policies and procedures, social stereotypes, and personal prejudices that adversely affect their degree of success.

The Nondiscrimination Approach to EEO

Confronted with several policy options for guaranteeing equal employment opportunity to all citizens, governments generally adopted a *nondiscrimination approach*. This approach involves identifying specific categories of individuals who are judged to be in need of legal protection and prohibiting employers from discriminating against them on the basis of such factors as race, gender, national origin, and religion. Victims of discrimination are authorized under specific pieces of legislation to pursue individual remedies through the judicial system. In addition, government agencies are often authorized to impose administrative remedies by canceling government contracts or withholding government funds. The nondiscrimination approach thus sanctions government regulation while attempting to preserve, as much as possible, the principles of merit, individual liberty, and employer autonomy.

The nondiscrimination approach stands in sharp contrast to the affirmative action approach described in Chapter 8. In philosophical terms, the nondiscrimination approach is based on the principle of equal treatment and relies on the judicial system to correct wrongs done to the victims of discrimination. By contrast, the affirmative action approach relies on the willingness of employers to take race, ethnicity, and gender into account when making personnel decisions to achieve a greater degree of substantive equality.

EXHIBIT 7.1

THE NONDISCRIMINATION APPROACH TO EEO: KEY LANDMARKS

Civil Rights Act of 1866 Guarantees to all persons (i.e., nonwhites and noncitizens) the same legal rights as "white citizens" (42 U.S.C. sec. 1981). The Civil Rights Act of 1991 broadened Section 1981 to clarify that it prohibits racial harassment and discrimination in employment as well as in the making of contracts. Individuals may sue local governments as employers, but not state or federal agencies.

Fourteenth Amendment to the U.S. Constitution (1868) Contains a clause prohibiting states from depriving any person of life, liberty, or property without due process of law, or from denying any person of the equal protection of the laws.

Civil Rights Act of 1871 Allows citizens to sue local government officials, and even some private individuals, who deprive citizens of any constitutional or federal statutory rights (42 U.S.C. sec. 1983).

Executive Order 8802 of 1941 Issued by FDR to prohibit employment discrimination in the federal civil service and by defense contractors. Established the Fair Employment Practices Committee to investigate and resolve complaints of discrimination.

Equal Pay Act of 1963 An amendment to the Fair Labor Standards Act of 1938 prohibiting discrimination in compensation on the basis of sex for work requiring equal skill, effort, and responsibility and performed under similar working conditions.

Civil Rights Act of 1964 (Title VII) Prohibits employers, employment agencies, and labor organizations from discriminating on the basis of race, color, religion, sex, and national origin. As amended in 1972, it applies to both public and private employers with 15 or more employees.

Exhibit 7.1 identifies key landmarks in the federal government's efforts to secure greater equality of employment opportunity. Collectively, they represent the nondiscrimination approach to EEO.

Title VII of the Civil Rights Act of 1964

Before the 1960s, several states had enacted "fair employment practices" laws prohibiting discrimination on the basis of such factors as race, religion, and national origin. In the absence of adequate funding and enforcement mechanisms to accomplish their purposes, these laws remained generally ineffective. Not until 1964 did events converge to assure enactment of the nation's first civil rights law comprehensively addressing discrimination in housing, voting, public accommodations, and employment. Bolstered by a large Democratic majority in Congress, and supported by individuals and groups shocked by the violence in Birmingham, President Johnson succeeded in maneuvering a bill through Congress containing stronger civil rights requirements than those proposed by President Kennedy the year before.

It is Title VII of the Civil Rights Act of 1964 that addresses discrimination in employment. Although one of the least controversial sections at the time of enactment, Title VII has proven to be an important weapon in the struggle by women and mi-

EXHIBIT 7.1 *(continued)*

Age Discrimination in Employment Act of 1967 Prohibits discrimination on the basis of age in hiring, discharge, and terms, conditions, and privileges of employment by employers with 20 or more employees and by unions and employment agencies. As amended in 1986, it specifically protects individuals who are 40 years of age and older. State and local governments have been covered as employers since 1974.

Equal Employment Opportunity Act of 1972 Amendments to the Civil Rights Act extending coverage to public sector employers and providing the Equal Employment Opportunity Commission with enforcement powers.

Rehabilitation Act of 1973 Prohibits the federal government, government contractors, and programs receiving federal financial assistance from discriminating against individuals on the basis of physical or mental disability.

Pregnancy Discrimination Act of 1978 An amendment to the Civil Rights Act prohibiting employers from discriminating against individuals on the basis of pregnancy, childbirth, or medical conditions related to childbirth.

Americans with Disabilities Act of 1990 (Title I) Prohibits all employers with 15 or more employees, private and public, from discriminating against the disabled in employment, and requires them to make "reasonable accommodation" for disabilities unless it involves "undue hardship."

Civil Rights Act of 1991 Allows individuals to receive punitive and compensatory damages under the Civil Rights Act, Americans with Disabilities Act, and Rehabilitation Act, if they can establish "malice or reckless indifference" to federally protected rights. It also places the burden on the employer to defend practices that adversely affect individuals in protected categories.

norities to obtain equal employment opportunity. Originally regulating only private sector employers, employment agencies, and labor organizations, Title VII was amended by the Equal Employment Opportunity Act of 1972 to cover public sector employers as well. These amendments also extended coverage to employers with 15 or more employees (the original act applied to those with 25 or more employees), and gave authority to the Equal Employment Opportunity Commission (EEOC) to sue employers on behalf of individuals whose Title VII rights it believed had been violated (the original act provided the EEOC with no enforcement powers). Exhibit 7.2 summarizes key provisions of the Civil Rights Act as amended.

Title VII Complaint Procedures

Nearly every state has its own civil rights legislation and enforcement agency. In many instances state law is more comprehensive in its coverage than federal law. State and local employees normally file complaints with local enforcement agencies under state law, but "consolidated complaints" are often filed when both state and federal laws are allegedly violated. For illustrative purposes, the analysis that follows focuses on complaints brought under the federal Civil Rights Act.

EXHIBIT 7.2

SUMMARY OF KEY PROVISIONS OF TITLE VII AS AMENDED

Organizations Covered Title VII applies to all employers with 15 or more employees (including state and local governments and school systems), employment agencies, and labor organizations.

Categories of Individuals Protected Individuals are protected on the basis of race, color, religion, sex, and national origin.

Unlawful Employment Practices Chief among the employment practices defined as unlawful are the following (42 U.S.C sec. 2000e-2, 1982)

1. to fail or refuse to hire or to discharge any individual, or otherwise to discriminate against any individual with respect to his compensation, terms, conditions, or privileges of employment, because of such individual's race, color, religion, sex, or national origin.

2. to limit, segregate, or classify his employees or applicants for employment in any way which would deprive or tend to deprive any individual of employment opportunities or otherwise adversely affect his status as an employee, because of such individual's race, color, religion, sex, or national origin.

Major Exemptions from Coverage Among the many exemptions from coverage are the following

a. Personnel decisions may be made on the basis of an individual's religion, sex, or national origin "in those certain instances where religion, sex, or national origin is a bona fide occupational qualification reasonably necessary to the normal operation of that particular business or enterprise. . . ." This is known as the BFOQ exception.

b. Schools owned or supported by a particular religion may hire employees on the basis of their religious affiliations.

c. Use of "different standards of compensation, or different terms, conditions, or privileges of employment pursuant to a bona fide seniority or merit system, or a system which measures earnings by quantity or quality of production or to employees who work in different locations" is lawful as long as such practices are not motivated by an intent to discriminate.

Enforcement The Equal Employment Opportunity Commission investigates charges of discrimination to determine whether there is reason to believe each charge is true, and if so, to resolve it through conciliation. If conciliation efforts fail, the EEOC may file a civil suit in federal court. It cannot, however, bring suit against a government or government agency. Charges involving state and local governments are referred to the Attorney General for possible litigation.

Judicial Remedies After a finding of intentional discrimination, the court may order the employer to cease engaging in unlawful practices and may order appropriate remedies, including reinstatement, hiring a rejected job applicant, and back pay. As amended by the Civil Rights Act of 1991, individuals may also receive punitive and compensatory damages if they can establish "malice or reckless indifference" to federally protected rights (except that punitive damages usually cannot be recovered from government employers). Courts are also given discretion to award the costs of attorney's fees to the prevailing party.

Government employees who believe their Title VII rights have been violated will normally follow agency complaint procedures as spelled out in collective bargaining agreements, administrative rules, and/or general personnel policies. Resolving complaints internally allows all parties to avoid lengthy and costly litigation. However, employees who fail to pursue internal complaint procedures do not necessarily lose their right to file a charge with the EEOC or to take their complaints to court. Employees of federal agencies are an exception. They must exhaust internal remedies before they may appeal the agency's decision to the EEOC or before they may file a civil suit. Internal grievance procedures in the federal service typically involve efforts by an EEO Counselor to resolve the complaint informally, filing of a formal, written complaint with the agency if informal efforts fail, and an opportunity for a formal hearing before a decision is rendered by the agency head.[1] When a formal hearing is requested, a complaints examiner or administrative judge considers the testimony presented at the hearing and recommends to the agency head an appropriate course of action. The federal employee or job applicant may then appeal the agency's decision to the EEOC's Office of Review and Appeals, or file a civil action in federal court.

Complaints Handled by the EEOC

Except in the federal service, employees and job applicants who believe Title VII rights have been violated may file a complaint directly with the EEOC. Charges may also be filed by any person or organization on behalf of such individuals. Whether or not a complaint is first pursued internally, a charge must be filed with the EEOC within 180 days of the alleged unlawful employment practice.

Once a charge is filed, the EEOC must notify the employer of the charge within ten days. If the regional office of the EEOC determines that there is "reasonable cause" to believe that the charge is true, it attempts to resolve the complaint "by informal methods of conference, conciliation, and persuasion" as required by Title VII. Successful efforts typically result in a conciliation agreement. These out-of-court settlements minimize harmful publicity, are less costly than litigation, and offer assurances of confidentiality and protection from future lawsuits. The employer may agree, for example, to eliminate discriminatory practices and offer some form of remedy to those it has harmed, including hiring an excluded job applicant or reinstating a discharged employee with back pay. In some instances the employer may agree to remediate discrimination against whole classes of individuals by, for example, offering monetary awards to all employees or job applicants affected and/or establishing affirmative action timetables and hiring goals.

If conciliation efforts fail in private sector cases, the EEOC is authorized to file a civil suit against the employer on the complainant's behalf. It has no such authority, however, in public sector cases. Although the EEOC is responsible for investigating complaints against state and local governments, once conciliation efforts have failed it refers such cases to the Attorney General with recommendations regarding the merits of proceeding with litigation. To file a private civil suit against a state or local government, an employee or job applicant must first obtain a right-to-sue letter from the EEOC or state civil rights agency. Because the EEOC is so far behind in its case load, it rarely completes its investigation within 120 days after the complaint is filed, as Congress intended. As a result, individuals are routinely given the right to sue if it is requested.

Title VII Complaints Handled by State Agencies

Congress mandated that state or local civil rights agencies be given the first opportunity to remedy alleged discrimination if state law prohibits the same forms of discrimination prohibited under Title VII. As a result, complaints filed with the EEOC are routinely referred to a local agency for a period of 60 days. These agencies are called "706 agencies," reflecting the section of Title VII that authorizes them to handle complaints under contract with the EEOC. Their task is to investigate complaints and attempt to resolve them through conciliation. If no mutually acceptable agreement is reached, the 706 agency will make a decision regarding whether there is reasonable cause to believe that the charge is true and will forward its decision to the regional EEOC office. The EEOC automatically assumes jurisdiction after 60 days, but in practice it takes no action as long as the state agency is continuing to investigate and negotiate.

Pattern or Practice Suits

In addition to filing civil actions on behalf of individual employees or job applicants, the U.S. Attorney Generals office may on its own authority file suits against state and local governments who are thought to be in significant violation of Title VII. This authority is derived from section 707, which allows suits against persons "engaged in a pattern or practice or resistance to the full enjoyment" of Title VII rights.

Collectively Bargained Grievance Procedures

Collective bargaining agreements usually establish procedures by which members of the bargaining unit may grieve adverse employment decisions. Employees are not required to exhaust such internal remedies before filing a complaint with a civil rights agency. Even in cases where a labor arbitrator has found against an employee in binding arbitration, the employee may still take his or her Title VII complaint to the EEOC or state 706 agency.

Recordkeeping and Reporting Requirements

State and local governments with 100 or more employees must file a report with the EEOC every two years containing information on employees by protected category, job classification, and salary. Information regarding employees' sex, race, or ethnic background may be obtained by visual survey or by the maintenance of postemployment records if it is allowed under state law. The particular report filed by state and local governments is called the Local Government Information Report, or EEO-4 Report. Public elementary and secondary schools must also keep such records; school systems with more than 100 employees must file an EEO-5 report biennially. Finally, institutions of higher education, public or private, must keep such records and file an EEO-6 report biennially.

Theories of Discrimination and Judicial Enforcement

As noted earlier, managers and personnel officers require a broad working knowledge of civil rights law, including an understanding of what constitutes unlawful discrimination and what is required for personnel practices to conform to legal requirements. To assist in this regard, Exhibit 7.3 defines key terms that often arise in the context of litigation.

The Civil Rights Act neither defines discrimination nor offers guidance regarding how to establish a connection between an adverse employment decision and an employee or applicant's protected status. As a result, the courts have had to take responsibility for interpreting congressional intent and establishing judicial procedures for

---

EXHIBIT 7.3

KEY TERMS IN CIVIL RIGHTS LITIGATION

Adverse Impact Term used when a selection procedure for a particular job or set of jobs, such as an employment test or a promotion review, produces a substantially lower selection rate for women or minorities than for the group with the highest selection rate.

Bona Fide Occupational Qualification (BFOQ) Refers to a necessary and therefore legitimate job qualification. It provides an exception to the Civil Rights Act's prohibition against discrimination on the basis of sex, religion, and national origin. Thus, requiring a women's washroom attendant to be female is a BFOQ. According to case law, race or color can never be a BFOQ.

Business Necessity The principal defense used by an employer to justify continued use of an otherwise neutral employment practice that has had an adverse impact on women or minorities. It is an argument that the practice is necessary to the safe and efficient operation of the organization and that no alternative practice is available that would have less adverse impact.

Class Action Suit A lawsuit brought by one or more individuals on behalf of themselves and all "similarly situated" individuals. It is often used in disparate (or adverse) impact suits so that remedies can be provided to all individuals who were adversely affected by a particular employment practice.

Conciliation Agreement A negotiated settlement between the EEOC (or state enforcement agency) and an employer in which the employer agrees to resolve a discrimination complaint in specified ways without acknowledging wrongdoing.

Consent Decree A negotiated settlement similar to a conciliation agreement except that compliance is enforced by the courts. It is often used to settle expensive class action suits by providing monetary awards to the victims of discrimination or establishing timetables for eliminating the underrepresentation of women or minorities.

Disparate (or Adverse) Impact Discrimination The kind of discrimination that occurs when an otherwise neutral employment practice produces an adverse impact on women or minorities and the practice is not demonstrably related to job requirements (e.g., in a case involving a job qualification) or predictive of subsequent job performance (e.g., in a case involving an employment examination).

EXHIBIT 7.3 *(continued)*

Disparate Treatment Discrimination The kind of discrimination that occurs when members of protected groups are intentionally treated differently in employment situations than are members of other groups because of their race, religion, sex, or national origin.

Four-fifths Rule A rule of thumb suggested by the EEOC for determining the point at which adverse impact occurs. If the success rate for women or minorities in a particular selection process is less than four-fifths (or 80 percent) of the success rate for other groups, then adverse impact has occurred.

706 Agency A state fair employment practice agency that under Section 706 of the Civil Rights Act is given the first opportunity to resolve discrimination complaints under federal law. Such agencies contract with the EEOC to process claims involving federal rights. They sometimes possess authority to rule on disputed issues without filing civil suits.

Reasonable Accommodation Employers are required under federal law to accommodate the religious preferences and known disabilities of job applicants and employees when it is reasonable to do so. This might involve, for example, rearranging a work schedule so that an employee may have a religious holiday off, or hiring a reading assistant for a visually impaired employee. Stricter standards of "reasonableness" are applied in disability cases than in cases involving religion.

Undue Hardship Employers are required to provide reasonable accommodation in cases involving religion and disability unless doing so will pose an undue hardship. The Americans with Disabilities Act, for example, requires courts in determining whether undue hardship exists to look at such things as the nature and cost of the accommodation, and the size and financial resources of the employer.

---

enforcing Title VII. During the first decade of litigation, two theories of discrimination emerged from judicial rulings. The first of these, *disparate treatment theory,* may be stated as follows:

> *Discrimination occurs when an employer, as the result of ill will or some other impermissible motive, intentionally treats a member of a protected class differently from other similarly situated individuals on the basis of that individual's race, religion, sex, or national origin.*

Disparate treatment may occur, for example, when an employer:

- refuses to consider blacks for employment either because of racial hostility or because the employer believes "whites make better employees."
- refuses to promote women because of stereotyped views regarding their abilities or social roles.
- pays a woman a lower wage than a man for performing essentially the same work.
- disciplines a member of a racial or ethnic minority when nonminorities committing the same offense receive lesser or no discipline.

One type of disparate treatment involves use of employment policies or job qualifications that distinguish between job applicants or employees explicitly on the basis of race, religion, sex, or national origin. Examples include a policy of not hiring women for particular kinds of jobs, or a job qualification that requires applicants to be males. These examples represent *prima facie violations* of Title VII (they are discriminatory on their face), and employers have no defense except to invoke the bona fide occupational qualification (BFOQ) exception. In a BFOQ defense the employer argues that the qualification is necessary for reasons of privacy (such as requiring women's washroom attendants to be female) or to ensure that job duties are performed safely and efficiently (such as requiring mandatory retirement for state troopers at age 65, in the context of the Age Discrimination in Employment Act).

A second type of disparate treatment involves personnel decisions (rather than official policies) that intentionally treat employees or job applicants differently on the basis of race, religion, ethnicity, or gender. Examples include disciplining hispanics more harshly than nonhispanics for similar offenses, and hiring men with young children while rejecting women with young children. Because direct evidence of a discriminatory motive is difficult to produce, cases are generally built around circumstantial evidence. The plaintiff attempts to show disparate treatment by comparing his or her treatment with that received by other "similarly situated" persons. If the employer can offer no convincing, nondiscriminatory reason for its actions, then the court may infer that an impermissible motive was involved in the employer's action.

Congress, when it enacted Title VII, held a disparate treatment view of discrimination. Its primary concern was to prohibit overt acts of exclusion, intentional segregation in the workplace, and flagrant racial hostility. This view, however, ignores the more pervasive forms of discrimination built into institutional practices that, although not intended to be discriminatory, nonetheless adversely affect the employment opportunities of women and minorities. As long as the disparate treatment view of discrimination prevailed, victims of institutional discrimination were unable to obtain remedy through the courts. This situation changed in 1971 when the Supreme Court issued its decision in *Griggs v. Duke Power Co.*[2] Arguing that the underlying purpose of Title VII included improving the economic condition of women and minorities, the Supreme Court ruled that Congress intended to prohibit employment practices that are discriminatory in effect as well as in motive.

The *Griggs* case was initiated by a group of black employees at Duke Power's Dan River Steam Station in Draper, North Carolina. Before passage of the Civil Rights Act, Duke Power had purposefully employed blacks only in the labor department, where the highest paying jobs paid less than the lowest paying jobs in the station's other four departments. When Duke Power abandoned its practice of restricting blacks to the Labor Department in 1965, it established a high school diploma and passing scores on two aptitude tests as qualifications for placement in any of the other four departments. These qualifications were not discriminatory on their face. Nor had Duke Power applied different standards to white and black employees. Yet because of the effects of past discrimination in both education and employment, black employees failed to meet these qualifications in larger numbers than white employees. The effect, whether intended or not, was to restrict the employment opportunities of blacks. A court of appeals ruled that employment practices having an adverse impact on members of protected groups do not constitute unlawful discrimination in the absence of proof of an employer's intent to discriminate. The Supreme Court, however, disagreed. It concluded that "practices, procedures, or tests neutral on their face, and even neutral in terms of intent, cannot be maintained if they operate to 'freeze' the status quo of prior discriminatory employment practices."

The Supreme Court in *Griggs* thus articulated a second theory of discrimination, *disparate (or adverse) impact theory*. This theory may be stated as follows:

> *Discrimination occurs when otherwise neutral employment policies, selection criteria, or other institutional practices adversely affect individuals protected by Title VII when they are not valid predictors of an individual's ability to perform the job in question or are not demonstrably related to actual job requirements.*

Disparate impact may occur, for example, when an employer:

- uses height and weight requirements established without regard to the actual requirements needed to perform particular jobs (such requirements may adversely affect women and members of certain racial or ethnic groups).
- uses standardized employment tests that have not been validated in terms of how well they measure the abilities of applicants to perform specific job requirements (such tests may adversely affect women or minorities, depending on the nature of the biases contained in them).
- requires that all employees be able to speak English fluently, although it is not essential to the satisfactory performance of the jobs in question (fluency requirements may adversely affect members of certain racial or ethnic groups).

The Court's decision in *Griggs* proved of great importance in expanding employment opportunities. First, it provided a legal theory with which women and minorities could attack institutional and systemic forms of discrimination in court. In addition, because disparate impact suits are often brought as class actions, the courts could enforce remedies on behalf of large numbers of employees or job applicants. Second, in contrast to disparate treatment cases, plaintiffs bringing disparate impact suits need not show that the employer intended to discriminate on the basis of race, religion, sex or national origin. The Court ruled in *Griggs* that ". . . good intent or absence of discriminatory intent does not redeem employment procedures or testing mechanisms that operate as "built-in headwinds" for minority groups . . . Congress directed the thrust of the Act to the *consequences* of employment practices, not simply the motivation." Finally, the *Griggs* decision significantly altered the practice of human resource management. In stating that "any test used must measure the person for the job and not the person in the abstract," the Court ruled that screening tests used as a condition for employment or promotion must relate directly to requirements of the job. Employers, as a result, began hiring industrial psychologists to validate employment tests, taking additional steps to assure that other personnel instruments met the test of "job-relatedness" and, in some instances, hiring more women and minorities solely for the purpose of avoiding disparate impact suits.

The *Griggs* decision remains the subject of much controversy. Some critics continue to argue, for example, that Congress did not intend to outlaw disparate impact when it enacted the Civil Rights Act and that the Supreme Court erred in the *Griggs* decision.[3] Critics also point to the practical difficulties faced by employers in defending themselves against charges of discrimination. Although in theory an employer can win a disparate impact suit by proving that the challenged selection criterion is valid, this is often difficult to do in practice.

The EEOC Uniform Selection Guidelines of 1978

Employers have had little difficulty understanding what is required to avoid *disparate treatment* complaints. They must simply ensure that all employees and applicants are treated equally. But because *disparate impact* charges could be filed against them in instances where their policies and practices were facially neutral and where they did not intend to discriminate, employers demanded guidelines from the federal government defining adverse impact and clarifying what they must do to avoid disparate impact suits. Although a uniform set of guidelines was clearly needed, the various federal agencies responsible for enforcing nondiscrimination requirements were slow to agree on their contents. As a result, the EEOC was not able to issue its Uniform Guidelines on Employee Selection Procedures until 1978.

The Uniform Guidelines are designed to assist employers in complying with the requirements of federal nondiscrimination law in general and in avoiding adverse impact in particular. They state, first, that the use of any selection procedure which has an adverse impact on members of protected groups will be considered discriminatory unless they have been validated. Second, they describe methods by which selection procedures may be validated (see Chapter 9). Third, they require employers to use the procedure having the least adverse impact where two or more procedures are equally valid. Fourth, they require employers to keep records to determine whether adverse impact is occurring. Finally, they offer the Four-fifths Rule as a rule of thumb in determining whether adverse impact has occurred.

The Fourth-fifths (or Eighty Percent) Rule states that federal enforcement agencies will regard as evidence of adverse impact a selection rate for any race, sex, or ethnic group which is less than 80 percent of the rate for the group with the highest selection rate. For example, if the selection rate for blacks is less than 80 percent of that for whites, or the promotion rate for women is less than 80 percent of that for men, then adverse impact has occurred and the employer is obligated to seek out its cause and eliminate the offending selection procedure or ensure its validity.

To avoid liability resulting from adverse impact suits, the Guidelines suggest routinely analyzing selection rates by race, sex, and national origin both in hiring and promoting employees. The period for which such data is analyzed will depend on what length of time will produce statistically valid comparisons. Consider the following hypothetical example involving a municipal police department during a one-year period:

$$\frac{30 \text{ blacks selected}}{100 \text{ blacks applied}} = .3 \text{ (selection rate for blacks)}$$

$$\frac{500 \text{ whites selected}}{1000 \text{ whites applied}} = .5 \text{ (selection rate for whites)}$$

$$\frac{.3}{.5} = 60\% \text{ (the ratio of success of blacks to whites)}$$

Because 60 percent is less than 80 percent, the police department has violated the Four-fifths Rule in the overall hiring process and is vulnerable to a disparate impact suit.

Selection processes often involve several components. An applicant to the police department, for example, may be subject to a written examination, a physical abilities test, and an interview. The "bottom line" rule states that federal enforcement agencies will not investigate further if the results of the total selection process are within the limits set by the Four-fifths Rule. This means that an employer need not analyze every component of the selection process for evidence of adverse impact unless the Four-fifths Rule is violated for the selection process as a whole. In 1982 the Supreme Court invalidated the bottom line defense in *Connecticut v. Teal*,[4] ruling that employers must make sure that no members of protected groups are adversely affected by any component of the selection process regardless of whether the final selection rates are nondiscriminatory. The EEOC, however, generally investigates only the bottom line when deciding whether to take enforcement action.

Evidence of adverse impact does not mean that the employer is guilty of discrimination or that particular selection procedures must be eliminated. Job qualifications may in fact be job related, and tests may in fact be valid predictors of future job performance. The EEOC Uniform Guidelines simply suggest that if employers wish to avoid disparate impact suits or EEOC investigations they should keep relevant statistics on applicant flow, evaluate selection procedures for evidence of adverse impact, and eliminate offending practices or ensure their validity. Because it is often difficult or expensive to validate selection procedures, employers may be tempted to discriminate in favor of women and minorities to stay within the boundaries of the Four-fifths Rule. This kind of strategy, however, is clearly not sanctioned by either the Civil Rights Act or the Uniform Guidelines.

Shifting Burdens of Evidence in Judicial Proceedings

Individuals pursuing charges of discrimination in court must show a connection between a particular action by an employer (e.g., a decision to discharge them) and their status as members of a protected class (e.g., their race, gender, religion, or national origin). They may attempt to establish this connection by relying on disparate treatment theory, disparate impact theory, or both, depending on the particular circumstances. The flow of evidence is essentially the same, but the kinds of evidence presented and the defenses offered may vary. Although the burden of proof ultimately remains with the plaintiff, it is nonetheless useful to understand the "shifting burdens" involved as each party to a suit presents evidence. Exhibit 7.4 outlines the three basic steps involved as the burden of presenting evidence shifts back and forth between plaintiff and the employer as defendant.

Discrimination on the Basis of Race or Color

Disparate treatment may involve official or unofficial policies of excluding racial minorities from employment, denying them promotional opportunities, disciplining them more severely than nonminorities, or treating them in more disparaging or undignified ways. In such instances, it is irrelevant whether the discrimination is motivated by racial bigotry, sympathetic "concern for how minority employees may fit

EXHIBIT 7.4

FLOW OF EVIDENCE IN TITLE VII CASES

Step One
Plaintiff must establish a prima facie case of discrimination by providing evidence that the employer is guilty of unlawful discrimination.

Strategies in Disparate Treatment Cases
The plaintiff provides evidence that he or she is a member of a protected group who was treated differently than similarly situated employees or job applicants who are not members of a protected group. This creates an inference that discrimination has occurred.

As one example of how this might be done, the Supreme Court in *McDonnell Douglas Corp. v. Green*[5] laid out the following four-part test for establishing a prima facie case The plaintiff must show (1) that he or she belongs to a racial minority; (2) that he or she applied and was qualified for a job for which the employer was seeking applicants; (3) that, despite his or her qualifications, he or she was rejected; and (4) that after this rejection, the position remained open and the employer continued to seek applicants from persons with similar qualifications. This test applies equally to promotions and to members of any protected class.

Strategies in Disparate Impact Cases:
a) A Showing of Restricted Policy The plaintiff provides evidence that the employer had a policy (official or unofficial, written or unwritten) that, although neutral on its face, produced a substantial adverse impact on a protected class or classes.

b) Disparate Rejection Rates The plaintiff offers statistical evidence that the rejection rates in hiring or promoting members of protected groups is significantly higher than for other applicants or employees. This raises an inference that specific screening instruments are producing adverse impact.

c) Population Comparisons The plaintiff offers statistical evidence that the percentage of employees in the employer's workforce who are members of a protected group is significantly lower than their percentages in the local population.

Employers are provided an opportunity to rebut evidence of disparate treatment or disparate impact. If the employer succeeds, the court may choose to dismiss the case at this point.

Step Two
If the plaintiff succeeds in establishing a prima facie case, the burden shifts to the employer to rebut the presumption of discrimination.

Possible Defenses in Disparate Treatment Cases:
a) Legitimate Reason Defense Employer may argue that what appears to be unequal treatment actually reflects a legitimate organizational purpose. An employee may have been discharged, for example, not because of race but because of excessive absenteeism.

b) BFOQ Defense Title VII allows personnel decisions to be made on the basis of religion, sex, or national origin in those rare instances where religion, sex, or national origin is a bona fide occupational qualification. There is no BFOQ defense in cases involving racial discrimination.

EXHIBIT 7.4 *(continued)*

c) Bona Fide Seniority or Merit System Defense Title VII also allows employers to treat individuals differently where such treatment results from a "bona fide seniority or merit system, or a system which measures earnings by quantity or quality of production," if such practices are not motivated by an intent to discriminate.

Possible Defenses in Disparate Impact Cases:
a) Job-Relatedness/Business Necessity Defense Employer attempts to show that an employment practice (e.g., a qualification, policy, or test) is a valid predictor of job performance or is in some other way clearly based on job requirements, and is thus necessary to the efficient and safe operation of the organization. For this defense to be successful, the legitimate business purpose must be sufficiently compelling to override its discriminatory impact. (The Civil Rights Act of 1991 countered the Supreme Court's 1989 *Wards Cove* decision by clarifying that the burden is on the employer to demonstrate business necessity.)
b) Lack of "Qualified" Applicants Defense Employer argues that it should not be held liable for adverse impact produced by a particular selection procedure because it tried but failed to attract "qualified" applicants.

Step Three
The burden shifts to the plaintiff to rebut evidence presented by the employer.

Disparate Treatment Cases:
The plaintiff may argue that the reason advanced by the employer is a pretext for discrimination by reaffirming evidence of discriminatory motive or by challenging the employer's credibility.

Disparate Impact Cases:
The plaintiff may dispute evidence presented during the employer's defense, or argue that other instruments are available that would produce less adverse impact.

in," or a desire to conform with the attitudes and preferences of co-workers or clients. Since the *Griggs* decision, the central issue for employers has been identifying and addressing selection policies and procedures that may have an adverse impact on racial minorities. In the public sector, for example, much attention has been directed at the underrepresentation of blacks and hispanics in municipal, county, and state police forces and fire departments.

Color is identified in the Civil Rights Act as a protected category because it is theoretically possible for employers to argue that individuals were not discriminated against because of their race but because of their color, lighter skin tones being preferred by them over darker tones. In practice, however, charges of discrimination based on color are rare.

Discrimination on the Basis of National Origin

What is meant by the term "national origin" is not entirely clear. National origin discrimination, according to the EEOC, includes denials of equal opportunity because of an individual's place of origin or that of his or her ancestor's, or because of an individual's physical, cultural, or linguistic characteristics that may be associated with a particular nationality.[6] Although noncitizens are not explicitly protected as a group by Title VII, requiring employees to be citizens may be illegal if it has the purpose or effect of discriminating against individuals on the basis of national origin. In addition, the Immigration Reform and Control Act of 1986 prohibits employment discrimination against noncitizens who have been lawfully admitted to the United States and have filed their intent to become citizens.[7] This Act is intended to protect individuals in those instances where Title VII may not apply.[8]

One issue of concern in this area is the adverse impact that height and weight requirements may have on persons of some nationality groups. For this reason EEOC Guidelines specifically call on employers to examine such requirements for adverse impact. Where adverse impact is found, only those that are reasonably necessary to the performance of a particular job are considered lawful. A second issue involves requiring employees to be fluent in English. Because such requirements may result in either disparate treatment or disparate impact, employers must be prepared to defend their use. A fluency requirement, for example, may be validly related to the functions of a public relations officer, but bears little relationship to the functions performed by most blue-collar workers. Finally, the EEOC interprets Title VII as prohibiting harassment on the basis of national origin. Employers have a duty to maintain a working environment free of harassment. Under circumstances defined in EEOC Guidelines, ethnic slurs and other forms of conduct related to an individual's national origin may constitute unlawful harassment.

Discrimination on the Basis of Sex

Women, like racial and ethnic minorities, have faced a long history of discrimination in the United States. Discrimination against women is often the product of social stereotypes regarding their "proper roles" in society. As examples, women have been viewed as being responsible for child rearing rather than bread winning, requiring protection from certain occupational hazards or working conditions, and being "suited" for a limited range of occupational pursuits. As the following cases indicate, the courts have used Title VII to strike down a broad range of stereotype-based employment practices:

Child Care–Related Discrimination When Ida Phillips applied for a job as Assembly Trainee with the Martin Marietta Corporation, she was told that it was company policy not to accept job applications from women with preschool-aged children. Applications from men with preschool-aged children were readily accepted. (*Phillips v. Martin Marietta Corporation* 400 U.S. 542, 1971).

Marital Status–Related Discrimination   Stewardess Mary Sprogis was discharged by United Air Lines in 1966 for violating company policy requiring stewardesses to be unmarried. No such policy was applied to male stewards. (*Sprogis v. United Air Lines, Inc.* 444 F.2d 1194, 1971)

Sex Role–Based Discrimination   Celio Diaz, a man, was rejected for a position as a flight cabin attendant by Pan American Airways in 1967 because of Pan Am's policy of hiring only women as flight attendants. Pan Am argued that women were superior to men in nonmechanical aspects of the job such as "providing reassurance to anxious passengers" and "giving courteous, personalized service." Gender-based stereotypes can clearly limit employment opportunities for men as well as for women. (*Diaz v. Pan Am Airways, Inc* 442 F.2d 385, 1971)

Pay-Related Discrimination   Alberta Gunther received a salary as a jail matron that was 70 percent of that received by male correctional officers at the Washington County Jail in Oregon. Washington County set the rate at 70 percent although its own analysis established that jail matrons deserved to be paid at a rate 95 percent of that received by correctional officers. (*County of Washington v. Gunther* 452 U.S. 161, 1980).

Sexual Harassment   Deborah Ann Katz, an air traffic controller, was subjected to intensely humiliating sexual slurs, insults, and innuendos while employed by the FAA. Male employees were not subjected to such harassment. (*Katz v. Dole* 709 F.2d 251, 1983).

Excluding Women from Certain Jobs

Title VII, as interpreted by the courts, requires employers to evaluate male and female employees on the basis of their individual capacities to perform a particular job, rather than on the basis of stereotypes about their abilities as a class or their roles in society. As a result, the paternalistic laws that before 1964 excluded women from certain job categories have been superseded by Title VII. Despite such changes, vestiges of paternalism continue to influence employment policies and practices. Employers have, for example, excluded women from jobs involving heavy lifting, arguing that women as a class are unable to perform safely and efficiently the duties of the jobs involved. The courts have not generally been convinced by such arguments. In *Weeks v. Southern Bell Tel. Co.*, for example, a federal court of appeals ruled that Southern Bell's refusal to consider women for the job of switchman was unlawful despite evidence that the job was "strenuous."[9] The company had no reasonable basis, the court ruled, for concluding that all or substantially all women would be unable to perform job duties.

Even where women are not excluded as a group, they may still be excluded from certain jobs by the way job qualifications are set. An employer may have a facially neutral policy, for example, excluding all applicants who cannot lift 100 pounds.

When confronted with the fact that such job requirements have a disparate impact on women, the employer may argue that it is a job-related requirement and thus justified as a "business necessity." However, the employer will be expected to demonstrate that lifting 100 pounds is reasonably necessary to performing the requirements of the job in question and that a system is in place for testing the strength of all job applicants.

"Sex Plus" Cases

"Sex plus" cases are those in which the employer does not distinguish between individuals *solely* on the basis of sex, but does distinguish on the basis of sex plus some other factor such as marital status or parenthood. These situations involve employment standards that are applied to one sex but not to the other. Employers have argued that such distinctions are not prohibited by Title VII because they are not based solely on sex. In the *Sprogis* case cited above, United Airlines argued that its policy did not discriminate against women because of their sex but against a subclass of women because of their marital status. The courts have ruled, however, that where disparate treatment involves the fundamental rights of childbearing and marriage, such practices are prohibited by Title VII as sex-based discrimination. In short, it is not necessary for an employment practice to be directed at all members of a sex for it to be unlawful. It is only necessary that gender be a substantial factor in the discrimination. Policies that set different grooming standards (e.g., length of hair) for men and women, by contrast, have not been found unlawful because they involve neither immutable sex-related characteristics nor fundamental rights.

Mixed Motive Cases

Mixed motive cases, such as *Price Waterhouse v. Hopkins*,[10] demonstrate just how complex judicial enforcement of Title VII can be. Despite having helped secure a $25 million contract with the State Department, Ann Hopkins was not granted a partnership in the accounting firm of Price Waterhouse. The firm's motives were "mixed." The decision reflected a legitimate concern about her abrasive personality and poor interpersonal skills. However, impermissible, stereotype-based views of how women should behave also played a role in the decision. One partner described her as "macho," a second suggested that she "overcompensated for being a woman," a third advised her to take "a course at charm school," and a fourth suggested that her chances would improve if she would "walk more femininely, talk more femininely, dress more femininely, wear make-up, have her hair styled, and wear jewelry."[11]

The Supreme Court had to address two key issues. First, did Price Waterhouse unlawfully take Hopkins' gender into account when making its decision? Justice Brennan, writing for the majority, answered in the affirmative: It does not "require expertise in psychology to know that, if an employee's flawed 'interpersonal skills' can be corrected by a soft-hued suit or a new shade of lipstick, perhaps it is the employee's sex and not her interpersonal skills that has drawn the criticism."[12] Second, should Price Waterhouse be held liable for a violation of Title VII given that it also had a legitimate motive for withholding the partnership? Here the Court answered that an employer should not be held liable *if* it can prove that it would have made the same decision even if it had not taken gender into account.

The case was remanded to the district court to determine whether the employer should be held liable. The story does not end here, however. Realizing that the Court's ruling made it easier for employers to avoid liability, Congress included language in the Civil Rights Act of 1991 stating that an employer violates Title VII any time race, religion, sex, or national origin is a factor, even if the decision is made primarily for legitimate reasons. Although liable, an employer can nonetheless avoid paying compensatory and punitive damages by showing that it would have taken the same action despite the influence of an impermissible motive.

Pregnancy-Related Discrimination

Before 1978 it was common, particularly in the private sector, for employers to refuse to hire pregnant women. It was also common to discharge women who became pregnant or to require them to take mandatory, unpaid pregnancy leave. Excluding pregnancy-related disabilities from medical leave policies and benefit plans was also a common practice. When General Electric denied pregnancy-related benefits to a group of female employees in the early 1970s, the women filed a class action lawsuit claiming that General Electric's policy constituted sex-based discrimination. The Supreme Court disagreed, ruling in *General Electric Co. v. Gilbert* that distinctions based on pregnancy cannot be equated with distinctions based on sex. The class of nonpregnant employees, the Court reasoned, contained both men and women, and therefore the employer's policy could not reflect discrimination on the basis of sex.[13]

Congress quickly responded to the *Gilbert* decision by enacting the Pregnancy Discrimination Act of 1978. This Act amended the definition of sex discrimination in Title VII to include employment practices that discriminate "on the basis of pregnancy, childbirth, and related medical conditions." This means that employers cannot lawfully refuse to hire a pregnant job applicant if she is able to perform the major functions of the job. Pregnant employees must be allowed to work as long as they are able and then must be treated the same as all other employees who become temporarily disabled. Although the Act does not require employers to maintain maternity leave policies, it does require them to extend the same disability leaves and benefits to pregnant employees that are extended to other employees with temporary disabilities. The Family and Medical Leave Act of 1993 now requires employers with 50 or more employees to provide unpaid parental leaves.

Sexual Harassment

Sexual harassment is defined by the EEOC as "unwelcome sexual advances, requests for sexual favors, and other verbal or physical conduct of a sexual nature. . . ."[14] The latter refers to such things as suggestive comments, leering, gestures, physical touching, symbolic harassment such as prominent displays of nude pictures, and, in extreme cases, physical assault. Sexual harassment is perpetrated mainly by men against women, although men are often victims of sexual harassment as well. A 1987 survey of federal employees, for example, found that approximately 42 percent of all women and 14 percent of all men had experienced some form of uninvited and unwanted sexual attention.[15] Unlawful harassment can involve homosexual as well as heterosexual advances.

Harassment against women is particularly difficult to eradicate from the workplace because of lingering sex-role stereotypes, including perceptions of women as economically subservient and sexually submissive. In addition, because men frequently exercise authority over women in the workplace, they are often in a position to exploit the economically dependent status of female employees. Whether perpetrated by supervisors or co-workers, harassment can be intensely humiliating and degrading, and reactions frequently include extreme anger, depression, and greatly reduced self-esteem.[16] The economic costs of sexual harassment can also be enormous. The federal government, for example, has estimated that between 1985 and 1987 sexual harassment cost it $267 million. These costs resulted from increased turnover and absenteeism due to harassment, paying medical insurance claims for employees seeking professional counseling in dealing with the effects of harassment, and reduced individual and work group productivity.[17]

The courts did not initially define sexual harassment as unlawful, viewing it instead as private conduct between workers for which the employer was not responsible. Today, however, the judicial system recognizes two kinds of unlawful sexual harassment.[18] The first is sometimes called "quid pro quo" harassment because it involves the exchange of sexual favors for employment-related benefits. An employee, for example, who is denied a job, promotion, or other employment benefit because of his or her refusal to consent to sexual advances has a legitimate Title VII complaint. Similarly, an employee not involved in a quid pro quo bargain who nonetheless believes that an employment opportunity or benefit has been lost because another employee was rewarded for submitting to sexual favors also may have a legitimate Title VII complaint.

A second kind of unlawful sexual harassment is generally referred to as "hostile work environment" harassment. It refers to situations where no exchange of employment benefits for sexual favors is involved, but where conduct of a sexual nature becomes so hostile or abusive that it negatively affects an employee's work performance. According to EEOC guidelines, such conduct is a violation of Title VII when it has "the purpose or effect of unreasonably interfering with an individual's work performance or creating an intimidating, hostile, or offensive working environment." Courts were initially reluctant to recognize such claims because they failed to specify what economic benefit had been denied to employees as the result of sexual harassment. This issue was finally addressed by the Supreme Court in 1986 in *Meritor Savings Bank, FSB v. Vinson.*[19] The Court ruled that no tangible economic benefit need be lost for an employee to establish a Title VII claim. Because the right to work in an environment free from harassment can be viewed as a condition of employment, conduct that denies employees this right, according to the Court, may represent a Title VII violation. An employee need only show in court that the harassment was unwelcomed and that it was sufficiently pervasive or severe to alter the conditions of employment by creating a hostile or abusive work environment.

The courts also had to sort out the circumstances under which an employer could be held liable for the actions of supervisors and co-workers. In cases involving co-workers, the courts and the EEOC have been in general agreement. The employer is responsible for paying economic damages to victims of sexual harassment by co-workers where the employer knew or should have known about the harassment and failed to take immediate corrective action. In situations involving supervisors, by contrast, the issue of liability is less clear. The EEOC considers employers responsible for the actions of its supervisors whether or not they have knowledge that harassment is occurring. However, the Supreme Court in *Vinson* implied that strict liability is not always warranted in hostile work environment cases where higher management has prohibited such behavior and has no reasonable basis for knowing of its existence.

Because many of the causes of sexual harassment are embedded in the larger American culture, it is probably not realistic to expect to eliminate it from the workplace entirely. Nonetheless, management has an affirmative duty under Title VII to prevent sexual harassment from occurring and there are steps it can take toward this end. EEOC guidelines, court rulings, and common sense tend to support the following actions: First, management should establish clear policies defining and prohibiting sexual harassment and setting out severe penalties for violators. These policies should also establish procedures for pursuing complaints of harassment, including avenues for bypassing supervisors who may be unsympathetic or actually involved in harassing employees. Second, management should establish training programs to inform all employees about organizational policies and to sensitize them to the importance of eliminating harassment, including the elimination of sexually oriented language, jokes, and gestures. Because unlawful sexual harassment is defined as "unwelcomed" conduct, employees should also be told that they have an obligation to communicate to appropriate individuals which behaviors they consider offensive. Third, supervisors should be trained to recognize violations and educated regarding the importance of taking immediate corrective action. Finally, support groups should be established in departments where harassment and retaliation are difficult to see and control. The city of Madison, Wisconsin, created such groups after concluding that women firefighters, police officers, bus drivers, and maintenance employees "work in extraordinarily complex male dominated subcultures where loyalty to the crew often takes precedence over all else and is seen as a prerequisite for survival on the job."[20]

Discrimination on the Basis of Religion

Title VII prohibits employers from discriminating against individuals because of their particular religious faith and the practices associated with that faith. In 1972, Congress amended Title VII to clarify that employers have a duty to "reasonably accommodate" religious practices unless the employer can prove that doing so would result in "undue hardship" on the conduct of business. Practices that employers are expected to accommodate include observance of a Sabbath or religious holiday, prayer breaks during working hours, dietary requirements, mourning periods for deceased relatives, religious prohibitions against membership in labor organizations, and practices concerning dress and other personal grooming habits.

The key legal issue in most discrimination cases involving religion is whether an employer has fulfilled its duty to reasonably accommodate the religious practices of an employee or prospective employee. Complaints often arise because of a conflict between an employee's work schedule and his or her desire not to work on the Sabbath or on certain religious holidays. The employee may be accommodated, for example, by locating an employee with similar qualifications who might volunteer to work on

Saturdays, Sundays, or religious holidays, flexible work hours or shifts, lateral transfers or changes of assignments, or excused absences for religious observances. The difficulty lies in determining when such accommodations constitute an undue hardship. According to EEOC guidelines, "an employer may assert undue hardship to justify a refusal to accommodate an employee's need to be absent from his or her scheduled duty hours if the employer can demonstrate that the accommodation would require more than a *de minimis* cost."[21] The cost involved in occasionally arranging shift changes or allowing a day off is unlikely to be "more than a *de minimis* cost." By contrast, if shift swaps cannot be arranged, and the employee cannot simply be excused from work, the salaries paid to a substitute may represent an undue hardship. In *Trans World Airlines, Inc. v. Hardison*,[22] for example, the Supreme Court ruled that TWA was justified in discharging an employee after efforts to accommodate the employee's refusal to work Saturdays through providing days off and arranging shift swaps had failed.

Discrimination on the Basis of Age

Recognizing the unique characteristics of discrimination based on age, Congress opted to enact separate legislation rather than include age among the categories protected by the Civil Rights Act. In 1967 Congress passed the Age Discrimination in Employment Act (ADEA), which, as amended in 1974 and 1986, prohibits private employers with more than 20 employees and state and local governments from discriminating against individuals who are 40 years of age and older.

Age discrimination occurs because employers want to avoid paying the higher salaries and more expensive benefits generally earned by older employees, or because of unwarranted concerns about the physical deterioration that occurs with age and the negative effects of such deterioration on work performance or safety. Before enactment of the ADEA, it was not uncommon for employers to advertise for "young applicants," exclude applicants over a certain age, find reasons to discharge older workers, or adopt mandatory retirement ages. The ADEA now prohibits age-specific employment policies affecting persons older than 40 unless age can be shown to be a BFOQ, or unless the differentiation is based on a bona fide seniority system, bona fide benefit plan, or "reasonable factors other than age."[23]

State and local governments often use the BFOQ exception to justify the use of mandatory retirement and maximum hiring age policies in police and firefighting occupations. Despite specific language in the ADEA allowing bona fide hiring and retirement plans in these occupations, such policies are not always upheld. In *EEOC v. Missouri State Highway Patrol*, for example, a federal district court struck down a policy requiring retirement of state troopers at age 60.[24] The court concluded that the Highway Patrol had not produced evidence that all or substantially all troopers older than 60 are unable to perform job duties safely and efficiently. Nor had it demonstrated that it was impractical to determine which troopers may no longer be qualified because of age-related deteriorations in their abilities. The court was apparently convinced by evidence that many simple and inexpensive tests exist for assessing balance, flexibility, agility, speed, power, and endurance. Recent court decisions seem to favor the use of physical fitness tests over mandatory retirement policies in safety-sensitive occupations. As an alternative, the Older Workers Benefit Protection Act of 1990 specifically allows use of early-retirement incentive plans as long as they are truly voluntary.

Individuals who believe their ADEA rights have been violated must file a complaint with the EEOC within 180 days of the alleged violation or within 300 days if the complaint is first referred to a local 706 agency. If conciliation efforts fail, the EEOC is authorized to sue the employer on the employee's behalf. Alternatively, the employee may file a private civil suit after 60 days from the time the complaint was filed if the EEOC has not already filed a suit. In contrast to its authority under Title VII, the EEOC may file suits against state and local governments as well as private employers.

Federal employees are covered by a separate section of the ADEA. As with Title VII cases, complaints are first pursued within the agency, with the employee reserving the right to a formal hearing and the right to appeal the agency head's decision to the EEOC.[25] Alternatively, federal employees may file their own private civil suits as long as they give the EEOC at least 30 days' notice of their intent and the notification is within 180 days of the alleged violation.

The implications of the ADEA for management are relatively clear. Management is responsible for posting notices informing employees of their ADEA rights and maintaining payroll and personnel records as required by the EEOC. Management must also scrutinize all age-specific policies and practices to ensure they can be defended under one of the ADEA's exceptions. Finally, managers must not allow the age of job applicants or employees to affect their employment decisions, at least as regards persons older than age 40. These responsibilities may be even broader under state law because some states protect all employees and job applicants from age discrimination, not just those who are 40 years of age or older.

Discrimination on the Basis of Disability

The difficulties disabled Americans face in pursuing employment opportunities result from the nature of their impairments and the attitudes imposed on them by society. Historically, disabled persons have been stigmatized as inferior and treated as social outcasts. Feelings of aversion, paternalism, or pity have influenced the screening, testing, and interviewing processes to cause the rejection of many qualified disabled applicants.[26] Social stereotypes and stigmas are not without serious consequences. They reduce the self-esteem of disabled persons, increase their social isolation, and produce feelings of inferiority that may further discourage them from seeking employment.[27] They also reinforce the mistaken belief that hiring disabled workers will result in higher accident rates, increased legal liability, higher insurance premiums, higher training costs, or lost productivity. Such concerns have led employers to adopt employment policies excluding "the blind," "epileptics," "diabetics," or "persons with bad backs" regardless of their individual situations or the requirements of specific jobs. Finally, disabled Americans have been constrained by access barriers, including narrow walkways, absence of curb ramps, inaccessible restrooms, and lack of elevators. By the early 1970s Congress decided it was time to take action to eliminate as many of these barriers as possible. Today two key pieces of federal legislation address discrimination on the basis of disability: the Rehabilitation Act of 1973 and the Americans with Disabilities Act of 1990.

The Rehabilitation Act of 1973

Although the Rehabilitation Act is not a comprehensive nondiscrimination law, it does prohibit discrimination by three types of employers. Section 501 prohibits federal agencies from discriminating against qualified physically or mentally handicapped persons. Disabled employees and job applicants are required to pursue their complaints internally. If not satisfied with the results, they may then appeal the agency head's decision to the EEOC. The EEOC acts as an appeals board with power to uphold or overturn agency decisions. Federal employees also have a private right to sue after internal remedies have failed.

Section 503 requires government contractors with contracts in excess of $2,500 to "take affirmative action to employ and advance in employment qualified handicapped individuals." State and local government agencies having contracts with the federal government are subject to Section 503 requirements. This might be the case, for example, where a state department of fish and game has contracted to operate a federal fish hatchery. Complaints are investigated by the Department of Labor's Office of Federal Contract Compliance Programs (OFCCP), which has authority to enforce contractual obligations either through the courts or by enforcing administrative remedies such as withholding payments due on contracts, terminating contracts, or debarring contractors from future contracts.

Finally, Section 504 prohibits discrimination against disabled persons by any program receiving federal financial assistance or conducted by any executive branch agency. Because they receive federal assistance, many state and local agencies, as well as public school and university systems, are subject to these requirements. They are prohibited from discriminating both in their roles as employers and as providers of program benefits and services.

Section 504 complaints are filed with the federal department distributing the funds in question. For example, an individual who believes he or she has been discriminated against by a university receiving federal financial assistance from the Department of Education must file a complaint with the Department's Office for Civil Rights (OCR). OCR investigates complaints and attempts to resolve them through conciliation. If conciliation efforts fail, OCR may seek compliance by suspending or terminating federal aid. Individuals may also file a private civil suit after exhaustion of administrative remedies.

Before 1988 it was unclear whether state and local agencies were subject to Section 504 requirements as a whole, or whether only the particular programs receiving federal funds were subject to these requirements. The Civil Rights Restoration Act of 1988 added language to Section 504 to make it clear that an entire department or agency is covered if any part of it receives federal funds. Generally speaking, however, only the specific program found guilty of discrimination runs the risk of losing federal funds.

The Americans with Disabilities Act of 1990

The Americans with Disabilities Act (ADA) is a truly comprehensive piece of legislation that extended civil rights protections to an estimated 43 million Americans with mental and physical disabilities. It goes well beyond the Rehabilitation Act of 1973 by prohibiting discrimination by all employers, public and private, with 15 or more employees. It prohibits discrimination in employment, public services, and public accommodations. Because of the special barriers confronting the disabled, it also requires public transportation systems, other public services, and telecommunications systems to be accessible to persons with disabilities.

It is Title I of the ADEA that specifically addresses employment-related discrimination. Title I requires employers to reasonably accommodate the known physical and mental limitations of an otherwise qualified job applicant or employee unless doing so would impose an undue hardship on the employer. Important provisions with which managers and personnel officers should be familiar include the following:[28]

Definition of Disabled Person   Like the Rehabilitation Act, the ADA defines disability with respect to any given individual as:

a. a physical or mental impairment that substantially limits one or more of the major life activities of such individual;

b. a record of such an impairment; or

c. being regarded as having such an impairment.

The second of these categories is significant because it extends protection to persons with past impairments such as rehabilitated drug abusers, persons recovered from heart attacks, and former cancer patients. The third category is significant because it extends protection to those individuals who have never suffered a substantially limiting impairment but who are nonetheless perceived as disabled. An individual who is discriminated against because he or she is thought to have AIDS, for example, has legal recourse under this definition. The third category also protects individuals whose impairments do not substantially affect their work abilities but who are erroneously judged to be substantially limited nonetheless.

Definition of Qualified Disabled Person   Because employers are prohibited from discriminating against *qualified* individuals with disabilities, the key issue for managers is knowing who is and is not qualified. According to the ADA, a qualified individual with a disability is "an individual who, with or without reasonable accommodation, can perform the essential functions of the employment position that such individual holds or desires." This means that employers must assess each person's work abilities in relation to the specific requirements and essential functions of each job. Essential functions are those that are central to a job and cannot be transferred to other employees. As discussed in Chapter 5, essential functions are ideally determined through job analysis and are recorded in a job description.

The Duty of Reasonable Accommodation   According to the ADA, reasonable accommodation includes making workplace facilities accessible and usable, restructuring jobs and work schedules, acquiring or modifying work equipment or devices, modifying examinations and training materials, and providing qualified readers or interpreters. An employer has a duty to accommodate known physical or mental limitations so that an otherwise qualified applicant or employee is fully capable of performing the job's essential functions, unless it would impose an undue hardship.

Definition of Undue Hardship   An undue hardship is an action requiring significant difficulty or expense. The ADA identifies several factors to be considered in determining whether undue hardship exists, including the nature and cost of the accommodation and the organization's financial resources. In practice this is often left to the courts to determine on a case-by-case basis.

Definition of Discrimination Generally speaking, the ADA prohibits treating individuals differently on the basis of disability, testing and selecting individuals in ways that adversely affect persons with disabilities, maintaining qualification standards or other selection criteria that tend to screen out individuals with disabilities unless they can be shown to be job-related and consistent with business necessity, and failing to provide reasonable accommodation. Employers also cannot require preemployment medical examinations, although they can make job offers contingent on passing such an examination after an offer is extended, if everyone is treated equally in this regard and confidentiality is protected.

Exceptions Employers are allowed to maintain qualification standards that require that individuals "not pose a direct threat to the health or safety of other individuals in the workplace." The burden is on the employer, however, to show that the individual poses "a significant risk" that cannot be eliminated by reasonable accommodation. The ADA also identifies homosexuals, bisexuals, transvestites, and persons currently using illegal drugs as not falling within the category of "qualified individual with a disability."

Enforcement The provisions of the ADA are enforced by the EEOC with the same remedies available as under Title VII of the Civil Rights Act.

Implications for the Selection Process

Employers cannot safeguard the rights of disabled applicants if they do not know which applicants are, or consider themselves, impaired. Although they are only required to accommodate *known* impairments, employers will be expected to provide opportunities for applicants to make their impairments known. This can be accomplished by including a statement of the following kind on job application forms:

> *The employer is committed to making reasonable accommodation to any known disability that may interfere with an applicant's ability to compete in the selection process or ability to perform the duties of the position for which he or she is applying. If you would like us to consider such accommodation, please attach a description of the desired accommodation.*

A statement of this kind helps to reassure job applicants that supplying the information is voluntary, that they may participate in determining whether reasonable accommodation is possible, and that the information is intended to be used for lawful purposes. By responding, the applicant informs the employer that he or she may be protected from discrimination under the law.

Meeting an employer's legal obligations is particularly difficult in those situations where an apparently disabled applicant does not make his or her impairments known. The ADA specifically precludes asking whether an individual has a disability. For this reason an applicant should not be asked during an interview whether he or she is disabled, even where it is apparent to the interviewer that the applicant is in fact impaired. To avoid treating applicants differently, the interviewer should instead review job requirements with each applicant and then ask whether the applicant possesses any impairments that may restrict his or her ability to perform them efficiently and safely. An affirmative answer may lead to discussions of accommodation, and a negative answer should be accepted as truthful until events prove otherwise.

The ADA does not require selecting a disabled person over a clearly more qualified, nonimpaired applicant. Rather, it requires ensuring that the disabled individual is not screened out by considerations related to an impairment that is either unrelated to job demands or can be accommodated without undue hardship. With this task in mind, Exhibit 7.5 summarizes key decisions in a selection process in which disabled applicants are known to be competing.

AIDS in the Workplace

Persons with Acquired Immune Deficiency Syndrome (AIDS) have failed immune systems that leave them susceptible to opportunistic infections that eventually result in death. As the AIDS epidemic spreads, employers will increasingly confront difficult situations involving employees or job applicants with AIDS. Because of the fear generated by AIDS, for example, managers may be pressured by other employees to segregate or discharge employees who have AIDS or who have tested positive for the HIV virus. Or they may be tempted to discriminate against such individuals because they anticipate resistance from co-workers, believe it will increase their legal liability to hire individuals with a contagious disease, or fear it will drive up their medical insurance costs.

As noted earlier, however, the ADA prohibits discrimination against persons with disabilities as long as they do not pose a direct threat to the health or safety of others and are able to perform essential job duties. Guidelines issued by the Center for Disease Control emphasize that AIDS cannot be transmitted by casual workplace contact and that people with AIDS may continue on the job without endangering their co-workers or the public in most occupational settings. Fear of contagion thus does not provide a legitimate basis for rejecting applicants or discharging employees who are HIV positive or have AIDS. A federal court, for example, recently found the District of Columbia Fire Department guilty of discrimination for discharging a firefighter who had tested positive for HIV.[29]

Under ADA requirements, current employees must be allowed to continue to work as long as they are able to perform essential job duties, with or without reasonable accommodation. Reasonable accommodation in such situations might include flextime, job restructuring, leave with or without pay, more frequent rest breaks, or transfer to a different position. Once AIDS has incapacitated employees to the point that they can no longer perform essential job functions, they may be accommodated with a disability leave. When disability benefits are exhausted and there is little reason to believe they will be able to return to work in the near future, a decision to discharge them may be appropriate.

Many government agencies have established policies describing the rights of persons with AIDS and have initiated programs for educating employees about AIDS in an effort to reassure them that they do not run a significant risk of contracting AIDS from casual workplace contact. In addition, many agencies are training supervisors about the disease, how to handle workplace situations that may arise, and the importance of maintaining the confidentiality of medical information concerning individual employees.

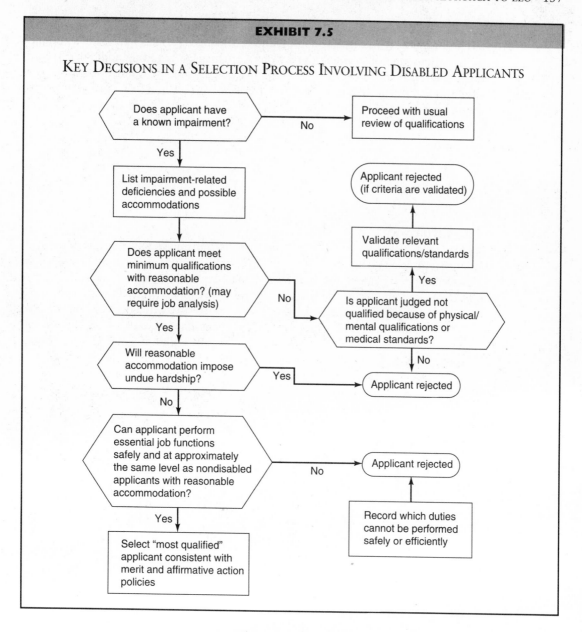

EXHIBIT 7.5

KEY DECISIONS IN A SELECTION PROCESS INVOLVING DISABLED APPLICANTS

The Nondiscrimination Approach: A Final Word

Externally imposed legal requirements concerning civil rights have had an enormous impact on the practice of human resource management since 1964. In practice, managers and personnel officers must be familiar with the major provisions of state law as well as the federal laws discussed in this chapter. State laws are sometimes more restrictive than federal laws and managers and personnel officers are be held responsible for safeguarding employee rights under both.

Although the nondiscrimination approach has done much to define and protect civil rights in the workplace, it is not without controversy. It has resulted in a complex set of regulations constraining the actions of managers, requiring additional record-keeping systems, and creating a responsibility for ensuring the validity of selection devices that is difficult to satisfy. Even more controversial, however, is the affirmative action approach to EEO, an approach that is examined in the next chapter.

■ **CASE 7.1** Aids in the Workplace[30]

The Situation

You are the Chief of the Eligibility Determination Bureau. You oversee a staff of 12 eligibility technicians who review the applications of persons seeking public assistance to determine if they meet state and federal eligibility criteria. Remarks made by other employees lead you to believe that one technician is widely viewed by other employees as being gay. He does exhibit behavioral characteristics stereotypically associated with gays. In addition, he has recently missed several days of work because of a respiratory infection and does not appear to be in the best health. It is not long before co-workers reach the conclusion that the technician has AIDS.

Fear quickly spreads through the Bureau. A delegation of workers visits your office and announces that the technician in question should be tested for the AIDS virus and given a leave of absence until the test results are complete. They make it clear that they consider his presence in the workplace a threat to their health and they want the situation resolved immediately.

The Problem

This situation poses a number of ethical, legal, and practical problems for management. Apprised of the situation, the Department Director decides it should not be treated as an isolated occurrence. He elects to implement a policy covering this and similar situations that may arise in the future. You are asked to be part of the management team given responsibility for drafting agency policy. How will you respond to the following policy issues:

1. Will the policy require mandatory AIDS testing for job applicants or current employees? Might this expose the agency to legal risk?
2. If the person with AIDS experiences disabling conditions and requests a medical leave of absence, will the policy allow such a leave?
3. Will the policy allow the release of information about a person's health status, as employees are demanding?
4. Will the policy require that employees who refuse to work with persons with AIDS be disciplined?
5. Will the policy attempt to allay the fears of employees about AIDS? If so, how?

▲ **EXERCISE 7.1** Sexual Harassment in the Workplace

Instructions

Form into groups of three to five and appoint one person to record the group's responses. Discuss and, if possible, agree on the appropriateness of the behaviors listed below using the following scale:

1—Always appropriate
2—Usually appropriate
3—Neutral
4—Usually inappropriate
5—Never appropriate

For each behavior, record the group's reasons for assigning a particular score. The class as a whole may then compare group ratings and discuss what obligations, if any, management has in each instance.

Behaviors

1. A supervisor invites a subordinate to lunch.

2. A co-worker calls you at home repeatedly to request a date after you have told him/her you are not interested.

3. A supervisor routinely puts his/her arm around subordinates while talking to them.

4. A subordinate agrees to date his/her supervisor after a mutual attraction has developed.

5. A male member of a work crew tells sexually-oriented jokes in front of a female employee.

6. A supervisor promotes his girlfriend as his administrative assistant even though other promotable men and women are available.

Notes

1. 29 C.F.R. Sec. 1613.231 (1992).

2. 401 U.S. 424.

3. Michael Evan Gold, "Grigg's Folly: An Essay on the Theory, Problems, and Origin of the Adverse Impact Definition of Employment Discrimination and a Recommendation for Reform," *Industrial Relations Law Journal* 7 (No. 4, 1985):429–598.

4. 457 U.S. 440, 1982.

5. 411 U.S. 792, 1973.

6. 29 C.F.R. Sec. 1606.1 (1992).

7. Codified at 8 U.S.C. 1324(b) and 1103(a).

8. 28 C.F.R. Sec. 4.100 (1992).

9. 408 F.2d 288, 1969.

10. 490 U.S. 228, 1989.

11. Ibid., 228.

12. Ibid., 256.

13. *General Electric Co. v. Gilbert* (429 U.S. 125, 1976).

14. 29 C.F.R. Sec. 1604.11 (1992).

15. U.S. Merit Systems Protection Board, *Sexual Harassment in the Federal Government: An Update* (Washington, D.C.: MSPB, 1988), 2.

16. James C. Renick, "Sexual Harassment at Work: Why It Happens, What to Do About It," *Personnel Journal* 59 (August 1980):658–662.

17. U. S. Merit Systems Protection Board, *Sexual Harassment*, 4.

18. Robert K. Robinson et al., "Sexual Harassment in the Workplace: A Review of the Legal Rights and Responsibilities of All Parties," *Public Personnel Management* 22 (Spring 1993):123–135.

19. 477 U.S. 57.

20. Jeri Spann, "Dealing Effectively with Sexual Harassment: Some Practical Lessons from One City's Experience," *Public Personnel Management* 19 (Spring 1990), 64.

21. 29. C.F.R Sec. 1605.2(e) (1992).

22. 432 U.S. 63, 1973.

23. Joseph M. Pelicciotti, ""Exemptions and Employer Defenses Under the ADEA, *Public Personnel Management* 20 (Summer 1991):233–261.

24. 555 F.Supp. 97, 1982.

25. 29 C.F.R. Sec. 1613.501 (1992).

26. U.S. Commission on Civil Rights, *Accommodating the Spectrum of Individual Abilities* (Washington, D.C.: Government Printing Office, 1983).

27. Kent Hull, "Forward—The Specter of Equality: Reflections on the Civil Rights of Physically-Handicapped Persons," 50 *Temple Law Quarterly* 50 (No. 4 1977):944—952.

28. See, for example, Harvey R. Boller and Douglas Massengill, "Public Employers' Obligation to Reasonably Accommodate the Disabled Under the Rehabilitation and Americans with Disabilities Acts," *Public Personnel Management* 21 (Fall 1992):273–300.

29. See "Firefighter Applicant with AIDS Virus Qualified for Job," *IPMA News* (September 1992), 12.

30. The situation described in this case is derived in part from William S. Waldo, "The Work Environment: A Practical Guide for Dealing with AIDS at Work," *Personnel Journal* (August 1987), 135.

CHAPTER 8

The Affirmative Action Approach to EEO

Learning Objectives

After mastering the material contained in this chapter, you will be able to:

1. Explain the defining characteristics of the affirmative action approach to equal employment opportunity.
2. Identify five affirmative action methods.
3. Describe and compare three types of preferential affirmative action programs.
4. Identify and evaluate five arguments made by those who oppose affirmative action as public policy.
5. Explain the goals of diversity management programs.

Even as the Civil Rights Act was working its way through Congress, civil rights advocates understood that prohibiting discrimination would not guarantee equal employment opportunity for women and minorities. Although the Civil Rights Act represented an important first step, educational disadvantages, insufficient work experience and skills, and the adverse effects of social stereotypes would continue to cause women and minorities to be underrepresented in most organizations. Recognizing that these kinds of barriers could not be addressed effectively through litigation, civil rights advocates pressed for faster, more aggressive measures for achieving substantive equality. In short, they demanded affirmative action.

The *affirmative action approach* to EEO refers to various efforts that deliberately take race, sex, and national origin into account to remedy past and current effects of discrimination. Its primary goal is to ensure that women and minorities are widely represented in all occupations and at all organizational levels. Like the nondiscrimination approach, it has greatly influenced the practice of human resource management. It has resulted in special recruitment and training programs, new systems for tracking the numbers of women and minorities in each occupational category, hiring goals and timetables, and preferential selection policies.

Affirmative action policies and programs, and the political controversies that surround them, have greatly altered the landscape of human resource management. This chapter examines these changes by defining the affirmative action approach to EEO, describing three types of preferential affirmative action programs, evaluating affirmative action as public policy, and exploring the growing interest in diversity management.

Origins of the Affirmative Action Approach

The concept of affirmative action originated with the realization that some of the more intractable barriers to EEO cannot be addressed effectively through litigation. Educational disadvantages, for example, continue to affect racial and ethnic minorities as they pursue employment opportunities. Historically, blacks often attended the poorest schools and were socialized not to aspire to other than menial occupations. Low socioeconomic status, itself partly a result of past and current discrimination, has made it difficult for many blacks to take full advantage of available educational opportunities. The *Griggs* case provides an example. Although a high school diploma was required of whites and blacks alike, blacks were adversely affected because only 12 percent of black males graduated from high school in North Carolina in the early 1960s, compared with 34 percent of white males.[1] The effects of educational disadvantages of this kind are often cumulative. As individuals are denied employment opportunities because they lack the required educational qualifications, they also fail to accumulate valuable work experience. As a result, they may fall farther behind in the competition for available jobs each time an employment opportunity is denied to them.

Social stereotypes represent another significant barrier to equal employment opportunity. Women in particular have been adversely affected by stereotypes regarding their work aptitudes or their "proper" roles in society. Traditionally, parents, teachers, and guidance counselors have discouraged women from pursuing educational opportunities that might prepare them for careers in traditionally male-dominated occupations. Similarly, hiring authorities have steered women into low-level secretarial and clerical jobs, regardless of their work aptitudes or abilities. Regardless of their intent, these actions reinforce prejudicial stereotypes and deny women a wide range of employment opportunities.

Women moving into career tracks once dominated by men are encountering a subtle yet possibly more serious form of stereotyping. There is now considerable evidence that unconscious expectations about the behaviors that are "appropriate" for women are limiting their ability to advance up the organizational hierarchy. Men, for example, are expected to be assertive and to perform leadership roles, and their behaviors are approved when they do. Women exhibiting the same behaviors, by contrast, are often greeted with disapproval. The *Price Waterhouse* case provides an example. Ann Hopkins was criticized for her assertiveness and asked to walk, talk, and dress more femininely. A different set of expectations apparently applied to her male counterparts. The existence of such biases have been confirmed by experimental research. In one recent experiment, for example, men and women were trained to lead small group discussions and to present the same sets of arguments.[2] Researchers recorded the nonverbal reactions of other group participants. In groups led by women, participants, both male and female, responded negatively to the arguments, whereas in groups led by men, participants reacted positively. Such studies seem to confirm that leadership behaviors are not expected from women; they are expected to be more passive and deferential. These stereotype-based expectations no doubt contribute to what has been called the *glass ceiling*, the level in an organizational hierarchy beyond which few women advance. Significantly, these expectations appear to operate at a largely unconscious level, affecting even those who hold egalitarian views of gender roles. This makes them particularly difficult to address.

Economic and educational disadvantages, and the persistence of gender, racial, and ethnic stereotypes, continue to contribute to the underrepresentation of women and minorities in the workplace, especially at higher organizational levels. During the 1960s, affirmative action gradually emerged as a strategy for addressing workforce imbalances. The term first appears in President Kennedy's Executive Order 10925 of 1961. It required federal agencies to review their employment practices and recommend "additional affirmative steps" for eliminating discrimination. It also required government contractors to take "affirmative action" to ensure that applicants and employees are treated "without regard to their race, creed, color, or national origin." Consistent with the nondiscrimination approach, Kennedy viewed these "additional affirmative steps" as remedial in nature, designed to eliminate institutional and informational barriers that interfered with equal employment opportunity.

A commencement address given by President Johnson at Howard University in 1965 signaled the beginning of a subtle shift in emphasis from equal opportunity to substantive equality:

> You do not take a person who, for years, has been hobbled by chains and liberate him, bring him up to the starting line of a race and then say, "you are free to compete with all the others," and still justly believe that you have been completely fair.
>
> Thus it is not enough to open the gates of opportunity. All our citizens must have the ability to walk through those gates.
>
> This is the next and the more profound stage of the battle for civil rights. We seek not just freedom but opportunity. We seek not just legal equity but human ability, not just equality as a right and a theory but equality as a fact and equality as a result.[3]

Three months later, President Johnson issued Executive Order 11246 requiring government contractors to submit "compliance reports" to the Secretary of Labor. This was a critical step in the development of affirmative action as a strategy for achieving balanced workforces. According to Revised Order 4, issued in 1971 for purposes of implementing Executive Order 11246, these reports had to include hiring goals and timetables for rectifying the underrepresentation of women and minorities.

During the 1960s and 1970s, affirmative action programs in the federal government became increasingly institutionalized. In 1969 President Nixon issued Executive Order 11478 requiring formal affirmative action programs in each federal agency. Under regulations drawn up by the EEOC, federal agencies were henceforth expected to use the same aggressive, results-oriented procedures mandated earlier for private contractors. The growing commitment to social equity received renewed attention in 1978 when the Civil Service Reform Act created special recruitment programs to reduce minority group underrepresentation in federal agencies. Despite hostility to affirmative action during the Reagan years, affirmative action programs and policies have remained very much a part of human resource management at the federal level.

Although the degree of commitment to affirmative action varies greatly from one jurisdiction to the next, formal affirmative action programs are now very much a part of institutional life at the state and local level as well. This is the result of many factors, including federal regulations requiring agencies receiving federal funds to maintain affirmative action programs, and political pressures from various interest groups for greater social equity. Changing demographic characteristics are also playing a role. By the late 1980s, affirmative action began to enter a new phase. With greater numbers of women and minorities entering the labor force, and with governments having to compete more aggressively for qualified job applicants, the benefits of affirmative action programs are becoming more apparent. Governments are beginning to appreciate that the underutilization of women and minorities represents an unnecessary waste of human potential, and aggressive recruitment and training programs are now increasingly a matter of institutional necessity as well as civil rights. As a result, emphasis is shifting from preferring individuals for employment on the basis of their gender or skin color to effectively managing the diversity that already exists in the workplace. This theme is developed more fully toward the end of the chapter.

The Spectrum of Affirmative Action Methods

The nondiscrimination approach to EEO is relatively passive. It requires little of employers beyond a willingness to treat everyone equally. The affirmative action approach to EEO, by contrast, relies on positive, results-oriented practices to ensure that women and minorities are equitably represented in the organization's workforce. Where the nondiscrimination approach calls on employers to be gender neutral and color blind, the affirmative action approach requires them to deliberately take race, sex, and national origin into account in their employment practices. It is the rejection of the equal treatment principle, if only for a short time, that makes the affirmative action approach so controversial. Pursuing affirmative action goals without unduly harming the interests of white males can be an immensely difficult task.

Debates over affirmative action, however, tend to lose sight of the fact that there are many methods available and some of them do less violence to the equal treatment principle than others. Although many people equate affirmative action with hiring goals and quotas, there are other methods that do not involve employment preferences. Because managers and personnel officers are often caught up in the controversies that surround affirmative action programs, the distinctions between these methods are worth exploring.

Five key methods of affirmative action are described below:

1. *Special Recruitment Programs*—By visiting college campuses, and by placing job announcements where women and minorities are likely to see or hear them, employers can increase the number of qualified women and minorities in the applicant pool. To help break the glass ceiling, aggressive recruitment programs are now being used to attract qualified applicants for upper-level as well as entry-level positions. Special recruitment programs increase access to qualified applicants, but they do not require that subsequent selection decisions be made on the basis of gender, race, or national origin.

2. *Special Training Programs*—Because women and minorities often lack the work experience and skills needed to advance within the organization, training programs

provide an important means for improving the representation of women and minorities at higher organizational levels. Training programs may involve technical training, on-the-job training, or management development courses. Although special programs may be designed with the needs of women and minorities in mind, they do not exclude others from participating.

3. *Adverse Impact Analysis*—As established by the *Griggs* decision, this strategy involves scrutinizing job qualifications, employment examinations, and other selection devices for evidence of adverse impact. Steps are taken to ensure that qualifications are demonstrably related to job requirements and examinations are valid predictors of subsequent success on the job. This method may also involve reducing reliance on educational credentials and pencil and paper tests by substituting tests that assess job skills, abilities, and aptitudes.

4. *Workforce Analysis*—This method involves tracking the number of women and minorities in each occupational category relative to their numbers in the external labor force, determining whether the agency is "underutilized" in particular occupational categories, and establishing numerical hiring goals to achieve an appropriate balance. Hiring authorities are expected to keep affirmative action goals in mind but are not told that women and minorities must be given preference. Rather, women and minorities are selected on a "tie-breaker" basis when they are "substantially equally qualified" with other top-rated candidates.

5. *Mandated Quotas*—This method involves hiring or promoting a mandated number of women or minorities until underutilization problems are corrected. Because it requires preferring candidates on the basis of gender, race, or national origin without strict reference to their relative qualifications, it is lawful only when ordered by a court or when it results from a negotiated settlement. However, it is sometimes practiced unofficially to correct underutilization problems that expose employers to legal risk.

As illustrated in Exhibit 8.1, these methods can be viewed as lying along a continuum. The farther one moves to the right, the greater the violence done to the equal treatment principle and the higher the resulting controversy. The first three methods represent the kinds of affirmative action envisioned by President Kennedy. They take

---

EXHIBIT 8.1

A SPECTRUM OF AFFIRMATIVE ACTION METHODS

Low Threat to Equal
Treatment Principle

High Threat to Equal
Treatment Principle

X	X	X	X	X
Recruitment Programs	Training Programs	Adverse Impact Analysis	Workforce Analysis and Hiring Goals	Mandated Quotas

race, gender, and national origin into account but do not involve employment preferences. As explained more fully below, workforce analysis and hiring goals were sanctioned by President Johnson. This method has been called a "soft quota system" because it sometimes involves preferring less qualified candidates over more qualified ones, depending on how much pressure is exerted by upper-level management or enforcement agencies. The final method, mandated quotas, is used only rarely. It is nonetheless viewed by many people as synonymous with affirmative action.

Preferential Affirmative Action Programs

Most government agencies today maintain formal affirmative action programs. Many of these go beyond specialized recruitment and training programs to include policies that sanction preferential treatment of women and minorities in employment decisions. The discussion below distinguishes between three kinds of preferential affirmative action programs: court-ordered programs, programs mandated by and approved under Executive Order 11246, and programs voluntarily adopted by government agencies.

Court-Ordered Affirmative Action Programs

This type of affirmative action program is established by court order to remedy the effects of intentional acts of discrimination by an employer. Such programs are characterized by the use of hiring ratios or quotas to obtain a workforce that is representative of the number of women or minorities in the local labor force. It is a drastic kind of remedy generally ordered only where women or minorities are significantly underrepresented and there has been a long history of discrimination. In most instances this kind of remedy is not needed. When individuals are harmed by employment discrimination, courts normally pursue a "make whole" remedy intended to restore victims of discrimination to their "rightful place." Such remedies typically include hiring an excluded job applicant or reinstating a discharged employee, and compensating him or her for economic losses suffered as the result of lost pay, benefits, or seniority. Such individual remedies are not practical, however, to correct systematic, long-term discrimination against whole classes of individuals. In these instances courts have used the authority given to them under the Civil Rights Act to correct the effects of discrimination through the use of race- or gender-conscious hiring ratios or quotas. Such remedies are also found in negotiated consent decrees monitored by the courts.

An example of court-ordered affirmative action is found in *United States v. Paradise.*[4] Finding that the Alabama Department of Public Safety had systematically excluded blacks when hiring state troopers, a federal court in 1972 ordered the Department to hire one black for every one white until 25 percent of state troopers were black. Because the Department continued to discriminate against blacks by promoting them at slower rates than whites, the court intervened again in 1983 by temporarily imposing a one black for one white promotion ratio. The Supreme Court upheld the orders of the district court, rejecting claims that the use of race-conscious hiring and promotion ratios constitutes reverse discrimination.

The concept of "reverse discrimination" rests on the argument that extending employment preferences to individuals on the basis of their race or gender is itself a form of discrimination. According to this view, affirmative action adversely affects white males and therefore violates both Title VII and the 14th Amendment to the Constitution. At issue is the scope of a court's authority in ordering remedies for discrimination. Section 706(g) of Title VII reads:

> If the court finds that the respondent has intentionally engaged in or is intentionally engaging in an unlawful employment practice charged in the complaint, the court may enjoin the respondent from engaging in such unlawful employment practices, and order such affirmative action *as may be appropriate, which may include, but is not limited to, reinstatement or hiring of employees, with or without back pay. . . ,* or any other equitable relief as the court deems appropriate (emphasis added).

Relying on the discretion apparently granted to courts by section 706(g), the Supreme Court has consistently ruled that the use of affirmative race- or gender-conscious remedies is permitted. Further, court-ordered remedies need not be restricted to the actual victims of discrimination. In *Local #28 of Sheet Metal Workers' International Assoc. v. EEOC,* for example, the Supreme Court ruled that the purpose of affirmative action "is not to make identified victims whole, but rather to dismantle prior patterns of employment discrimination and to prevent discrimination in the future."[5] Nonetheless, before imposing stringent remedies involving quotas, the Supreme Court requires the lower courts to carefully determine whether the employer has been guilty of intentional discrimination. Several Supreme Court Justices have also expressed the view that such remedies should not be imposed except in cases involving the most egregious forms of discrimination.

The use of race- and gender-conscious ratios and quotas has also been upheld by the courts when they are contained in consent decrees. In *Local 93 v. City of Cleveland,* for example, the Supreme Court ruled that Title VII does not preclude the use of such remedies as part of mutually agreed on consent decrees.[6] Despite such legal victories, the EEOC has been reluctant in recent years to approve consent decrees containing quotas.

Affirmative Action Programs Established Under Executive Order 11246

President Johnson signed Executive Order 11246 in September 1965. As amended, it prohibits employment discrimination on the basis of race, color, religion, sex, or national origin by employers holding federal contracts and subcontracts. In addition, it requires contractors and subcontractors to establish affirmative action plans to ensure equal employment opportunity. Compliance with Executive Order 11246 is monitored by the Department of Labor's Office of Federal Contract Compliance Programs (OFCCP). This agency investigates complaints of discrimination by job applicants and employees and takes steps to negotiate a conciliation agreement where such complaints have merit. The Secretary of Labor may impose sanctions in the event of noncompliance such as canceling or suspending contracts, or declaring the contractor ineligible for future contracts. In situations where substantial violations of the law appear to exist, the Secretary may refer complaints to the Attorney General with a recommendation to pursue contract compliance through the courts. Finally, individual complaints of discrimination may be referred to the EEOC for investigation of possible Title VII violations.

The defining characteristics of this type of affirmative action program are worth exploring because federal agencies are required to maintain similar programs, and state and local governments often do so voluntarily. Programs established under Executive Order 11246 are different from voluntary or court-ordered affirmative action programs in two important ways. First, unlike voluntary plans, they must conform to requirements carefully spelled out in government regulations. As explained below, these include analyzing "areas within which the contractor is deficient in the utilization of minority groups and women" and establishing goals and timetables for correcting identified deficiencies. Second, unlike court-ordered affirmative action plans that are imposed after a finding of unlawful discrimination, programs established under Executive Order 11246 are required of government contractors regardless of whether they have violated nondiscrimination laws. They also rely on nonbinding, numerical hiring goals pursued in good faith rather than on mandatory ratios or quotas.

Regulations for implementing Executive Order 11246 are found in Revised Order No. 4 issued by the Secretary of Labor in December 1971.[7] Revised Order No. 4 defines specific affirmative action requirements for federal contractors and subcontractors with contracts in excess of $50,000 and covering 50 or more employees. These employers must develop and implement written affirmative action plans, which are submitted to and approved by OFCCP and are updated annually.

As noted above, when President Johnson used the term affirmative action in Executive Order 11246, he had in mind nonpreferential forms of affirmative action such as aggressive recruitment efforts and greater use of training programs. By the time Revised Order No. 4 was issued in 1971, however, affirmative action had come to include the use of numerical goals and timetables to help correct gender and racial imbalances. Revised Order No. 4 requires contractors to collect data on the number of women and minorities in their workforces, determine whether women and minorities are "underutilized" in major job categories in relation to their availability in the external labor force, and establish numerical goals and timetables for bringing the composition of the organization's workforce into line with the composition of the external labor force. Each of these elements is described below.

Utilization Analysis Utilization analysis is a process for determining whether women and minorities are being underutilized. "Underutilization" is defined in Revised Order No. 4 as "having fewer minorities or women in a particular job group than would reasonably be expected by their availability." The first step, called workforce analysis, is to list all job titles in each organizational unit as they appear in collective bargaining agreements or payroll records. For each job title the total number of employees, the total number of male and female employees, and the total number of male and female employees in each of the following groups is recorded: Whites, Blacks, Hispanics, Asians, and Native Americans. Exhibit 8.2 provides an example of what the data might look like for the job of Computer Programmer I.

The second step is to combine job titles into major job groups. A job group is defined as "one or a group of jobs having similar content, wage rates and opportunities." How these job groups are defined is relatively arbitrary. They should contain enough actual positions for the numbers of women and minorities to be statistically significant. It would not make sense, for example, to collect data on the number of

---

EXHIBIT 8.2

WORKFORCE ANALYSIS FOR ONE JOB TITLE

Title	Total		White		Black	
	Male	**Female**	**Male**	**Female**	**Male**	**Female**
Computer Prog. I	9	3	7	2	0	0

	Hispanic		Asian		Native American	
	Male	**Female**	**Male**	**Female**	**Male**	**Female**
	1	0	1	1	0	0

---

women and minorities in a job group comprising only three positions. To return to the example in Exhibit 8.2, state and local agencies attempting this kind of analysis may collect data for a group composed of all technical jobs where the numbers are small, or just for the group of computer programmers where the numbers are large enough to be statistically useful.

The third step is to collect data on the availability of women and minorities in the relevant labor force. Although Revised Order No. 4 requires collecting data on eight factors, in practice the following four are the most relevant:

1. The percentage of minorities and women in the civilian labor force in the immediate labor area.
2. The percentage of minorities and women with requisite skills in the immediate labor area.
3. The percentage of minorities and women with requisite skills in the relevant recruitment area.
4. The percentage of minorities and women among those promotable or transferable within the employer's establishment.

Generally speaking, the appropriate labor force from which to draw data is the geographical area from which applicants for a particular job group are typically recruited. Unskilled workers, for example, are typically recruited from the local labor force, whereas technical and professional workers are often recruited statewide or nationally.

A more difficult question is whether availability analysis should be based on the *total* number of women and minorities available, or on the number of *qualified* women and minorities available. The answer to this question must be determined separately for each job group. The minority or female representation in the *total* labor force in the immediate area is an appropriate measure of availability for all relatively unskilled jobs (data source #1). Because these jobs can be performed by most people, an agency can be expected to employ minorities and women in numbers consistent with their total labor force availability.

EXHIBIT 8.3

AVAILABILITY ANALYSIS FOR ONE JOB GROUP

		Minority Availability			
Job Group	**Female Availability**	**Black**	**Hispanic**	**Asian**	**Native American**
Computer Programmer	33%	8%	3%	3%	1%

Data on total labor force availability, however, may not be appropriate for professional, technical, and skilled jobs because of the specialized credentials required. Agencies cannot be expected to achieve a 45 to 50 percent female representation in jobs such as engineering if a relatively small proportion of women possess engineering degrees or experience in the field. For jobs of this kind, the minority or female representation in the *qualified* labor force (all those with the minimum education and experience requirements) is a more realistic measure of availability (data source #3). An agency recruiting for skilled jobs nationally, for example, would base its utilization comparisons on the proportion of female and minority persons with the minimum qualifications for those jobs in the national labor force. Information supplied by the Department of Labor is useful in determining the availability of qualified persons in each field.

Exhibit 8.3 provides an example of utilization analysis for the job group of computer programmers based on hypothetical data for the qualified labor force in a particular state.

The final step is to use the data derived from the workforce and availability analyses to determine if any underutilization exists. For example, based on the availability of female computer programmers in the state labor force (Exhibit 8.3), we would expect 33 percent of the 12 computer programmers to be women. Because three of nine programmers are in fact women, no underutilization exists. We would also expect eight percent of the 12 computer programmers to be black. Because none are black, the agency is underutilized by one. Analysis is conducted separately for women and minorities. Thus, if this agency hires a black female, the utilization ratios will improve for both women and minorities.

Establishment of Goals and Timetables Revised Order No. 4, as well as some voluntary programs in state and local government, require the employer to establish annual goals and timetables for correcting underutilization. Goals and timetables must be both realistic and attainable as determined by the circumstances in each case. Such circumstances might include the extent of underutilization in the job group, the number of openings that become available in the job group each year, the availability of qualified women or minorities, and the organization's ability to compete successfully for them. The following is an example of a goal and timetable statement for the computer programmer job group described above:

> *Increase the representation of blacks by at least one over the next two years. Continue efforts to recruit Native Americans and to increase the representation of females.*

Goals and timetables are intended to be used as management tools. They remind managers of the agency's commitment to equal employment opportunity and represent yardsticks against which to measure the agency's progress in achieving an equitable representation of women and minorities. There is always a possibility, however, that personal commitments or pressures from enforcement agencies or higher-level administrators may cause hiring authorities to treat goals as inflexible quotas rather than desired targets. As a result, they may occasionally extend job offers to unqualified female or minority candidates. If a balance is to be maintained between the principles of EEO and merit, it is important that hiring authorities be encouraged to make good faith efforts toward achieving their goals without being subject to negative sanctions if quick results are not achieved.

Methods for Attaining Numerical Goals In the final analysis the use of goals and timetables is not as controversial as the methods selected for attaining them. Wishing not to violate the equal treatment principle, some employers rely on nonpreferential methods such as aggressive recruitment efforts, extensive use of on-the-job training to facilitate internal promotions, and revision of selection criteria and procedures so that qualified women and minorities are not unnecessarily excluded. Other employers, however, may select methods for attaining hiring goals that involve some form of preference on the basis of race, gender, or national origin. Selective certification rules, for example, may allow hiring authorities to go beyond the limits set by the rule of three or rule of five to assure that women or minorities are included in the final selection pool.

A second method is to allow hiring authorities to consider race, gender, or national origin as one of several legitimate factors in choosing among qualified, top-ranked candidates. Sometimes called a tiebreaker preference, this involves selecting a female or minority applicant from among the final pool of "substantially equally qualified" candidates without strict regard for the order in which they may have been ranked. A third method is to encourage the selection of a certain ratio of minorities or females from among qualified applicants over a specified period. However, to be consistent with Revised Order No. 4 and court decisions, hiring ratios should not be used except to remedy serious imbalances arguably caused by prior discrimination and should not take the form of rigid quotas.

Voluntary Affirmative Action Programs

Since the 1970s, the U.S. Commission on Civil Rights and the EEOC have encouraged government agencies to establish their own voluntary affirmative action programs similar to those required of contractors under Executive Order 11246. Agencies are encouraged to maintain statistical information regarding the race, gender, and national origin of their employees, determine the extent of underutilization, and establish voluntary hiring or promotion goals in each underutilized job category. They are free to choose their own methods for achieving affirmative action goals as long as they remain within boundaries set by the courts.

Many state and local government agencies have established voluntary affirmative action programs, but not always for the reasons that the EEOC and Civil Rights Commission intended. As judicial decisions and EEOC rules began clarifying legal obligations in the wake of the *Griggs* decision, employers sometimes found themselves in a difficult situation. When the number of minorities or women in various job categories was substantially lower than their numbers in the area's labor force, the employer was vulnerable to potentially costly lawsuits. Some of these employers, both public and private, viewed the *Griggs* decision as offering a fundamental choice: demonstrate that selection procedures are validly job-related, or neutralize the effects of adverse impact by adopting race- and gender-conscious affirmative action programs. Because the former generally proved difficult to achieve, some employers established affirmative action programs solely to avoid adverse impact suits. Ironically, doing so exposed them to charges of reverse discrimination.

The Supreme Court's first decision regarding the legality of voluntary affirmative action programs came in the 1979 landmark case of *United Steelworkers v. Weber.*[8] In 1974, Kaiser Aluminum and Chemical Corporation and the United Steelworkers of America negotiated an affirmative action program designed to increase the number of black employees in skilled positions at 15 plants. At the Louisiana plant, for example, fewer than two percent of the skilled craft positions were held by blacks, although they composed 39 percent of the local labor force. To increase job skills among blacks, an on-the-job training program was established that reserved 50 percent of the openings for black employees. This resulted in the selection of black employees with less seniority than some of the white employees who applied for the program but were rejected. One of the rejected employees, Brian Weber, filed a lawsuit claiming that he had been the victim of "reverse discrimination." The Supreme Court disagreed. It ruled that Title VII does not prohibit employers from voluntarily establishing race-conscious remedies where the program is a temporary, remedial measure designed to eliminate manifest racial imbalances in the workforce and does not represent an absolute barrier to white advancement. To conclude otherwise, the Court reasoned, would be to frustrate congress' desire to open opportunities in occupations that have been traditionally closed to women and minorities. In subsequent cases, the Supreme Court relied on similar arguments to uphold the use of voluntary affirmative action plans in the public sector.

Public sector programs may be challenged in court on the grounds that they violate the Constitution as well as Title VII. The key argument in such cases is that policies that treat classes of individuals differently on the basis of race or gender violate the 14th Amendment's equal protection guarantees. Although the Supreme Court in *Wygant v. Jackson Board of Education* struck down an affirmative action plan that protected minorities with less seniority than whites during layoffs, it nonetheless stated that "remedying past or present racial discrimination . . . is a sufficiently weighty state interest to warrant the remedial use of a carefully constructed affirmative action program."[9] In short, affirmative action programs are not inherently unconstitutional.

Another key issue is whether there must be evidence that an employer has been guilty of past discrimination, either by self-admission or by enforcement agency investigation, to justify the use of voluntary programs. In 1987 a divided Supreme Court ruled in *Johnson v. Transportation Agency of Santa Clara County* that employers may take voluntary affirmative action without admitting discrimination.[10] The case involved a situation that occurs often in public employment. In 1979 Diane Joyce and Paul Johnson competed for a promotion to the position of road dispatcher in the Santa Clara County Transportation Agency. Both had the minimum four years of experience in road maintenance that was required, but Paul Johnson had more years of experience in total. The agency's affirmative action plan authorized hiring authorities to set flexible promotion goals in positions where women were underrepresented and to take gender into account when making decisions. When Diane Joyce received the promotion pursuant to the affirmative action plan, Johnson sued, arguing that the Santa Clara Transportation Agency was guilty of reverse discrimination under Title VII for promoting a less-qualified woman. Although the district court agreed with Johnson, its ruling was overturned on appeal. When the case reached the Supreme Court, a majority of justices upheld the plan, ruling that its purpose was to eliminate manifest gender and racial imbalances, was flexible in nature, and did not unnecessarily harm the interests of male employees. Significant statistical disparities between the number of women and minorities in certain job categories and the proportion of qualified women and minorities in the relevant labor force, according to the Court, is sufficient indication that a Title VII violation has occurred.

This does not mean that all voluntary affirmative action programs will be upheld by the courts. A review of recent cases indicates that to survive judicial scrutiny voluntary plans must possess the following characteristics. First, the purpose of the plan must be to correct problems of underrepresentation specific to the organization, the plan must be "narrowly tailored" to address those problems, and it must be temporary in nature. Decisions by the supreme Court contain a subtle distinction in this regard. Although affirmative action plans cannot seek to *maintain* racial or gender balance simply to promote social justice (this is prohibited by section 703(j) of Title VII), they *can* legitimately seek to *attain* racial or gender balance where there is reason to believe that existing imbalances reflect historical discrimination. The reasonableness of such remedies is easier to demonstrate where there is evidence that unlawful discrimination has occurred, but requiring the employer to acknowledge its responsibility for past discrimination is not required because of the chilling effect such a requirement would have on the willingness of employers to establish affirmative action programs.

Second, affirmative action plans must be flexible in nature. In *Johnson*, hiring authorities were simply allowed to take race or gender into account as one of many factors in selection decisions. The plan did not treat goals as if they were rigid quotas. Finally, the affirmative action plan cannot "unduly trammel" the interests of males or nonminorities. In *Firefighters Local Union 1784 v. Stotts*, for example, a plan protecting minorities with low seniority during a layoff was struck down because it resulted in nonminorities actually losing their jobs.[11]

Affirmative Action for the Disabled

Section 503 of the Rehabilitation Act requires government contractors with contracts worth more than $2,500 to take affirmative action to employ and promote qualified handicapped individuals. Those having contracts worth $50,000 or more and having 50 or more employees must also prepare written affirmative action plans consistent with OFCCP regulations. Development of numerical goals and timetables is not required, however, because it is simply not possible to maintain data on the availability of qualified persons with disabilities. Whether a disabled person is qualified for a particular position must be determined on a case-by-case basis. Section 503 nonetheless requires employers to maintain records regarding the numbers of disabled applicants and employees and their relative success rates in being hired or promoted. Although Section 503 applies only to those state and local agencies actually participating in work under a federal contract or subcontract, all state and local agencies may be subject to similar requirements under state statutes or administrative rules.

In addition to their nondiscrimination and reasonable accommodation requirements, both Section 503 and the Americans with Disabilities Act require employers, including state and local agencies, to take special steps to remove employment barriers. These include removing architectural barriers, actively recruiting qualified disabled individuals, facilitating the advancement of disabled employees through training, career development, and counseling, and eliminating all physical and mental job requirements that tend to screen out qualified individuals that cannot be shown to be necessary to the safe and efficient performance of the jobs in question.

The affirmative action obligations of federal agencies are defined in Section 501 of the Rehabilitation Act. Each agency is required to develop and maintain an affirmative action program for hiring, placing, and advancing handicapped individuals. The federal government has declared itself a model employer in these regards. As one example of its commitment, federal regulations allow severely disabled and retarded individuals with two years of service in noncompetitive positions to be hired into competitive positions without going through the normal examination process.[12] In addition, the federal government has committed itself to accommodating the needs of alcoholic employees and encouraging their rehabilitation in ways that are not required of other employers.

Key Components of Affirmative Action Programs

Formal affirmative action programs are found today in all but the smallest political jurisdictions. These programs generally have four components. The first is an office that has been assigned primary responsibility for the equal employment opportunity/affirmative action (EEO/AA) program as a whole. It is typically charged with developing and implementing affirmative action policies, coordinating the various affirmative action efforts, compiling workforce data, and drafting the affirmative action plan. Individuals within each agency are also assigned affirmative action roles. Agency directors, for example, are typically given ultimate responsibility for programs within their agencies. In addition, EEO/AA officers are assigned such duties as collecting workforce data, training managers, counseling employees, and investigating barriers to equal employment opportunity. In large jurisdictions, the position of EEO/AA officer or counselor is created to perform these duties, whereas in smaller jurisdictions they are performed by already overburdened personnel officers.

A second component is the EEO/AA Policy Statement. It expresses in succinct fashion the organization's commitment to EEO/AA. Ideally, it is developed through a process that allows considerable input from managers and other agency personnel. This increases the sense of ownership in the policy and the likelihood that it will be taken seriously. Once completed, the policy statement is disseminated to all current and prospective employees and recruitment sources.

A third component is the arsenal of affirmative action methods to be used. Fundamental decisions must be made by the EEO/AA office regarding what combination of the five methods described earlier in the chapter will be used to accomplish program goals. In addition to special recruitment and training efforts, systems for conducting workforce and utilization analyses are often established.

A final component is the affirmative action plan itself. The plan is generally composed of the EEO/AA policy statement, an explanation of who has been delegated authority for various EEO/AA responsibilities, a description of ongoing recruitment and training programs, and identified deficiencies along with goals, timetables, and other actions for addressing them. Because results can be achieved best when they are based on clearly defined and measurable objectives, the affirmative action plan represents a useful planning and management tool. By setting hiring goals and timetables, it directs the attention of managers and personnel officers to what needs to be accomplished and how. To make sure that affirmative action policies and goals are taken seriously, performance appraisal systems are sometimes modified so that managers are evaluated on their degree of commitment to them.

EXHIBIT 8.4

KEY COMPONENTS OF AN AFFIRMATIVE ACTION PROGRAM

1. A written policy describing the agency's commitment to equal employment opportunity and affirmative action.
2. Dissemination of the agency's EEO/AA policy to all current and prospective employees and recruitment sources.
3. Assignment of overall EEO/AA responsibilities to a high-ranking administrator with sufficient authority and resources to assure program effectiveness. Assignment of specific responsibilities to department heads, program managers, line supervisors, personnel officers, and EEO officers.
4. Identification of deficiencies by conducting workforce and utilization analyses, and development of numerical goals and timetables for correcting identified deficiencies.
5. Routine analysis of selection procedures for evidence of adverse impact, including analysis of applicant flow and rejection rates.
6. Design and implementation of special recruitment, training, and test validation efforts to overcome barriers to female and minority employment and advancement.

Affirmative Action as Public Policy

As public policy, affirmative action is a strategy for achieving greater substantive equality by ensuring that women and minorities are fairly represented in the workforce at all organizational levels. It is generally understood and justified as a temporary, remedial means of compensating for decades of discrimination against women, blacks, and other minorities.[13] But as often happens in various areas of public policy, the two policy approaches to EEO sometimes move in contradictory directions, creating special problems for those—such as managers and personnel officers—who must implement them. For example, whereas the nondiscrimination approach requires that personnel decisions be made in a gender-neutral and color-blind fashion, the affirmative action approach requires that race, gender, and national origin be taken into account. And whereas the nondiscrimination approach relies on the principle of equal treatment, some affirmative action methods rely on the principle of compensatory treatment. As a result, the line that separates the pursuit of equal opportunity from the pursuit of equal results is often blurred. Given these contradictions, it is not surprising that there remains considerable debate regarding the direction EEO policies should take.

Many critics, including some women and minorities, advocate abandoning the affirmative action approach altogether. Their arguments are worth reviewing. First, affirmative action is said to harm the very individuals it is intended to benefit by stigmatizing women and minorities as the beneficiaries of special treatment.[14] Members of protected groups who achieve success, according to this view, must constantly defend themselves against the charge that their success was not earned but came as the result of affirmative action.

Second, many opponents object to compensating women and minority group members collectively for the harms done to them by society. They argue that affirmative action is inconsistent with legal principles of compensatory justice because it does not involve "making whole" the discrete victims of discrimination. Affirmative action programs extend employment preferences to women or minorities regardless of whether they have been personally disadvantaged by acts of discrimination, and they impose costs on other job applicants who are innocent of wrongdoing. The result, according to this view, is unjustified reverse discrimination.

A third argument is that affirmative action represents unwarranted "social engineering."[15] According to this view, efforts to achieve substantive equality by engineering balanced workforces rests on the questionable assumption that underrepresentation of women and minorities is principally the result of discrimination. Thomas Sowell, one of the most outspoken critics of affirmative action, believes that underrepresentation of racial and ethnic minorities is commonplace in societies generally and that it is the result of many factors other than discrimination.[16] These factors include variations between groups in cultural aspirations, in socioeconomic status, and in the skills that are passed on to each new generation. In many of these societies, the groups holding privileged positions are groups without the power and resources to have obtained their privileged positions by exploiting or discriminating against members of other social groups. Sowell's conclusion is that governments should not seek to engineer balanced workforces without first obtaining stronger evidence that underrepresentation is principally the result of discrimination.

Fourth, some opponents argue that the most fundamental barriers to equal employment opportunity are related to socioeconomic status and access to educational opportunities. Affirmative action, in their view, addresses the effects of these inequalities but does not address the causes. As a result, affirmative action programs tend to benefit only the relatively advantaged minority and female applicants who can get into final selection pools on the basis of their merits. Because affirmative action does not address the underlying inequalities, these critics believe existing programs will prove to be neither as effective nor as temporary in duration as proponents claim.

Finally, many opponents argue that in allowing exceptions to the equal treatment principle, affirmative action violates or seriously threatens the merit principle. According to this view, selecting less qualified candidates to attain affirmative action goals inevitably undermines the quality of the public workforce. The best way to assure that agencies are productive and efficient, according to these opponents, is to treat all applicants equally by evaluating them on their merits.

Affirmative Action and Merit

If the latter claim is correct, then affirmative action threatens the effectiveness of government in general and human resource management in particular. For this reason it is a claim that deserves closer scrutiny. No doubt there are times when the practice of affirmative action interferes with the operation of the merit principle. If employers, for example, treat numerical goals as quotas rather than as ways of measuring progress, or if clearly less qualified or unqualified applicants are selected simply to avoid legal liability, then the merit principle is certainly compromised. This does not mean, however, that the two principles are inherently opposed. Nothing in Revised Order No. 4, for example, requires employers to hire unqualified persons, or even to prefer lesser qualified individuals over more qualified individuals on the basis of gender, race, or national origin. Nor does it require employers to lower valid selection standards to meet established goals.

If a female or minority applicant is selected over at least one better qualified person on the basis of gender, race, or national origin, then preferential treatment has occurred. However, this does not mean that the merit principle or the quality of the public workforce has been sacrificed. If all of the top-rated applicants in the final selection pool are "substantially equally qualified," then a choice of any one of them is consistent with merit. The perception of unfairness arises because of the unjustified faith that Americans have in scored selection procedures. In *Johnson v. Transportation Agency of Santa Clara County,* for example, Paul Johnson received 75 points, and Diane Joyce received 73. His argument that reverse discrimination had occurred rested on the assumptions that their qualifications had been accurately scored, that he was "best qualified" by virtue of a two-point difference in score, and that he was therefore entitled to the promotion. As the Supreme Court noted, each of these assumptions is flawed. Employment tests and scoring systems simply do not have a high degree of validity (see Chapter 9), a two-point difference in score is not likely to have an appreciable impact on subsequent job performance, and possessing the highest score does not create a job entitlement. Hiring authorities have it within their discretion to base their decisions on many criteria, including gender, if it is pursuant to a narrowly tailored affirmative action policy. In short, although from one perspective the interests of white males are harmed in such instances, it is not clear that the merit principle is sacrificed in the process. The term "best qualified" is often a convenient fiction.

From Affirmative Action to Diversity Management

Affirmative action is undergoing a natural evolution, not so much in government policy as in organizational practice. Nearly two-thirds of those now entering the national labor force are women, native-born minorities, and newly arrived immigrants. Workforces are becoming much more culturally and socially diverse as a result. Demographic changes are manifesting themselves in the form of language barriers, inadequate educational backgrounds, and culture-based values and behaviors that are easily misunderstood. This reality is creating new challenges for organizations, as well as new opportunities. In response, some employers are now establishing diversity management programs. Although they may be linked to existing EEO/AA structures, they are fundamentally different from traditional affirmative action programs in several important regards.

First, in contrast to affirmative action, which focuses on overcoming barriers to initial organizational entry, diversity management focuses on facilitating upward mobility within the organization. With many entry barriers removed, and with more women and minorities entering the labor force, the larger challenge today lies in realizing their potential at every level, especially in management and leadership positions.[17] This is apparent at all levels of government. Exhibit 8.5 illustrates the situation in federal employment. Although nearly half of all white-collar positions are held by women (improving from 41 percent in 1974 to 48 percent in 1990), women are not well represented at the higher administrative and professional levels. Because they are promoted at much lower rates than men at grades GS-9 and GS-11, they quickly reach a "glass ceiling" beyond which it is difficult to advance. As shown in Exhibit 8.6, women hold only 19 percent of administrative and professional positions at grades GS-13 through 15, and only 11 percent in SES or equivalent positions. Similar patterns are found at the state level. For example, although the number of female agency heads in state government increased from 2 percent in 1964 to nearly 20 percent by 1990, women clearly remain underrepresented at the higher levels of government.[18] Diversity management emphasizes training and development as the primary means of facilitating upward mobility.

Second, the driving force behind diversity management is not social equity but a pragmatic concern for utilizing human resources as fully and as effectively as possible. Diversity management policies and practices do not focus exclusively on the needs of women and people of color. Rather, they focus additionally on a full range of individual needs arising from differences in values, cultural backgrounds, ages, abilities and disabilities, educational levels, and the realities of raising families.[19] Diverse ideas and creative abilities are viewed as assets to be valued, developed, and utilized for the benefit of employer and employee alike. This in turn entails a shift in emphasis from assimilating new employees to integrating them. According to R. Roosevelt Thomas, Executive Director of the American Institute for Managing Diversity, the usual prac-

EXHIBIT 8.5

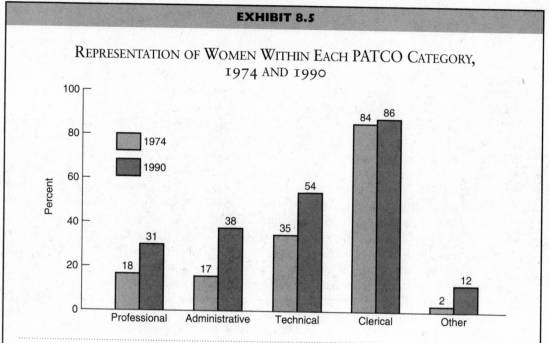

REPRESENTATION OF WOMEN WITHIN EACH PATCO CATEGORY, 1974 AND 1990

From U.S. Merit Systems Protection Board, *A Question of Equity: Women and the Glass Ceiling in the Federal Government* (Washington, D.C.: MSPB, 1992), 8.

EXHIBIT 8.6

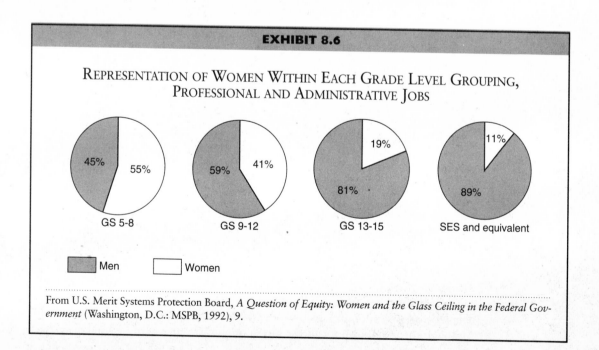

REPRESENTATION OF WOMEN WITHIN EACH GRADE LEVEL GROUPING, PROFESSIONAL AND ADMINISTRATIVE JOBS

From U.S. Merit Systems Protection Board, *A Question of Equity: Women and the Glass Ceiling in the Federal Government* (Washington, D.C.: MSPB, 1992), 9.

tice is to drop "blacks, Hispanics, women, and immigrants . . . into a previously homogenous, all-white, all-Anglo, all-male, all native-born environment" and to place the burden of cultural change on the newcomers.[20] The newcomers, according to Thomas, will no longer tolerate such an approach. The entire organizational culture must be prepared to change by embracing diversity.

Finally, diversity management does more than affirmative action to address the root causes of inequality. The key lies in training and development. First, managers are trained to cope with interpersonal conflicts, language barriers, and other problems associated with increased diversity. They are also trained to manage diversity by altering their management practices as dictated by the situations at hand. Second, all employees receive training in cross-cultural awareness in an effort to break down the prejudices and stereotypes that contribute to interpersonal conflicts and continue to create barriers to equal employment opportunity. Finally, training and development programs are used as vehicles for providing all employees with the competencies they will require to advance in the organization and realize their full potentials. The key question that every manager should be asking, according to Thomas, is "Am I fully tapping the potential capacities of everyone in my department?"

It must be emphasized that the foregoing analysis describes the conceptual underpinnings of what is now being called diversity management. Only rarely have attempts been made to implement diversity management programs in any comprehensive fashion. Beyond a few workshops and isolated experiments, the concept of diversity management remains relatively untested. Nonetheless, it offers a promising direction for exploration because its assumptions are consistent with those of the human resource management perspective as described in Chapter 1 and because it promises to be less socially divisive than affirmative action. Whether government employers choose to move in this direction remains to be seen.

■ **CASE 8.1**   The Johnson Decision

Background

In December 1978 the Santa Clara County Transit District Board of Supervisors adopted an affirmative action plan for the County Transportation Agency. On December 12, 1979, the Agency announced a vacancy for the position of road dispatcher in the Roads Division. In accordance with the affirmative action plan, Diane Joyce was subsequently promoted. Another applicant, Paul Johnson, then filed a suit claiming reverse discrimination. As noted earlier in this chapter, the Supreme Court upheld the Agency's voluntary affirmative action plan. Because the plan is typical of many found in the public sector, the facts of the case and the issues involved are worthy of discussion.

The Facts

1. The affirmative action plan authorized the Agency to consider the sex of the applicant as one factor in making promotions to positions within a traditionally segregated job classification in which women have been significantly underrepresented. Although the plan did not call for hiring quotas, it did identify a long-term goal:

filling 36 percent of Agency jobs with women (their proportion in the area labor force).

2. At the time of the promotion decision, none of the 238 Skilled Craft Worker positions was held by a woman.

3. Nine applicants, including Joyce and Johnson, possessed the minimum qualification of four years of dispatch or road maintenance experience.

4. Diane Joyce had worked for the County since 1970, including four years as a road maintenance worker. She occasionally worked out of class as a road dispatcher.

5. Paul Johnson had worked for the County since 1967, ten years as a road yard clerk and two as a road maintenance worker. He also occasionally worked out of class as a dispatcher and had experience as a dispatcher in the private sector 13 years previously.

6. The interviews were scored. Paul Johnson tied for second with a score of 75, and Diane Joyce ranked next with 73. A second interview was conducted, and Joyce was recommended for the promotion.

7. The Agency Director, relying on the recommendation of the Affirmative Action Coordinator as well as the selection committee, promoted Joyce.

The Issues

Leaving aside the narrower legal issues with which the Supreme Court dealt, address the following policy questions:

1. Is the historical underrepresentation of women in skilled craft jobs sufficient cause to justify affirmative action plans of this kind?

2. Are the systems used in testing and interviewing candidates sufficiently reliable to justify selecting applicants in order of their scores? Similarly, does a higher number of points or an additional year of experience establish an applicant as the most meritorious?

3. What role, if any, should other, possibly more subjective criteria be allowed to play in selection decisions? Should management be able to consider agency needs broadly and select freely from among those who are substantially equally qualified?

4. Could the Transportation Agency have dealt with the problem of underrepresentation in a less divisive way? If so, how?

Notes

1. 420 F.2d 1225, note 6 at 1239.

2. Doré Butler and Florence L. Geis, "Nonverbal Affect Responses to Male and Female Leaders: Implications for Leadership Evaluations," *Journal of Personality and Social Psychology* 58 (January 1990):48–59.

3. Lyndon Johnson, *Lyndon B. Johnson: Public Papers of the Presidents of the United States, 1965, Book II* (Washington D.C.: Government Printing Office, 1965), 636.

4. 107 S.Ct. 1053 (1987).

5. 106 S. Ct. 3019 (1986).

6. 106 S. Ct. 3036, (1986).

7. 41 C.F.R. 60.2 (1992).

8. 443 U.S. 193 (1979).

9. 476 U.S. 267 (1986).

10. 480 U.S. 624 (1987).

11. 467 U.S. 561 (1984).

12. 5 C.F.R. 3.1(b), (1993).

13. See, for example, John C. Livingston, *Fair Game? Inequality and Affirmative Action* (San Francisco: W. H. Freeman, 1979).

14. Thomas Sowell, "Affirmative Action: A World Wide Disaster," *Commentary* 88 (December 1989):21–41.

15. Morris B. Abram, "Affirmative Action: Fair Shakers and Social Engineers," *Harvard Law Review* 99 (April 1986):1312–1346.

16. Sowell, "Affirmative Action."

17. R. Roosevelt Thomas, Jr., "From Affirmative Action to Affirming Diversity," *Harvard Business Review* 68 (March/April 1990), 108.

18. Angela M. Bullard and Deil S. Wright, "Circumventing the Glass Ceiling: Women Executives in American State Governments," *Public Administration Review* 53 (May/June 1993):189–202.

19. David Jamieson and Julie O'Mara, *Managing Workforce 2000: Gaining the Diversity Advantage* (San Francisco: Jossey-Bass, 1991).

20. Thomas, "From Affirmative Action to Affirming Diversity," 112.

CHAPTER 9

Employee Recruitment and Selection

Learning Objectives

After mastering the material contained in this chapter, you will be able to:

1. Explain the relative advantages of internal versus external recruitment.
2. Write a job announcement containing the kinds of information required by prospective job applicants.
3. Identify eight strategies for predicting which job applicants will prove to be superior performers.
4. Purge nonjob-related inquiries from application forms and interview questions.
5. Distinguish between assembled and unassembled employment examinations.
6. Develop and use a scored application supplement.
7. Identify seven types of assembled employment tests and their primary uses.
8. Explain the importance of validating employment tests and describe how it is accomplished.
9. Develop and conduct a structured interview based on the results of job analysis.
10. Conduct a reference check without exposing your employer to legal risk.

Staffing is perhaps the most critical of human resource functions. The agency that fails to aggressively recruit the best available talent, distinguish superior applicants from adequate ones, and secure the services of those it selects will lack the capacity to achieve mandated objectives and maintain credibility with the public. To appreciate this truth, one need only consider what would happen if such efforts were not made. Serious mismatches between a worker's abilities and job requirements are likely to result in poor work performance, reduced morale within the work group, higher training costs, and a greater number of voluntary and involuntary severances. Higher turnover rates in turn translate into higher costs for recruiting, selecting, and training new employees. Finally, because the quality of an agency's human resources directly affects the quality of services provided, mismatches between employee abilities and job requirements impose costs on society as well.

Attracting and securing highly qualified job applicants is not easy under the best of circumstances. It is becoming all the more difficult as the growth rate of the labor force declines, competition for individuals with special skills increases, and government salaries continue to lag behind those offered in the private sector. With these special challenges in mind, this chapter examines how to recruit qualified applicants and how to select those whose qualifications best match the requirements of open positions.

Employee Recruitment

Agencies naturally wish to obtain the best talent available. This is something they cannot do if talented individuals are not among those in the applicant pool. The essential task of recruitment is to encourage qualified persons to explore career opportunities with an agency and apply for specific job openings. By casting their nets as widely as possible, agencies can obtain a diverse mix of applicants and increase the likelihood that the applicant pool will contain several first-rate candidates.

Despite these benefits, most government agencies do relatively little recruiting. Overwhelmed by floods of job applications, they have traditionally kept the numbers down to manageable proportions by simply reporting job openings to state employment agencies and posting notices of civil service examinations. Three factors are now changing government's passive attitude toward recruitment. First, many agencies are recruiting more aggressively to meet their affirmative action goals. Second, increased delegation of hiring authority to the agency level is encouraging more agencies to actively seek out the kinds of employees they most need and want. Finally, public agencies can no longer assume that individuals with needed skills and abilities will be found in their applicant pools. Although there is generally high interest in government employment, particularly during periods of economic downturn, demographic factors are changing, and individuals with special skills are becoming increasingly scarce. A recent study by New York State cites with concern the "growing shortage of workers with appropriate skills to perform the available jobs."[1] The Volcker Commission reached a similar conclusion in its study of the federal executive service: "Gone are the days when the brightest students would line up for a chance at a government job. Gone, too, is the buyer's market that came with the huge baby boom generation."[2] As government work becomes more specialized and labor markets become tighter, government agencies will increasingly find themselves competing with each other and with private employers for qualified job applicants. The willingness to recruit aggressively may well determine who is most successful.

Institutional Versus Job-Specific Recruitment

Recruitment programs typically combine two kinds of activities. The first, *institutional recruitment,* is conducted on a continuous basis and is designed to inform potential job applicants of career opportunities with a government or government agency. Methods include visiting college campuses to speak with students face to face, setting up exhibits at job fairs, and distributing pamphlets outlining career opportunities in public service. Although expensive, use of pamphlets and face-to-face meetings are important for attracting individuals who may not otherwise consider public service careers. New demographic realities, for example, "will demand a recruiting strategy more heavily directed toward two-earner couples, minorities, and single mothers."[3]

Job-specific recruitment, by contrast, is initiated as needed to fill job vacancies. Methods include posting job announcements, notifying state employment services and organizations considered to be good recruitment sources, and placing advertisements in newspapers, professional newsletters, and sometimes on radio and television. How widely to recruit and what sources to use depend in large part on the type of job. Clerical, unskilled, and semiskilled employees, for example, are typically recruited locally by posting job announcements, listing openings with state employment services, and occasionally by placing advertisements in local newspapers. Files may also be maintained in the personnel office for "walk-ins." Technical and professional employees, by contrast, are typically recruited regionally or nationally by mailing job announcements to organizations considered to be good recruitment sources and by advertising in professional and trade journals.

Internal Versus External Recruitment

A recurring question, for which there is no final answer, is whether to recruit internally to fill higher level positions or to open the competition to external candidates as well. Limiting job opportunities to internal applicants holds several advantages. Current employees are more likely than outside candidates to be committed to the organization and its goals, remain with the organization longer, be better known in terms of their abilities, and require less orientation and training. The most important benefit, however, is the potentially positive effect on employee morale and work performance. By promoting internally, managers send a message to employees that their work is valued and that opportunities for professional growth truly exist.

These benefits aside, there are times when it may make sense to solicit external candidates. The first occurs when available internal candidates clearly lack the necessary qualifications to perform job duties successfully. In such situations an agency is well advised to recruit externally. A second occurs when new people with fresh perspectives are needed. Hiring only from within tends to cause "inbreeding" and it may prove advantageous to open competition to external candidates for this reason. A third occurs when women and minorities are underrepresented at upper levels of an agency and recruiting from within only perpetuates existing patterns. Confronted with this possibility, hiring authorities may choose to expand recruitment efforts to attract qualified female and minority applicants.

Although it may seem advantageous to promote from within except in the situations identified above, the issue is far from settled. Some commentators assert that all job vacancies above the entry level should be open to both internal and external candidates. According to this view, if internal candidates are truly the best qualified, they should be able to demonstrate their competence in an open competition. This may be true enough in the abstract, but agencies that implement such a policy often confront the situation in which internal candidates are rejected in favor of outsiders. The morale and work performance of rejected candidates may suffer, and the individual hired may face discontented or hostile co-workers. In such situations supervisors will need to exercise considerable skill in explaining to rejected candidates why they did not receive the promotion and what steps they can take to improve their chances of success in the future.

The choice to recruit externally or internally is sometimes constrained by union contracts and merit system rules. Union contracts, for example, often specify that employees within a work unit must have an opportunity to bid for a job before its availability is announced more widely. This is accomplished through a practice known as job posting. Descriptions of open positions are posted on designated bulletin boards or routed internally, and interested persons are invited to "bid" for the job. In some situations managers may possess authority to promote an individual to an available position without going through any selection process at all. In formal merit systems, by contrast, hiring authorities usually must conduct an open competition to demonstrate which candidate is best qualified. The choice to recruit internally or externally may also be influenced by ease and timeliness of selection. Because of the complex nature of many government selection systems, it is often easier and quicker to simply promote from within.

Obstacles Created by Centralized Hiring Systems

Highly centralized hiring systems—legacies of the nineteenth century reform movement—are frequently cited as obstacles to successful recruitment. According to a recent General Accounting Office (GAO) report, for example, there is widespread agreement that the federal hiring system is "time-consuming, cumbersome, and ineffective in a competitive labor market."[4] Many of the nation's best prospects are discouraged from applying for available jobs as a result. The nature and extent of this problem is described in the Volcker Commission Report:

> Even when the public sector finds outstanding candidates, the complexity of the hiring process often drives all but the most dedicated away. Perceptions of public service as a lackluster career are compounded by the belief among potential candidates that getting a government job is an exercise in frustration. For example, only a third of the honor students surveyed by the Commission said they would know how to obtain a government job even if they wanted one, and only 3 percent actively sought federal employment.[5]

To address these concerns, the Volcker Commission recommended delegating greater authority to agencies to set their own recruitment and selection rules, offering recruitment incentives for hard-to-fill jobs, and hiring both undergraduate and graduate students on-the-spot to minimize paperwork and delay.[6] Despite some movement in these directions, simplification efforts in the federal government have not progressed far. To improve the effectiveness of recruitment programs, governments at all levels will have to do more to streamline their selection processes. The difficulty lies in granting greater discretion to agency officials while safeguarding the merit principle from potential abuses of delegated authority.

Job Announcements

The goal of job-specific recruiting is to ensure that the applicant pool contains enough qualified individuals so that a good job/person match can be made. Whether vacancies are publicized through posted notices, recruiting bulletins, consolidated listings, or advertisements, the job announcement plays a central role in the recruitment process. The job announcement is an abbreviated version of the position description designed to assist prospective applicants in deciding whether to apply. They must be written with care because the selection criteria used to hire an individual must be consistent with the job requirements and qualifications as stated in the job announcement. For this reason the recruitment process should not begin until the agency is satisfied that the position description is a valid representation of the requirements of the position to be filled.

Exhibit 9.1 provides a sample job announcement derived from the position description presented in Chapter 5 (see Exhibit 5.7). Job announcements provide information about job duties and responsibilities, minimum job requirements and qualifications, salary ranges, and explanations of how to apply. This information performs two important functions. First, openly announcing job requirements establishes the basis on which the merit principle can operate. Subsequent steps in the selection process, if pursued with integrity, define who is most meritorious in terms of these requirements. Second, the information facilitates a process of self-selection by potential applicants. Information contained in the announcement encourages those who are genuinely interested and qualified to apply, while discouraging those without sufficient interest or qualifications. Statute law or administrative rules often specify how and where vacancies are to be announced and how long the position must remain open so that all interested persons have an opportunity to apply.

The Selection Process: An Overview

Recruitment ends and selection begins with the arrival of the application deadline. The one person who can best perform the duties of the job in question must now be identified. How this is accomplished may vary greatly from one jurisdiction to another, or even within the same agency. Generally speaking, however, the basic stages in the selection process are those shown in Exhibit 9.2. Important information is gathered at each stage to assist in making the final decision. Applications are reviewed to screen out those who do not possess minimum qualifications. The remaining applicants are typically scored and ranked based on an evaluation of their credentials and work history as revealed in the application form or on the results of one or more employment tests. An applicant's final score or rank order is viewed as an indicator of how well he or she meets job requirements. According to some predetermined criterion, such as the rule of three, a set of job finalists is identified. Interviews and reference checks are then conducted before the final selection decision is made.

Selection Strategies

Selecting the best applicant is an enormously difficult task. First, it requires predicting future work performance based on very limited information. Second, it is complicated by the fact that performance is a product of so many different variables, including technical knowledge, job-related abilities, interpersonal skills, and motivation and effort. As a result, each agency seeking to design an effective selection system must decide which determinants of performance to measure and which selection techniques to use. This decision in turn requires adoption of a deliberate selection strategy (or strategies). Each of the following strategies is founded on a specific hypothesis regarding how to predict future work performance.

EXHIBIT 9.1

SAMPLE JOB ANNOUNCEMENT

Position Title: Personnel Specialist

Location: Human Resources Office, Department of Commerce

Salary: $26,750–$32,450

Closing Date: March 31, 1994

Position Summary

The personnel specialist provides personnel and equal employment opportunity services to the Department of Commerce. Under general supervision this position is responsible for recruiting, monitoring EEO/Affirmative Action policies, employee training and development, and classification actions.

Primary Duties

1. Responds to requests for reclassification by conducting desk audits, determining whether the position is correctly classified, and preparing necessary documentation to record action with the State Classification Bureau.
2. Provides advice/assistance to supervisory personnel in classifying new or existing positions as a result of reorganizations or changes in staffing patterns.
3. Develops and conducts training workshops and seminars to improve the knowledge, skills, and abilities of Department employees.
4. Monitors agency personnel decisions to assure compliance with EEO/Affirmative Action requirements.
5. Supervises collection of workforce data for EEO/Affirmative Action reports.
6. Provides technical assistance for individual hiring, including developing appropriate selection devices, determining suitability of experience and educational qualifications of applicants, developing position announcements, and conducting initial screening of applicants.

Qualifications

Working knowledge of the principles, practices, and techniques of public human resource management. Must be familiar with state and federal regulations pertaining to classification, wage and hour, nondiscrimination and affirmative action, and other law as it relates to this area of personnel. Must have excellent interpersonal relations skills and the ability to interpret and defend decisions. These knowledges and abilities are typically acquired through a B.A. in a related field and three years of progressively more responsible experience in human resource management.

How to Apply

Applications may be obtained from the Office of Human Resources, Department of Commerce. An EEO/AA Employer.

EXHIBIT 9.2

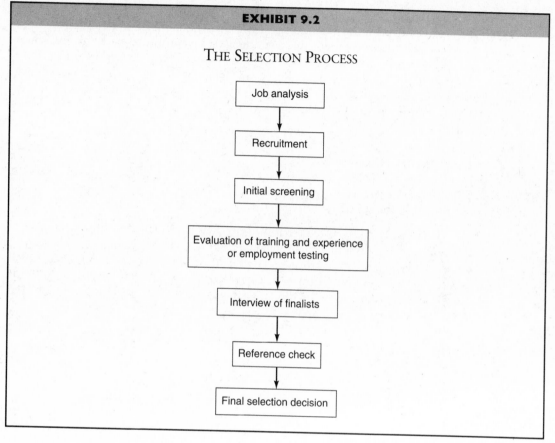

THE SELECTION PROCESS

Job analysis

↓

Recruitment

↓

Initial screening

↓

Evaluation of training and experience
or employment testing

↓

Interview of finalists

↓

Reference check

↓

Final selection decision

The KSA Strategy

Hypothesis: an applicant's job performance may be predicted from the degree of match between his or her knowledge, skills, and abilities (KSAs) and those KSAs determined to be necessary for successful job performance.

This strategy typically involves reviewing an applicant's educational background and work history as stated on the application form or personal resume. It may also entail testing applicants for specific knowledge, skills, or abilities. Although it is the principal strategy employed in the public sector, it reveals very little about an applicant's motivation, potential for growth, or fit with the organizational environment.

Track Record Strategy

Hypothesis: An applicant's job performance may be predicted from evidence of superior performance in the past.

This strategy rests on the belief that past performance is the best predictor of future performance. It involves reviewing application forms and interviewing candidates to determine whether they have produced specific results in similar work environments.[7] Candidates may be asked, for example, to describe past accomplishments that suggest that they will be successful in achieving specific work-related objectives in the future. Advocates of this strategy argue that it is superior to other strategies because work experience is not the same thing as demonstrated performance, educational attainment may indicate little more than an ability to do well in academic settings, technical knowledge does not guarantee high performance, and ability tests do not measure effort. However, this strategy is not appropriate for filling entry-level positions where applicants have not had sufficient opportunity to establish track records.

Learning/Intelligence Strategy

Hypothesis: An applicant's job performance may be predicted from his or her ability to learn how to perform work tasks effectively or, relatedly, from his or her general intelligence.

This strategy relies on tests that measure general mental abilities, including such things as reasoning ability, visualizing ability, verbal comprehension, memory, and numerical ability. High scores are assumed to indicate the applicant's ability to learn job tasks quickly and perform them well. This strategy is seldom used in the public sector because of doubts about the validity of intelligence tests and concerns about potential adverse impact on minority applicants.

Aptitude Strategy

Hypothesis: An applicant's job performance may be predicted from his or her general interest in or aptitude for certain kinds of jobs or occupations.

This strategy relies on the results of aptitude tests to determine what kinds of work applicants are best suited for. It assumes that individuals with an interest in or aptitude for certain kinds of work are more highly motivated to do well than those who do not. But because test results are relatively crude indicators of future performance, this strategy is probably more relevant to placement decisions. The latter seldom arise in the public sector because applicants are typically placed in those positions for which they applied.

Personality Trait Strategy

Hypothesis: An applicant's job performance may be predicted from a comparison between his or her personality traits and those traits believed to be positively or negatively related to successful job performance.

This strategy focuses on complex issues of motivation and personal stability as a means of predicting who will make the best employees. It assumes that relationships between certain traits and job performance exist and it relies on personality tests or interviews to assess those traits. Tests and interviews, for example, may focus on forcefulness, flexibility, need for approval from peers, need for approval from superiors, tolerance for uncertainty, ability to delay gratification, and need for security. Because the goal is to understand a person's inner qualities rather than to document KSAs or past accomplishments, this strategy places a heavy burden on interviewers and those who interpret test results. It is seldom employed in the public sector because personality traits are relatively poor predictors of future performance even when they can be assessed accurately.

Work Sample Strategy

Hypothesis: An applicant's job performance may be predicted from his or her performance of actual or simulated work samples.

This strategy rests on the assumption that the best way to determine how applicants will perform on the job is to measure how well they perform on some of the job's basic tasks. An applicant for a secretarial position, for example, may be given a typing test. Or candidates for a promotion to a higher management level may participate in an assessment center involving several exercises that simulate actual work situations. It is a strategy currently receiving increased attention because the use of work sample tests to predict future work performance promises a high degree of validity.

Networking Strategy

Hypothesis: An applicant's job performance may be predicted from his or her reputation for successful job performance as reported by credible contacts.

Some organizations, particularly in the private sector, encourage employees to maintain professional networks and to identify or contact individuals who they believe will make good job candidates. Networking can be an important part of an agency's affirmative action program, and recommendations from knowledgeable persons can result in the selection of superior employees. As often practiced in the past, however, this strategy operated in the form of "old-boy networks" that circumvented the merit system, denied equal employment opportunity to others, and produced the kind of inbreeding that inevitably occurs when a homogenous group of individuals selects others with similar backgrounds.

Situational Strategy

Hypothesis: The job performance of applicants may be predicted from what they say they would do in job-related situations.

This strategy involves identifying critical behaviors necessary to successful job performance and determining through the use of tests or interviews whether an applicant is likely to exhibit such behaviors on the job. During a structured interview, for example, an applicant may be offered job-specific situations and asked to describe how he or she would respond. Although this strategy, if pursued with care, is likely to satisfy the job-relatedness standard put forth in *Griggs*, it rests on the questionable assumption that applicants will actually behave on the job in the ways indicated during the selection process.

The foregoing strategies are not mutually exclusive. Because each tends to focus on a different determinant of work performance, organizations ordinarily adopt a combination of strategies to improve their ability to identify the best job applicants. Generally speaking, the more determinants of performance are measured, the greater the predictive validity of the selection process. The difficulty lies in deciding what combination of strategies to adopt, which selection techniques to use, and how each technique is intended to contribute to the quality of the final selection decision. A number of factors must be considered when making these decisions, including the validity and legal defensibility of various selection methods, their feasibility, merit system constraints, and the resources available.

Applicant Screening

Screening is the process of determining which applicants possess minimum job qualifications and which do not. Those who do not are removed from further consideration. A review of the application form is the primary method of applicant screening. It entails comparing information about an applicant's work history and educational attainment with stated job requirements. In this way evaluators can address the merit system's most fundamental concern: "Does the applicant have the education and experience needed to do the job?" The screening process occasionally extends beyond a review of the application form. Applicants for jobs as patrol officers, for example, are often required to meet minimum height and weight requirements and receive passing scores on achievement and physical abilities tests. In such situations multiple screening devices ("pass-fail tests") are used to establish the pool of *qualified* job applicants. Qualified applicants are usually rank-ordered for purposes of final selection.

During the 1970s, the National Civil Service Reform League (NCSL) launched an attack upon traditional public sector screening practices. Executive Director Jean Couturier argued that traditional practices were intended to screen applicants out for the sake of administrative convenience rather than to fully assess their job potentials.[8] According to Couturier, the overreliance on educational credentials, employment tests, and the rule of three only assured that many minority applicants would not be given an opportunity to prove their worth. Largely for this reason, the NCSL's 1970 Model Civil Service Law recommended elimination of the rule of three and the adoption of pass-fail tests in which all those with passing scores would be accorded equal consideration for job openings.

Height and weight requirements also came under attack in the years following the *Griggs* decision because they tend to screen out a disproportionate number of female and minority applicants. A New York court, for example, found that requiring State Police to be at least five feet nine inches tall eliminated 75.9 percent of all adult male hispanics nationally and 80.6 percent in New York.[9] In a similar case a height requirement of five feet two inches and a weight requirement of 120 pounds excluded 40 percent of all women in the United States as candidates for correctional counselor but only 1 percent of male candidates.[10] The courts have ruled in such cases that height and weight requirements are appropriate only if they are a "business necessity," i.e., essential to the safe and efficient performance of the duties of a particular job.

The Job Application and EEO

In 1971 the Supreme Court articulated the principle that employment tests "must measure the person for the job and not the person in the abstract."[11] Because reviews of job applications are considered tests under the law, employers must be prepared to demonstrate the "job-relatedness" of all questions asked on the application form. In the wake of the *Griggs* decision the EEOC and other enforcement agencies expressed concern that questions contained on application forms were screening out applicants unnecessarily and providing information that could bias hiring authorities. In the final analysis, purging application forms of irrelevant information makes sense whether or not an agency is concerned with avoiding charges of discrimination. It simply helps ensure that persons involved in making employment decisions are not biased, intentionally or otherwise, by knowledge of job applicants that is not relevant to their ability to perform job duties.

Although the EEOC cannot expressly forbid an agency from requesting certain kinds of information on an application form, Burrington suggests that any question "that cannot be strictly justified as a business necessity, cannot be proven to be a valid predictor of job success, or might screen out disproportionate members of protected group applicants should not be included as part of any preemployment inquiry."[12] As shown in Exhibit 9.3, application forms used by state governments in 1981 could not meet the standards set by the *Griggs* decision. A follow-up study in 1993 found that many pre-employment inquiries had been purged from application forms, whereas others had been qualified by language explaining that the inquiries were solely for EEO reporting purposes.

Inquiries of the following kinds are particularly troublesome from an EEO perspective:

Gender, Race, National Origin   An applicant's gender, race, or national origin is rarely, if ever, relevant to job requirements. Nonetheless, public agencies are required by federal law to record information of this kind. This creates an obvious problem—how to obtain the required information without potentially biasing those making selection decisions. As shown in Exhibit 9.3, most states now request such information but include disclaimers explaining that the information is used only to satisfy EEO reporting requirements. At least twenty-seven states now request the information on separate or detachable survey forms.

Marital Status   The courts consider marital status to be closely associated with gender and will look very closely at an organization's reasons for inquiring about it. Asking which title an applicant prefers (Mrs. Ms, Miss) or about an applicant's maiden name may be viewed by the courts or the EEOC as a backdoor approach for determining marital status. No state now asks about preferred title, and only two states ask about marital status, both in the EEO reporting section. Ten states asked about other names the applicant may have been known under but primarily for the purpose of verifying education and work history.

Date of Birth/Age   Federal law protects persons older than age 40 from discrimination, and state laws are often more inclusive. If the law requires a person to be at least 18 or 21 to hold a particular job, then an application may legitimately ask whether the applicant meets the relevant age requirement. Only five states now ask for the applicant's birthdate other than in the EEO reporting section. Although clues

EXHIBIT 9.3

PRE-EMPLOYMENT INQUIRIES MADE BY THE 50 STATES

	1981 N = 50		1993 N = 48	
	No.	%	No.	%
1. Are you known or have you been known by any other name(s)?	4	8%	10	21%
2. Which title do you prefer? Mr., Mrs., Miss, or Ms.?	5	10%	0	0
3. What is your birthdate? (With EEO disclaimer)	16	32%	26	54%
4. What is your birthdate? (Without EEO disclaimer)	23	46%	5	10%
5. What is your birthplace? (Without EEO disclaimer)	2	4%	0	0
6. What was your age on your last birthday? (With EEO disclaimer)	12	24%	13	27%
7. What was your age on your last birthday? (Without EEO disclaimer)	4	8%	0	0
8. What is your sex? (With EEO disclaimer)	37	74%	42	88%
9. What is your sex? (Without EEO disclaimer)	7	14%	1	2%
10. What is your race or ethnic group? (With EEO disclaimer)	35	70%	43	90%
11. What is your race or ethnic group? (Without EEO disclaimer)	4	8%	0	0
12. Do you have any handicaps or physical defects? (With EEO disclaimer)	28	56%	22	46%
13. Do you have any handicaps or physical defects? (Without EEO disclaimer)	7	14%	2	4%
14. What is your marital status? (With EEO disclaimer)	3	6%	2	4%
15. What is your marital status? (Without EEO disclaimer)	3	6%	0	0
16. What is your height and weight?	4	8%	0	0
17. What are the dates of your education or degrees?	47	94%	37	77%
18. Have you ever been convicted of a crime?	20	40%	31	65%
19. Do you possess a valid driver's license?	24	48%	20	42%
20. Do you have transportation to work?	5	10%	0	0
21. Do you read and write English?	2	4%	0	0
22. What is the lowest pay you will accept?	12	24%	6	13%
23. Are you willing to travel?	8	16%	8	17%
24. Are you willing to work shifts/overtime?	5	10%	18	38%
EEO survey detachable from application	13	26%	22	46%
EEO survey on separate sheet	8	16%	5	10%

Source: Data for 1981 are adapted from Debra D. Burrington, "A Review of State Government Employment Application Forms for Suspect Inquiries," *Public Personnel Management* 11 (Spring 1982), 58. Data for 1993 are based on research by the author.

to an applicant's age may be obtained from the dates that educational degrees were obtained, 37 states clearly consider the question justified by business necessity.

Mental or Physical Disabilities   Although agencies need to know whether applicants have the mental and physical capacity to perform a job successfully, or whether they pose a safety threat to themselves or others, to enquire generally about the health of all applicants violates the Americans with Disabilities Act of 1990. Twenty-two states ask about disability status for EEO purposes. Two additional states ask about disability status but do not include a disclaimer.

Arrest Records   Courts have ruled that employers may not ask about arrest records because of its adverse impact on minorities and because arrest is not evidence of guilt. Asking about convictions may also adversely impact minorities, but an agency may be able to justify such inquiries if the conviction is recent (e.g., within five years) and the nature of the crime raises legitimate concerns about the applicant's fitness for a specific job. To protect themselves from negligent hiring suits, 31 states now ask about convictions but most inform the applicant that convictions are not an absolute bar to employment and that they will be assessed in the context of specific job requirements.

Travel/Transportation/Driver's License   Questions of this kind may adversely affect women and minorities (as well as others) who do not own a car, do not have a driver's license, or cannot travel extensively because of family obligations. Such questions are appropriate only if related to specific job requirements. No state currently asks about having transportation to work, only eight ask about availability for traveling, and among the 20 states asking about a valid driver's license, six instruct applicants to answer the question only if it is relevant to the job for which they are applying.

Job resumes are sometimes requested by employers as substitutes for or supplements to application forms. This is particularly true when recruiting for professional and administrative positions. From an EEO perspective, however, it is best not to request them or encourage their submission because they often include personal, non-job-related information. Agencies serious about keeping extraneous information to a minimum will rely instead on application supplements that structure the kinds of additional information required.

Examinations: Assembled and Unassembled

Nineteenth-century reformers turned to scored examinations to break the back of the patronage system. By testing job candidates for specific knowledge and skills and ranking them according to their scores, reformers hoped to obtain competent employees and reassure the public that employment opportunities in government are distributed fairly. Today public employers rely heavily on two kinds of examinations: unassembled and assembled.

Unassembled examinations include various techniques for systematically evaluating a candidate's training and experience. They are "unassembled" in the sense that no examination is put together. Nor does the applicant actually take a test. Application forms and resumes are simply scored by personnel specialists according to predetermined selection criteria. This type of examination is used most often for managerial and professional positions above the entry level. Candidates for such positions have usually established track records that can be evaluated through the use of scored applications and interviews. *Assembled examinations,* by contrast, include a variety of written and performance tests for assessing job-related abilities and aptitudes. They are often used for filling clerical positions, positions requiring special knowledge or skills, and entry level professional and managerial positions. As a legacy of the reform movement, written examinations are used more extensively in the public sector than the private sector and their design relies heavily on the KSA strategy described above.

Unassembled Examinations: The Scored Application Form

Application forms may be used not only to screen out unqualified applicants but also to score and rank order those applicants possessing minimum qualifications. Federal examiners in the Office of Personnel Management, for example, score the information provided on Standard Form (SF) 171 by assigning points to ascending levels of knowledge, experience, and achievement. The results determine how competitive applicants will be in securing available jobs. To ensure the validity of the evaluation process, scoring systems must be designed so that points are awarded based on how much each job requirement contributes to job success. For example, if the new employee will spend 80 percent of his or her time performing classification duties, then 80 percent of the total points should relate to knowledge of and experience with classification.

For the sake of economy and efficiency, standardized application forms are often used by government agencies for all job openings. Unfortunately, standardized forms ask for information that is often irrelevant to the position to be filled and insufficient to adequately assess job candidates. One solution is to supplement the standardized form with a questionnaire tailored to the competencies necessary for a particular job. These are often called Supplemental Application Forms (SAFs) or Tailored Application Blanks (TABs). Questions contained in the application supplement are designed to guide applicants in describing their proficiencies, achievements, and accomplishments in ways that are relevant to the demands of the job to be filled. Information provided can then be scored against preestablished standards by evaluators who are familiar with the job in question. Exhibit 9.4 provides an example of an application supplement.

The advantages of the application supplement over the traditional application form are readily apparent. Once an appropriate scoring system is devised for the application supplement, evaluation can proceed in a more structured and thorough fashion. An example of a scoring system for the position of Insurance and Legal Division Administrator is presented in Exhibit 9.5.

In many instances the panel of evaluators will invite the highest scoring candidates for an interview that is structured around the same job-related criteria. A final selection decision and job offer will follow. The results of assembled examinations may also play a role in the final selection decision.

EXHIBIT 9.4

SAMPLE APPLICATION SUPPLEMENT

The following information is requested to enable the selection committee to establish your qualifications for the position of Administrator in the Insurance and Legal Division. The information submitted will become a basis for our evaluation of candidates. It is not necessary to have experience in all the areas listed.

1. Please indicate in your application if you are: a) currently licensed in this State, or b) qualified to practice law in this State.

2. Please detail your litigation experience in the following areas:
   a. defense of contract claims
   b. prosecution of actions to enforce statutory or administrative law
   c. defense against writs of mandamus, prohibition, or other common law or equitable reliefs
   d. civil jury trials concerning negligence claims

3. Please detail your abilities or experience as an administrator. Indicate the nature/extent of your experience in such areas as budgeting, work planning, supervision of professional staff, policy development and related activities. You may include experience from private or governmental practice.

4. Please explain your training or experience in the field of insurance coverage. Indicate your knowledge of risk calculation methods, investigation, premium determination, administration of self-insurance programs, defense of coverage suits, or related tasks and duties.

5. Please explain your training or experience in the field of administrative law. Include information on your experience in developing administrative rules, conducting public hearings, defending/prosecuting contested cases under the Administrative Procedures Act, or judicial review.

6. Please describe your general legal services experience, including the types of client organizations you advised, and the organization's size and diversity. You should include any experience you have in drafting opinions, providing daily legal services to management, and lobbying activities.

Developing and using an application supplement for each new hire requires considerable time and effort. For this reason standardized application forms are often scored without a supplement. For many positions in the federal government, for example, applicants are scored and certified to agencies based only on the information contained in the SF 171. This poses two problems. First, standardized forms cannot by their nature supply adequate, job-specific information about a candidate. Second, those applicants that know the scoring rules can tailor the information provided in advantageous ways by using the right words and emphases in describing their education and work experience.

Assembled Examinations: Types and Uses

Assembled examinations are relatively efficient and objective procedures for screening and ranking large numbers of job applicants. They are used extensively in the public sector, particularly among large jurisdictions with formal merit systems. Most of the

EXHIBIT 9.5

BENCHMARKS FOR EVALUATING TRAINING AND EXPERIENCE OF CANDIDATES FOR POSITION OF ADMINISTRATOR, INSURANCE AND LEGAL DIVISION

1. Minimum Qualifications: x = yes; blank = no
   Licensed to practice law in the State or qualified to obtain license.

   _____

2. Litigation Ability (weight 50 points maximum)

   Preferred (50):
   Successful, extensive litigation experience including:
   (a) defense of contract claims;
   (b) defense against writs of mandamus, prohibition, and other common law and equitable reliefs;
   (c) prosecution of actions to enforce statutory and administrative law. Generally five or more years of such experience including two to three civil jury trials concerning negligence claims.

   Acceptable (35):
   Less than five years' experience including all the areas above <u>or</u> more than five years' experience in at least two of the areas listed above.

   Unacceptable (0):
   No experience as legal counsel in civil jury trials concerning negligence claims.

3. Administrative Ability (10 points)

   Preferred (10):
   Two or more years directing the activities of staff attorneys. Experience to include such activities as establishing a budget for operations, hiring/supervising professional staff, and developing agency policy, workplans, and related activities.

   Acceptable (7):
   Two or more years supervising a staff of professional-level employees (nonattorneys) including the activities listed above. Management of private practice or governmental practice.

   Unacceptable (0):
   No demonstrable supervisory experience that included supervision of professional staff and preparation of budget workplans, etc.

4. Insurance Experience (10 points)

   Preferred (10):
   General responsibility for the operation of a self-insurance program, including determination of coverage, premium determination, appraisal investigation services, and claims adjustment.

EXHIBIT 9.5 *(continued)*

Acceptable (7):
Experienced in procurement of a variety of insurance coverages with responsibility for defending coverage disputes and a working knowledge of the principles of self-insurance.

Unacceptable (0):
No insurance administration experience.

5. Administrative Law Experience (10 points)

Preferred (10):
Experienced in developing administrative rules, conducting public hearings <u>and</u> defending or prosecuting contested cases under the Administrative Procedures Act (APA) or during judicial review.

Acceptable (7):
Has served as legal counsel in administrative law contested cases of a nature applicable to Department of Administration operations.

Unacceptable (0):
No actual experience in administrative law.

6. General Legal Services Experience (20 points)

Preferred (20):
Served as legal counsel to an organization with diverse operational requirements. Such experience to include providing daily legal advice to management; drafting legal opinions; lobbying legislative branch.

Acceptable (14):
Served as legal counsel to an organization with a narrow range of activities. Such activities to include activities listed above.

Unacceptable (0):
No staff legal counsel experience.

Source: Department of Administration, State of Montana, *Training and Experience Evaluation/Application Supplements,* 1983.

selection strategies outlined earlier in this chapter rely on one or more of the tests described below.

Achievement Tests   These measure an applicant's acquired knowledge in a particular occupational area, such as accounting or engineering. They are appropriate for use when successful job performance requires mastery of a specific body of knowledge. Although test results provide important information about job applicants, they should not be relied upon exclusively in making selection decisions because possession of knowledge alone is not a guarantee of superior work performance.

Intelligence Tests   General intelligence tests measure such things as memory, numerical ability, verbal comprehension, perceptual speed, and deductive and inductive reasoning. Their use rests on the belief that the higher the level of an applicant's mental abilities, the more quickly an applicant will learn job tasks and the better they will perform them. The term *intelligence* is now understood by most psychologists to be an artificial construct referring to several mental abilities, rather than to a single innate ability. What is less clear is whether "IQ scores" are primarily measures of acquired abilities or hereditarily determined abilities. If they tend to reflect socioeconomic background more than native ability, then they may unfairly disadvantage the already disadvantaged. Tests of general intelligence are rarely used in the public sector because of their adverse impact on minorities and the difficulty of demonstrating their validity. Specialized tests of mental ability, as opposed to tests of general intelligence, are used more frequently because they can be tailored to particular job categories. Tests of memory, vocabulary, and perceptual speed, for example, have been found to predict performance in clerical jobs.

Aptitude Tests   These measure aptitudes for particular kinds of work, such as working with people, machines, numbers, or words. Someone who demonstrates an aptitude for working with people, for example, may be a good prospect for a position in social work. Aptitude tests, however, only indicate general areas of ability or interest. Although they may provide clues about an applicant's level of motivation, they are not very useful for filling the narrowly defined positions commonly found in the public sector.

Personality Tests   These measure personality traits such as self-confidence, need for approval, aggressiveness, cooperativeness, flexibility, and tolerance for uncertainty. Their purpose is to evaluate intangibles that may affect work performance such as motivation and personal stability. Although the relationship between personality and performance seems obvious at first glance, many practical difficulties are associated with the use of these tests. First, they often take the form of personality inventories in which applicants select phrases that are most descriptive of themselves or their attitudes. Tests of this kind are susceptible to faking by applicants who attempt to guess which answers are most acceptable to the organization. Second, the more sophisticated forms of personality tests require the use of trained psychologists to interpret the results—something that is rarely done. Third, it is more difficult than one might think to establish statistically that a particular personality trait is a valid predictor of job success. For these reasons, among others, personality tests are not widely used in the public sector.

Physical Abilities Tests   These tests measure physical abilities such as speed, strength, agility, and stamina. They are appropriate for use when a job places extraordinary physical demands on its incumbents. They are used frequently, for example, in the selection of police and firefighters.

Performance or Work Sample Tests These tests require applicants to perform actual or simulated work tasks. The classic example is a typing test for persons seeking secretarial positions. A key assumption is that tests that measure work performance directly possess a high degree of validity. Although this is not always the case, the validity of performance tests is generally equal to or greater than that for other types of tests.[13] Evidence also suggests that they produce less adverse impact on minorities than pencil and paper tests. The reason that they are not used more frequently is that they are expensive to administer and are simply impractical for many types of jobs. It is difficult, for example, to ask candidates to actually fight a fire, apprehend a felon, or conduct a feasibility study.

Assessment Centers Pioneered by AT&T in the 1950s, assessment centers are used primarily to identify employees who show the greatest potential for promotion to higher levels of management. Assessment centers are both a place and a process.[14] Candidates are brought together in one place to participate in a series of group and individualized exercises over a two- or three-day period during which they are assessed by expert appraisers. The process begins by defining the behavioral characteristics that are most predictive of future job success. These may include such things as problem solving, leadership, and interpersonal skills. This step is important because the validity of the assessment process is dependent on measuring only those behaviors that are essential to performing higher-level job duties effectively. Once these behavioral dimensions are identified, appropriate tests can be developed for assessing them. Although the results of interviews and paper-and-pencil tests are often factored into a candidate's final score, the heart of the assessment process is a set of realistic but simulated performance tests that allow measurement of critical job behaviors. Four kinds of exercises are typically used:

IN-BASKET EXERCISES
Candidates are given information of the kind that might appear in the job incumbent's in-basket, including phone messages, letters, memos, and reports. Candidates are asked to take appropriate action by specifying what will be done and in what order of priority. This provides appraisers an opportunity to evaluate time management, organization, decision-making, and delegation skills.

LEADERLESS GROUP DISCUSSIONS
A group of candidates is given a problem to discuss and told to formulate a group response. No one is identified as group leader. This exercise provides appraisers an opportunity to assess behaviors related to problem-solving, interpersonal, and leadership skills.

ASSIGNED ROLE PLAY
A group of candidates is asked to discuss problems faced by government but with each given a specific role to play. Each candidate is asked to sell their point of view to the others. This provides an opportunity to assess the exercise of personal influence.

INDIVIDUAL EXERCISES
Candidates are asked individually to make an oral presentation or to respond in writing to a policy problem by analyzing the issues involved and offering appropriate recommendations. This allows assessment of analytical, problem-solving, and written communication skills.

These exercises are observed and assessed by trained psychologists or assessors drawn from management. Assessors rate the candidates on "assessor report forms" after each exercise is completed and then meet at the end of the two- or three-day session to discuss the results and reach consensus on each candidate.

Because evaluation is based on observable behaviors, and because multiple assessment techniques are used, assessment centers generally possess a high degree of validity. A study by Bray and Grant at AT&T found that individual work sample tests had higher predictive validity than paper-and-pencil tests, and that a candidate's composite score from multiple tests was a better predictor of subsequent job success than the results of any single test.[15] The major disadvantage of assessment centers is that they are expensive to design and administer and are appropriate to a relatively small range of positions.

Government agencies have experimented extensively with assessment centers, but not always in the comprehensive manner developed at AT&T.[16] A survey conducted by Ross found that many of them could not satisfy basic methodological requirements, such as completing thorough job analysis, using multiple assessors and pooling their judgments, and ensuring that assessors are well trained.[17] Although these low-budget assessment centers may demonstrate higher predictive validity than more traditional methods, it is important nonetheless that they satisfy basic methodological requirements. Simply copying or purchasing assessment center techniques used elsewhere will prove of little value unless their relevance to specific positions can be demonstrated.

Using Multiple Assessment Techniques

As noted earlier in this chapter, the federal Civil Service Commission established a tradition in the late 1800s of using written achievement tests for measuring job-related knowledge and abilities. Congress and the American public found these tests to be more acceptable than the highly abstract, academic tests used in the British system. Although a few psychologists were actively promoting the use of intelligence and personality tests by the 1920s, they have never been used extensively in government. In recent years, however, public agencies have shown a greater willingness to use tests other than the traditional achievement test. Research indicates that the key to successful hiring lies in using different types of tests, each designed to measure an essential skill or body of knowledge. Although it is not always practical to do so, using multiple assessment techniques promises to improve the quality of selection decisions. The scores from several tests may be combined to produce a composite score for each candidate or, alternatively, tests may be arranged sequentially with candidates needing a certain score or ranking on one test to be eligible for the next.

Testing and Veterans' Preference

The federal government and each of the 50 states extend some kind of employment preference to veterans. These policies are justified either as a means of reintegrating veterans into society or as a reward for service to their country. The nature of the preference varies from one jurisdiction to another according to who is eligible (wartime or peacetime veterans, veterans only, or spouses or dependents as well), the duration of the preference (e.g., one-time use only, preference limited to a specified number of years, or lifetime preference), and the use of the preference (e.g., initial hire only, initial hire and promotion, protection from layoffs).

Employment preferences may be relative or absolute. An absolute preference requires hiring authorities to select a veteran from the pool of qualified applicants, regardless of the relative qualifications of other applicants. A relative preference, by contrast, involves adding points to the test scores of eligible veterans. This is by far the more common approach. In federal employment, for example, eligible nondisabled veterans receive 5 extra points, and eligible disabled veterans (or persons related to a deceased or fully disabled veteran) receive 10 extra points.[18]

Employment preference for veterans is an issue that brings into conflict some of society's most cherished values. One conflict is between the desire to assist veterans and the desire to safeguard the values of merit and government efficiency. Extending a preference often means that persons who score highest "on their merits" are passed over for employment on the basis of nonmerit considerations. This causes some critics to fear that hiring the "less meritorious" endangers the quality of the public service. A second conflict is between the desire to assist veterans and the pursuit of affirmative action goals. Extending employment preference to veterans tends to reduce employment opportunities for women (because most veterans are men) and for nonveteran minority and disabled persons. For that matter, it tends to reduce employment opportunities for nonveteran white males as well.

Test Validity

Imagine the quandary that the *Grigg's* decision created for employers. Regardless of how pure their intentions, employers whose selection devices adversely affected members of protected groups found themselves facing the very real possibility of being summoned to court to defend their use. Not surprisingly, test validity emerged as a major issue in the 1970s.

Test validity refers to how well a test measures what it purports to measure. All employment tests, in one way or another, purport to measure the ability of applicants to perform job duties well. Some tests measure job performance directly (e.g., a typing test for secretarial positions), and others measure job performance in ways that are very indirect. A personality test, for example, may ask applicants to describe their relationship to their parents or siblings. Answers are then used to draw inferences regarding how well applicants are likely to perform on the job. The relationship between attitude and performance is indirect, and the validity of test results are more difficult to establish. Whether job performance is measured directly or indirectly, establishing the validity of the test is important. Use of invalid tests is unfair to applicants who may be wrongly rejected and it defeats the whole purpose for testing. Unless a correlation exists between scores and subsequent work performance, a test is useless as a selection device.

Although simple in concept, demonstrating the validity of tests can be immensely difficult and costly in practice. The essential task of validation is to provide evidence that tests successfully distinguish those applicants who will prove to be superior performers from those who will not. The two primary strategies for doing so are criterion-related and content validation.

Criterion-Related Validity

Demonstrating criterion-related validity requires showing that test scores (the predictors) are related to some measure of job performance (the criterion). In most validation studies of this kind the criterion is performance appraisal ratings. If the study finds a significant correlation between test scores and performance appraisal ratings, then the test can claim to be valid—at least to the extent that people with higher scores tend to perform better on the job. Criterion-related studies rely on experimental research designs that are costly and confront serious methodological difficulties. Experimental research is highly valuable when experimental conditions are carefully controlled, but this is rarely the case in employment settings. As a result, although the criterion-related strategy appears best in theory, it may be the least practical in fact.

Criterion-related validity may be established through either of two kinds of studies. Studies based on *predictive validity* seek to verify a relationship between the test scores of applicants and subsequent performance appraisal ratings. Studies based on *concurrent validity*, by contrast, seek to verify this relationship by testing current employees rather than job applicants. In both types of studies validity is expressed as coefficients of correlation, indicating the extent to which test scores and the criterion are related.

Studies of predictive validity involve testing all applicants, hiring a proportion of them at random, and evaluating their performance after they have been on the job for a period of several months. Because a group of persons selected randomly should contain individuals ranging from poor to good performers, an employer should be able to test the hypothesis that test scores will correlate with job performance. In practice, however, several difficulties arise. First, conducting a valid experiment requires hiring poor as well as good employees. This is something that no employer wishes to do and something that most public employers cannot do because they are legally required to select employees on the basis of job-related abilities. Second, an experiment of this kind requires a relatively large number of applicants for the same or similar jobs for the results to be statistically meaningful. Seldom can agencies hire enough applicants for similar positions to satisfy this requirement. Third, the accuracy of the results of the experiment is dependent on the accuracy of the performance appraisal ratings. Unfortunately, performance appraisal ratings are notorious for their susceptibility to bias. Finally, such studies are often immensely time consuming and expensive and thus beyond the abilities of smaller jurisdictions to afford.

The impracticality of hiring employees through random selection makes concurrent validation more attractive at first glance. In this type of experiment a test is administered to *current* employees and their scores are correlated with their most recent performance appraisal ratings. A test may be judged valid if those with the highest test scores are also those with the highest performance ratings. However, the credibility of the results is open to challenge for at least two reasons. First, it is easier for a test to distinguish good from bad applicants than it is to distinguish good from better employees. Because the poorer, rejected applicants are not included in the study, the strength of the correlation between scores and performance appraisal ratings is likely to be lower than it would have been otherwise. Second, it cannot be known with certainty that the test is measuring capabilities of employees at the time they were hired. It may be that test scores reflect capabilities developed on the job. If this is the case, then very little is learned from concurrent studies about the ability of the test to distinguish among candidates at the time they apply. Concurrent studies also confront the difficulties of obtaining a large enough sample size to allow for meaningful results and ensuring the accuracy of performance appraisal scores. Because of the difficulties associated with conducting criterion-related studies, the EEOC and the courts are now less insistent than they were in the 1970s and early 1980s that employers attempt to conduct such studies. Other strategies for establishing test validity may be equally legitimate.

Content Validity

Establishing the content validity of a test does not involve correlating test scores with some criterion of performance. Rather, it involves showing a direct relationship between the content of the test and the nature of job duties. This is done by identifying tasks and behaviors that are critical to successful job performance and including a sample of those tasks and behaviors in the test. Although content validation cannot show that those with higher scores tend to be the best performers, it can at least raise the inference that this should be the case. If, for example, the questions asked or exercises performed in the test bear an obvious relationship to job requirements, then the test, logically, should be a valid predictor of subsequent job performance.

Content validation is an appropriate strategy for those tests, such as achievement and performance tests, that measure required knowledge or behaviors directly. It is not an appropriate strategy for validating selection procedures that purport to measure traits or constructs such as intelligence, aptitude, personality, judgment, and spatial ability.[19] The basic goal of content validation is to construct tests that reflect directly the knowledges and behaviors required to perform the job rather than the aptitudes or underlying abilities thought to be involved in the job.

The best way to ensure content validity is to construct tests according to the results of careful and systematic job analysis. Through job analysis, critical tasks or behaviors may be identified and test questions or exercises constructed around them. If typing, for example, is essential to the successful performance of secretarial duties, then a typing test as a sample of work actually performed should possess content validity. As another example, if job analysis shows that firefighters must frequently carry people from burning buildings, then a physical abilities test that requires an applicant to carry 170 pounds up a 20-foot ladder might be judged to have content validity (despite potential adverse impact on women). In both of these examples, the exercises required of applicants are intended to sample actual job duties. Establishing the content validity of written tests is more difficult. If, for example, the ability to react appropriately in stressful situations is determined to be a critical behavior for police, then a multiple-choice question that asks how an applicant would respond in a given situation may be judged to have content validity if both the question and the preferred response are consistent with the results of thorough job analysis.

Demonstrating the relationship between test questions and subsequent job performance to the satisfaction of a court is often difficult. Written examinations used by police and fire departments, for example, have been struck down by the courts on numerous occasions. One court laid out the following minimum requirements for establishing content validity:[20]

1. Knowledge, skills, and abilities tested for must coincide with some of the knowledge, skills, and abilities required to perform jobs successfully.
2. Attributes selected for the examination must be critical and not merely peripheral to successful job performance.
3. The various portions of the examination must be accurately weighed to reflect the relative importance to the job of the attributes for which they test.
4. The level of difficulty of the examination must match the level of difficulty for the job.

Courts have also required that the cut-off score for passing an examination be set at a point that clearly distinguishes those who are minimally competent from those who are not—a requirement that makes sense in the abstract but is often very difficult to accomplish in practice.[21] Good faith efforts to establish content validity are important but do not alone guarantee that a test will be upheld in court. The case described in Chapter 5 involving the New York State Police represents an employer's worst fear—that a test constructed at great expense by professionals using a well-respected method of job analysis may nonetheless be struck down in court.

Issues of Test Fairness

Tests are said to be fair when persons with equal probabilities of success on the job have equal probabilities of being hired. Because a person's ability to obtain employment is often dependent on test scores, it is crucially important for tests to be fair and accurate predictors of job performance. Unfortunately, this is not always the case. Three issues related to test fairness have received considerable attention in recent years.

The first issue is whether tests are sufficiently predictive of job success to justify their use. Generally speaking, tests are rather poor predictors of job performance. It is not unusual, for example, for a test to possess a correlation coefficient of .2. This means that there is only 20 percent chance that a person scoring in the top fifth on the test will be among the top fifth in terms of actual job performance.[22] In short, the probability that the test will fail to accurately predict the future performance of job applicants is relatively high. When a highly qualified applicant is rejected because of a score that falls below the passing mark, the result is called a "false negative." The frequency with which false negatives occur raises serious doubts about the fairness of basing selection decisions on the results of scored examinations. As McClelland states, "We are in danger of creating a meritocracy based on false predictors of merit."[23]

A second issue, which follows in part from the first, is the tendency to attach more importance to test results than is warranted. Individuals receiving high test scores naturally believe that they are more meritorious than persons with lower scores. Indeed, merit system examiners often share this point of view. Unfortunately, this assumption does not withstand close scrutiny in light of relatively low test validities. Although the person who scores 96 may feel more qualified than a person who scores 92, it cannot be said with certainty that the scores are a true measure of their respective abilities—let alone that the first is exactly four increments more meritorious than the second. The validity of rank-ordering and selecting candidates according to test scores has been challenged often, particularly in situations involving police and firefighters, because women and minorities tend to be underrepresented among top scorers. What is fair in such situations is hard to sort out. Is it fairer to assume that the scores are valid predictors of job performance and select candidates in strict numerical order, or to treat all applicants with passing scores as substantially equally qualified and hire according to affirmative action guidelines?

The third issue is whether tests unfairly discriminate against minorities. The fact that minority applicants as a group tend to do less well on tests than nonminorities has led some to conclude that tests contain biases that cause them to be less valid for some groups than for others. Recent evidence, however, suggests that this is not the case. Generally speaking, the ability of tests to predict subsequent job performance tends to be the same for all groups regardless of race or gender.[24] Differences in group scores are nonetheless troubling. According to a National Academy of Sciences study, if the top 20 percent of whites are chosen for a job, only three percent of blacks are chosen at the same cut-off.[25] In short, comparatively larger proportions of blacks and Hispanics are screened out when they are tested and ranked according to test scores. This fact brings into conflict the use of tests to maximize workforce productivity and the desire to distribute the benefits of employment as widely as possible.

The expense of validating examinations, and uncertainties associated with defending them in court, led to a decline in the use of tests during the 1970s and 1980s. The Uniform Guidelines on Employee Selection Procedures, intended to assist employers in complying with federal law, proved to be too stringent. As a result, useful tests were abandoned or struck down along with the bad.[26] The federal government itself opted to discontinue use of the Professional and Administrative Career Examination (PACE) in the early 1980s because it adversely affected minority applicants. Although it temporarily lost an efficient way of screening the thousands of applications received each year for entry-level professional positions, OPM introduced a replacement in 1990 designed to achieve a better balance between the values of government productivity and social equity. The new examination consists of six broad-based tests, each covering a range of related occupations.[27] Test questions are less academic in nature and are based on situations a person might encounter in federal employment. Developed at a cost of about $100,000 each, OPM hopes they will produce less adverse impact than PACE.

Despite valid concerns about the fairness of employment tests, two key facts weigh against eliminating their use altogether. First, the predictive validity of tests is no worse and often is better than nonstandardized selection devices such as the job interview. Second, employment tests, with all their limitations, remain a valuable source of information about prospective employees. By using one or more tests in combination with other screening devices, the quality of final selection decisions can be greatly improved. It is simply unrealistic to expect any one test to be a powerful predictor of job performance. Each tends to focus narrowly on only one of the many factors that determine job success.

In the final analysis tests remain a relatively efficient, standardized means for screening large numbers of job applicants. They are also a relatively objective and equitable way of distributing valuable resources. They help ensure, for example, that selection decisions are not based on ascribed characteristics such as age, race, gender, religion, social status, or family connections—characteristics over which we have little control and that are seldom relevant to how well we perform our jobs. Properly designed and used, assembled examinations are an important guarantee of merit-based selection.

The Job Interview

The job interview is an oral technique used either to screen all job applicants or to assist in making a choice between job finalists. The latter represents the most efficient use of the interview technique because conducting interviews can be extraordinarily time consuming. The primary advantage of the interview over an employment test is that it allows an employer to evaluate a broader range of determinants of job performance. Its use is not restricted, for example, to explorations of a particular ability or body of knowledge. This advantage aside, the value of the interview's contribution to the selection process depends on the type of interview used and how it is conducted. Two basic types are the nondirective and structured interviews.

The *nondirective interview* is the type traditionally relied on in the private sector. It allows the interviewer to ask any questions that come to mind in exploring the candidate's qualifications or personal fit for the job. In practice this means that each candidate will be asked a different set of questions. Sometimes this type of interview takes the form of an oral personality test in which the interviewer explores various personality traits. For example, the interviewer may seek to draw conclusions regarding whether the candidate comes across as highly motivated, cuts the "right" image, or appears to be someone who will get along well with others.

The nondirective interview, despite its apparent usefulness, cannot satisfy basic professional standards of reliability and validity. As a selection technique, it is time consuming, highly subjective, and very low in predictive validity. Unlike an employment test, it cannot be standardized because different questions are asked of each applicant and there are no right or wrong answers against which to score the applicant.

It involves an interaction between interviewer and applicant that varies in form and content from one interview to the next no matter how consistent the interviewer attempts to be. In addition, candidates are often evaluated on personality traits by individuals who do not possess the training in psychology needed to accurately interpret candidate responses.

The *structured interview* involves a series of job-related questions asked of all candidates. The basic procedure begins with the creation of a committee of three or more persons who will subsequently ask uniform, job-related questions of applicants and score them according to predetermined, "preferred" answers. Committee members develop interview questions based on systematic job analysis and reach a consensus regarding what are and are not acceptable answers. Questions generally focus on required competencies and job-related behaviors rather than personality traits. The latter are included only if they are critical to successful job performance and if they can be defined as desired behaviors rather than as abstract traits. Follow-up questions are asked as needed to probe areas of concern. Finally, ratings are recorded immediately after the conclusion of each interview, and candidates are rank ordered by the committee after all interviews are completed.

Questions asked during the structured interview may be of several kinds. Examples include the following:

Situational Questions: How would you handle the following hypothetical situation?

Knowledge-based Questions: What is the definition of a bona fide occupational qualification?

Experience Clarification Questions: Your application indicates that you have experience writing class specifications. Would you please clarify what that experience entailed?

Job Requirement Questions: This position may require you to relocate after a period of several months. Would you be able to relocate if it becomes necessary?

Interview questions may also focus on psychological attributes if they are job-related and if the responses do not require extensive interpretation.

The structured interview is being used with increasing frequency in the public sector because it promises greater reliability and job-relatedness than more traditional, less structured kinds of interviews. The *situational interview* is a particular type of structured interview that involves asking job candidates how they would respond to specific job-related situations. Candidates may also be asked to perform simulations of the kind used in assessment centers. Exhibit 9.6 presents a sample rating guide for a situational interview question. It specifies the critical behaviors, tasks, and competencies addressed by the question and indicates their importance (or weight) to successful job performance. It also provides a model answer and rating scale.

Rating guidelines of the kind shown in Exhibit 9.6 direct the rater's attention to the specific competencies being assessed and the specific responses that are preferred. In the nondirective interview, by contrast, there is a tendency to judge candidates against a stereotype of the ideal applicant rather than against actual job requirements.

Despite a reputation for high subjectivity and low validity, the job interview can make an important contribution to the hiring decision if designed and administered carefully. Although testing may be more appropriate in some cases, such as for clerical and technical jobs, interviewing may be the best available selection technique for many professional and managerial jobs. Managers used to free-flowing kinds of interviews are likely to view structured interviews as cold and impersonal. Nonetheless, their greater reliability and job-relatedness outweigh the constraints imposed on the interviewer. As Smart notes, "The subjective elements of rapport, chemistry, and hitting it off with candidates are truly important, but only within the context of a valid, balanced, thoughtfully planned approach."[28]

Job Interviewing and EEO

An earlier section of this chapter emphasized the importance of purging all irrelevant and potentially discriminatory questions from the job application form. The same is true for questions asked during interviews. The wide-ranging, informal chats that once characterized the interview process are no longer appropriate if hiring authorities are to stay within the boundaries set by EEO regulations. To ensure equal treatment, the same questions should be asked of all applicants. Irrelevant or potentially discriminatory questions should not be asked unless business necessity can be demonstrated. For example, questions once asked frequently, such as "Do you intend to have more children?" or "Are you using contraceptives?" (generally asked only of women), are clearly inappropriate today.

Reference Checks

Reference checks are used to verify factual information supplied by candidates on application forms and to obtain additional information about them. To save time and expense they are often conducted only for job finalists. The reference check may be the last step before the final selection decision or it may be conducted just before interviewing the job finalists. The advantage of the latter approach is that it allows areas of concern identified during the reference check to be addressed during the interview. Most reference checks are conducted by telephone.

Reference checks vary in nature according to the kinds of questions asked and the persons to whom they are directed. One type of reference check involves contacting previous employers to verify dates of employment, job titles, duties performed, and attendance records. Providing false information is not unusual, and conducting reference checks of this kind is a prudent action to take. Courts have usually upheld the right of an employer to refuse to hire or to fire an employee who has lied on an application form, assuming that the employer had a legitimate reason for asking the questions in the first place. This type of reference check may also include asking past supervisors about the applicant's motivation, technical competence, and cooperativeness. A second type of reference check involves contacting personal references listed by the applicant who are knowledgeable about the quality of the applicant's work or personal character. Persons listed as references are likely to be favorably disposed toward the candidate, but they often supply honest appraisals nonetheless.

EXHIBIT 9.6

SAMPLE INTERVIEW QUESTION RATING GUIDE

Position Title <u>Water Rights Technician</u>

Date _____

Question Number <u>2</u>

1. a. Job Behavior or Task
   Researches water rights data to answer questions (in writing and in person) from applicants and claimants using a knowledge of water rights law and agency policy manuals.

   b. Required Knowledge, Skill, or Ability
   Ability to remain calm and provide effective service to the public, occasionally under stress.

2. Question—In this type of work we sometimes encounter irate people engaged in heated water disputes who are generally discontented with state government. It's five minutes before closing, and you have already spoken to more than two dozen people, many of whom are angry; an irate rancher storms into your office requesting assistance. He is loud and verbally abusive. How would you handle this situation?

3. Weight (A, B, C)
   B

4. Model Answer—(Handling stressful public contact)
   Applicant demonstrates a knowledge of basic human behavior and the fundamentals of effective communication (a speaker and a listener) by expressing the intent not to get into a shouting match; by listening to the irate person; by asking appropriate questions to get to the source of his problem; by assuring him that we will assist him to our best ability; by answering his problem directly or taking his name, address, and phone number and getting pertinent information so that another staff member can contact him, etc.

   <u>5</u>

   Applicant does not have as thorough an understanding as above, but does express the intent not to get into a shouting contest and at least tries to get his name, address, and phone number so someone else can contact him.

   <u>3</u>

   Applicant fails to express his ability to relate to the irate rancher at all; provides no assurances, gets no information, gives no direction or recourse to the rancher.

   <u>0</u>

Legal realities make conducting reference checks both necessary and problematic. Depending on the nature of the job, there may be a strong obligation to investigate a person's background because of the possibility of a negligent hiring suit.[29] A social services agency may put its clientele at risk, for example, by hiring a sex offender. Such suits arise when an employer hires an applicant without sufficient investigation and it is subsequently discovered that the individual has a background or history indicating a propensity for some kind of serious misconduct. A third party can often sue public employers for injuries caused by the employee. At the same time, however, conducting reference checks may lead to defamation of character suits. Defamation suits arise when an employer injures a former employee's subsequent opportunities for employment by the responses given during a reference check. It is one of the many ironies of human resource management that a manager or personnel officer may risk a lawsuit by saying too much (defamation) and asking too little (negligent hiring).

Obtaining useful information through reference checks is much more difficult in today's legal climate. Headline-grabbing defamation cases have been won by litigants, and employers are understandably more reluctant as a result to respond to reference checks. It is not unusual for organizations today to establish policies requiring all questions to be directed to the personnel office and to provide only information regarding job titles, dates of employment, or other information of a factual nature. Policies may also state that the organization will respond only to written inquiries on official letterhead. This is done to verify that the request is legitimate and to establish a written record of the information subsequently supplied. To avoid defamation suits some employers are also training their employees to provide only factual and easily verified information and to avoid answering trap questions (e.g., would you consider rehiring this employee?).

As a result of such defensive policies, persons conducting reference checks must often work hard to establish rapport with references to obtain the desired information. This is done by reassuring them that only information of a factual and verifiable nature is being sought. Whether information is solicited from past employers or character references, it is prudent to work from a list of structured questions and to ask essentially the same questions of all references. Candidates should not be rejected on the basis of negative information without first attempting to verify it.

The Final Selection Decision

Final selection occurs after screening and testing procedures have been completed. In formal merit systems hiring authorities are usually required to choose from among a limited number of candidates referred to them by the central personnel office. In less formal systems they are free to identify job finalists themselves. In either case, a good selection decision requires them to engage in two kinds of matching processes. The first is the applicant-job match. It is assessed in terms of an applicant's possession of required job competencies (KSAOs). The second is the applicant–work environment match. Work environment factors may include working conditions, characteristics of the local community, opportunities for advancement, and the dispositions of supervisors and co-workers. Assessing the applicant–work environment match is important because it bears on such issues as potential job satisfaction, motivation, turnover, and the quality of working relationships with others in the organization.

Often the applicant–work environment match is not considered until job finalists are identified and interviewed. Assessment may involve evaluating personal qualities such as common sense, poise, creativity, enthusiasm, loyalty, and personableness. These qualities typically cannot be measured accurately through testing techniques and are therefore frequently referred to as "subjective selection criteria." The use of subjective criteria tends to take on added importance during the final selection process when hiring authorities must make difficult choices among substantially equally qualified candidates. The final decision is often the result of largely intuitive, highly subjective judgments regarding the relative "fit" of job finalists.

Although the use of subjective criteria can contribute to the selection of first-rate employees, hiring authorities have an obligation to ensure that they do not involve unfair stereotypes or prejudices. For example, in *Price Waterhouse v. Hopkins* (see Chapter 7), a well-known accounting firm refused to offer a partnership to a female manager, despite her extraordinary success in obtaining client contracts, partly because she was perceived as too masculine. One of her supporters suggested that her chances of obtaining a partnership might improve if she would "walk more femininely, talk more femininely, dress more femininely, wear make-up, have her hair styled, and wear jewelry."[30] The Supreme Court subsequently upheld the district court's decision that she had been the victim of sex discrimination. In short, assessments of how well a candidate will "fit in" should not involve judgments tainted by harmful stereotypes or personal prejudices.

Employee Selection and Governmental Effectiveness

The importance of employee selection to organizational effectiveness bears repeating. Public agencies cannot be as effective as citizens have a right to expect when the quality of the workforce is undermined by poor hiring decisions. The amount of lost productivity represented by marginal workers who are not quite bad enough to fire but never good enough to promote can be enormous. Ironically, politicians try to save money by holding the line on labor costs when there are much larger savings to be had by improving systems of employee selection.[31] As one selection specialist put it, "If the wrong employee has been selected initially, no training program or motivational system—no matter how well conceived and designed —is likely to compensate adequately or offset the original error made in hiring such a person."[32]

■ **CASE 9.1**   A Failed Process? Or a Flawed Decision?

Although it seems like much longer, it was only three months ago that the Department of Commerce announced a job opening for an Administrative Clerk III position. Job qualifications included knowledge of business English and office procedures, skill in the use of personal computers, ability to read and understand instructions, and ability to maintain effective working relations with employees, other agencies, and the general public. Good judgment and interpersonal communications skills were also listed as essential qualifications. Finally, applicants were required to have a high school diploma or G.E.D. and three years of progressively responsible clerical experience.

Bryan Jones applied for the position, not because he particularly wanted to do clerical or secretarial work, but because the job market was extremely tight and he wanted to break into the state employment system any way that he could. He submitted the standard application form, the required application supplement, and a resume that mentioned his Master's degree in International Business and his fluency in Japanese.

During the screening process the members of the selection committee commented favorably on the value of having someone with Bryan's background in an office that dealt with interstate and some international business. After each applicant had been scored on the basis of previous training and experience, Bryan emerged as one of the three finalists for the position. He interviewed well and was given the position.

With the perspective provided by the intervening three months it is now clear that Bryan has poor communication skills, poor writing skills, and weak knowledge of grammar. He seems unmotivated and manages his time poorly. He also lacks people skills and quickly alienated other employees by letting them know that he is better than his secretarial status indicates.

Kathy Wainright, Division Administrator, was initially pleased that Bryan had accepted the position. She viewed his knowledge of international business as a valuable asset and believed that he was smart enough to overcome any deficiencies he may have. Now she is wondering where things went wrong. Office morale is lower than it has been in years, and productivity is declining. Wainright cannot put her finger on the problem. Nor is she sure what to do next.

1. What is the root cause of Wainright's predicament? A failed selection process, or a flawed selection decision?
2. How should "overqualified" applicants be treated in the selection process? Is the lesson in this case that overqualified applicants should not be chosen?
3. Did the selection process allow for a comprehensive and thorough assessment of each applicant's qualifications? If not, what improvements are needed?
4. What can or should Wainright do now?

▲ EXERCISE 9.1 Difficult Selection Issues

You are members of a selection committee charged with screening and evaluating applicants for the position of personnel specialist in the state's Department of Transportation. Minimum qualifications are a B.A. degree in a related field and three years of progressively more responsible experience in the field of human resource management. Initial screening has been completed and four applicants have emerged as finalists. Additional information about each applicant was revealed to you during routine reference checks. Your knowledge of the finalists may be summarized as follows:

Candidate #1: A woman who is only 6 credits short of her B.A. degree in business management and has served for five years as a personnel officer for the County. You learn that she is married to the Department's Deputy Director.

Candidate #2: A man who has a B.A. degree in a related field, worked previously for the Department, is a veteran who was released from active duty last month, and has had two years of personnel-related experience during military service.

Candidate #3: A woman who has a B.A. degree in a related field, has served as a personnel officer in another department for two years, and is the spouse of a 100% disabled veteran. During the reference check you also learn that she is pregnant and is due to deliver in two months.

Candidate #4: A male who has worked for 20 years as a personnel officer for several employers in the private sector. He has a B.A. degree in a related field and has published several articles on human resource management in professional journals. The reference check disclosed that he has a reputation for being an alcoholic.

Although you have not yet invited candidates for an interview, it is clear to you that the final selection decision is not going to be a simple one. You realize that there are several legal and policy-related issues that will require investigation before a final decision can be made. You decide to investigate these issues as fully as possible before scheduling interviews because there may be pertinent questions that you will want to ask of the candidates.

1. List all of the selection issues that are raised in this situation.
2. Some of the issues on your first list will require investigation. Prepare a second list identifying laws, regulations, and agency policies that must be consulted before a selection decision can be made.
3. Finally, list those questions that you have both a right and a responsibility to ask of your four candidates during the interview to protect the agency from legal risk and to ensure that the best qualified individual is selected. (Similarly, you may wish to identify those pieces of information that are irrelevant and should be ignored.)

Notes

1. Task Force on the New York State Public Workforce in the 21st Century, *Public Service Through the State Government Workforce: Meeting the Challenge of Change* (Albany, New York: Nelson A. Rockefeller Institute of Government, 1989), 13.

2. Volcker Commission Report, *Leadership in America: Rebuilding the Public Service* (Lexington, Massachusetts: D.C. Heath, Lexington Books, 1989), 23.

3. Ibid., 24.

4. U.S. General Accounting Office, *Federal Recruiting and Hiring: Making Government Jobs Attractive to Prospective Employees* (GAO/GGD-90-105, August 1990), 34.

5. Volcker Commission Report, *Leadership in America*, 28–29.

6. Ibid. 29.

7. See Charles A. Daily, *Using the Track Record Approach: The Key to Successful Personnel Selection* (New York: AMACOM, 1982).

8. Jean J. Couturier, "Court Attacks on Testing: Death Knell or Salvation for Civil Service Systems," *Good Government* 88 (Winter 1971):10–12.

9. *U.S. v. State of New York*, 21 EPD 30,314 (1979).

10. *Dothard v. Rawlinson*, 433 U.S. 321 (1977).

11. *Griggs v. Duke Power Co.*, 401 U.S. 424 at 436 (1971).

12. Debra D. Burrington, "A Review of State Government Employment Application Forms for Suspect Inquiries," *Public Personnel Management* 11 (Spring 1982), 56.

13. Richard D. Arvey, *Fairness in Selecting Employees* (Reading, Massachusetts: Addison-Wesley, 1979), 233.

14. Debbie Cutchin and David Alonso, "Solving Personnel Problems through the Assessment Center," in *Creative Personnel Practices: New Ideas for Local Government* (Washington, DC: International City Management Association, 1984). See also "Guidelines and Ethical Considerations for Assessment Center Operations," *Public Personnel Management* 18 (Winter 1989):457–470.

15. Douglas W. Bray and Donald L. Grant, "The Assessment Center in the Measurement of Potential for Business Management," *Psychological Monographs: General and Applied* 80 (no. 17, 1966).

16. William C. Byham and Carl Wettengel, "Assessment Centers for Supervisors and Managers: An Introduction and Overview," *Public Personnel Management* 3 (September/October 1974):352–364.

17. Joyce D. Ross, "A Current Review of Public Sector Assessment Centers: Cause for Concern," *Public Personnel Management* 8 (January/February 1979):41–46.

18. Veterans' Preference Act of 1944. See also, Office of Personnel Management, *Federal Personnel Manual* (Washington, D.C.: Government Printing Office, 1988).

19. See, for example, U.S. Equal Employment Opportunity Commission, "Uniform Guidelines on Employee Selection Procedures," *Code of Federal Regulations* (41 CFR Ch. 60, 1978).

20. *Kirkland v. Department of Correctional Services*, 7 FEP 694 (1974).

21. See Wayne F. Cascio, Ralph A. Alexander, and Gerald V. Barrett, "Setting Cutoff Scores: Legal, Psychometric, and Professional Issues and Guidelines," *Personnel Psychology* 41 (Spring 1988):1–24; and Richard E. Biddle, "How to Set Cutoff Scores for Knowledge Tests Used in Promotion, Training, Certification, and Licensing," *Public Personnel Management* 22 (Spring 1993): 63–79.

22. Alexandra K. Wigdor and Wendell R. Garner, eds., *Ability Testing: Uses, Consequences, and Controversies* (Washington, D.C.: National Academy Press, 1982).

23. David C. McClelland, "Testing for Competence Rather than for 'Intelligence'," in N. J. Block and Gerald Dworkin, eds., *The IQ Controversy: Critical Readings* (New York: Pantheon Books, 1976).

24. Margaret E. Griffin, "Personnel Research on Testing, Selection, and Performance Appraisal," *Public Personnel Management* 18 (Summer 1989):127–137.

25. Wigdor and Garner, *Ability Testing*.

26. Ibid., 143.

27. Judith Haverman, "Civil Service: Taking the Guesswork and Chance Out of Hiring," *Washington Post National Weekly Edition* (April 30–May 6, 1990):31.

28. Bradford D. Smart, *Selection Interviewing: A Management Psychologist's Recommended Approach* (New York: John Wiley & Sons, 1983), 2.

29. Robert J. Walter, "Public Employer's Potential Liability from Negligence in Employment Decisions," *Public Administration Review* 52 (September/October 1992):491–495.

30. *Hopkins v. Price Waterhouse* (618 F. Supp. at 1117, 1985).

31. James P. Springer, "The Importance of Selection in Public Sector Administration," *Public Personnel Administration* 11 (Spring 1982):9–12.

32. Erwin S. Stanton, *Successful Personnel Recruiting and Selection* (New York: AMACOM, 1977), 2.

Part 4

Performance Management

Analysis in Parts 2 and 3 focused on positions: how to define them, analyze them, evaluate them, and fill them. Little was said about the people that constitute the organization or how to manage human performance effectively. In Part 4 the focus shifts from managing positions to managing people. Because it is ultimately people who determine the success of organizations, the task of performance management is a critical one. As discussed in the chapters that follow, performance management entails setting goals and standards for work, training and developing employees, directing and motivating employees, evaluating their work performance, and rewarding them for superior efforts.

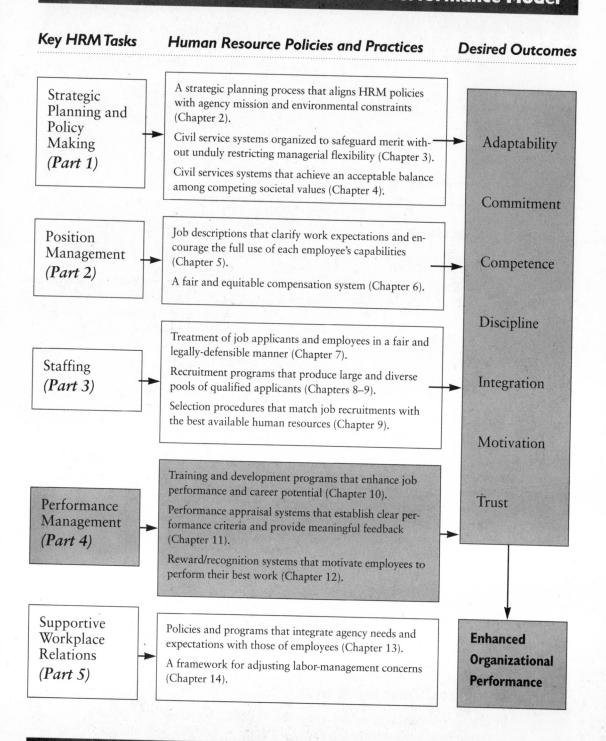

Linking HRM Tasks and Outcomes: A Performance Model

Key HRM Tasks	Human Resource Policies and Practices	Desired Outcomes

Strategic Planning and Policy Making (Part 1)

A strategic planning process that aligns HRM policies with agency mission and environmental constraints (Chapter 2).

Civil service systems organized to safeguard merit without unduly restricting managerial flexibility (Chapter 3).

Civil services systems that achieve an acceptable balance among competing societal values (Chapter 4).

Position Management (Part 2)

Job descriptions that clarify work expectations and encourage the full use of each employee's capabilities (Chapter 5).

A fair and equitable compensation system (Chapter 6).

Staffing (Part 3)

Treatment of job applicants and employees in a fair and legally-defensible manner (Chapter 7).

Recruitment programs that produce large and diverse pools of qualified applicants (Chapters 8–9).

Selection procedures that match job recruitments with the best available human resources (Chapter 9).

Performance Management (Part 4)

Training and development programs that enhance job performance and career potential (Chapter 10).

Performance appraisal systems that establish clear performance criteria and provide meaningful feedback (Chapter 11).

Reward/recognition systems that motivate employees to perform their best work (Chapter 12).

Supportive Workplace Relations (Part 5)

Policies and programs that integrate agency needs and expectations with those of employees (Chapter 13).

A framework for adjusting labor-management concerns (Chapter 14).

Desired Outcomes:

Adaptability

Commitment

Competence

Discipline

Integration

Motivation

Trust

Enhanced Organizational Performance

CHAPTER 10

Human Resource Training and Development

Learning Objectives

After mastering the materials contained in this chapter, you will be able to:

1. Explain how training and development contributes to organizational integration and adaptability, and employee competence, commitment, and motivation.
2. Explain why the training and development function is rising in importance and status.
3. Identify the purposes of employee orientation and three kinds of information required by new employees.
4. Describe four basic steps in creating and operating a training program.
5. Select appropriate methods of instruction for achieving identified learning objectives.
6. Explain the goals and purposes of management development and career development programs.

A manager fortunate enough to hire an individual with excellent potential for job success is not guaranteed a motivated, highly productive employee. Additional steps are necessary if the promised potential is to be realized. The new employee must be *oriented* to job requirements and organizational realities, *trained* to perform present job duties well, and *developed* so that he or she will be prepared to take on a variety of organizational roles in the future. These important tasks are the responsibility of the training and development function.

This chapter analyzes the importance of training and development, explains why it is currently receiving so much attention, describes the process of designing and implementing training programs, and assesses the promise and reality of this important area of human resource management.

The Training and Development Function

The responsibilities of the training and development function, as in other areas of human resource management, are shared jointly by line and staff officers and are performed at more than one organizational level. Each supervisor is responsible for providing on-the-job training and working with personnel officers to identify training needs that cannot be met on the job. Managers are responsible for establishing and implementing training policies and identifying organizational problems that may require training-related interventions. Finally, the training staff, assuming a government is large enough to maintain one, is responsible for providing training courses that meet the needs of broad categories of government workers. The federal government's Office of Personnel Management (OPM), for example, offers a broad range of courses to agencies in the Washington area through its Office of Washington Training and Development Services. OPM operates several regional training centers as well.

Not all governments rely on the central personnel office to provide training opportunities. The state of Kentucky, for example, relies on the Governmental Services Center at Kentucky State University to deliver a varied curriculum of training courses.[1] Montgomery County, Maryland, prefers to contract with private consulting firms to deliver management development courses.[2] Smaller governments often cannot afford to maintain their own training and development staffs. Training duties are typically performed by busy supervisors with the assistance of overworked personnel officers, or they are not performed at all. In-house training programs seldom exist, and out-of-house opportunities are provided only when discretionary funds are available. This does not mean that small governments cannot train and develop their employees. The North Central Texas Council of Governments, for example, has established a regional training center to provide training courses on a fee-for-service basis to member governments in the region.[3]

Training and Development Activities

The activities defined in Exhibit 10.1 illustrate the range of training opportunities provided to employees. Some of them may be placed under the heading of training, and others belong more appropriately under the heading of development. *Training activities* aim at improving the skills needed to perform current job duties effectively. They may focus on technical skills, such as computer programming, or "soft" skills, such as communications and problem solving.[4] *Development activities,* by contrast, are broader in scope and more future oriented. Their aim is to improve employee motivation and job satisfaction, prepare employees to perform a variety of organizational roles, and assist them in advancing within the organization.

The Goals of Training and Development

The training and development function exists to serve vital individual and organizational goals. Among the desired human resource outcomes identified in Chapter 1, training and development programs contribute to organizational integration and adaptability, and employee competence, commitment, and motivation.

First, training and development programs help *integrate* various aspects of human resource management, thereby improving the organization's ability to achieve strategic objectives. Consider the following examples. Performance appraisal systems can help identify skill deficiencies, but training opportunities are needed if these deficiencies are to be corrected. Human resource planning efforts can forecast a shortage of skilled workers, but current employees need to be retrained if the organization is to

---

EXHIBIT 10.1

TRAINING AND DEVELOPMENT ACTIVITIES

Apprenticeship Training A method used for centuries in skilled craft occupations in which apprentices acquire knowledge and skills under the guidance of experienced craftpersons. After a period of one to six years of on-the-job training, apprentices are certified as "journey workers" and deemed qualified to pursue their craft. Apprenticeship training is sometimes used in the public sector to train firefighters, police, and correctional officers.[5]

Career Development Programs that encourage employees to view learning as a lifelong process. As employees acquire new skills and abilities, they often experience the sense of satisfaction that comes with personal growth. They may also improve their opportunities for vertical and lateral movement within the organization. By developing its human resources in the aggregate, the organization obtains an increasingly well-qualified workforce and a talent bank to draw on as environmental circumstances and organizational needs change.

Cross-training A combination of on-the-job training and job rotation in which experienced workers are trained to perform other jobs, both to increase organizational flexibility and to develop individual talents. Clerical workers, for example, may be trained to perform a variety of jobs within the work unit or jobs in other units.

Employee Orientation Activities, including workshops and on-the-job training, designed to introduce new employees to their jobs and to the organization. It is a process of informing new employees of work expectations, organizational policies and operations, and employee benefits. It may also involve socializing them in organizational values and goals.

Job Rotation An employee development program in which employees acquire new skills and master new tasks by moving from one job to another at specified intervals. It is used most often with management trainees, but can be used to develop other employees as well. Through job rotation, employees can develop and practice new skills, broaden their understanding of organizational operations, and identify areas in which they can best use their talents in the future.

Management Training Training programs designed to improve the current or future performance of supervisors, managers, and executives by imparting knowledge, developing skills, or establishing new attitudes. Programs may include in-house training, out-of-house workshops, institute-based seminars, university degree programs, mentoring, and job rotation.

On-the-Job Training (OJT) A training method in which employees learn by actually performing job duties under the guidance of a supervisor or experienced co-worker. It is used to orient new employees to job requirements and to ensure a basic level of proficiency among new and old employees alike.

Organizational Development Training activities aimed at changing attitudes, values, and beliefs of employees to improve organizational functioning. Such activities are often prescribed after an investigation of an organizational problem by an outside consultant. A strategy for planned change is then established and appropriate interventions prescribed to achieve desired objectives. Interventions include such things as sensitivity training and team-building workshops.

Socialization Training Training activities designed to impart organizational rules and value perspectives to employees. It may involve socializing new employees about important organi-

EXHIBIT 10.1 *(continued)*

zational norms, ensuring that new employees have realistic expectations regarding work roles and resources, converting managers to a particular management philosophy, or communicating to all employees the importance of professional ethics and public accountability.

Structured Mentoring A program that pairs more experienced employees with less experienced employees to form mentor-protégé teams, usually for purposes of management development. The mentor develops the protégé by performing a number of roles, including coach, sponsor, and protector. Less structured programs simply reward experienced employees who voluntarily undertake mentoring roles.

Technical Training Training designed to ensure that employees possess the basic knowledge and skills needed to perform current job duties effectively.

Tuition Assistance A program established by agency policy that authorizes managers to reimburse employees for all or part of tuition costs while attending a college, university, or technical school for the purpose of developing knowledge and skills. Educational benefits of this kind serve as a recruitment device, a means for ensuring that critical skills are acquired, and a way to facilitate individual career advancement.

adapt successfully. Strategic planners may commit the organization to developing its human resources, but little will be accomplished unless managers are trained to be "people developers" and employees are socialized to value personal development. In short, training is an important component in any human resource management system. It can significantly enhance organizational effectiveness if it is properly integrated with other system components.

Second, training and development can play an important role in building *employee competence and commitment* by addressing important individual needs. Training and development opportunities, for example, are vehicles for achieving personal proficiency, job security, and career advancement. They help ensure that employees have the skills necessary for succeeding in their current jobs and for advancing to more challenging jobs in the future. Although much more research is needed, it is widely believed that a demonstrated willingness to satisfy developmental needs helps produce loyal and committed employees—employees who are more likely to identify with the organization's goals and values and more willing to work hard on its behalf.

Third, a well-trained and well-developed workforce increases an organization's ability to *adapt* successfully to a changing environment. The ability to adapt requires employees who possess skills and abilities that go beyond those needed in their current jobs. It may prove necessary to ask employees to do different things or to do existing things differently as technologies, strategic plans, political directives, legal requirements, and social values change. By investing in its human resources, an organization can build reserves of special talents to draw on when confronted with changing circumstances and emerging challenges. The ability to adapt also depends on the foresight of the training and development staff in anticipating changing needs and providing appropriate training and development opportunities. In short, training and development can be a powerful agent for planned change.

Finally, training and development programs, if designed and implemented with care, can increase individual *motivation*. Personal growth, for example, often results in higher self-esteem and job satisfaction, and advancement to more challenging jobs can increase intrinsic motivation. According to W. Edwards Deming, there is a certain pride or "joy" that comes with continuous self-improvement that is essential to motivating employees and maximizing quality.[6]

The Rising Status of Training and Development

Despite the clear benefits to be derived from human resource training and development, training budgets are traditionally among the first to be cut during periods of fiscal stress.[7] At such times central staffs are reduced in size, and line managers, who often must pay for training out of their discretionary funds, are compelled to reduce training opportunities to satisfy competing demands. But times change. The status of training and development is now on the rise as government agencies search for ways to respond appropriately to changes occurring in their environments. These changes, as described in the *Workforce 2000* report, include greater workforce diversity, growth in the number of jobs requiring specialized knowledge and skills, and increased competition for skilled workers.[8]

The implications of these trends for training and development are several. First, competition for qualified workers is expected to become intense in some areas of the nation. The predicted gap between the skill levels of new workers and the skill requirements of jobs is especially troubling for governments because they rely heavily on jobs requiring specialized skills. Forty-eight percent of federal employees, for example, hold professional, technical, and managerial jobs, compared with 25 percent in the economy as a whole.[9] The number of such jobs is expected to increase in the years ahead. Faced with the difficulty of obtaining skilled workers in increasingly competitive labor markets, governments will be forced to shift their focus from recruitment and selection to training and development. As the *Civil Service 2000* report states,

> *Federal agencies can either "buy" or "make" the skills they need. In other words, they can recruit and hire highly skilled, qualified workers from the national labor market, or they can invest in their current workers and teach them what they need to know. Since many Federal employers will continue to face difficulties in competing for the best-qualified workers, Federal agencies should systematically invest more in their existing workforces. This will not only make the Federal government a more attractive place to work, it will be a cost-effective way to build Federal skills.[10]*

In short, recruitment problems will increase the strategic value of human resource training and development. Technical and professional workers recruited successfully at the entry level will require continuous development if they are to advance to higher level positions. Cross-training, which involves learning to perform new job duties and organizational roles, is one means of developing human resources. It is accomplished through job rotation, job enrichment, and work sabbaticals. Through cross-training, agencies at all levels can develop multitalented workforces to draw on as needed.

Second, the rapid rate of technological change is expected to alter the character of many types of jobs. As a result, employees require continuous retraining if their skills are not to become obsolete. Desktop computers, for example, are now available to most white-collar workers, creating extensive training needs in word processing, electronic spreadsheets, and data-based management. Computers are also breaking down traditional communications channels by allowing workers to communicate with others at will and to obtain access to all kinds of information. These changes place additional demands on training and development staffs. Managers need to be trained in how to manage more open, less hierarchical work units, and employees need training in how to work effectively in multidisciplinary teams.

Third, greater development opportunities may be needed to motivate members of the "baby-boom" generation who are facing limited opportunities for advancement as they reach mid-career. Research on values shows that these workers are more likely to value personal growth than older workers.[11] Recognition of the importance of career development is increasing as the need to motivate these workers becomes more apparent.

Finally, as demographic changes create workforces that are more diverse in their racial, ethnic, and gender composition, training in diversity management will become more important. Many new employees may be burdened with lower levels of language competence, poorer educational preparation, culture-based behaviors that may be easily misunderstood, and difficulties associated with reconciling the demands of work and family. The goal of diversity management training is to provide managers and employees alike with the interpersonal skills and cross-cultural awareness necessary for working together effectively. Subjects often covered in diversity management courses include valuing diversity, overcoming stereotypes and assumptions about others, learning how to assist women and minorities to advance within the organization, and developing basic communications and interpersonal skills.

Despite the alarm bells sounded by the *Workforce 2000* report, it is far from certain that governments are placing a higher priority on training and development. Among those responding to a survey of local government officials in Virginia, 47.9 percent said they currently encourage career development and intended to increase its use in the future, and another 35.4 percent said they intended to increase career development efforts although they did not currently have programs in place.[12] Large percentages of respondents also said they intended to increase use of educational leave, tuition reimbursement, in-house employee training, and diversity management courses for managers. However, a study of state personnel directors by Hays and Kearney yielded less optimistic results.[13] Most policy responses are focusing on incremental adjustments to benefit systems (to meet the needs of a more diverse workforce) and performance assessment (as the basis for pay-for-performance systems), with very little being done in the area of employee development.

Employee Orientation

Beginning a new job, especially when it is with a new employer, can be a profoundly unsettling experience. New employees bring a variety of personal hopes and fears to their jobs. They naturally wonder whether their expectations will be matched by reality, whether they will like and be liked by their colleagues, and whether their abilities are adequate for the challenges they soon will face. The employee and employer have their own expectations and needs, and it is far from certain that a mutual accommodation between them can be achieved. If it cannot, the new employee is likely to leave after a short period or remain with the organization as an unmotivated, possibly disgruntled worker. Successfully integrating new workers into the organization is a vitally important management task, and employee orientation is the principal means of achieving it.

Employee orientation is the process of introducing new employees to their jobs and to the organization. Edgar Schein, a noted authority on career dynamics, suggests that the orientation process should lead to the formation of a psychological contract between employee and employer:

> *Entry into the organization is, from the individual's point of view, a process of breaking in and joining up, of learning the ropes, of figuring out how to get along and how to make it. The same process from the point of view of the organization is one of induction, basic training, and socialization of the individual to the major norms and values of the organization and of testing new employees to make it possible to place them correctly in a job and career path. The two processes can be seen as a kind of negotiation between the "recruits" and the organizational members with whom they deal, leading to a viable psychological contract—a matching of what the individual will give with what the organization expects to receive, and what the organization will give relative to what the individual expects to receive.*[14]

If handled properly, orientation activities can reduce anxieties, lessen adjustment problems, and assist in forming a psychological contract between employee and employer to the benefit of both.

Employee orientation is essentially an informational process. First, new employees need information about their job duties and responsibilities, performance expectations, and the limits of their authority. This information is usually provided by the employee's immediate supervisor or an experienced lead worker. Mentoring relationships may also be established to integrate new employees into the organization. For example, a "buddy system" may be established in which a co-worker is trained to serve as a mentor or guide for the new employee.

Second, new employees need information about the organization's operations and policies. They need to know, for example, how to get on the payroll, what benefits they are entitled to, what personnel policies apply to them, and what rights and obligations they have as employees. This information is often compiled in employee handbooks and reviewed during group orientation sessions. In large governmental jurisdictions these sessions are usually conducted by the central training and development staff. They may range from brief introductions to formal presentations lasting several days.

Finally, new employees need information regarding the attitudes and patterns of behavior expected of them. Organizational cultures tend to include norms regarding how work should be done, how a good employee is expected to behave, and how best to fit in and progress within the organization.[15] These cultural norms are typically communicated by supervisors and co-workers. Learning them helps to reduce the anxieties often experienced by new employees. According to Schein, if the necessary psychological contract is not established early, the organization is likely to lose the considerable investment it has already made in recruiting, selecting, and training the new employee.

Orientation sessions also provide opportunities to socialize new workers in organizational values and philosophies. The goal is to establish common purposes and shared commitments. Until recently, however, few government agencies have attempted to socialize employees through well-defined organizational philosophies. They have relied instead on policy directives, standard operating procedures, and behavioral rules. This is now beginning to change. A recent book by Osborne and Gaebler emphasizes the benefits to be derived from replacing rule-driven government with mission-driven government.[16] Excellence in government can be achieved, they argue, by defining each agency's mission, formulating an organizational philosophy, and using employee orientation programs as opportunities to socialize new employees. According to Osborne and Gaebler, once the mission is understood and its values internalized, employees will achieve a closer identify with the organization, feel a stronger commonality of purpose, and be more motivated to achieve organizational goals.

Orientation programs are no guarantee that employees will adjust to workplace demands and remain with the organization. Nonetheless, by clarifying job expectations and communicating what the organization is all about, they can do much to ease the transition into a new job and form the psychological contract necessary to becoming a motivated and productive employee.

Training as a Systematic Process: Four Steps

Employees may be properly oriented to their jobs but lack the training needed to perform their duties effectively. These employees will not experience the intrinsic rewards that come with knowledge of a job well done. Nor can they expect to receive the usual organizational rewards accorded successful workers. In short, training is an important contributor to individual motivation and productivity.

Training is essentially a matter of determining what knowledge and skills employees require and finding the means to develop them. Successful training requires a systematic approach involving four steps:

1. Needs assessment
2. Curriculum design
3. Training delivery
4. Training evaluation

As shown in Exhibit 10.2, these steps represent a systematic approach to the design and evaluation of training programs. Each of these steps is described below.

Needs Assessment

Efficient and cost-effective training programs are designed and delivered in response to identified training needs. As shown in Exhibit 10.2, needs assessment is an information-gathering process involving job, person, and organization analysis.[17] *Job analysis* involves determining the KSAOs required to perform job duties successfully. *Person analysis,* by contrast, involves appraising the performance of employees to determine which KSAOs, if any, require further development. Supervisors, sometimes

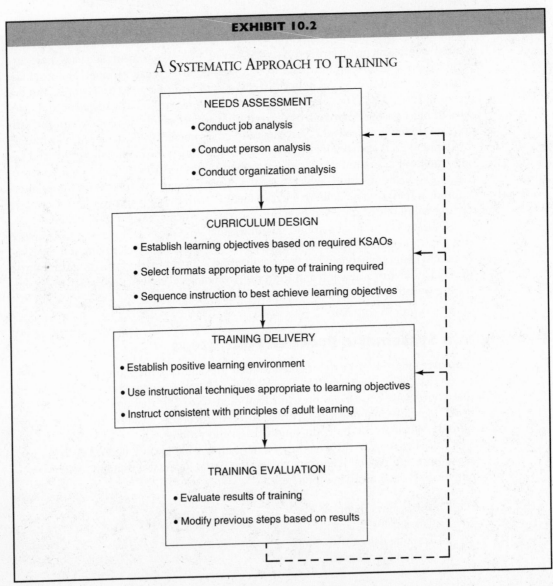

EXHIBIT 10.2

A SYSTEMATIC APPROACH TO TRAINING

NEEDS ASSESSMENT

- Conduct job analysis
- Conduct person analysis
- Conduct organization analysis

CURRICULUM DESIGN

- Establish learning objectives based on required KSAOs
- Select formats appropriate to type of training required
- Sequence instruction to best achieve learning objectives

TRAINING DELIVERY

- Establish positive learning environment
- Use instructional techniques appropriate to learning objectives
- Instruct consistent with principles of adult learning

TRAINING EVALUATION

- Evaluate results of training
- Modify previous steps based on results

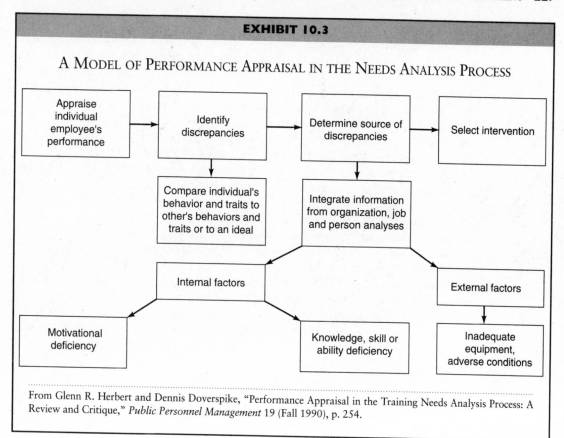

EXHIBIT 10.3

A MODEL OF PERFORMANCE APPRAISAL IN THE NEEDS ANALYSIS PROCESS

From Glenn R. Herbert and Dennis Doverspike, "Performance Appraisal in the Training Needs Analysis Process: A Review and Critique," *Public Personnel Management* 19 (Fall 1990), p. 254.

assisted by training specialists, assess the performance of subordinates and determine who will benefit from what types of training. Supervisors also watch for performance problems that may indicate the need for training. The best approach to needs assessment is one that relies on multiple sources. For example, training needs may be identified on a daily basis as performance problems are observed and discussed, on a routine basis during formal performance appraisals, and on a periodic basis by surveying employees regarding their perceived training needs.

The goal of job and person analysis is to identify the knowledge and skill requirements of a job, determine proficiency levels of the incumbent, and prescribe appropriate training to close the gap. The goal of *organization analysis,* by contrast, is to identify macro-level training needs so that resources can be concentrated in particular areas. For example, training specialists may identify a need to retrain employees in anticipation of newly emerging technologies, educate employees regarding new legal requirements, socialize workers in the importance of eliminating sexual harassment, or train supervisors in human relations skills.

Once a performance problem is identified, the next step is to determine what type of intervention is required. It cannot be assumed, for example, that training is always the proper response. Performance problems should be diagnosed systematically and training prescribed only where it is clearly warranted. Exhibit 10.3 presents a model for determining appropriate interventions using performance appraisal data. If discrepancies appear between an employee's performance and established performance standards, the sources of those discrepancies must be determined. These sources may be external to the employee, such as adverse policies and working conditions, poorly designed jobs, inadequate equipment, or lack of constructive feedback. They may also be internal to the employee, such as lack of motivation or deficiencies in knowledge and skills. It is the last of these that indicates a need for training. If an employee is fully capable of performing job duties effectively but chooses not to, motivational or disciplinary interventions are more appropriate than training.

Once training is identified as an appropriate intervention, the supervisor and employee should draft a plan identifying the type of training needed and how it will be obtained. Types of training include on-the-job training, remedial education, formal in-house or out-of-house training courses, commercially developed self-study programs, and courses taken through a local college or university. Which of these options to choose depends on organizational policies, the size of the training budget, and, most importantly, the objectives to be achieved.

Supervisors in large governments often find that the type of training needed by their employees is readily available from the central training and development office. One of the primary duties of this office is to assess the training needs of the workforce by conducting organization analysis. If large numbers of employees are found to need a particular type of training, the central staff is expected to design a course to meet that need. In practice, however, central staffs often pursue a smorgasbord approach, offering a wide range of courses without assessing whether they are actually needed. Course offerings also tend to be biased toward the needs of supervisory and managerial personnel at the expense of rank-and-file employees. Needs assessment, according to Schneier, Guthrie, and Olian, receives more lip-service than practice.[18] There are several reasons for this, including lack of knowledge of how to conduct needs assessments, inadequate staff resources, poor planning, management skepticism about its effectiveness, and a penchant for offering courses simply because they are in vogue.

Curriculum Design

A key to the success of training is a well-planned curriculum. This is equally true for a single course, a series of related courses, or the collective offerings of the training staff. Curriculum development begins where needs assessment leaves off—with the identification of learning objectives. Learning objectives are valuable because they communicate to trainees what is expected of them, provide guidance to trainers in choosing appropriate learning techniques, and establish the basis for evaluating training effectiveness. The following is an example of a learning objective for a course in diversity management: "at the end of this course, the manager-trainee will be able to assist women and minorities in advancing within the agency and increase cross-cultural awareness among employees."

Instructional design is a well-established field of study comprising several distinct approaches.[19] The traditional *school approach* defines instructional objectives in terms of conveying information and increasing knowledge. The subject matter is organized by an instructor into a logical, hierarchical sequence so that each new concept or piece of information builds on previous ones. The school approach is appropriate, for example, when the goal is simply to inform employees about changes in the law or organizational policies. Knowledge alone, however, is seldom sufficient to correct performance-related problems. The *behavioral approach* defines instructional objectives in terms of desired work behaviors. The sequence of instructional steps is planned to teach and reinforce behavioral objectives through constant repetition and feedback until the subject as a whole is mastered. It is best suited for blue-collar and clerical jobs involving repetitive, manual tasks. Regardless of what kind of instructional objectives and methods are ultimately chosen, the *andragogical approach* emphasizes the importance of actively involving the learner in selecting and defining them. This approach is useful in training professional and administrative personnel when combined with the *competency-based approach*. The competency-based approach uses a variety of instructional techniques to develop specific work-related competencies. A competency is simply a composite of capabilities that enable a person to excel in performance. Examples include problem-solving, communication, and listening skills.

Familiarity with adult learning theory is useful in selecting appropriate instructional techniques. Malcolm Knowles has popularized the term "andragogy" (the teaching of adults) to distinguish adult training from "pedagogy" (the teaching of children).[20] According to Knowles, adults learn differently than children in several ways: First, adults have a deep need to be self-directing. This suggests that instructors should act as facilitators, encouraging individual exploration and active involvement of students in their own learning, rather than as experts who convey information in an ordered sequence. Second, adults learn more effectively if they understand *why* they need to know or need to be able to do something. They are pragmatic learners who are motivated to learn when instruction is directly related to improving some aspect of their lives. This suggests the importance of explaining why they are at the training session (besides being sent by the boss) and what is in it for them. Third, learning for adults is more meaningful when it is tied to personal experience. This suggests that instruction should be problem centered rather than content centered, and trainees should be invited to relate new ideas to their past experiences. In addition, instructional techniques should offer many opportunities for active involvement, such as field trips, case study analysis, in-basket exercises, question and answer periods, role-playing exercises, simulations, games, and team assignments.

Finally, learning materials must be developed consistent with identified training objectives, the intended audience, and the organizational environment. Whether training takes place on the job or in the classroom, lessons must be logically sequenced to achieve training objectives. Supervisors and personnel officers asked to assist with curriculum development will find it a challenging task.

Training Delivery

The particular format used to deliver training is determined during the curriculum development process. Standard delivery formats include the following. *On-the-job training (OJT)* involves learning a job by actually performing its duties. It is typically provided to new employees, and for many it is the only training they receive. Supervisors or experienced workers are assigned to coach new employees in the basic elements of the job. Often, however, they are not trained as trainers and they resent the time it takes to "break in" new employees. Although the effectiveness of OJT can be enhanced by establishing a structured program of instruction, most often it is treated as an informal, unstructured process in which supervisors orient and train employees as they choose.

A special type of on-the-job training is *job instruction training (JIT)*. Developed for manufacturing jobs during the Second World War, JIT involves listing all job tasks in their natural sequence, showing the worker how to perform each task, providing step-by-step instructions for each, and having the worker practice each step repeatedly until it is mastered.

Programmed learning is a behavioral method for developing job skills. A series of questions or problems are presented in a workbook or by a computer, the learner is given time to respond, and feedback is immediately offered regarding the accuracy of the learner's responses. This method assumes that effective learning requires mastering one thing at a time through constant repetition and reinforcement, and it is best suited for jobs requiring basic technical knowledge and skills.

Computer-assisted instruction (CAI) is a specific type of programmed learning in which learners are provided self-paced, individualized lessons on a computer, are given immediate feedback on their answers, and are tested periodically so that progress can be monitored. Lessons may involve tutorials, drill and practice exercises, instructional games, or problem-solving exercises. Its use is limited mainly to jobs involving technical knowledge and skills, and it is relatively expensive.

Classroom instruction is the most frequently used training format in the public sector. Depending on the audience and training objectives, a variety of learning techniques may be used to supplement the standard lecture format, including simulations, group exercises, and audiovisuals. Instructor-led training is appropriate for a wide range of training needs. It is a relatively dynamic approach because an instructor is present to respond to the needs and interests of trainees. In addition, courses can be developed relatively quickly and delivered at moderate expense.

Effective classroom instruction requires creating and maintaining a positive learning environment. Setting the proper climate, according to Malcolm Knowles, is the single most crucial element in the entire training process:

> If the climate is not really conducive to learning, if it does not convey that an organization considers human beings its most valuable asset and their development its most productive investment, then all the other elements in the process are jeopardized. There is little likelihood of having a first-rate program of human resource development in an environment that is not supportive of learning.[21]

Knowles suggests that the physical surroundings be pleasing and comfortable and organized for active learning. Tables, for example, can be arranged in a U-shape configuration to allow formal face-to-face interaction. Knowles also emphasizes the importance of establishing a positive psychological environment characterized by collaborativeness (rather than competitiveness), supportiveness, mutual trust, active inquiry, and openness.

Finally, effective training delivery requires each agency to establish policies that distribute training opportunities broadly and fairly. Before such policies can be formulated, policy makers must address some difficult questions:

Will training opportunities be made available to all agency personnel, or only to targeted groups of employees?

How much money will be set aside for training purposes?

Will employees be compensated for tuition and travel costs?

Will employees be allowed time off with pay to attend training sessions?

Will employees be allowed to take advantage of out-of-house opportunities as well as in-house training programs?

Will training opportunities be treated as employee benefits to be distributed widely, or as training and development interventions to be authorized only after systematic needs assessment?

These questions are thornier than they first appear. For example, if past managers have distributed training opportunities as a reward for hard work by sending employees "to fun places," then employees may be slow to appreciate a new policy that distributes opportunities consistent with strategic training and development decisions. Similarly, if opportunities have been distributed on a "now-it's-your-turn" basis, then employees may resist policies that authorize training only after systematic needs assessment. Once established, the integrity of new policies must be carefully protected. Resentments arise quickly if managers are perceived as "playing favorites" in flagrant disregard of existing policies.

Evaluation of Training

The final component of a systematic training process is the evaluation of training efforts. The training and development literature is replete with references to the importance of this step. By evaluating training it is possible to determine whether training courses and programs are accomplishing their stated objectives. It can be determined, for example, whether performance deficiencies are being corrected, attitudes changed, or behaviors altered. Second, it allows the training and development staff to identify areas where particular courses, or the training program as a whole, may be strengthened. Third, it provides data for assessing the cost-effectiveness of the training program. For budgeting purposes, managers need to know whether they are getting their money's worth from investments in training.

Accomplishing these purposes is complicated by the fact that there are several kinds of evaluation available, many of them methodologically complex and expensive. Jack Phillips, building on a model originally proposed by Donald Kirkpatrick, identifies four distinct "levels" of evaluation. Each level requires a more complex methodology than the previous one:[22]

Level	Questions
Reaction	Were the learners pleased with the program?
Learning	What was learned from the program?
Behavior	Did the learners change their behaviors based on what was learned?
Results	Did the change in behavior positively affect the organization?

Most organizations do not evaluate beyond level 1. At the conclusion of a course, trainees are simply given a questionnaire (sometimes called a "smile sheet") asking them how satisfied they were with course content, instructor, and facilities. Although it is the most frequently used type of evaluation, it provides the least amount of useful information. It cannot be determined from the results, for example, whether learning took place or whether job performance will improve. Its advantage is that it is both easy and inexpensive to administer.

Organizations occasionally attempt to evaluate at level 2. This involves testing the knowledge of trainees before and after training to determine how well they have understood and absorbed the material. Increased knowledge and understanding, however, do not necessarily translate into improved work performance. Evaluation at level 3 requires the use of relatively complex methodologies to determine whether work performance has actually improved. This type of evaluation is problematic for at least two reasons. First, it is an expensive, labor-intensive task to evaluate changes in performance for even a small sample of those participating in a training program. It also requires experimental research designs in which training is delivered in an inflexible fashion so that all variables can be strictly controlled. Second, studies of this kind usually rely on the results of employee performance appraisals conducted before and after training. Most performance appraisal instruments simply are not sensitive enough to detect modest but meaningful changes in work performance.

Results of level 4 evaluation are potentially of great value to high-level administrators who wish to know whether their investment in training is paying dividends. Unfortunately, the methodological difficulties involved in conducting valid cost-benefit analyses are often insurmountable. Economic impacts are extremely hard to measure because it is difficult to control all the other variables that may be producing changes in behaviors or unit performance. In addition, many kinds of training aim at developing the abilities of employees over an extended period. Analysts cannot expect to determine the organization's return on investment immediately.

Because it is not always practical to use quantitative methods of evaluation, some training experts advocate the use of alternative methods.[23] Among them is Malcolm Knowles:

> Of all the aspects of adult learning, there is not one that causes more of a sense of inadequacy, guilt, and dissatisfaction than evaluation. We have been living for the last 40 years in a mythical world that has laid a burdensome load of unrealistic expectations on us—the world of quantitative measurement. The assumption that the significant effects of learning can be measured and reported quantitatively is simply not true.[24]

Knowles suggests that it is often more practical to use qualitative methods of evaluation, including participant observation, in-depth interviews, case studies, and personal journals. Similarly, A. C. Hamblin argues that the "right" approach in any given situation is the one which is most practically feasible and useful.[25] Hamblin advocates a "discovery" approach in which evaluation is continuous and intermingled with training. The purpose of this approach is to obtain useful feedback rather than to prove that learning objectives have been achieved.

Evaluation remains an important component of systematic training despite the methodological difficulties involved. Without evaluative data, managers cannot determine the relative effectiveness of various training options nor make informed human resource management decisions. For this reason, managers should obtain as much evaluative data as possible within the boundaries of what is methodologically sound and what they think they can afford.

Employee Development

Development programs expand the capabilities of employees so that they will be able to perform many organizational roles effectively. Unlike technical training, which can provide immediate pay-offs in terms of enhanced productivity, development programs represent long-term investments. They allow employees to grow and change with the organization to the benefit of both. Organizations obtain much-needed flexibility by developing a broad talent pool on which to draw, whereas employees benefit from personal growth, enhanced motivation, and career advancement. Several kinds of development programs are currently in use. Foremost among these are management development and individual career development programs.

Management Development Programs

Management development programs are designed to improve the current or future work performance of managers by developing the skills and abilities required to perform managerial duties effectively. Providing development opportunities to employees is important because it is neither practical nor desirable to recruit managers solely from outside the organization. Tapping the talents of current employees is the principal means by which organizations satisfy their management needs. It cannot be taken for granted, however, that employees with appropriate skills and abilities will always be available to fill vacant managerial positions. Individuals promoted on the basis of technical expertise are often totally unprepared for management responsibilities. In short, managerial skills and abilities are resources that must be carefully developed.

The need for management development programs is particularly acute in the public sector because merit systems tend to recruit and select white-collar professionals on the basis of technical expertise rather than aptitude for management. Professionals may be highly competent within their areas of expertise but lack the training and experience necessary for success in managerial roles. The Volcker Commission Report, for example, found this to be the case for many federal white-collar employees:

> *In any given year, roughly 60,000 to 70,000 white-collar employees join the federal civil service. What is most surprising, according to the Commission's Task Force on Education and Training, is how few of these employees had specific training to be government executives. Most were hired because of specific skills, not because they were generalist managers. Only 808, or 2.7 percent, of the new professional employees hired in 1987 had degrees in public administration or political science, while 23 percent had degrees in engineering and 24 percent in business and accounting.*[26]

The Volcker Commission concluded that many, if not most, of these employees will require training and development if they are to move successfully into management positions.

Employees experience different development needs as they advance through the management ranks. Those preparing for supervisory positions, for example, often require training in basic principles of supervision, including how to motivate, appraise, coach, discipline, schedule work, and maintain positive employee relations. Individuals preparing to move into mid-management positions, by contrast, often require training in planning, organizing, budgeting, team building, and problem solving. Finally, those entering the executive ranks may need development training in such areas as strategic planning, public relations, and legislative operations.

Employees typically gain access to management development opportunities in one of two ways. They can either request authorization from their supervisors to pursue opportunities that are consistent with their individual career plans or they are nominated by their superiors through a formal nominations process. Development opportunities may take a variety of forms, including in-house training courses, on-the-job mentoring, job rotation, workshops, institute-based seminars, and university-based degree programs. At the state level the central training and development office often delivers an integrated series of training courses for supervisors and managers. Some of these programs award employees a certificate on completion. At the federal level the larger agencies operate their own institutes for specialized management training. In addition, the Government Executive Institute provides training for SES executives, SES candidates, and senior managers from all government departments and agencies in the Washington area. Most offerings are short, intensive programs that can be fitted into busy schedules. They focus on subjects such as legislative operations, negotiating skills, and public policy briefings. SES members and senior managers can also attend a four-week residential program at the Federal Executive Institute in Charlottesville, Virginia.

Career Development Programs

Career development programs provide opportunities for personal growth to employees in general. They are founded on the twin beliefs that workers want to experience personal growth and that employers have an obligation to help them achieve their fullest potentials. According to Beverly L. Kaye, a carefully planned and thoughtfully implemented career development program can

> (1) help identify individual talents and desires and place employees in work situations that are personally meaningful because of relevance to those talents and desires, (2) assist employees to view the organization as one that respects their unique abilities and encourages their utilization and growth, (3) involve employees in communicating their needs and aspirations at all levels of the organization, and (4) enable individuals to continually develop their potential and to be challenged by future learning possibilities.[27]

In short, by developing its human resources, an organization can simultaneously establish a pool of capable workers to draw on and address some of the causes of turnover, low morale, and decreased productivity.

Career development may involve nothing more than an informal discussion between supervisor and employee about the latter's career goals and available opportunities for professional growth. Alternatively, formal programs can be established to encourage systematic self-development. Agency policies, for example, may require supervisors and employees to sit down at least once a year to draft a career development plan identifying learning objectives and the means for achieving them. They may also set target dates for accomplishing objectives and specify ways to measure progress toward them. A second type of program relies on career development workshops organized and delivered by the training and development staff. Employees are taught how to assess their own values and goals, and are informed about alternative career opportunities that the organization may have to offer. A third approach involves the use of self-paced, self-study workbooks to help employees explore personal values and career interests. Those who are reluctant to discuss personal goals in front of others tend to prefer the workbook over the workshop approach. Perhaps the most effective approach is to combine all three into a single, integrated program. Employees may, for example, attend workshops to learn of opportunities within the organization, work their way through self-diagnostic workbooks at their own pace, and sit down with their supervisors to discuss specific learning objectives. Another type of comprehensive program is offered by the U.S. General Accounting Office's Counseling and Career Development Branch.[28] Assistance is provided for both personal problems and performance or career-related matters. Services include orientation and developmental workshops, a career resource center, individual counseling with psychologists, and assistance to supervisors and managers in counseling employees regarding job performance and career development.

Career planning encourages employees to evaluate career opportunities and restraints realistically. Even when opportunities for upward advancement are limited, employees can still find satisfaction in their work through alternatives such as lateral moves, skill acquisition, and job enrichment. Because people are motivated differently, career planning must be done on an individual basis. Some employees aspire to perfect their abilities in their current jobs, others desire new experiences constantly, and still others demonstrate no interest in opportunities for development whatsoever. Most career development programs are also voluntary. This is because it is the employee who is ultimately responsible for assessing interests and abilities, gathering the information needed to set career goals, and communicating goals to supervisors.

Although not all employees need or desire developmental opportunities, some do. Professionals, for example, need to keep abreast of changes in their fields. A tuition assistance program may provide the incentive they need to develop their job-related skills and to return to work with renewed vigor and fresh ideas. Employees who find themselves "structurally plateaued" are also prime candidates for employee development. These are individuals who believe they should be moving upwards in the organization but find themselves with few possibilities for advancement.[29] Such individuals must be encouraged to pursue lateral moves rather than vertical advancement and greater depth and breadth of experience whether or not it leads to higher status and pay. A third category includes those who are "content plateaued." This occurs when the content of a job is mastered so well that there is no further challenge and employees feel stagnant and unmotivated as a result. Career development programs can help identify those who feel plateaued and offer them new challenges. For such individuals the opportunity for continuous learning may represent a form of empowerment and may be the key to maintaining their job satisfaction and productivity.

Career development programs are not without their critics. Development programs can be expensive and the return on investment difficult to assess. Training and development budgets can be quickly depleted if every employee wishes to take advantage of available opportunities. Managers in this situation find it necessary to screen all requests carefully and assess each of them in terms of expected payoffs. Sometimes they have to say no. This can be difficult when employees genuinely believe that a conference or workshop will be a wonderful learning experience. Such decisions become even more difficult when a manager is forced to choose between preparing individuals for anticipated promotions and facilitating personal growth. Faced with these difficulties some managers decide that they cannot support development opportunities that are not clearly linked to organizational advancement.

A second criticism is that career development programs create false expectations that organizations cannot hope to realize. Supervisors and managers often resist the concept of employee development, fearing that it will cause employees to believe they are more mobile in the organization than they actually are. False expectations need not develop, however, if aspirations are discussed openly and in the context of what is realistic.[30] Managers may also fear that it will cause them to lose their best employees, leaving them to continually train new staff members. To overcome resistance of this kind upper management may have to create incentives for mid-managers to view development as something that is good for the organization as a whole.

The Training Function and Organizational Development

Some training specialists favor shifting the focus of the training and development staff from individual training to organizational development (OD). Organizational development involves diagnosing systemwide problems, collecting information about them, planning the means for solving them (training may be one of many options), and evaluating the results.[31] OD interventions are often designed to restore organizations to health by creating a supportive organizational culture, positive interpersonal relations, and enhanced commitment and morale.

OD is seen by its advocates as a way of pursuing planned change. In their view, simply designing and delivering training courses based on real or imagined needs is not sufficient to ensure proper organizational functioning. Instead, the training and development staff must become a problem-solving staff adept at assessing problems and prescribing appropriate interventions, including training, discipline, job enrichment, job redesign, and new reward systems.

Most agencies could benefit from systematic analysis of performance problems and thoughtfully planned interventions. But it is far from clear that the training and development staff is capable of performing a problem-solving and consulting role. Such a shift in focus would take it well beyond its traditional role of providing technical training and facilitating employee development. An alternative might involve creating ad hoc teams of training specialists and managers to tackle identified performance problems.

The Promise and the Reality

The training and development literature promises many benefits to organizations willing to commit the necessary resources. Workers will be more productive, supervisors will learn how to motivate employees better, managers will use their tools with greater skill, and everyone will be united by a shared sense of purpose. The reality is somewhat different. Promises often remain unfulfilled for a variety of reasons. Among them are management's failure to accept responsibility for training, poor execution of training programs, lack of knowledge about the learning process, and inadequate budgets.[32]

But if the benefits to be derived from training are difficult to realize, the pursuit of those benefits is no less important. Organizational excellence is not achieved without sustained effort. It remains for management to develop better training policies, encourage greater use of needs assessment and on-the-job training, provide additional opportunities for professional development, lobby for larger training budgets, and forge the kind of line-staff partnership necessary for ensuring that all employees are fully trained and developed.

■ CASE 10.1　Who Failed Whom?

Tracy Armstrong was hired as an accountant to handle the contracts her state agency had with the federal government. Armstrong had worked for state government several years earlier, was familiar with computers, and was highly knowledgeable about accounting principles and procedures. However, she had very little knowledge of the state's new accounting system.

Armstrong's supervisor, Adam Cooper, oriented Armstrong to her job by sitting down at the computer and showing her the steps for accessing the applicable computer programs. He also gave her a list of the accounts and told her verbally what she would be responsible for. During her first two weeks on the job Armstrong received a total of four hours of training.

Because of the stress of his many duties, Cooper often worked with his door closed. He told Armstrong not to bother him when his door was closed. Armstrong took pride in her work and had always earned praise from her supervisors. She saw the new accounting system as a challenge but expected to master it successfully as she always had in the past. Because Cooper's door was often closed, she got into the habit of asking others in the office for help when she needed assistance with the new accounting system.

After six weeks Cooper issued Armstrong a verbal warning because her productivity was not what he expected. The warning surprised and upset Armstrong, but she resolved to try harder. She began coming to work earlier and she enrolled in a class at the local vocational technical school to learn more about the state accounting system, at her own expense.

A month later Cooper issued another reprimand, which was placed in Armstrong's personnel file. It almost seemed as if Cooper had already decided to fire her and was just building the necessary case against her. Armstrong nonetheless redoubled her efforts.

About halfway through Armstrong's six-month probationary period, Cooper took a three-week vacation. He left a list of tasks to complete during his absence. Armstrong completed everything except for two items that involved procedures she was unsure about. One in particular concerned a computer program she wasn't yet trained in, as it had been out of service her first two months of employment. Rather than risk a major mistake, Armstrong decided to wait to ask Cooper about the two items when he returned.

Cooper was not sympathetic when Armstrong explained why she had not completed the mandated tasks. He issued yet another written reprimand. With the necessary paper trail in place, Cooper informed Armstrong three weeks before her probationary period ended that she would not be hired permanently.

1. What human resource management issues are raised in this case?
2. To what might Armstrong's "failure" be attributed?
3. Was the outcome in this case inevitable? What might each have done differently so that an otherwise hard-working employee is not let go?

▲ EXERCISE 10.1 A Training and Development Tracking System

A study recently commissioned by the City Council turned up three startling facts:

1. Fully 78 percent of City employees strongly desire additional opportunities for skill development and professional growth;
2. 66 percent of city departments are underspending the training budgets allocated by the Council; and
3. 81 percent of managers had no clear understanding of the training needs and desires of their employees.

You constitute the three- to five-person committee appointed by the Mayor to outline the basic components of a new training policy and tracking system. Your goal is to create the means for ensuring that the City's human resources are trained and developed systematically. You decide to begin by discussing and recording answers to the following questions:

1. What should be the goal(s) of the new training policy and what issues should it address?
2. Who should be given responsibility for assessing the needs of employees for both technical training and employee development, and how will it be accomplished? (This is a city of 70,000 inhabitants with no training staff and a three-person personnel office).
3. Will you recommend a computer-based tracking system for ensuring that employees are receiving appropriate training and that funds are being spent in a cost-effective manner? If so, what information should be collected, how, and by whom? (The goal here is to obtain useful information without overburdening busy managers with paperwork).

Notes

1. Gene W. Childress and John A. Bugbee, "Kentucky's Across-the-Board Effort at Making HRD Work," *Public Personnel Management* 15 (Winter 1986):369–376.

2. Dennis I. Misler, "Management Development and More: Contracting Out Makes It Possible," *Public Personnel Management* 15 (Winter 1986):389–393.

3. Barbara Carpenter, "Being "Regional": A Key to Training Success," *Public Personnel Management* 15 (Winter 1986):383–388.

4. See, for example, Michael Stanton, "Workers Who Train Workers," *Occupational Outlook Quarterly* 33 (Winter 1989–90):2–11.

5. Norma M. Riccucci, "Apprenticeship Training in the Public Sector: Its Use and Operation for Meeting Skilled Craft Needs," *Public Personnel Management*, 20(Summer 1991):181–193.

6. W. Edwards Deming, *Out of the Crisis* (Cambridge: Massachusetts Institute of Technology, 1986).

7. Terry Newell, "The Future and Federal Training, *Public Personnel Management*, 17 (Fall 1988):261–271.

8. William B. Johnston, *Workforce 2000: Work and Workers for the 21st Century,* (Indianapolis: Hudson Institute, June 1987).

9. William B. Johnston and others, *Civil Service 2000* (Washington, D.C.: Office of Personnel Management, June 1988), 6–7.

10. Ibid., 32.

11. Daniel Yankelovich, *New Rules: Searching for Self-fulfillment in a World Turned Upside Down* (New York: Random House, 1981); Newell, "The Future and Federal Training"; Blue Woolridge and Jennifer Wester, "The Turbulent Environment of Public Personnel Administration: Responding to the Challenge of the Changing Workplace of the Twenty-first Century," *Public Personnel Management* 20 (Summer 1991):207–224.

12. Woolridge and Wester, "The Turbulent Environment of Public Personnel Administration."

13. Steven W. Hays and Richard C. Kearney, "State Personnel Directors and the Dilemmas of Workforce 2000: A Survey," *Public Administration Review* 52 (July/August 1992):380–388.

14. Edgar H. Schein, *Career Dynamics: Matching Individual and Organizational Needs* (Reading, MA: Addison-Wesley, 1978), 81–82.

15. Ibid., 82.

16. David Osborne and Ted Gaebler, *Reinventing Government: How the Entrepreneurial Spirit is Transforming the Public Sector* (Reading, MA: Addison-Wesley, 1992).

17. Analyses required for needs assessment are described in a classic work by William McGehee and Paul W. Thayer, *Training in Business and Industry* (New York: John Wiley & Sons, 1961).

18. Craig Eric Schneier, James P. Guthrie, and Judy D. Olian, "A Practical Approach to Conducting and Using the Training Needs Assessment," *Public Personnel Management* 17 (Summer 1988), 203.

19. See, for example, William J. Rothwell, "Curriculum Design in Training: An Overview," *Personnel Administrator* 28 (November 1983):53–57.

20. Malcolm S. Knowles, *The Adult Learner: A Neglected Species* (Houston: Gulf Publishing Co., 1978).

21. Malcolm S. Knowles, "Adult Learning: Theory and Practice," in Leonard Nadler, ed., *The Handbook of Human Resource Development* (New York: John Wiley & Sons, 1984), 6.17.

22. Jack J. Phillips, "Evaluation of HRD Programs: Quantitative," in Nadler, ed., *The Handbook of Human Resource Development*; Donald L. Kirkpatrick, "Evaluation of Training," in Robert L. Craig, ed., *Training and Development Handbook* (New York: McGraw-Hill, 1986), 18–2.

23. Knowles, "Adult Learning: Theory and Practice,"; George M. Alliger and Elizabeth A. Janak, "Kirkpatrick's Levels of Training Criteria: Thirty Years Later," *Personnel Psychology* 42 (Summer 1989):331–334; A. C. Hamblin, *Evaluation and Control of Training* (London: McGraw-Hill, 1974).

24. Knowles, "Adult Learning: Theory and Practice," 6.21.

25. Hamblin, *Evaluation and Control of Training.*

26. Volcker Commission Report, *Leadership in America: Rebuilding the Public Service* (Lexington, Massachusetts: D.C. Heath, Lexington Books, 1989), 42–43.

27. Beverly L. Kaye, *Up is Not the Only Way: A Guide to Career Development Practitioners* (Englewood Cliffs, New Jersey: Prentice-Hall, 1982), 5.

28. Kaye, *Up is Not the Only Way,* 47.

29. Zandy B. Leibowitz, Beverly L. Kaye, and Caela Farren, "What to Do About Career Gridlock," *Training and Development Journal* 44 (April 1990):29.

30. Barbara Moses, "Giving Employees a Future," *Training and Development Journal* 41 (December 1987):25.

31. Rothwell, "Curriculum Design in Training."

32. McGehee and Thayer, *Training in Business and Industry,* 19.

CHAPTER 11

Performance Appraisal and Counseling

Learning Objectives

After mastering the material contained in this chapter, you will be able to:

1. Identify four purposes of performance appraisal and explain how the design and operation of the appraisal process changes according to which purpose is emphasized.
2. Explain the obstacles that must be addressed in designing and conducting effective performance appraisals.
3. Describe the defining characteristics of ranking techniques, rating scales, management by objectives, and methods that use performance standards.
4. Design an effective performance appraisal system given a particular set of organizational goals and circumstances.
5. Conduct an appraisal interview that provides useful feedback without threatening the employee's self-esteem.

Performance appraisal is the process of communicating work expectations, evaluating employee performance, and encouraging performance improvements. If done with care it can provide a wide range of organizational benefits. Its results can be used to determine training needs, identify candidates for promotion, and allocate organizational rewards such as merit pay. The feedback given to employees can also improve motivation and productivity. In practice, however, appraisal systems are widely condemned despite their potential benefits. Employees, for example, often express doubts about their accuracy and supervisors view them as unpleasant and burdensome chores. Latham and Wexley suggest that they are a lot like seatbelts: "Most people believe they are necessary, but they don't like to use them."[1] Apparently performance appraisals rarely deliver in practice what they promise in theory. This is a paradox well worth exploring.

This chapter defines the purposes of performance appraisal, describes major types of appraisal methods, and identifies potential obstacles to their successful design and use. A central theme is that effective human resource management requires accurate assessment of work performance and feedback that encourages employee development as well as improved productivity.

Four Purposes of Performance Appraisal

Performance appraisal is a management tool that may be used to direct and control employee behavior, distribute organizational rewards, improve work performance, or develop employee capabilities. Its design and use vary according to which of these purposes it is intended to serve. Each of these purposes is described below.

Directing and Controlling Behavior

The measurement criteria and performance standards contained in appraisal systems direct the attention of employees to what is to be done and how. Because job retention, promotions, and pay bonuses often depend on performance ratings, appraisals can also be used to control employees. The implicit threat of withholding desired rewards, for example, can help ensure that employees are submissive to authority. Organizations using appraisals for this purpose are generally more concerned about securing compliance to organizational directives than encouraging creativity or improving work performance. They are not likely to burden supervisors with the task of coaching and counseling employees. Nor are they likely to involve employees in defining work standards or setting performance goals.

Validating Administrative Decisions

The most frequently cited reason for maintaining appraisal systems is to provide the data needed to make administrative decisions. To accomplish this purpose, supervisors are asked to compare employees with each other, either directly or indirectly, and to assign an overall performance score or ranking to each. Scores or rankings are then used to determine which employees are most deserving of promotion, transfer, financial bonuses, or discipline. No counseling sessions or employee participation are needed to achieve this purpose.

Improving Work Performance

Performance appraisals may also be used to improve each employee's work performance. This is accomplished by clarifying work expectations, identifying work deficiencies, and determining how to improve future performance. It may be determined, for example, that some employees need additional training and others lack the necessary motivation. In the latter instances, coaching and counseling, goal setting, and various rewards may be used to motivate employees and reinforce positive work behaviors.

Developing Employee Capabilities

The appraisal interview provides an opportunity to encourage employees to develop their capabilities. Creating a talent pool to draw on as circumstances change allows organizations to strengthen their capacity to adapt to future challenges. Intrinsic rewards derived from personal growth also enable organizations to motivate and retain their best workers. To achieve this purpose, employees are encouraged during the appraisal interview to obtain training and professional development beyond that which is needed to perform current job duties.

Most organizations do not attempt to achieve these purposes in equal measure. Some purposes are more important to them than others, and they will design and operate their appraisal systems accordingly. For example, organizations concerned primarily with performance improvement and employee development are less likely to compare employees with each other or to use appraisals as means of controlling employee behavior. Explicit comparisons between employees can lead to morale problems and an overemphasis on control can have demotivating effects. Both are inconsistent with a management philosophy based on developing and utilizing employee talents. Such organizations are more likely to coach and counsel employees individually without reference to the performance of others. In short, because the purposes described are partially incompatible, it is unrealistic (and probably undesirable) to expect a single performance appraisal instrument to accomplish all four purposes at once.

Obstacles to Effective Performance Appraisal

All too often performance appraisals fail to achieve their intended purposes and leave all parties disillusioned. The gulf between what appraisals promise and what they deliver is the result of several obstacles that undermine their effectiveness. These include lack of organizational commitment, inadequate appraisal instruments, rater biases, a natural distaste for judging and being judged, and the difficulty of defining meaningful measures of performance. These obstacles are so formidable, viewed as a whole, that a growing number of critics are questioning whether performance appraisals should be conducted at all.

As shown in Exhibit 11.1, obstacles to effective performance appraisal may arise from the rating instrument, rater judgment, or the appraisal process itself. Understanding these obstacles is important if they are to be addressed successfully. Each of them is discussed in turn below.

Inadequate or Inappropriate Rating Criteria

For best results performance appraisal instruments should contain appraisal criteria (e.g., typing speed) or performance standards (e.g., 60 words per minute) that are job related and explicitly defined. Supervisors require clear criteria on which to base judgment if they are to justify their ratings and any personnel actions taken on the basis of them. Similarly, subordinates cannot be held accountable for meeting performance expectations that they are not aware of. Finally, if organizational rewards are to have any motivational value, employees must be confident that they are distributed based on accurate assessments of their work performance. Too often, however, supervisors are asked to rate or rank subordinates without benefit of clearly stated appraisal criteria or performance standards, resulting in legitimate questions about the accuracy of ratings and the integrity of the process.

Even more troublesome is the difficulty involved in identifying meaningful measures of performance. Critics such as W. Edwards Deming advocate abandoning traditional performance appraisal systems for precisely this reason.[2] Deming's attack is aimed specifically at annual performance ratings in which the productivity of each employee is measured and financial rewards are distributed based on the results. The only verifiable measure of performance, according to Deming, is usually a short-term count of some kind, such as student test scores for measuring the productivity of teachers. Deming finds such measures inappropriate because work productivity is usually affected by factors beyond the control of the employee, including the efforts

---

EXHIBIT 11.1

OBSTACLES TO EFFECTIVE PERFORMANCE APPRAISAL

Rating Instrument	**Rater Judgment**	**Appraisal Process**
Absent or vague appraisal criteria or performance standards	Personal biases: • Favoring some employees over others • Prejudice related to race, gender, age, disability	Insufficient organizational commitment
Appraisal criteria or performance standards that are insufficiently job related	Judgment errors: • Contrast effects • First impression error • Halo effect • Similar-to-me effect • Central tendency error	Insufficient employee feedback The natural distaste for judging others
Use of inappropriate measures of performance	Deliberate manipulation of ratings	The natural distaste for being judged

---

of many other people and the system in which the employee works. The traditional performance review, according to Deming, only creates ill will, undermines teamwork, and distracts all concerned from the true causes of poor product or service quality: systemic flaws in the work process itself. Finally, it allows managers an all too easy way to abdicate their responsibility for the continuous management of human performance.

Rater Biases and Judgment Errors

Performance appraisal is inherently subjective. As a result, ratings are often influenced by factors other than the behaviors or achievements of those being rated. Such factors include personal biases, judgment errors, and intentional manipulations. Because they undermine the validity of the entire appraisal process, these factors represent serious obstacles to effective performance appraisal.

First, ratings may be influenced by the personal biases or prejudices of raters. They may be positively or negatively skewed, for example, according to how well the rater likes particular individuals. Similarly, ratings may be affected by personal prejudices related to race, gender, age, or disability. Although raters may not be conscious of their biases or intend to harm particular employees, the accuracy of performance ratings are undermined nonetheless.

Second, accuracy may be undermined by rating errors. These are errors in judgment that occur in a relatively systematic fashion during the appraisal process. Common rating errors include the following:[3]

Contrast Effects This refers to the tendency to rate employees relative to each other rather than to actual job requirements. A good performer, for example, may be given an "average" rating for no other reason than that he or she did not perform quite as well as someone else. Some organizations require supervisors to rate employees in a comparative fashion, but even in these instances a rating such as "average" should be determined in relation to how well a given individual has met performance standards.

First Impression Error This refers to the tendency to rate individuals based on first impressions and then to ignore or discount information that does not support those first impressions. An employee who fails to perform well when first hired, for example, may continue to receive poor ratings even after performance has improved.

Halo Effect This refers to the tendency to rate an individual consistently high or low across all performance dimensions based on only one aspect of job performance. A supervisor, for example, who is impressed with an individual's interpersonal skills in dealing with clients may generalize this favorable impression to other areas of the individual's work performance whether or not such generalizations are warranted.

Similar-to-Me Effect This refers to the tendency to judge persons more favorably who are perceived to be similar to one's self. The troubling implication of this is that raters may evaluate the same work behaviors differently depending on their own race, gender, educational background, or organizational roles.

Central Tendency Error This refers to the tendency to rate all individuals close to the midpoint of a scale regardless of their actual levels of performance. It occurs because raters are unable or unwilling to carefully differentiate between distinct levels of performance. Some supervisors, for example, give only average ratings because they believe there is always room for improvement, and others simply play it safe by refusing to label individuals as either superior or poor performers.

Rating errors occur for various reasons. One of the most fundamental reasons is insufficient information to evaluate job performance accurately. Many supervisors perform their job duties physically separated from their subordinates. As a result, they are not able to observe a representative sample of work behaviors. Similarly, the work of subordinates may be so highly specialized that supervisors are simply not qualified to assess the adequacy of their work.

Rating errors occur in any process involving human judgment. But although such errors can never be eliminated completely, steps can be taken to reduce the frequency of their occurrence. The use of precise measurement scales may help reduce errors by providing greater guidance to raters. Efforts to train raters to understand and avoid common errors may also help. Evidence suggests that simply making raters more knowledgeable about potential errors and warning them to avoid such errors does not prove effective. Latham and Wexley suggest using an intensive workshop approach in which participants observe rating errors being made on videotaped simulations, practice rating individuals shown on the videotapes, and are provided feedback about their ratings.[4] Because such training programs require considerable investments of time and money, some organizations prefer a strategy of increasing the number of individuals involved in the appraisal process. By combining the supervisor's ratings with peer ratings, for example, employees are given greater assurance that their ratings are not unduly affected by the biases or judgment errors of any one person.

Third, rating accuracy may be affected by deliberate efforts to manipulate the results. Some supervisors, despite being trained to avoid rating errors, feel justified in giving ratings that are higher or lower than employees deserve. Reasons for inflating evaluation scores include a desire to obtain merit increases for as many subordinates as possible, show empathy for someone whose work is suffering because of temporary personal problems, avoid confrontation with a difficult employee, and encourage a marginal employee whose performance seems to be improving.

Not all judgment errors can be eliminated from the appraisal process, and perhaps not all forms of conscious manipulation are equally undesirable. Each organization must take a realistic view, deciding which errors and biases are most destructive and taking necessary steps to contain them within acceptable boundaries.

Insufficient Organizational Commitment

Improving work performance and developing employee capabilities requires considerable time and effort and a genuine commitment by all concerned. Unfortunately, appraisal systems are often imposed by a central personnel office on reluctant managers without benefit of training and without building the necessary commitment. This encourages managers to think of performance appraisal as a peripheral duty—a burdensome chore to be gotten out of the way as quickly as possible—rather than an important management responsibility. Treated as a hollow formality, performance appraisal quickly becomes another example of the "triumph of technique over purpose." Ensuring that appraisals are treated as an important management responsibility is as difficult as it is necessary. To succeed in this regard top management must be clear about the goals of the appraisal system, must communicate them clearly and often, and must hold supervisors and managers accountable for achieving them. One way to accomplish this is to evaluate supervisors and managers on the basis of their commitment to the performance appraisal process and reward them accordingly. In addition, commitment from employees can be increased by involving them in designing and implementing the appraisal system. Finally, commitment can be increased by encouraging the personnel staff to act as facilitators and consultants rather than enforcers.

Insufficient Employee Feedback

Agencies concerned with securing minimally acceptable levels of performance from employees or in obtaining data on which to base administrative decisions need not be overly concerned with providing employee feedback. By contrast, agencies interested in developing their human resources and motivating employees to be more productive risk losing all of the benefits of an otherwise well-designed appraisal system by failing to discuss the results of appraisals with employees. According to Locke and Latham, goal setting and feedback are the primary elements of most theories of motivation.[5] This suggests that it is not enough to simply rate an employee on an appraisal form and forward it to the personnel office. An appraisal interview must also be scheduled so that the supervisor and employee can discuss performance-related strengths and weaknesses and set goals for improving performance. To provide meaningful feedback supervisors must develop effective coaching and counseling skills and commit considerable time and effort to the task. Their frequent failure to do so represents a major obstacle to effective performance appraisal.

A Natural Distaste for Judging and Being Judged

Even the best performance appraisal systems face a fundamental and intractable problem: how to overcome the natural reluctance of people to judge others and to be judged themselves. Douglas McGregor captured the essence of this dilemma in an article written in 1957:

> The conventional approach, unless handled with consummate skill and delicacy, constitutes something dangerously close to a violation of the integrity of the personality. Managers are uncomfortable when they are put in the position of "playing God." The respect we hold for the inherent value of the individual leaves us distressed when we must take responsibility for judging the personal worth of a fellow man. Yet the conventional approach to performance appraisal forces us, not only to make such judgments and to see them acted upon, but also to communicate them to those we have judged. Small wonder we resist![6]

McGregor argued that this dilemma is compounded by asking supervisors to coach and counsel their subordinates at the same time that they are asked to judge them. Successfully performing both roles (judge and coach/counselor) is difficult because the act of passing judgment is likely to threaten the self-esteem of employees, strain the supervisor's relationship with subordinates, and do more to inhibit motivation than to encourage it. This point is illustrated with humor in Exhibit 11.2. The story of the Company Man could just as easily be the story of the Agency Man.

To avoid asking supervisors to perform incompatible roles and to reduce the likelihood of damaging employee self-esteem, McGregor suggested substituting an employee-centered approach for the conventional top-down approach. Specifically, McGregor suggested giving employees primary responsibility for establishing performance goals and appraising progress toward them, focusing the appraisal interview on job performance rather than personality, and training supervisors to coach and counsel employees rather than to criticize or place blame. Although decisions must still be made regarding who should receive promotions or monetary bonuses, McGregor argued that appraisals can be conducted in more sensitive, less judgmental ways. Twenty-five years later W. Edwards Deming echoed McGregor's argument, stating that "A leader, instead of being a judge, will be a colleague, counseling and leading his people on a day-to-day basis, learning from them and with them."[7]

Performance Appraisal and EEO

Performance appraisals are subject to the EEOC's Uniform Selection Guidelines if ratings are used to make decisions affecting the employment status of employees (e.g., promotions, discharges, merit awards). Although it is relatively rare for courts to find against an employer because of the inadequacies of their appraisal systems, there are a few notable exceptions. A review of existing case law suggests that the reliability, validity, and legal defensibility of appraisals can be enhanced in the following ways.[8]

1. *Develop evaluative criteria through systematic job analysis.* The criteria on which employees are evaluated and the standards that define good and poor performance

---

EXHIBIT 11.2

THE COMPANY MAN

I work for a big company. I'm small. I'm much smaller than the company. My boss told me so himself. He said, "The company is much bigger than you."

I work out of a cell. The company calls it an office but to me it's a cell. . . .

The man who occupies the cell next to mine is small. The other day, he was smaller. He's a good company man. He uses words like "interface" and "input." But the other day he passed by my office in a daze, as if he had just been smashed by a demolition ball.

"That man," I said to myself, "just got reviewed."

Sure enough, he had.

He got a "fair" on appearance and cooperativeness, an "average" on initiative and productivity. "I didn't get one 'outstanding,'" he said.

He didn't show up the next day. I think he was home crying. I think he's destroyed.

Two days ago, I got reviewed.

"Let's interface," said my boss.

My boss is small, but I'm smaller. He's a good man, my boss. I'm also a good man.

"You're a good man," he said, and he put a check mark next to "good." Not "outstanding."

Well, I said to myself, so I'm not an "outstanding" man. Who is? But I'm punctual.

"Yes, you are," my boss said, and he checked off "above-average" for "punctuality."

But do I comb my hair nicely, wear trim, dark suits, my tie in a corporate knot?

"I don't know," said my boss, mulling me over. "Your hair is kind of long. Your shoes could use a shine."

---

should be determined by using proven techniques of job analysis. Developing the performance appraisal instrument from systematic job analysis strengthens an employer's case in the event of a lawsuit. The Supreme Court ruled in *Albemarle Paper Company v. Moody* that because the company had made no attempt to analyze each job and determine what constituted good and poor performance, it could not validate the use of its highly subjective rating standards. In fact, the Court concluded, "There is no way of knowing precisely what criteria of job performance the supervisors were considering, whether each of the supervisors were considering the same criteria or whether, indeed, any of the supervisors actually applied a focused and stable body of criteria of any kind."[9]

2. *Use outcome or behavioral measures.* Appraisal systems are more easily defended if they focus on outcome measures (e.g., the number of applications processed) or work behaviors (e.g., typing manuscripts without errors), rather than personal traits (e.g., loyalty, dependability). Courts have found trait-based criteria to be too subjective and therefore open to misinterpretation and manipulation. For example, a federal district court ruled in *Wade v. Mississippi Cooperation Extension Service* that,

> *a substantial portion of the evaluation rating relates to such general characteristics as leadership, public acceptance, attitude toward people, appearance and*

EXHIBIT 11.2 *(continued)*

I got an "average" for "appearance." That didn't hurt because back in the days when I was a rugged individualist I used to be downright "slovenly," I prided myself in being a "slob" and in slurring my words like Marlon Brando.

"You know," my boss said, "you slur your words like Marlon Brando."

So I got a "poor" for "speech."

All right, but despite these drawbacks, these flaws of character, I do "get along with people."

"You don't 'get along with people,' do you?" my boss said.

That was a slap in the face.

"Who don't I get along with?" I asked.

"You're a loner."

I am? Yes, I am. I got a "poor" in "cooperativeness."

It was downhill from there. I didn't get one "outstanding." Not for "initiative." Not for "creativity." Not for "productivity." Funny, I used to think I was creative and productive. I even used to think of myself as cooperative and attractive. All I am, it turns out, is "punctual."

I didn't show up for work today. I'm home. Should I go on living? My wife says yes. She thinks I'm at least average. She thinks I ought to go back to work and tell him off, my boss. I can't do that, of course—and that's no way to get even. What I can do tomorrow is review my secretary. I'm small, but I'm bigger than she is.

Source: Jack Engelhard, "The Company Man," *New York Times*, February 6, 1982, p. 23. Copyright © 1982 by the New York Times Company. Reprinted by permission.

grooming, personal conduct, outlook on life, ethical habits, resourcefulness, capacity for growth, mental alertness, and loyalty to organization. As may be readily observed, these are traits that are susceptible to partiality and to the personal taste, whim, or fancy of the evaluator. We must thus view these factors as presently utilized to be patently subjective in form and obviously susceptible to completely subjective treatment.[10]

3. *Communicate performance standards to employees.* A few courts have ruled that it is unreasonable to hold employees accountable for meeting standards of performance that they are not aware of. In *Rowe v. General Motors Corporation,* for example, the Court chastised the employer for not making promotion criteria known to employees.[11] In *Zell v. U.S.,* by contrast, the federal government was upheld when it could demonstrate that promotion criteria were job related, Zell was aware of the criteria, and her scores were considerably lower than her promoted colleagues.[12]

4. *Provide supervisors with adequate training.* A few courts have ruled that to ensure the accuracy of ratings supervisors should be trained in the use of the rating instrument and how to apply performance standards. In *Rowe,* for example, the court criticized the employer for not providing adequate training.

In short, in the relatively few instances in which courts have scrutinized the technical aspects of appraisal systems they have indicated that appraisals should be based on systematic job analysis, be standardized in format, and be as fair and objective as possible. For the most part they have simply insisted that well-established principles of human resource management be observed in practice.

Appraisal Criteria and Performance Standards

Appraisal criteria are work-related dimensions on which job performance is evaluated (e.g., typing skills). Performance standards, by contrast, are measurable levels of performance that job incumbents are expected to achieve (e.g., 60 words per minute). Appraisal criteria are standard features of appraisal systems, whereas performance standards are used only when an organization wishes to assess the results or outcomes of work performance. Specifying appropriate criteria and performance standards is the most difficult aspect of developing an effective appraisal system. What is involved in this task thus deserves a brief review.

Three Types of Appraisal Criteria

Appraisal systems may evaluate personal traits, employee behaviors, or work results. Schneier, Beatty, and Baird suggest that if what people ARE at work counts, appraise personal characteristics (traits); if what people DO at work counts, appraise employee behaviors; and if what people ACHIEVE at work counts, appraise results.[13] Examples of these three types of appraisal criteria are provided in Exhibit 11.3.

Trait-Based Systems Traits are personal characteristics assumed to contribute to effective job performance. Trait-based criteria require virtually no time and expense to develop, and because they are assumed to be applicable to most jobs in the organization, a single appraisal form can be used to evaluate nearly all employees. As noted earlier in this chapter, however, the courts have found trait-based criteria to be

---

EXHIBIT 11.3

EXAMPLES OF THREE TYPES OF APPRAISAL CRITERIA

Trait-Based	Behavior-Based	Results-Based
Dependability	Submits reports on time	Number of clients served
Leadership	Provides sufficient on-the-job training to ensure efficient use of equipment and materials	Number of applications processed
Cooperativeness		
Initiative		Number of projects completed
Loyalty	Keeps informed regarding changes in EEO law	Number of days without an accident
	Praises employees for things they do well	Amount of money saved

highly subjective. Because they are seldom derived from systematic job analysis, their use is difficult to defend in court. Another problem is that trait-based criteria provide very little feedback to employees. For example, telling employees to be "dependable" may be good advice but communicates very little about what they should be doing and how. Finally, the accuracy of ratings is undermined because criteria such as "dependability" provide little guidance to the rater regarding how they are to be defined.

Behavior-Based Criteria   These criteria focus more directly on what workers actually do and are therefore more readily observable than traits. It is difficult to know, for example, when "dependability" is observed, but much less difficult to know when an employee "submits reports on time." This improves the accuracy of ratings and puts employers in a better position to defend their appraisal systems in court. Feedback is facilitated because behavioral criteria provide employees with a clearer understanding of what they must do differently to improve future ratings. Finally, because behavioral criteria are often relevant to a variety of jobs, a different set of criteria may not have to be developed for each job individually.

Results-Based Criteria   One disadvantage of behavior-based criteria is that they do not focus on what employees actually accomplish. From a managerial perspective, it is not sufficient for employees to exhibit desired behaviors if they never seem to accomplish anything. Results-based criteria send a clear message to employees that the organization is interested in achieving results. An additional advantage is that results are easier to measure in quantitative terms than are behaviors. For this reason they are sometimes referred to as "hard" or "objective" measures. This does not mean that they are necessarily more accurate indicators of performance. Results, for example, are often determined by factors beyond an employee's control. The use of results-based criteria may also skew assessments toward those tangible work outcomes that are easily measured and away from qualitative and process-related aspects of performance. The number of clients served, for example, may be an important aspect of performance, but so too is how well they have been served. Finally, emphasis on results may foster a harmful level of competitiveness among employees and a results-at-any-cost mentality. It is concerns such as these that led W. Edwards Deming to advocate abandoning the use of appraisal systems of this kind.

Exhibit 11.4 provides a summary of how well each type of appraisal format achieves the objectives of performance appraisal. Although formats using behavioral criteria appear to be superior in most regards, the final choice depends on the priorities established among organizational purposes and the nature of work to be appraised. The best strategy may be to incorporate both behavior- and results-based criteria into the organization's appraisal instrument as individual situations warrant. In this way organizations may obtain the advantages of both appraisal formats while avoiding the disadvantages that arise when either is used alone.

Developing Appraisal Criteria

Perhaps the most troublesome task in developing a performance appraisal instrument is the identification of appropriate appraisal criteria for specific jobs. It may be accomplished either through a task-oriented approach that derives appraisal criteria

EXHIBIT 11.4

A GENERAL EVALUATION OF THREE APPRAISAL FORMATS BASED ON THEIR ABILITY TO ACHIEVE SPECIFIED OBJECTIVES

Objective / Format	Feedback/ Development	Assessing Training Needs	Identification of Promotion Potential	Reward Allocation	Measurement Accuracy
Trait-based	Poor	Poor	Poor to fair	Poor to fair	Poor to fair
Behavior-based (if behaviorally-anchored)	Very good to excellent	Very good	Very good	Very good	Good
Effectiveness- or results-based	Fair to good	Fair to good	Fair to good	Very good to excellent	Very good to excellent

Source: Adapted version of Figure 3 from Craig Eric Schneier and Richard W. Beatty, "Integrating Behaviorally-based and Effectiveness-based Methods," *Personnel Administrator* 24 (July 1979): 68. Reprinted with the permission of HRMagazine (formerly Personnel Administrator) published by the Society for Human Resource Management, Alexandria, VA.

from knowledge of job tasks or a worker-oriented approach that derives appraisal criteria from knowledge of the behaviors that contribute to effective job performance.

The Task-Oriented Approach The first step in this approach is to develop a comprehensive list of job tasks. A shorter list is then developed containing only those tasks deemed important enough to include on the appraisal instrument. This is typically accomplished by questioning job experts (e.g., incumbents and supervisors) about the frequency with which tasks are performed and the consequences of error associated with each. At this point organizations may choose to implement an unsophisticated method of performance appraisal in which supervisors are given the list of job tasks and are asked to rate incumbents on how well each task is performed. More sophisticated methods require job experts to identify desired work behaviors or performance standards against which to appraise employees. The major methodological weakness of the task-oriented approach is that deriving appraisal criteria from a list of tasks involves inferential leaps that may be difficult to defend.

The Worker-Oriented Approach In this approach appraisal criteria are derived from behaviors that contribute to effective job performance. These behaviors are identified using the critical incident technique described in Chapter 5. Similar behaviors may be combined, for example, under a performance dimension labeled "motivation," as shown below:

PERFORMANCE DIMENSION: MOTIVATION

Effective Behaviors:
1. Employee assists co-workers with their assignments after his or her own job responsibilities are met.
2.
3.

Ineffective Behaviors:
1. Employee criticizes co-workers who work more rapidly than others.
2.
3.

Once identified, appropriate behaviors can be selected for use as appraisal criteria and measurement scales can be constructed around them.

Performance Appraisal Methods

The development process does not end with the identification of appraisal criteria. They must be incorporated into some kind of appraisal method. Although countless varieties of appraisal methods exist, most fall into one of the following categories: rating scales, ranking techniques, management by objectives (MBO), and methods that use performance standards. The method or methods selected depend on the purposes to be achieved and the type of appraisal criteria chosen for use. It may also depend on the nature of the work being performed. An MBO method may be used, for example, to evaluate managers, and a behaviorally based rating scale may be used to evaluate employees below the managerial level.

Rating Scales

All rating scales require raters to evaluate employee performance along a continuum that is anchored by numbers (e.g., 1 through 6) or adjectives (e.g., excellent to unacceptable). One or more scales are developed for each appraisal criterion and raters are asked to mark the point on each scale that best indicates the level of performance attained by job incumbents. Points on the scale are often given numerical values so that scores can be added together to determine which employees are most deserving of organizational rewards.

Trait-Based Scales   These scales are constructed around traits such as loyalty, dependability, and cooperation. Examples of trait-based scales are shown in Exhibit 11.5. A series of scales can be arranged on an evaluation form and used for evaluating all or most employees. Because they are simple and inexpensive to develop and easy to use, these scales have been the method of choice among both public and private employers. Their popularity has declined in recent years, however, because the courts have found them to be highly subjective and not sufficiently job related. Note, for example, that only the fifth scale shown in Exhibit 11.5 attempts to explain what is meant by the term *cooperation*. With certain modifications, some of the shortcomings of trait-based scales can be overcome. For example, traits can be defined in behavioral terms and raters can be asked to indicate whether a particular trait is relevant to the duties performed by each employee.

Behaviorally Anchored Rating Scales (BARS) BARS are rating scales anchored with specific behaviors that characterize effective and ineffective levels of performance. Appraisal criteria may be stated as knowledges, skills, abilities, job duties, or personal characteristics. The behavioral anchors are developed by using the critical incident technique. As shown in Exhibit 11.6, behavioral anchors are usually arranged

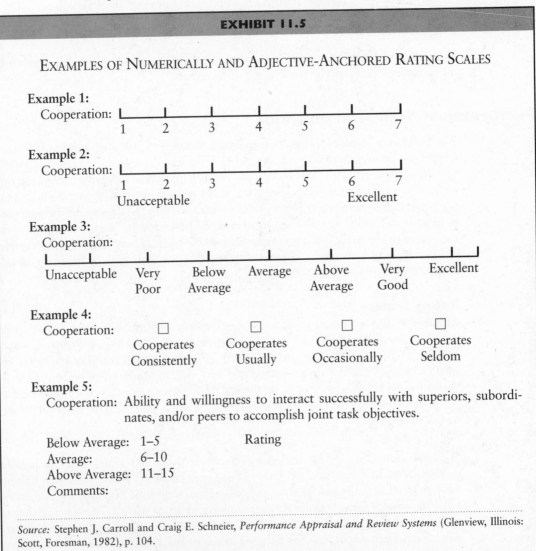

EXHIBIT 11.5

EXAMPLES OF NUMERICALLY AND ADJECTIVE-ANCHORED RATING SCALES

Example 1:
Cooperation:
    1   2   3   4   5   6   7

Example 2:
Cooperation:
    1   2   3   4   5   6   7
    Unacceptable   Excellent

Example 3:
Cooperation:

| Unacceptable | Very Poor | Below Average | Average | Above Average | Very Good | Excellent |

Example 4:
Cooperation:

☐ Cooperates Consistently   ☐ Cooperates Usually   ☐ Cooperates Occasionally   ☐ Cooperates Seldom

Example 5:
Cooperation: Ability and willingness to interact successfully with superiors, subordinates, and/or peers to accomplish joint task objectives.

Below Average: 1–5   Rating
Average: 6–10
Above Average: 11–15
Comments:

Source: Stephen J. Carroll and Craig E. Schneier, *Performance Appraisal and Review Systems* (Glenview, Illinois: Scott, Foresman, 1982), p. 104.

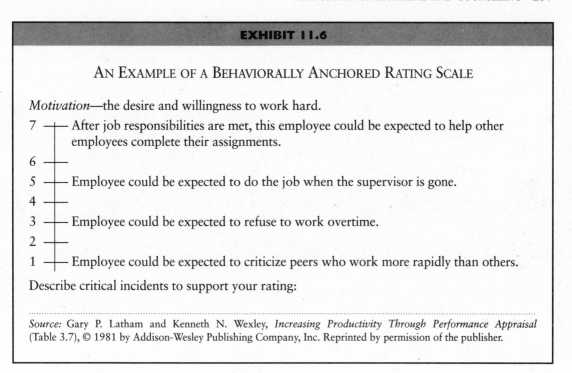

EXHIBIT 11.6

An Example of a Behaviorally Anchored Rating Scale

Motivation—the desire and willingness to work hard.

7 —— After job responsibilities are met, this employee could be expected to help other
employees complete their assignments.

6 ——

5 —— Employee could be expected to do the job when the supervisor is gone.

4 ——

3 —— Employee could be expected to refuse to work overtime.

2 ——

1 —— Employee could be expected to criticize peers who work more rapidly than others.

Describe critical incidents to support your rating:

Source: Gary P. Latham and Kenneth N. Wexley, *Increasing Productivity Through Performance Appraisal* (Table 3.7), © 1981 by Addison-Wesley Publishing Company, Inc. Reprinted by permission of the publisher.

vertically, with each one representing a higher level of job performance. At appraisal time the rater simply selects the descriptive statement on each scale that best characterizes the worker's level of performance.

A key advantage of the BARS method is that it removes the necessity of making inferences about an employee's knowledge, skills, and abilities by focusing the rater's attention on representative behaviors that are readily observable. In addition, because scales are developed for each major job category after systematic job analysis, the job relatedness of this method is easily defended in court. Yet another advantage is that the descriptive anchors communicate to employees in a relatively precise way what behaviors are expected of them and what is required to receive good ratings.

The BARS method has disadvantages as well. First, because the points along the scale are not always mutually exclusive, raters may be uncertain about which point to select. More than one of the anchors, or possibly none of them, may seem to describe a particular employee. Second, because of the complexity involved in defining the behavioral anchors and the necessity of developing separate scales for each major job category, the BARS method requires large investments of time and money. Jacobs, Kafry and Zedeck reviewed several studies involving the use of BARS and found no evidence that the potential gains in reliability warrant the additional costs.[14] Finally, as with other behavior-based methods, there may exist important job dimensions, such as analytical abilities, that cannot be reduced to observable behaviors.

Behavioral Observation Scales (BOS) Behavioral observation scales are also developed using the critical incident technique. Similar critical incidents are combined into a single "behavioral item," such as "praises and rewards subordinates." As shown in Exhibit 11.7, a Likert scale is then constructed for each behavioral item and raters are asked to indicate how often each employee engages in the desired behaviors. During the development process, job incumbents review the scales to ensure that all critical behaviors are represented and that the items are written unambiguously.

Behavioral Observation Scales possess all of the advantages of BARS, including involvement of employees in the development process, job relatedness, and the ability to provide information useful for identifying training needs, making administrative decisions, and facilitating employee development. In addition, BOS offer certain advantages over BARS. BOS state desired work expectations in a clearer, more straightforward fashion. In addition, once behavioral items are identified, there is no need to develop complex scales such as those used in the BARS method. Likert scales are easy to develop and use. Behavioral observation scales are not, however, without disadvan-

---

EXHIBIT 11.7

EXAMPLES OF BEHAVIORAL OBSERVATION SCALES (BOS)

Appraisal Criterion: Interaction with subordinates

1. Treats all employees in a fair, consistent, uniform manner.
   Almost Never   1   2   3   4   5   Almost Always

2. Asks subordinates to do things rather than ordering them.
   Almost Never   1   2   3   4   5   Almost Always

3. Avoids responding with hostility or defensiveness
   when interacting with subordinates.
   Almost Never   1   2   3   4   5   Almost Always

4. Praises employees for things they do well.
   Almost Never   1   2   3   4   5   Almost Always

5. Explains the rationale behind rules and regulations.
   Almost Never   1   2   3   4   5   Almost Always

6. Stresses the importance of safety to subordinates.
   Almost Never   1   2   3   4   5   Almost Always

7. Clearly describes changes in policy or procedures to subordinates.
   Almost Never   1   2   3   4   5   Almost Always

8. Encourages subordinates to assist in problem solving.
   Almost Never   1   2   3   4   5   Almost Always

9. Asks employees if they need help in developing their skills and abilities.
   Almost Never   1   2   3   4   5   Almost Always

10. . . . .

Source: Gary P. Latham and Kenneth N. Wexley, *Increasing Productivity Through Performance Appraisal,* (pp. 227–231), © 1981 by Addison-Wesley Publishing Company, Inc. Reprinted by permission of the publisher.

tages. Perhaps the most significant disadvantage is that they only measure the frequency of desired behaviors. They do not provide additional information about the quality of an employee's work performance or indicate how often the particular behavior *should* be exhibited.

Ranking Techniques

Ranking techniques ask raters to compare the performance of job incumbents with that of other employees in the same or similar jobs. Supervisors may be asked, for example, to rank subordinates from best to worse in terms of overall performance. Rankings are used primarily to make administrative decisions regarding promotions, monetary bonuses, and the distribution of other organizational rewards. Because the accuracy of ratings may be threatened by personal biases and the inherent difficulty of combining rankings made by different supervisors, Graves suggests using a scaled comparison method. This involves ranking individuals two at a time on each performance dimension according to the degree of difference in their levels of performance.[15] Multiple comparisons for all relevant employees can then be fed into a computer and an overall ranking generated.

One disadvantage of ranking techniques is that they only provide feedback to employees regarding their relative standings in the work unit. This is not the kind of feedback needed to develop employee capabilities or improve work performance. Making direct comparisons among employees may also discourage teamwork and undermine employee self-esteem. Although advocates insist that comparisons are needed to make administrative decisions, opponents argue that such decisions can be made without direct comparisons.

Management By Objectives (MBO)

MBO focuses on work outcomes. It is used to measure and reward employee achievements rather than desired traits or behaviors. As defined by Peter Drucker in the early 1950s, MBO is a comprehensive planning process in which top administrators formulate organizational goals, organizational units establish performance goals and objectives consistent with them, and each individual establishes performance goals and objectives consistent with those of the unit and the organization as a whole. This "cascading of goals" focuses the attention of all units and individuals on achieving desired results in an integrated fashion.

Today the term management by objectives is often used in a more limited sense to refer to performance appraisal systems in which employees set work-related objectives and are evaluated according to their degree of success. Of the steps shown in Exhibit 11.8, most attention is usually given to steps 3 through 9. Objectives are set jointly by the supervisor and subordinate, and the subordinate takes primary responsibility for developing an action plan for accomplishing the agreed-on objectives. Accomplishments are reviewed at the end of the appraisal period and new objectives are established. A goal is something the employee wishes to accomplish in the job and is stated in general terms. An objective, by contrast, is a specific action that must be accomplished to reach a goal and is stated in measurable terms, such as improving response time by 20 percent over the next six months. Routine objectives deal with basic responsibilities. They may include, for example, reducing error rates or increasing response times. Problem-solving objectives focus on solving particular difficulties in

---

EXHIBIT 11.8

The Management by Objectives Process

Steps

1. Analyze environment.
↓
2. Set organizational goals.
↓
3. Set goals for individuals and groups derived from organizational goals.
↓
4. Develop action plans for each goal.
↓
5. Determine performance indicators to use in evaluating goal progress and accomplishment.
↓
6. Periodically review goal progress.
↓
7. Conduct final review of goal accomplishment at end of time period.
↓
8. Establish self-improvement objectives for next period based on any deficiencies identified in goal accomplishment in previous period.
↓
9. Establish performance objectives for the next period.

Source: Stephen J. Carroll and Craig E. Schneier, *Performance Appraisal and Review Systems* (Glenview, Illinois: Scott, Foresman, 1982), 140.

---

the job or unit. Finally, self-improvement objectives focus on overcoming knowledge or skill deficiencies that adversely affect an employee's current job performance or ability to advance within the organization.

The high degree of supervisor-employee interaction helps improve communications and clarify work expectations. In addition, the goal-setting features characteristic of these methods can facilitate increased motivation. Research evidence suggests that setting specific, challenging goals, for example, can improve the level of employee performance significantly. But MBO methods have disadvantages as well. First, the MBO process can involve considerable time and paperwork. Second, the use of output measures can cause employees to respond in undesired ways. Employees, for example, may pay too little attention to the quality of their work, use questionable methods to achieve their goals, or become overly competitive at the expense of collegiality. Finally, it is difficult to compare employees for purposes of making administrative decisions because goals may vary greatly in their degree of difficulty, and their attainment may be affected by situational factors beyond the employee's control. Despite these limitations, MBO remains a popular means of appraising managerial personnel.

Methods That Use Performance Standards

Another approach to measuring work outcomes is to design the evaluation instrument around performance standards. These are defined levels of performance that job incumbents are expected to achieve. An important characteristic of performance standards is that they are stated in ways that are easily measured, such as typing 60 words per minute, or answering the phone by the third ring. Their use is premised on the belief that employees can be held accountable for the quantity and quality of their work only if management specifies desired levels of performance, appraises work performance against these standards, and distributes organizational rewards and sanctions according to how well they are met. Consistent with this premise, the 1978 Civil Service Reform Act mandated performance-based appraisal systems for federal employees. Many state and local governments followed the federal government's example. Thus, although no states used performance-based methods in 1975, 40 percent were using them by 1982.[16]

The appraisal form is developed by identifying key duties and responsibilities and two to five performance standards for each. Supervisors normally draft tentative standards and finalize them through discussions with job incumbents. An agency may develop separate standards for each position or one set of standards for a class of similar jobs. Once the form is developed, supervisors evaluate employees periodically and discuss the ratings during the appraisal interview. Exhibit 11.9 provides an example.

Appraisal systems that evaluate employees on the basis of performance standards share many of the advantages and disadvantages of other results-oriented methods. Performance standards communicate work expectations very clearly and provide a means of holding employees accountable. However, defining meaningful standards for work outputs in the public sector can be difficult. As a result, standards may focus on those aspects of performance that are easily measured at the expense of those that are not. Finally, such methods may have little motivational value unless they are used in conjunction with goal-setting and reward systems that encourage performance above the standard.

Who Should Conduct the Appraisal

Analysis to this point has assumed that appraisals are conducted by supervisors because this is the practice in most organizations. Other options, however, are worth exploring. The evaluator should be knowledgeable about the job's objectives, able to observe the employee performing the job frequently, and capable of determining whether work performance is satisfactory. Because supervisors often cannot satisfy these conditions, others may have to be involved in the appraisal process to ensure the validity of the results.

Supervisors remain a logical choice for conducting appraisals because they are responsible for developing employees and distributing rewards and sanctions. As supervisors they will know much about job requirements and employee performance. Nonetheless, their knowledge may be incomplete and personal biases or judgment errors can affect the ratings of particular employees. Some organizations have experimented with self-appraisals as an alternative. They provide important information to supervisors regarding how employees view their performance and they encourage employees to think about their strengths and to set goals for future improvement.

EXHIBIT 11.9

AN APPRAISAL FORM USING PERFORMANCE STANDARDS

Name: Jordan Smith	Class Title: Secretary 1	Outstanding	Above Standard	Standard	Needs Improvement	Unacceptable	Date: September 23, 1994
Duties/Responsibilities	Performance Standards						Comments
1. Composes responses to routine requests from correspondence to answer basic informational or procedural questions.	a) Responses are mailed within 2 days of receipt of inquiry.						Response time has been less than 2 days.
	b) Information provided is responsive to inquiry, clearly stated, and consistent with agency rules and procedures in 9 out of 10 responses.						Majority of responses are accurate; approximately 1 in 10 have indicated a lack of understanding of the inquiry.

The primary disadvantage is that the agreement between self-appraisals and supervisory appraisals is often low. Some studies have found self-appraisals to exceed those given by supervisors, and others have found self-appraisals to be lower.[17] One solution is to combine supervisory and self-appraisal ratings by having each complete a standardized appraisal form independently. If they cannot reach agreement during the appraisal interview, their differences can simply be stated as such in the evaluation report.

A second alternative is peer appraisal. Peer ratings have been shown to produce much higher levels of reliability than either supervisory or self-appraisals. This occurs because the average of several ratings is usually more reliable than a single rating and because of the greater knowledge of job performance that comes with the constant interaction among peers. For ratings to be reliable, however, peers must work closely together performing similar kinds of work. In addition, steps must be taken to overcome the natural reluctance of employees to judge each other. Employees may think it is a form of snitching or worry that they will cause harm to their colleagues. These concerns can be alleviated by having peers complete the appraisal document anonymously and instructing supervisors to use the results only for purposes of counseling and development. Supervisors can then encourage employees to discuss ratings without putting them in a position of having to defend them.

Yet another alternative is to use multiple sources of appraisal information. This increases the probability of obtaining a comprehensive and reliable view of each employee's contribution to the organization. The disadvantage is that using a combination of supervisory, self-, and peer appraisals increases the complexity of the process, and the expected gains may not outweigh the added costs as a result. Ultimately, decisions regarding who should conduct appraisals must be made on the basis of organizational goals and resources, the organization's human resource management philosophy, the degree of interaction and trust among particular groups of employees, and the nature of the work.

Conducting the Appraisal Interview

The appraisal interview is a discussion between a supervisor and subordinate about the latter's performance and the steps that can be taken to correct work deficiencies and facilitate further growth and development. For the organization that places a high value on the latter, the appraisal interview and how it is conducted is far more important strategically than the choice of the appraisal method. Essential prerequisites for performance improvement and employee development include feedback, goal setting, and positive reinforcement. It is only at the interview stage of the appraisal process that these prerequisites can be satisfied.

The Role of the Supervisor
The effectiveness of feedback, goal setting, and positive reinforcement depends on the manner in which the interview is conducted. Too little time and effort is typically given to the interview process because organizations tend to underestimate its importance and supervisors often dread face-to-face encounters. Lacking confidence in their interpersonal skills or simply wishing to avoid conflict, supervisors often treat the interview superficially or fail to conduct it altogether.

Despite the inherent difficulties, steps can be taken to ensure that this important part of the appraisal process achieves its intended purposes. The first step is to define a role for the supervisor that is least likely to evoke hostile and defensive reactions from those being appraised. Studies have shown that employee reactions during interviews become increasingly negative as the amount of unfavorable evaluation increases.[18] Studies have also found that status differences between supervisors and subordinates can be significant barriers to open and honest communication. The role of the supervisor in the interview process must be defined with these realities in mind.

According to Maier's classic formulation, there are three basic approaches to conducting the appraisal interview.[19] As shown in Exhibit 11.10, two of these place the supervisor in the role of judge and the third emphasizes the role of helper. In the Tell and Sell Approach the supervisor explains how well the employee has performed, tries to convince the employee that the ratings are an accurate reflection of performance, and attempts to get the employee to agree to a plan for improving performance. Because of its emphasis on one-way communication, this approach is most compatible with an authoritarian style of management. The Tell and Listen Approach encourages

EXHIBIT 11.10

THREE TYPES OF APPRAISAL INTERVIEWS

Method	Tell and Sell	Tell and Listen	Problem Solving
Role of Interviewer	Judge	Judge	Helper
Objective	To communicate evaluation To persuade employee to improve	To communicate evaluation To release defensive feelings	To stimulate growth and development in employee
Assumptions	Employee desires to correct weaknesses if he knows them Any person can improve if he so chooses A superior is qualified to evaluate a subordinate	People will change if defensive feelings are removed	Growth can occur without correcting faults Discussing job problems leads to improved performance
Reactions	Defensive behavior suppressed Attempts to cover hostility	Defensive behavior expressed Employee feels accepted	Problem-solving behavior
Skills	Salesmanship Patience	Listening and reflecting feelings Summarizing	Listening and reflecting feelings Reflecting ideas Using exploratory questions Summarizing
Attitude	People profit from criticism and appreciate help	One can respect the feelings of others if one understands them	Discussion develops new ideas and mutual interests
Motivation	Use of positive or negative incentives or both (Extrinsic in that motivation is added to the job itself)	Resistance to change reduced Positive incentive (Extrinsic and some intrinsic motivation	Increased freedom Increased responsibility (Intrinsic motivation in that interest is inherent in the task)

EXHIBIT 11.10 *(continued)*

THREE TYPES OF APPRAISAL INTERVIEWS

Method	Tell and Sell	Tell and Listen	Problem Solving
Role of Interviewer	Judge	Judge	Helper
Gains	Success most probable when employee respects interviewer	Develops favorable attitude to superior, which increases probability of success	Almost assured of improvement in some respect
Risks	Loss of loyalty Inhibition of independent Face-saving problems created	Need for change may not be developed	Employee may lack ideas Change may be other than what superior had in mind
Values	Perpetuates existing practices and values	Permits interviewer to change his views in the light of employee's responses Some upward communication	Both learn since experience and views are pooled Change is facilitated

Source: Norman R. F. Maier, "Three Types of Appraisal Interview," *Personnel* 34 (March/April 1958):39.

employees to respond to the supervisor's assessment of their strengths and weaknesses. The supervisor listens attentively and changes the ratings if the discussion warrants it. Employees tend to experience a greater sense of satisfaction with this approach because of the two-way communication that occurs, but specific goals for performance improvement are not set and the supervisor continues to act in the role of judge. In the Problem-Solving Approach the employee is encouraged to actively participate through self-appraisal. Together the supervisor and employee explore ways to solve problems related to work performance and reach agreement on improvement goals. Problems discussed may relate to work procedures, lack of resources, lack of needed skills, or misunderstandings about job requirements. The key difference between this approach and the others is that the supervisor emphasizes the role of helper. By focusing on solving problems rather than identifying personal faults, the appraisal process is depersonalized and defensive reactions are less likely to occur. In the role of helper the supervisor can also promote employee development by discussing the employee's career goals and how to obtain the qualifications needed to move vertically or laterally within the organization.

Maier found that the problem-solving approach produces more positive reactions from employees and more work-related improvements than the others. Although routinely recommended in the performance appraisal literature, it is by no means easy to implement. It requires a special commitment to employee involvement and supervisors who are well trained in the techniques of goal setting, feedback, and positive reinforcement.

Goal-Setting, Feedback, and Positive Reinforcement

The appraisal process can do little to improve employee motivation unless specific goals are set, employees are provided feedback about their progress, and positive achievements are reinforced. The appraisal interview provides an opportunity to accomplish all three. Discussion may focus on desired traits, behaviors, or outcomes—depending on the nature of the appraisal instrument. After the results of the evaluation have been discussed, goals can be set for further work improvement and personal development. As discussed in Chapter 12, goals are an effective means of motivating employees if they are both challenging and attainable. Goals must also be personally meaningful, relating to each employee's interests as well as organizational objectives. Forced, rigid goal setting can actually inhibit the motivation of self-directed employees by diverting attention away from what is intrinsically motivating about their work. Once new goals are established, employees must receive feedback about how well they are doing on a daily basis.

Positive achievements may be reinforced either through merit pay awards or praise. Praise is the more efficient reinforcer of the two because it is cheaper, can be given continuously, and is less likely to contribute to morale problems. Linking goal-setting and praise to desired job behaviors is a proven means of increasing employee motivation and productivity. This linkage can be achieved, for example, by beginning the appraisal interview with a summary of what the employee has done that is deserving of recognition and why it is deserving. New goals can then be set and progress can be reinforced by offering praise on a daily basis. All of this requires supervisors who are able to devote large blocks of time to the task, possess good interpersonal skills, and enjoy working closely with their fellow employees. In practice, however, even the most dedicated supervisors often have too little time and too few training opportunities to fulfill their counseling and coaching responsibilities adequately.

Factors Contributing to Appraisal System Effectiveness

This chapter has described the main components of a performance appraisal system, including appraisal criteria, an appraisal instrument or method, and an appraisal interview. It has also reviewed findings from the rather extensive body of research regarding factors that contribute to their reliability and effectiveness. These factors include the following:

1. Use of job analysis to develop appraisal criteria
2. Use of both behavior-based and results-based appraisal criteria
3. Use of an appraisal instrument that communicates work expectations clearly and allows accurate evaluation of work performance

4. Involvement of employees in developing the appraisal system and appraising performance
5. Training for supervisors on the use of the appraisal instrument, how to avoid judgment errors, and how to coach and counsel employees
6. Use of goal setting, feedback, and positive reinforcement techniques
7. A problem-solving approach to the appraisal interview that avoids placing blame or finding fault
8. A strong message from upper management that the supervisor's appraising and counseling responsibilities are to be taken seriously

From Performance Appraisal to Performance Management

Performance appraisals—as noted at the beginning of the chapter—rarely deliver in practice what they promise in theory. The reason seems to lie once again with the legacy of scientific management.[20] Formal appraisal systems were first adopted in the early 1900s as a means of directing and controlling employee behavior through the scientific measurement of human performance. The underlying faith in science continues to influence the design and use of appraisals today. Indeed, much of the analysis in this chapter focused on how to improve the accuracy and reliability of appraisals. The unfortunate consequence of treating performance appraisal as a scientific technique is that it quickly becomes an end in itself. Boxes are checked, the appraisal form is forwarded to the personnel office, and very little is ultimately accomplished. In short, the traditional appraisal process allows managers to avoid dealing with human beings and their performance-related problems.

The prevailing disillusionment with performance appraisal can only be reversed by shifting the emphasis from appraising performance to effectively managing it. Although appraisal instruments may still be useful in communicating expectations, the central focus must shift from checking boxes to motivating employees and solving their performance-related problems. This shift is particularly important as government agencies search for ways to establish more flexible and team-based work arrangements. Although traditional appraisal systems may have been appropriate for directing and controlling production workers in the early 1900s, they are much less so for motivating and developing the semiautonomous professionals that work for government today. Governments in the twenty-first century are likely to rely much more on peer appraisals and problem-solving sessions as a result.

■ **CASE 11.1**   Managing Performance from Afar

Tom Benson has a problem and it's only getting worse. As district manager for a human services agency, he is responsible for the performance of both the main office and a rural suboffice located 60 miles away. Each office employs family assistance counselors, a clerical support staff, and an office manager. Because Tom works out of the main office, he relies heavily on the suboffice manager to handle the day-to-day business of that operation. Six months ago Tom hired Brenda to manage the suboffice. Brenda came highly recommended as a hard-working and fastidious manager.

This gave Tom reason to hope that she could correct the problems caused by the casual style of the previous manager. Although Tom is free to visit the office only once every two weeks, he is determined to be more vigilant in monitoring its operations. Part of Tom's problem is how to appraise and manage Brenda's performance when he is rarely present to observe her work.

The more immediate problem, however, is that the counselors are complaining that she is micromanaging everything they do. Brenda, it seems, is not only a dedicated public servant but also a perfectionist. She works at least 60 hours a week and tends to hold the office staff to the same standards that she demands of herself. In addition, her obsession with paperwork has apparently created the perception that she is more concerned with documenting the services provided than with achieving results. The counselors are complaining that the attention to detail she requires in staff reports is causing unnecessary delays in providing services.

When Tom raised these concerns with Brenda, she defended her style in the same meticulous and detailed fashion that was causing the staff distress. Tom realized that his problem went beyond how to observe and counsel her from a distance. The agency's trait-based performance appraisal system was totally inadequate for addressing a situation in which a manager is hardworking yet overly dedicated to doing things "by the book."

The problem is getting worse. Morale is continuing to decline and a few counselors are threatening to quit. Tom is reluctant to discipline a manager who is undeniably a hard-working and dedicated public servant. He believes the answer must lie with performance appraisal and counseling, but he is not sure what to do or where to begin.

1. What human resource management issues are raised in this case?
2. Do you agree with Tom that this situation calls for better performance management rather than discipline? Or, is discipline a necessary part of performance management?
3. Given that Tom's office is 60 miles distant, how might the performance appraisal system be changed so that Tom can manage Brenda's performance more effectively?

▲ **EXERCISE 11.1**   Providing Constructive Feedback

Instructions

Form into groups of two and take turns performing the role of supervisor in the two scenarios given below. The goal is to provide clear and useful feedback in a constructive manner. Give some thought to what you think should be said, then talk to the "employee."

The Facts

Employee: recreation specialist
Supervisor: you
Time of observation: about 10 minutes ago
General topic: local community recreation plan

Scenario One The recreation specialist has written a summer recreation plan for the town of Castleford. You have just read the draft, and you consider it deficient in several areas: the goals were vague and unmeasurable, no implementing activities were included, the budget estimates were unrealistic in the face of recent cuts, and the projected timelines were so broad as to be meaningless.

One approach: "Darn it, it seems hopeless to think you'll do anything right. Just look at this plan you wrote—it stinks! More of the type of mistakes you've been making all the time lately. Now take this draft and revise it into the proper format and content, okay?"

What is your approach?

Scenario Two The recreation specialist has written a summer recreation plan for the town of Grangeville. You have just read the draft, and you find it exceptional—a welcome change from recent plans by this employee. It contains all the necessary elements, concisely laid out—specific, measurable goals; relevant activities; an exact budget estimate, including alternatives; and specific, realistic timelines. The writing is entirely correct—in fact, it's a pleasure to read.

One approach: "Hey, nice job!"

What is your approach?

Notes

1. Gary P. Latham and Kenneth N. Wexley, *Increasing Productivity Through Performance Appraisal* (Reading, Massachusetts: Addison-Wesley, 1981), 2.

2. W. Edwards Deming, *Out of the Crisis* (Cambridge, Massachusetts: Massachusetts Institute of Technology, 1986), 101–103.

3. See, for example, Latham and Wexley. *Increasing Productivity*, 100–103.

4. Ibid., 104–113.

5. Edwin A. Locke and Gary P. Latham, *Goal-setting: A Motivational Technique that Works!* (Englewood Cliffs, New Jersey: Prentice-Hall, 1978).

6. Douglas McGregor, "An Uneasy Look at Performance Appraisal," *Harvard Business Review* 35 (May/June 1957), 90.

7. W. Edwards Deming, *Out of the Crisis,* 117.

8. See Gerald V. Barrett and Mary C. Kernan, "Performance Appraisal and Terminations: A Review of Court Decisions Since Brito v. Zia with Implications for Personnel Practices," *Personnel Psychology* 40 (Autumn 1987):489–503.

9. 422 U.S. 405 (1975), at 433.

10. 372 F. Supp. 126 (1974), at 142.

11. 457 F.2d 348 (1972).

12. 472 F.Supp. 356 (1979).

13. Craig Eric Schneier, Richard W. Beatty, and Lloyd S. Baird, "How to Construct a Successful Performance Appraisal System," *Training and Development Journal* 40 (April 1986):40.

14. Rick Jacobs, Ditsa Kafry, and Sheldon Zedeck, "Expectations of Behaviorally Anchored Rating Scales," *Personnel Psychology* 33 (Autumn 1980):595–640.

15. J. Peter Graves, "Let's Put Appraisal Back in Performance Appraisal," in John Matzer, Jr., ed., *Creative Personnel Practices: New Ideas for Local Government* (Washington D.C.: International City Management Association, 1984):57–74.

16. Charlie B. Tyer, "Employee Performance Appraisal in American State Governments, *Public Personnel Management* 11 (Fall 1982):199–212.

17. Latham and Wexley, *Increasing Productivity,* 83.

18. See, for example, Stephen J. Carroll and Craig E. Schneier, *Performance Appraisal And Review Systems* (Glenview, Illinois: Scott, Foresman, 1982), Chapter 7.

19. Norman R. F. Maier, "Three Types of Appraisal Interview," *Personnel* 34 (March/April 1958):27–40.

20. See, for example, Charles J. Fox, "Employee Performance Appraisal: The Keystone Made of Clay," in Carolyn Ban and Norma M. Riccucci, eds., *Public Personnel Management: Current Concerns—Future Challenges* (New York: Longman, 1991):58–72.

CHAPTER 12

Employee Motivation and Productivity

Learning Objectives

After mastering the materials contained in this chapter, you will be able to:

1. Demonstrate a clear conceptual understanding of employee motivation and productivity.
2. Draw on three types of motivational strategies in developing an effective human resources strategic plan.
3. Explain the relevance of Herzberg's two-factor theory to the attainment of a highly motivated, committed, and productive workforce.
4. Use an expanded definition of productivity to identify appropriate performance measures for an agency with which you are familiar.
5. Distinguish ad hoc throughput strategies for improving productivity from participative management programs such as Quality of Work Life and Total Quality Management.
6. Identify at least four roles that managers and personnel officers are often asked to perform in improving productivity.

Because the quality of our lives depends in no small measure on the services that governments provide, a wasteful and ineffective government is an affront to all of us. It is particularly offensive to taxpayers who have a legitimate right to expect "the biggest bang for the buck." Although organizational performance is the product of many factors, a highly motivated and productive workforce is unquestionably among them. Unfortunately, one of the central failings of contemporary human resource management is that planning and administering programs receives more time and energy than does the management of human performance. Although lip service continues to be paid to the view that human resources are an organization's most valuable assets, too little of the typical manager's day is spent ensuring that human resources are developed and utilized to the maximum benefit of all parties to the employment contract.

Securing a highly motivated and productive workforce is too important to leave to chance. It requires careful planning, considerable knowledge of human motivation, and strong commitment from top management. It also requires personnel policies and systems that do more to liberate human energies than to constrain them. The important task of this chapter is to define motivation and productivity in ways that are meaningful for both managers and personnel officers, review strategies for motivating employees, and evaluate existing performance monitoring and productivity improvement programs. Analysis begins with the individual worker and the complex phenomenon known as motivation.

Directing, Controlling, and Motivating

Countless books and articles assert that motivating employees is the key to productivity. Rarely, however, do they offer a clear definition of motivation. Nor do they take the time to distinguish motivation from other aspects of human resource management such as direction and control. In fact, the term *motivation* has been used in many ways to mean a wide variety of things. If managers and personnel officers are to make informed, strategic decisions regarding productivity improvement, they must have a clear understanding of what motivation entails. A few analytical distinctions will help in this regard.

When discussing the management of human performance, motivation is often confused or purposefully lumped together with direction and control. In fact they are analytically distinct. *Direction* involves focusing employee attention on what needs to be done and how. It is accomplished through structural and procedural mechanisms such as job descriptions, standard operating procedures, directives issued through the chain of command, training, and organizational policies. *Control* involves ensuring that work tasks are carried out as directed. It is accomplished through such means as close supervision, performance appraisals, production audits, enforcement of rules, sanctions, and employee socialization. Through direction and control, managers are able to achieve dependability and predictability of human behavior, compliance with authority, and at least minimally acceptable levels of work performance. *Motivation,* by contrast, is an internal state that energizes employees to produce at a level that goes well beyond what is minimally required. It also causes them to demonstrate special qualities such as enthusiasm, creativity, and a high regard for excellence.

The Internal Sources of Motivation

Motivation is that which energizes people to act in certain ways and to channel their behaviors toward particular goals. It begins with each individual's needs, desires, and expectations, and the relative priorities placed on them. According to most contemporary theories of motivation, the wish to satisfy deeply felt needs and desires creates a tension within people and drives them to find ways to satisfy their needs and desires so that the tension might be reduced. Personal motives may include the needs to belong to something larger than the self, contribute to activities that are consistent with one's values, be recognized by others who are held in respect, avoid pain or punishment, continue to experience personal growth, or obtain more pay so that material wants can be satisfied. No two individuals have the same motives because they arise out of each person's cumulative life experiences and the values derived from them.

The question, "how do we motivate our employees?" wrongly implies that all workers are motivated in more or less the same ways and that motivation is something that is dependent on actions taken by management.[1] In fact, individuals act in response to a broad range of personal motives and often do so without any particular action by management. Because they are motivated by factors that are uniquely relevant to them, they may or may not respond to the kinds of rewards that managers have to offer. Thus, if managers are to intervene constructively in the motivational process, they must find ways to link those behaviors required by the organization (such as dependable role performance) with the particular motives of each employee. Meyer makes this point as follows:

> For example, if I am motivated by the need to be recognized, and the organization (represented by my manager) doesn't provide me with personal and authentic recognition, my motivation doesn't change but my behavior does. It is channeled and directed away from the organization and toward another behavior that will provide me with a response to my need. The manager must discover from me what I consider "recognition" to be, so that he or she can manage the energy from that motive. It can be concluded that people aren't lacking in motivation; their motivation is merely not directed effectively toward organizational goals.[2]

Tapping each employee's full potential by assessing and responding to his or her personal motives is a daunting task precisely because individual motives are so diverse.

Although admittedly difficult, this task can be accomplished through the maintenance of a psychological contract in which the employee and employer periodically reaffirm their mutual commitment to satisfying each other's needs and expectations. In concrete terms, this is done by sharing mutual expectations at recruitment time, discussing mutual needs and desires during the performance appraisal conference, and reaffirming commitment through hard work and good attendance by employees and supportive policies and actions by management. Continuous feedback is the key to successfully maintaining the psychological contract. Depending on each person's needs and desires and contributions to organizational goals, a manager might offer feedback in the form of a financial reward, praise, greater challenge, or more opportunities for personal growth. The difficulty lies in providing feedback that is personally meaningful to each employee.

Managers can also facilitate the motivational process by removing barriers that impede successful goal attainment. This involves ensuring that structures and policies liberate rather than constrain motivational energies. It may mean, for example, limiting the use of control mechanisms to what is necessary to ensure accomplishment and coordination of work tasks, relying on mission statements rather than rules, and developing job descriptions that are flexible enough to allow full utilization of employee talents. Given the realities of organizational life in the public sector, this is easier said than done.

Motivation Toward What?

Organizational theorists tend to assume that if workers are motivated in some general sense, productivity will automatically result. In fact, employees may be motivated to achieve any number of personal objectives, some of which may be consistent with and contribute to organizational objectives, and others that may not. Part of management's task is to encourage a unity of interest between personal and organizational objectives.

But what are the specific behaviors that organizations hope to elicit from employees? According to Daniel Katz and Robert L. Kahn, three distinct categories of behaviors are required of employees:[3] First, organizations need talented individuals who will join and remain with the organization. A long-term commitment from employees not only contributes to organizational functioning but also helps reduce costs associated with absenteeism and turnover. Second, organizations need employees to perform their work roles dependably and to satisfy at least minimum quality and quantity performance standards. Finally, attainment of organizational objectives requires behaviors that go well beyond dependable role performance. These behaviors include, among others, dedication, cooperativeness, creativity, innovativeness, and a demonstrated willingness to do the little things that contribute so importantly to protecting and promoting organizational interests.

Eliciting these behaviors necessarily entails the use of different motivational strategies. For example, strategies that are successful in encouraging employees to join and remain with the organization may do little to encourage dependable role performance. An essential part of the strategic planning process involves analyzing the range of available motivational strategies and selecting those strategies most likely to elicit the behaviors required for effective organizational functioning.

Three Categories of Motivational Strategies

According to Katz and Kahn, the many available strategies for motivating employees tend to fall into one of three basic categories: legal compliance, external rewards, and internalized motivation. Each of these categories relies on different methods of motivation and each elicits different kinds of behaviors. Knowledge of the full range of available strategies and the behaviors they are designed to elicit is critically important when developing a human resource strategic plan.

Legal Compliance Strategies

Strategies in this category encourage obedience and conformity of behavior through the exercise of formal authority. They typically involve the development of extensive systems of rules and regulations and the use of sanctions to secure compliance. Employees are "motivated" to comply with the rules either because they accept their legitimacy or because they wish to avoid sanctions.

Given the variability and unpredictability of human behavior, all organizations must secure at least some minimum level of reliability from employees in the performance of their work roles. Organizational effectiveness is placed in serious jeopardy when employees do not come to work on time, do not cooperate with supervisors and co-workers, and do not perform work tasks dependably. Although labeled a motivational strategy, legal compliance clearly emphasizes direction and control over motivation. The issue for organizations is not whether to direct and control employees, but how and to what extent. Government agencies that are highly bureaucratic in structure and philosophy tend to rely heavily on legal compliance strategies. Reliability, predictability, and conformity of behavior are achieved through the enforcement of workplace rules, standard operating procedures, narrowly defined job descriptions, and organizational directives issued through a relatively rigid chain of command. Compliance is also encouraged by appealing to symbols of authority, socializing employees in prevailing bureaucratic norms, and issuing threats and sanctions.

Heavy reliance on legal compliance strategies is likely to prove counterproductive for several reasons. First, the routine use of sanctions often fosters resentment and organized resistance among employees, necessitates increasingly higher levels of fear to ensure compliance, and contributes to higher turnover rates. Second, placing employees in narrowly defined jobs and using standard operating procedures to limit their discretionary power constitutes an unnecessary waste of human potential. Reliability of performance may be achieved, but at the probable expense of innovative and creative behaviors, opportunities for personal growth, and the full use of human resources. Employees are less likely to identify with the organization and its goals in a work environment overly constrained by rules and sanctions. Third, rigidities of structure and process may deny employees the flexibility they need to serve their clients and may reduce the ability of the organization to adapt appropriately to changes taking place in its environment. Finally, legal compliance strategies tend to require large numbers of supervisors, which not only creates higher payroll costs, but also constrains efforts to achieve flatter, leaner, and more flexible service delivery systems.

In short, although legal compliance strategies can help ensure predictability, compliance with minimum work standards, and regular job attendance, they will not by themselves energize employees to perform above standard or exhibit innovativeness, creativity, loyalty, and commitment. System stability is only a part of what an organization requires for effective functioning.

External Rewards Strategies

Motivational strategies falling into this category rely on external rewards to secure desired behaviors. External rewards include such things as pay, benefits, promotions, praise, recognition awards, and pleasant working conditions. The logic behind this approach is that employees will work hard, not because the work is gratifying in itself, but because it is instrumental in obtaining desired rewards. The role of the manager, from this perspective, is to ascertain what employees value and to structure the workplace so that valued rewards are available, are within the reach of hard-working employees, and are distributed on the basis of demonstrated results.

According to Vroom's widely accepted expectancy theory, motivation increases when an employee values a particular reward highly and believes there is a reasonably good chance of achieving it.[4] However, certain conditions must be satisfied before external rewards can serve as effective motivators: work performance must be evaluated accurately and fairly; rewards must be contingent on superior job performance; employees must have reasonable opportunities to achieve specified goals and objectives; the value of the reward to the employee must be sufficient to induce the effort necessary for successful goal attainment; and the reward must be received as soon as possible to ensure positive reinforcement.

The effective use of external rewards is constrained in practice by the difficulties inherent in satisfying these conditions. First, general system rewards, those available to most or all employees by virtue of their membership in the organization, hold little motivational potential because they are not distributed on the basis of demonstrated performance. General system rewards include cost-of-living pay increases, positive working conditions, retirement benefits, and other fringe benefits. If the range and magnitude of these rewards are highly attractive relative to those offered by other employers, they may induce employees to remain with the organization and demonstrate a high level of commitment to it. However, general system rewards are not likely to result in higher levels of productivity. Nor will they necessarily foster innovation, creativity, and a commitment to excellence. Second, employees tend to have little confidence in the performance appraisals used to evaluate their performance or in the ability of their supervisors to rate them fairly and accurately. Third, as job tasks become more interdependent, and as organizations move toward team-based models of work, the ability to evaluate and reward employees on the basis of their individual contributions becomes all the more difficult. Although rewards may be distributed to members of a work team based on the group's performance, this tends to reward overachieving and underachieving team members alike. Fourth, rewards, particularly the financial rewards offered in the public sector, are seldom sufficient to induce greater work effort. A study of pay-for-performance systems in 23 states, for example, found that inadequate or inconsistent funding tended to undermine system goals.[5] Finally, it is seldom practical to distribute rewards with sufficient immediacy to reinforce desired behaviors. Merit awards and pay bonuses are typically distributed only once a year. Although rewards such as praise can be distributed more frequently, it is probably unrealistic to expect supervisors to voice approval every time an employee exhibits positive work-related behaviors.

The effective use of external rewards is particularly difficult in the public sector because of constraints on the range of rewards available for use by managers. Salaries, for example, tend to be tied to each position's classification, and pay increases are typically legislated or negotiated for groups of employees as a whole, regardless of each individual's level of performance. In the absence of a pay-for-performance system, public managers can seldom use pay as a reward for superior performance. Similarly, promotions have limited motivational value because there are relatively few opportunities for advancement in most public agencies. This is attributable in part to the small number of positions available at the top of hierarchically structured organizations and in part to the practice of opening competition for vacant positions to persons outside of the agency. Finally, although praise and recognition is always available to public sector managers, it is probably not realistic (and perhaps undesirable) to distribute them on a contingency basis. Praise and recognition may be more effective as motivators when they are used to support the total person rather than as an instrumental reward contingent on specific behaviors.

Recent interest in the use of external rewards in the public sector has focused primarily on development and implementation of pay-for-performance systems. Fourteen states adopted pay-for-performance systems during the 1980s, bringing the total to 23 states by 1990. These systems often combine merit pay with financial bonuses. Merit pay is a salary increase added to an employee's base pay as a reward for superior work performance. Financial bonuses, by contrast, are rewards for superior performance that are provided on a one-time basis and are not added to base pay. Although pay-for-performance systems have proven successful in raising productivity in some instances, a common set of problems tend to undermine their effectiveness. These include invalid performance appraisals, dysfunctions arising from the competition over rewards, and lack of adequate financial incentives.[6] The Performance Management and Recognition System (PMRS), which is the federal government's pay-for-performance system for 130,000 managers and supervisors in grades 13 through 15, provides a case in point. Studies by the Office of Personnel Management and the Government Accounting Office have found the results to be "generally disappointing."[7] Perry and Petrakis suggest that the current popularity of pay-for-performance systems among politicians may have more to do with their symbolic value than with their ability to improve government effectiveness:

> No matter how onerous merit pay may be to those immediately affected, it sends a message that the governed are in control and things are as they should be. It is this symbolic role of pay-for-performance which may explain its persistence despite its disappointing consequences.[8]

The key to the successful use of external rewards lies in determining when it is most appropriate to use them and in designing systems that address the practical difficulties just outlined. Where organizations have successfully overcome these practical difficulties, external rewards have proven effective in attracting workers to the organization, retaining them, and motivating them to meet and exceed quantitative and qualitative performance standards.

Strategies Based on Internalized Motivation

Internalized motivation refers to energies released from within as a result of intrinsic rewards obtained from work. Intrinsically motivated individuals engage in positive work behaviors not to obtain an external reward, nor in deference to formal authority, but because of the personal satisfaction derived from the work itself. According to psychologists, the root source of intrinsic motivation is the basic need of humans to be competent and self-determining in relation to their environment.[9] As will be seen, this basic need gives rise to other needs, such as the need for affiliation. The role of the manager, from this perspective, is to structure jobs and work relationships so that employees will be constantly self-motivating. Katz and Kahn identify three types of internalized motivation, as follows:

Value Congruence Self-motivation may result from congruence between the values of the employee and the values of the larger work group or organization. When values are congruent the employee derives satisfaction from knowing that he or she is engaged in work that is personally meaningful. Value congruence can result from either a natural matching process or deliberate socialization by the employer. In the first instance congruence occurs when an individual self-selects an organization because of an anticipated identity of values. Persons committed to preserving the environment, for example, may gravitate toward agencies engaged in environmental protection.

Congruence may also result from efforts by the employer to socialize employees in organizational values. The recent literature on symbolic management encourages employers to take a new look at socialization as a means of motivating employees.[10] Symbolic management entails developing mission statements embodying key organizational values and reinforcing those values through stories, speeches, and other symbolic actions that underscore the importance of the agency's mission. The underlying purpose is to foster greater commitment to the organization and dedication to its purposes. Advocates of this strategy argue that it not only produces superior work performance but also innovativeness, creativity, and a willingness to protect organizational interests.

Government agencies theoretically enjoy an advantage in this regard because their essential purpose is to serve the public interest. Contributing to the attainment of important societal values can be highly rewarding. The problem, of course, is that unwise organizational policies and controls, and the low esteem in which government work is held, tend to rob work of its intrinsic satisfactions. The solution to this, according to David Osborne and Ted Gaebler, is to get on with the task of replacing rule-driven government with mission-driven government.[11]

Satisfaction of Affiliation Needs   The need to affiliate with others has been identified by psychologists as one of the most basic of human needs. It includes the need to develop friendships, receive affection, and belong to something larger than the self. Affiliation needs can be satisfied by encouraging teamwork and involving employees in making key decisions. This strategy, according to advocates, will cause those with high affiliation needs to identify closely with the work group and become committed and dedicated workers as a result. Organizations can also create a sense of community among employees by demonstrating a commitment to the well-being of each of its members. The success of business enterprises in Japan, for example, is often attributed to their holistic concern for employee well-being, their emphasis on working in groups, and the sense of community that their organizational policies are designed to create.[12] (See Chapter 13 for a fuller discussion of this strategy).

Satisfaction of Ego and Growth Needs   People have a basic need to be competent and self-determining in relation to their environment. This need can be satisfied in part through the challenge and sense of accomplishment derived from work and the personal growth that results from the continued work experience. Human Resources theorists, following the lead of Douglas McGregor, Rensis Likert, and Frederick Herzberg, advocate participative management and job redesign techniques to foster intrinsic motivation of this kind. *Participative management* involves providing employees with greater discretion in determining the most appropriate ways of performing work operations, as well as greater involvement in making the policy decisions that affect them. Not only does the additional challenge elicit intrinsic motivation, but the opportunity for self-determination is intrinsically rewarding as well. Advocates of this strategy believe that when employees participate in determining what they will do and how, they become more ego-involved and committed to doing it.[13] *Job redesign,* by contrast, involves restructuring jobs so that they are more challenging and require greater resourcefulness. The resulting opportunities for personal growth and the exercise of personal competence are believed to be intrinsically motivating. Frederick Herzberg uses the term *job enrichment* to describe a particular kind of job redesign in which greater variety, complexity, autonomy, and responsibility are incorporated into a job or group of jobs. Exhibit 12.1 presents the principles of job enrichment and the motivators that are activated by them.

Although research has generally confirmed the effectiveness of participatory management and job enrichment as motivational techniques, their success or failure in specific situations is determined by many different factors. A job enrichment experiment among low-level clerical workers in a large federal agency in the 1970s helped to isolate some of these factors.[14] Low-level clerical workers in three units were asked to work as a team and were delegated discretionary authority to decide how to divide up and carry out their work responsibilities. Productivity went up and absenteeism and turnover went down as a result of these changes, but job satisfaction remained

---

EXHIBIT 12.1

PRINCIPLES OF VERTICAL JOB LOADING

Principle	Motivators Involved
A. Removing some controls while retaining accountability	Responsibility and personal achievement
B. Increasing the accountability of individuals for own work	Responsibility and recognition
C. Giving a person a complete natural unit of work (module, division, area, and so on)	Responsibility, achievement, and recognition
D. Granting additional authority to an employee in his or her activity; job freedom	Responsibility, achievement, and recognition
E. Making periodic reports directly available to the worker rather than to the supervisor	Internal recognition
F. Introducing new and more difficult tasks not previously handled	Growth and learning
G. Assigning individuals specific or specialized tasks, enabling them to become experts	Responsibility, growth, and advancement

Source: Reprinted by permission of *Harvard Business Review.* An Exhibit from "One More Time: How Do You Motivate Your Employees?" by Frederick Herzberg (HBR Classic, Sept/Oct 1987). Copyright © 1987 by the President and Fellows of Harvard College; all rights reserved.

surprisingly low. Researchers attributed the gains in productivity not to the motivational effects of job enrichment but to the fact that the employees worked more efficiently as a team than they had as individuals. They also concluded that the work had not been enriched to the point where intrinsic motivation could occur. This, in addition to the fact that positions were not reclassified upward despite increased levels of autonomy and responsibility, were offered as explanations for continued low job satisfaction. The results of the study suggest that it may be difficult to enrich lower-level jobs to the point where significant intrinsic motivation will occur and that many job incumbents many continue to expect extrinsic rewards in exchange for increased productivity. As other studies have shown, not all workers will desire or respond positively to enriched work. The central life interests of many workers will continue to revolve around activities outside of the workplace.

The three strategies of internalized motivation are consistent with the goals and assumptions of the human resource management perspective described in Chapter 1. By satisfying the need for affiliation, self-expression, and personal growth, these strategies help to promote employee development and the fullest utilization of their talents. For advocates of this perspective it is particularly frustrating that the public sector has been slow to adopt these motivational strategies. Organizational rewards still tend to focus on wages, hours, benefits, and working conditions. In light of the public sector's continued reliance on legal compliance and external rewards, it is interesting to speculate about whether the purported success of Japanese management systems is the result of their use of internalized motivation strategies. The elements of Japanese management identified by William Ouichi—intensive socialization in organizational values, emphasis on working in groups, open communication, consultative decision making, and a demonstrated holistic concern for employees—appear to be particularly well suited to satisfying the affiliation, ego, and growth needs of employees.[15]

Which Motivational Strategy to Choose

Which strategy or combination of strategies—legal compliance, external rewards, or internalized motivation—should an organization employ? Research has not and probably cannot offer a definitive answer. Perhaps the best answer is that each agency must choose that strategy or combination of strategies that is most consistent with its human resources philosophy, the nature of the jobs in question, and the relative availability of various kinds of rewards. Although it may seem logical to conclude that the most effective motivational strategy is one that relies on both extrinsic and intrinsic rewards, some caution is warranted. If, as many management theorists believe, the effects of intrinsic and extrinsic rewards are cumulative, then it makes sense to utilize both kinds of strategies together. However, it may be the case that the use of extrinsic rewards actually diverts attention from intrinsic satisfactions. Based on laboratory experiments, Edward Deci has concluded that the greater the use of extrinsic rewards, the greater the decrease in intrinsic motivation.[16] If Deci is correct, then management will need to decide in each situation whether the gains from extrinsic motivation are sufficient to warrant a potential loss of intrinsic motivation. Because civil servants have traditionally been asked to derive intrinsic satisfactions from their program commitments and professional pursuits, the sudden introduction of a pay-for-performance system, for example, may prove counterproductive.

The selection of motivational strategies and the design of reward systems involve fundamental choices that should not be taken lightly or made quickly. Such choices, if implemented thoroughly and consistently, will have enormous impacts on the structure of the organization, the design of jobs, the role of the personnel office, the nature of supervision, and the contents of personnel policies. It is important, therefore, that these decisions be made in the context of the strategic planning process and with considerable input from line managers, personnel officers, and other employees.

Job Satisfaction, Motivation, and Productivity

Management theorists once tended to assume that high job satisfaction led to heightened motivation and ultimately increased productivity. We now know that workers can be very happy with their jobs but not be particularly well motivated or productive. Development of an effective human resources strategy thus depends on distinguishing job satisfaction from motivation and productivity.

The distinction is expressed most clearly in Frederick Herzberg's two-factor theory of motivation. According to Herzberg, job dissatisfaction and job satisfaction (i.e., motivation) are independent dimensions resulting from two different sets of factors. Job dissatisfaction is produced by negative factors in the work environment, such as low pay, moronic policies, poor working conditions, and capricious treatment by superiors. Job satisfaction and increased productivity, by contrast, result from intrinsic satisfactions derived from the work itself. Intrinsic factors include achievement, recognition for achievement, the nature of the work, responsibility, and personal growth. As discussed above, these motivators are built into the job through job enrichment. Higher productivity is the expected outcome.

The two-factor distinction is important because it alerts us to the need to pursue two partly distinct courses of action if we wish to enhance productivity. First, proactive steps must be taken to remove the sources of dissatisfaction. This is necessary because high levels of job dissatisfaction undermine morale, reduce some aspects of motivation, and even drive some employees to seek employment elsewhere. Second, proactive steps must be taken to facilitate employee motivation. These steps, according to Herzberg, include the adoption of job enrichment, participative management, and other methods designed to elicit internalized motivation. In short, although removing the sources of dissatisfaction is important and necessary, it does not by itself produce a motivated and productive workforce.

Although critics argue that Herzberg's two-factor theory is overstated and oversimplified, the theory does serve to warn us of the dangers of thinking in linear terms about the relationships between job satisfaction, motivation, and productivity. It encourages us to tackle simultaneously those things that are destructive of morale and those things that constrain our ability to facilitate self-motivation. It encourages us to assess the diverse needs of employees and how best to satisfy them. Finally, it encourages us to define the behaviors required of employees and to choose appropriate strategies for eliciting them.

Goal-Setting as a Motivational Technique

According to Edwin A. Locke and Gary P. Latham, goal setting is the essential ingredient in the success of pay-for-performance, job enrichment, management by objectives, and various forms of participative management.[17] Locke and Latham use the term *goal* to mean anything that helps establish what needs to be achieved, including task statements, performance standards, quotas, objectives, deadlines, and budgets. Goal setting in their view contributes to improved organizational performance by directing the efforts of workers to what needs to be accomplished, providing the challenges that spark motivation, providing standards against which to measure individual or group success, and helping ensure that each person's talents are fully utilized. The underlying source of motivation is the sense of accomplishment and efficacy employees gain from achieving defined goals, apart from any extrinsic rewards they may also receive.

Research conducted in the laboratory and in the field led Locke and Latham to conclude that "people who are given specific, challenging goals perform better than people who are given specific, easy goals, vague goals (such as "do your best"), or no goals."[18] The process of goal setting involves seven key steps[19]:

1. Specify the general objective or tasks to be done.
2. Specify how the performance in question will be measured.
3. Specify the standard or target to be reached.
4. Specify the time span involved.
5. Prioritize goals.
6. Optional step: rate goals as to difficulty and importance.
7. Determine coordination requirements.

Although these steps have the greatest relevance to production jobs, they are also applicable to professional and managerial jobs and problem-solving teams. In the latter cases, upper management sets the basic goals to be achieved and then delegates responsibility for setting specific objectives and how they are to be accomplished. In some organizations this is done in the context of management by objectives (MBO), a process in which employees identify common goals and coordinate their efforts toward achieving them. (See Chapter 11 for a fuller discussion of MBO).

An Expanded Definition of Productivity

A motivated workforce does not guarantee a productive workforce. Although motivated workers are likely to be hard-working employees, a number of factors may limit the quality, quantity, and cost-effectiveness of their work outputs. These include lack of clear understanding of what needs to be accomplished, waste, poor job design, insufficient skills, inadequate resources and equipment, and bureaucratic constraints. In short, strategies are needed for enhancing work productivity as well as employee motivation.

Interest in improving government productivity is higher today than at any point since World War II. With demand for increased services outpacing government's capacity to generate additional revenues, citizens, politicians, and administrators alike are turning to productivity improvement for answers. Because they are designed to extract greater yield from available resources, productivity improvement efforts hold out hope for balancing budgets without increasing taxes, freeing up additional resources for new purposes, and restoring public confidence in government. But what citizens, politicians, and administrators mean by improved productivity, or how they hope to accomplish it, is not always clear. It is therefore important to clarify the meaning of productivity before exploring how organizational productivity might be improved.

Productivity is defined most often as a ratio of inputs to outputs. Its measurement is undertaken to determine the *technical efficiency* of an organization's productive efforts. Because there is no single measure of productivity, administrators must select those measures that are most appropriate to their purposes. For example, the productivity of a county road shop in maintaining roads during winter months may be measured in terms of the number of miles of road sanded per ton of gravel or the number of miles sanded per person-hour. Once appropriate measures are identified, data can be recorded on a routine basis and compared periodically with previous performance data or with the performance data of similar agencies in other jurisdictions. If there is reason to believe that productivity is low, steps can be taken to improve productivity either by accomplishing the same level of output with less resources (e.g., the same number of highway miles sanded but with less gravel or personnel) or by doing more with the same resources (e.g., more highway miles sanded with the same amount of gravel or personnel).

The problem with defining productivity in terms of technical efficiency alone is that the results tell us very little about the quality of an agency's products or services, or whether desired objectives are being achieved. Nor can it tell us much about fairness or citizen satisfaction—things that may ultimately be more important than saving dollars. Thus an expanded definition of productivity is needed if we are to evaluate organizational performance in any comprehensive way.[20] At a minimum, the definition of productivity should be expanded to include organizational effectiveness. *Effectiveness,* in contrast to efficiency, is a measure of how well goals and objectives are being achieved. It can be measured using quality, quantity, or outcome-based standards. These standards, according to Siegel, include accomplishment of goals and objectives, accomplishments having the desired impact on goals and objectives, quality of outputs, timeliness of outputs, fulfillment of public needs, and acceptance and use by customers.[21] It is worth keeping in mind that effectiveness has very little meaning outside of the particular criterion used to measure it.

Technical efficiency may contribute to effectiveness but does not guarantee it. In some instances efficiency and effectiveness may even be at odds with each other. A county road shop, to return to an earlier example, may speed up its snowplowing efforts, thereby removing greater quantities of snow but in the process outraging those citizens whose cars and driveways are buried as a result. This is one of the things that makes the concept of productivity so problematic. If the quality of a service decreases at the expense of improved efficiency, then productivity arguably has not been improved. In practice, difficult decisions may have to be made regarding the trade-offs among potentially competing values, including efficiency, effectiveness, equity, and citizen satisfaction.

Productivity measurement may be expanded to include efficiency and effectiveness, but it is ultimately *organizational performance* that agency administrators are most concerned about. Wu makes this point as follows:

In view of the possibility of productivity, efficiency, profitability and effectiveness moving in different directions, it would be useful to appraise performance as a whole. Performance, the primary criterion for judging organizations, "is a total concept," and includes the following aspects: (a) an organization's acquisition of input from its environment and its costs; (b) the ways and costs with which the organization transforms input into output; (c) the quantity and quality of the output; (d) the various effects (beneficial and otherwise) of the output; and (e) the side effects and ultimate results of the activities involved. . . . Performance thus includes not only productivity, efficiency and profitability (where applicable), but also effectiveness, taking into account the outcome (including side effects).[22]

Recognizing the importance of adopting an expanded definition of productivity, the federal government has pioneered a concept known as "Total Performance Measurement." Under this approach, measures of efficiency and effectiveness are combined with information on employee and customer attitudes, and the results are used to assist managers in identifying problem areas and taking corrective action.[23] Total performance measurement, however, lies largely in the domain of the policy analyst, program evaluator, auditor, and budget analyst. From the perspective of human resource management, greatest concern lies with those aspects of productivity that relate directly to work performance. Exhibit 12.2 identifies factors affecting employee productivity. The task for personnel officers and line managers is not so much to determine overall program effectiveness—this is typically left to others—but to measure and monitor work productivity as it relates to quality, quantity, and timeliness of work outputs.

The number and range of factors presented in Exhibit 12.2 provide an idea of the difficulties involved in achieving and maintaining high levels of employee productivity. Problems associated with any one or more of these factors—such as inability to recruit well-qualified employees, poorly designed jobs, obsolete equipment, overly restrictive policies, a culture of mistrust, or insufficient rewards—may greatly undermine employee productivity. The potential interactive effects among these factors makes the challenge even greater. Motivation, for example, is often affected by factors in the work environment and organizational culture, and organizational culture shapes and is shaped by factors in the work environment. But although Exhibit 12.2 does not capture all of the complexities involved, it nonetheless provides a starting point for thinking strategically about how to improve and sustain employee productivity.

Productivity Measurement

Once discredited as a holdover from the scientific management era, interest in productivity measurement is experiencing a rebirth. Wishing to maintain levels of service in the face of stagnant operating budgets, administrators are increasingly searching for ways to improve productivity. An essential prerequisite is a system for measuring productivity. Appropriate performance standards and measures of quality, quantity, and timeliness are needed to determine the productivity of individual workers, groups of workers, and entire programs. Information derived through productivity measurement allows administrators to identify problems, determine appropriate corrective actions, and evaluate the success of their efforts. Measurement systems also provide agencies with a means of focusing on what it is they are suppose to be accomplishing.

EXHIBIT 12.2

FACTORS AFFECTING EMPLOYEE PRODUCTIVITY

Job Design

Does the design of the job enhance work quality, efficiency, and timeliness?

Work Technology

Do work tools enhance work quality, efficiency, and timeliness?

Work Environment

Do organizational policies, physical settings, interpersonal relations, and managerial practices enhance job satisfaction and work quality, efficiency, and timeliness?

Organizational Culture

Does the underlying structure of shared values, beliefs, and assumptions enhance job satisfaction and work quality, efficiency, and timeliness?

Unit Structure and Operations

Do unit structures and the organization of work processes enhance work quality, efficiency, and timeliness?

Individual Motivation

Do reward systems channel human energies toward the simultaneous realization of individual and organizational goals?

Individual Qualifications

Do employees possess the knowledge, skills, and abilities they need to perform work tasks efficiently and effectively?

Employee Productivity

As measured by:

• Work quality

• Technical efficiency

• Timeliness

Measurement Strategies

Two productivity measurement strategies are engineered work standards and group output trend analysis.[24] *Engineered work standards* are specifications established through scientific study regarding the time it should take to complete a particular task or produce some unit of output. The actual output of workers is compared against the standard and the results are used as a measure of work efficiency. Engineered work standards are most useful when jobs are routine in nature and involve visible outputs that are easily counted. Although this does not describe most jobs in public agencies, engineered work standards have been used for clerical and street maintenance jobs. Experience suggests that they must be implemented with care because employees often feel threatened by the prospect of working harder while confronting possible layoffs because of increased efficiency. *Group Output Trend Analysis* involves measuring the output of groups of employees engaged in similar kinds of work, using appropriate indicators of productivity. Examples might include the number of applications processed, highway miles sanded, tons of garbage collected, clients served, fires extinguished, and arrests made. Once these output measures are developed, output data can be combined with input data (e.g., person-hours or employee-years) to provide standard measures of technical efficiency.

Constraints on Productivity Measurement

A report issued by the Senate Committee on Governmental Affairs in 1992 noted that despite evidence that performance measurement and reporting can improve decision making, accountability and responsiveness to citizens, and program performance, "performance measurement is still the exception rather than the norm in American government organizations."[25] Very little measurement seems to be done on a regular, ongoing basis. Perhaps the biggest reason for this is that most agencies simply lack the analytical capabilities required to develop measurement indicators, establish management information systems, and collect and analyze data on a routine basis. For this to be feasible at all, most agencies will need technical assistance from a central staff with expertise in productivity measurement. During the 1970s, for example, federal agencies received technical assistance from the Office of Management and Budget, General Services Administration, and the short-lived National Center for Productivity and Quality of Working Life. Participating agencies identified the output measures most meaningful for their operations, and the Bureau of Labor Statistics began routinely collecting data and expressing it in terms of output per staff-year. More recently, technical assistance has been provided by the National Productivity Group of the U.S. General Accounting Office (GAO). The National Productivity Group has pioneered a sophisticated model for measuring and improving agency productivity. The model rests on the belief that productivity improvement must be pursued as a systematic management process that is integrated with organizational procedures, appraisal systems, goal-setting practices, budget processes, management information systems, and human resource systems. The model itself involves setting up a computer-based productivity measurement system, assessing the agency's structural, procedural, and technological elements to identify productivity problems, analyzing the agency's management systems in terms of its capacity for ongoing measurement and productivity improvement, and offering specific recommendations regarding how to improve productivity.[26] The National Productivity Group's goal is to institutionalize a productivity measurement and management system in each federal agency.

Although most state and local governments still lack the capacity to develop productivity measurement systems, there are notable exceptions. Agency heads in Sunnyvale, California, for example, have long been required to measure the quantity, quality, and cost of every service they delivery. By collecting data on agency outputs, the City is able to maintain a Municipal Performance Index detailing its efficiency and effectiveness over time.[27]

Lack of analytical capacity provides only one of many possible explanations for why routine, ongoing productivity measurement is rarely seen in government. Adoption and implementation of productivity measurement and improvement systems face numerous constraints, both practical and political. First, politicians have few incentives for pursuing complex initiatives that pay political dividends only after a period of several years. Although they understand the public's anger over government waste and inefficiency, they also understand that the perception of action is more important to their political futures than the reality. Vague but symbolic references to budget ceilings and productivity improvement programs are often sufficient in this regard. Politicians also understand that some services and service levels are politically necessary even when they are grossly inefficient. Consolidating small school districts or closing a few state-owned liquor stores, for example, often proves to be infeasible politically despite the greater efficiencies they promise.

Second, agency administrators often lack incentives to implement productivity measurement and improvement systems. Budgeting procedures, for example, generally do not allow administrators to transfer the savings to other budgetary categories or to retain them beyond the end of the fiscal year. Their success in containing costs may only cause legislators to conclude that the agency is overfunded and to reduce its budget allocations as a result. Administrators may also feel threatened by the enhanced accountability that would be made possible if performance criteria were to be monitored by executive and legislative branch auditors. Finally, administrators may simply be too busy responding to problems to undertake productivity efforts, or they may feel uncomfortable about their lack of familiarity with what productivity measurement entails.

Third, employees may resist efforts to implement productivity measurement systems. Suspicious of management's motives, they may fear that they will result in work quotas and layoffs. Resistance to productivity measurement may also result from dissatisfaction with the carrot and stick philosophy on which many productivity improvement systems are based. Finally, employees may fear that they will be held accountable for productivity goals that are largely beyond their control. This is a realistic concern given that job performance in the public sector often is affected by the work of other employees, is dependent on actions taken by other agencies, and is constrained by many bureaucratic and environmental factors.

Fourth, productivity measurement faces a number of practical difficulties. For example, much of what is done in the public sector does not generate results that can be easily measured. A manager who spends considerable time studying problems and putting out brush fires may have little tangible product to show at the end of the day. Although appropriate output measures may be found for the program as a whole, measurement of each employee's work output may not be feasible. Another practical problem is that the use of quantitative measures can skew employee behaviors in counterproductive ways. It can, for example, cause employees to emphasize the measurable aspects of their jobs at the expense of those important, but less readily measurable aspects that contribute to the quality of their work. It may also encourage employees to tackle those goals that are easiest to achieve, such as finding jobs for those who are most easily placed or securing treatment for those who are most easily rehabilitated. Use of productivity measures may also encourage workers to overreport actual output. A final difficulty is that the time and effort involved in recording and analyzing data may actually reduce individual and unit productivity.

Productivity Improvement Programs

Productivity improvement efforts go well beyond the adoption of productivity measurement and monitoring systems. Numerous strategies are available for encouraging employees to work smarter, harder, more efficiently, and to interact with each other more effectively. To simplify matters, these strategies can be grouped into two categories: ad hoc throughput strategies and participative management strategies.

Ad Hoc Throughput Strategies

In the language of systems theory, productivity is a measure of the efficiency with which inputs are converted to outputs. The many factors involved in the conversion process are called throughputs. Among them are the factors presented above in Exhibit 12.2, including internal structures, work schedules, reward systems, organizational policies and procedures, and management styles. One obvious way to pursue productivity improvement is to analyze these factors in terms of their positive and negative consequences for productivity and to alter them as needed. Common throughput strategies include the following:[28]

Incentive-Based Strategies Despite political and legal constraints, many public sector organizations are altering their reward systems in an effort to increase employee motivation. Ensuring a highly motivated workforce is perhaps the most critical step an organization can taken in pursuing higher productivity. Strategies center on the use of performance-based evaluation and pay systems, gain-sharing plans, and rewards for cost-saving suggestions. Job enrichment efforts also fall into this category to the extent that they motivate workers to higher levels of productivity through the intrinsic rewards they provide.

Performance-Targeting Strategies Taking advantage of the motivational value of task clarification and goal setting, these strategies include management by objectives (MBO), appraisal by objectives (ABO), and engineered work standards.

Structural Reorganization Strategies These strategies involve analyzing organizational structures and procedures to identify those that are undermining operational efficiency or effectiveness. Corrective actions may involve such things as changing unit size, staffing procedures, organizational policies, physical arrangements, and budgetary systems.

Job Design and Workflow Strategies   These strategies involve redesigning specific jobs or the entire workflow of the unit so that work tasks are performed more efficiently. Changes might include putting similar units or jobs together, redesigning jobs so that routine duties can be delegated to paraprofessionals, or rearranging work tasks so that they can be performed on a team basis. The team approach may produce positive motivational effects as well as improved efficiency and effectiveness. A related strategy is the adoption of alternative work schedules, such as flextime or the 4/40 work week (See Chapter 13).

Technology Improvement Strategies   These strategies involve modifying work methods through the introduction of higher-order technologies so that greater productivity is achieved. Examples include the introduction of labor-saving equipment, management information systems, and tracking and control systems.

Training and Development Strategies   These strategies, described in Chapter 10, are designed to ensure that employees have the skills and abilities required to perform work duties in a superior manner. Specific strategies include retraining, cross-training, job rotation, mentoring, and encouraging continuing education.

Organizational Development Strategies   These involve efforts in planned change designed to improve interpersonal relations and communications within the organization. They are typically guided by consultants and involve the use of social science techniques. Strategies include sensitivity training, team-building, diversity management training, and management by objectives.

Participative Management Strategies

Productivity improvement strategies falling under the heading of participative management have enjoyed varying degrees of popularity in recent years. Strategies in this category bring line managers, personnel officers, and other employees together in new collaborative arrangements for the purpose of solving productivity-related problems. These arrangements often utilize throughput strategies but are implemented as ongoing programs. According to proponents, team-based, participative management programs can simultaneously increase trust and commitment, improve labor-management relations, and increase productivity.

To fully achieve their intended goals, participative management programs require a fundamental change in the nature of management itself, from a hierarchical, top-down system to one based on coordinated networks of teams and characterized by greater workplace democracy. For this reason participative management strategies rely to one extent or another on team-building techniques. Team building involves the use of various kinds of work groups to improve communication, cooperation, and ultimately organizational performance. John Greiner has identified three basic kinds of team efforts:[29]

OPERATING TEAMS

These are groups of employees who perform their day-to-day tasks as a team. Local government examples include team policing, custodial teams, and health care teams.

PROBLEM-ORIENTED TEAMS AND TASK FORCES

These groups come together on a temporary or permanent basis to discuss and recommend solutions to specific problems. Participation on the team is not considered part of an employee's regular job but an addition to that job.

MANAGEMENT TEAMS

These are groups of supervisory and management personnel who work together regularly to deal with operational problems, daily decisions, or objectives that fall between (or transcend) existing organizational boundaries.

In contrast to the ad hoc throughput strategies described above, participative management strategies are implemented as ongoing programs. Four kinds of participative management programs are described below: Joint Labor-Management Committees, Quality of Work Life Programs, Quality Circles, and Total Quality Management Programs.

Joint Labor-Management Committees

Composed of mid-managers and union members, these committees work in a nonadversarial fashion, outside of the collective bargaining process, to study problems and recommend actions involving productivity issues of mutual concern. Through this mechanism both sides can establish where their common interests lie, resolve roadblocks to higher productivity, and develop greater commitment to proposed solutions. Subjects discussed typically include the effects of technological change on jobs, job displacement, safety issues, and new incentive plans. Although they are "fragile institutions," joint labor-management committees have experienced some degree of success in the public sector.[30]

Quality of Worklife Programs

Quality of Worklife (QWL) programs use problem-solving teams to diagnose and correct workplace problems that are contributing to job dissatisfaction. Although QWL has its roots in the human resources and socio-technical theory of the 1960s, it took on the dimensions of a social movement in the United States after the publication in 1973 of a report entitled *Work in America*. Sponsored by the U.S. Department of Health, Education, and Welfare, the report concluded that job dissatisfaction was widespread in the workplace and that the alienating aspects of work pose a major threat to productivity.

The range of techniques used to improve productivity are much the same as those used by other participative, team-based programs. They include restructuring work so tasks can be performed on a team basis, job enrichment, flexible work schedules, greater worker involvement, and improved pay, working conditions, and benefits. What makes the QWL approach unique is that reform efforts are loosely tied together by common theoretical and philosophical principles. Work, according to these principles, must be personally rewarding and socially meaningful, and working conditions must be supportive of human dignity. Until these conditions are met, employers cannot expect high job satisfaction, motivation, or commitment. Advocates of QWL insist that increased government productivity is fully dependent on improving the quality of working life.[31] There is, however, little agreement on what constitutes improved quality of work life. Some improvement efforts focus on enriching work and democratizing the workplace; others seek to improve pay, fringe benefits, and working conditions as well.[32]

The public sector has been less willing to experiment with QWL programs than the private sector. Rosow suggests this is attributable in part to the absence of clear goals, a greater need for secrecy, and insufficient authority to pursue solutions.[33] Improving the quality of work life can also cost much more than governments are willing to pay. Finally, research has not clearly demonstrated that improvement in the quality of work life leads to improved job satisfaction or productivity. If Herzberg's two-factor theory is correct, improving environmental factors such as pay and working conditions may reduce dissatisfaction without necessarily increasing job satisfaction or productivity.

Quality Circles

In the late 1970s American businesses "rediscovered quality." Experiencing intense competition from abroad, key industries refocused their efforts on improving the quality of their products. Many of them began establishing quality circles, organizational devices that Japanese companies had been using for years. By the early 1980s, numerous public agencies at all levels of government had adopted the quality circle concept. The quality circle is a small group of workers in a particular organizational unit that meets weekly to identify, analyze, and solve problems they experience in their jobs. Participation is voluntary.

Because quality circles engage rank and file employees in planning and problem-solving activities, they represent a form of participative management. But although most forms of participative management only allow workers to provide input to a planning process or to review plans already developed by management, members of quality circles select which problems to tackle, receive intense training in problem solving, and are responsible for formulating and implementing their own solutions. If they lack the authority needed, circle members are expected to present their case to management. Quality circles thus represent a means of tapping the knowledge and expertise of those most intimately involved in work operations while also developing their capabilities.

Although their primary task is to solve quality-related problems, quality circles are usually authorized to tackle any problem related to work processes or working conditions that is sufficiently limited in scope to be manageable. This provides employees with a concrete means of addressing the many workplace frustrations that contribute to job dissatisfaction. Resulting changes in employee attitudes and behaviors may prove to be more important to the organization than anticipated cost savings. According to Gryna, for example, quality circles enable the individual to improve personal capabilities, increase the individual's self-respect, help workers change personality characteristics such as shyness, prepare workers to become the supervisors of the future, increase mutual respect between workers and supervisors, reduce conflict stemming from the working environment, help workers understand why many problems cannot be solved quickly, and instill in workers a better understanding of the importance of product quality.[34]

Securing these benefits is not a sure thing. The success of quality circles depends on several critical factors. First, team members must be given extensive training in team-building and problem-solving skills. Second, upper management must establish an organizational environment in which participative management can flourish. Quality circles do not perform well in an authoritarian and inflexible environment. Third, quality circles must be given sufficient authority to address the problems they identify and management must be willing to act on proposed solutions when action is warranted. Perhaps the largest cause of failure is not allowing circles to address significant problems and not giving them sufficient authority to act. Fourth, the quality circle process must be sustained by well-trained coordinators and group facilitators. Finally, quality circles should be just one component of a comprehensive quality improvement program. They can accomplish little if they are a token effort unsupported by a larger organizational commitment. Unfortunately, these conditions are difficult to satisfy in the public sector. Even when management is committed to the concept, the need for accountability, the nature of hierarchically ordered bureaucracies, the fragmentation of authority, and the rigidities of civil service systems make it very difficult for meaningful exercises in empowerment to flourish.

Total Quality Management (TQM)

Far too often innovations such as the quality circle are treated as panaceas. Little time or effort is taken to comprehend their underlying philosophies or to consider what it will take for them to succeed. In light of the counterproductive parade of fads that has characterized the search for organizational excellence, Total Quality Management (TQM) offers a ray of hope. It is a process for improving quality that is comprehensive in scope and based on definable principles. These principles are derived in large part from the work of W. Edwards Deming and Joseph Juran, who introduced methods of quality control to the Japanese in the period after World War II and who were largely ignored in the United States until the "rediscovery of quality" in the late 1970s.

Two key principles define what TQM is all about. First, the customer is the ultimate determiner of quality and customer satisfaction is the primary goal of organizations. This principle has particular relevance to public sector organizations since democratic governments exist to serve their citizens (or customers). Key steps in the TQM process include defining which particular customers the agency exists to serve (internally and externally), asking customers what they want, and structuring their service delivery systems to satisfy those wants. Osborne and Gaebler cite the example of the Madison, Wisconsin, police department, which surveys every 35th person it encounters, whether a victim of a crime, a witness, a complainant, or a criminal, asking them to rate service quality and to suggest how service might be improved.[35]

The second key principle is continuous improvement of the process by which services are delivered. According to Deming, only 15 percent of quality-related problems are the fault of employees, whereas fully 85 percent are the fault of the operating systems within which they work.[36] Although TQM follows no single set of steps, it typically involves the use of temporary project teams or permanent quality circles composed of both managerial and nonmanagerial personnel who define the customers they are responsible for serving, investigate systemic causes of inferior performance, gather all statistical data relevant to the service delivery process, and draw up plans for corrective action. Team members receive extensive training in problem-solving techniques, often including statistical measurement. A unique aspect of Deming's philosophy of quality control is that quality should be built into the product or service from the outset and that subsequent investigations should focus on identifying and rectifying sources of error in the work process rather than in the final product or service. This does not mean, however, that outcomes are unimportant. Continuous improvement requires defining standards of quality and regularly measuring agency success against those standards.

Taking these two principles together, TQM may be defined as a strategic process for achieving *customer satisfaction* by involving employees in problem-solving efforts designed to *continuously improve the process* of service delivery. It requires a new kind of organizational culture in which managers become process managers and facilitators of employee empowerment.

TQM is currently being used by the federal government and many state and local governments. Introduction of TQM in the public sector is an exciting prospect because it promises to reverse the public's perception of government bureaucracies as arrogant and uncaring. Nonetheless, the success of TQM in the public sector remains highly uncertain for several reasons. First, because of the extensive training required and the considerable amount of staff time expended in investigating problems, TQM is undeniably expensive. Second, to produce results TQM requires sustained commitment from political leaders, something that is often lacking. Few benefits accrue to politicians in the short term, and many TQM efforts fail when their champions leave office. Third, defining the agency's customers is often difficult because of the multiple goals and clienteles that public agencies exist to serve. Fourth, governments must find ways to reward agencies for seriously pursuing and achieving cost savings. The most obvious answer is to allow agencies to retain at least a portion of their savings to use for other purposes. Fifth, considerable skill and sensitivity is required to overcome potential opposition from organized labor. Finally, as with other quality improvement efforts in the public sector, TQM will confront bureaucratic constraints and resistance from mid-managers. Obstacles of this kind make exercises in employee empowerment difficult to implement and sustain.

Given these considerable difficulties, the success of TQM efforts may depend on the amount of institutional support they can muster. Federal agencies, for example, can now turn to the Federal Quality Institute for assistance. In addition to providing technical assistance, the Institute organizes conferences, networking systems, and a quality improvement award program. If the many obstacles cited above can be overcome successfully, and if it is not treated as just another management fad, TQM promises to be a powerful tool for improving organizational performance.

Productivity Improvement and Human Resource Management

The connection between productivity improvement and human resource management deserves a word of explanation. Personnel officers and line managers play important roles in any such efforts. First, personnel officers and managers may be asked to help collect and analyze data as part of a productivity measurement and monitoring program. Second, line managers often participate in making decisions as members of problem-solving teams and assist in implementing team decisions. Third, personnel officers may be asked to provide technical assistance, including such things as training quality circle members, assisting with job redesign, rewriting personnel policies, and consulting in the development of new reward systems. Personnel officers may also be asked to help sort out some of the difficult questions involved in setting up and coordinating quality circles and TQM teams. These may include determining who will be selected for teams and how, what kinds of training will be needed to develop team-building and problem-solving skills, and how team efforts will be coordinated and sustained. Finally, personnel officers may be asked to mediate between employees and management during the design and implementation of new initiatives. It will be their task to ensure that employee rights and interests are respected and that resistance from both employees and managers is successfully overcome.

All of these roles will pose new and unique challenges for the human resource function. The personnel staff, for example, must overcome its specialized and fragmented character if it is to contribute meaningfully to the design and operation of productivity improvement programs. And line managers will have to learn how to become effective facilitators, process managers, and empowerers if participative management programs are to succeed. Success in developing a highly motivated and productive workforce ultimately depends on the ability and willingness of personnel officers and managers alike to perform new and challenging roles.

■ CASE 12.1   Money, Morale, and Motivation

Mary Jacobson was hired as a Vocational Trainer I at a starting salary of $19,000. At the end of her first year she received a promotion to the position of Vocational Trainer II. This position involved higher-level duties and responsibilities and required her to attend to clients in two counties. Mary's new salary was $21,000, $2,000 less than her predecessor had received. Mary was surprised by the discrepancy in pay because her predecessor had worked for the agency only a few months longer than she had. At first she resolved to say nothing, but the more she thought about it the more it bothered her. When she finally asked her supervisor for an explanation she was told that her predecessor's salary had included a merit raise.

Mary later discovered that the "merit raise" had been given to every agency employee just two months before her initial employment. The same raise had been awarded to everyone without regard to years of service or job performance. Mary believed that her supervisor had not been totally forthcoming about the discrepancy in pay but she once again decided not to make a fuss.

After working for a year as a Vocational Trainer II, Mary asked to be given a raise to the level of her predecessor. Her duties had expanded to include legislative work and curriculum development, and she thought she had earned the "merit raise." Other workers in her job classification were receiving the higher salary. Mary submitted a formal request but was told there was no room in the budget to grant automatic annual pay increases. Mary was shocked by the response. Not only had she not requested an annual salary increase, but the agency's accountant had assured her that the budget still contained the $23,000 salary that her predecessor had received. Although she knew she probably shouldn't take the matter personally, she couldn't help but think that her hard work was unappreciated. Her commitment to the agency began to flag as a result.

Hoping to obtain an explanation that she could understand and accept, Mary took the matter to the agency Director. The Director responded that the budget simply couldn't accommodate the request. When Mary explained that the higher salary was already contained in the budget, the Director promised that she would "look into it." When several weeks passed without a response, Mary became disgruntled and quit.

1. Did Mary have valid reasons for being upset, or did she simply fail to understand the nature of compensation policies?
2. What does this case indicate about the relationships between pay, trust, morale, and motivation?
3. What could (or should) the Director have done differently?

Notes

1. Mary Coeli Meyer, "Motivation," in William R. Tracey, ed., *Human Resources Management and Development Handbook* (New York: AMACOM, 1985), 199.

2. Ibid., 200.

3. Daniel Katz and Robert L. Kahn, *The Social Psychology of Organizations* (New York: John Wiley & Sons, 1978), 402.

4. Victor Vroom, *Work and Motivation* (New York: John Wiley & Sons, 1964).

5. U.S. General Accounting Office, *Pay For Performance: State and International Public Sector Pay-For-Performance Systems* (GAO\GGD-91-1, October 1990).

6. James L. Perry, "Compensation, Merit Pay and Motivation," in Steven W. Hays and Richard C. Kearney, eds., *Public Personnel Administration: Problems and Prospects* (Englewood Cliffs, New Jersey: Prentice-Hall, 1990), 109.

7. U.S. General Accounting Office, *Pay for Performance*, 9.

8. James L. Perry and Beth Ann Petrakis, "Can Pay for Performance Succeed in Government?" *Public Personnel Management* 17 (Winter 1988):366.

9. See, for example, Edward L. Deci, *Intrinsic Motivation* (New York: Plenum Press, 1975).

10. See, for example, Tom Peters and Nancy Austin, *A Passion for Excellence: The Leadership Difference* (New York: Warner Books, 1985).

11. David Osborne and Ted Gaebler, *Reinventing Government: How the Entrepreneurial Spirit is Transforming the Sector* (Reading, Massachusetts: Addison-Wesley, 1992).

12. See William Ouichi, *Theory Z* (Reading, Massachusetts: Addison-Wesley, 1981); R. Pascale and A. Althos, *The Art of Japanese Management* (New York: Simon and Schuster, 1981); and Nina Hatvany and Vladimir Pucik, "Japanese Management Practices and Productivity," *Organizational Dynamics* 9 (Spring 1981):5–21.

13. Deci, *Intrinsic Motivation*, 223.

14. Edwin A. Locke, David Sirota, and Alan D. Wolfson, "An Experimental Case Study of the Success and Failures of Job Enrichment in a Government Agency," *Journal of Applied Psychology* 61 (December 1976):701–711.

15. Ouichi, *Theory Z*.

16. Deci, *Intrinsic Motivation*, 224.

17. Edwin A. Locke and Gary P. Latham, *Goal Setting: A Motivational Technique that Works!* (Englewood Cliffs, New Jersey: Prentice-Hall, 1984).

18. Ibid., 19.

19. Ibid., 27–37.

20. Gilbert B. Siegel, "Enlarged Concept of Productivity Measurement in Government: A Review of Some Strategies," *Public Productivity Review* 11 (Winter 1976):37–61.

21. Ibid., 41.

22. C. Y. Wu, "Refining Concepts of Performance in Development Effectiveness, Profitability and Productivity," *Philippine Journal of Public Administration* 17 (July 1973), 300.

23. Donald C. Kull, "Productivity Programs in the Federal Government," *Public Administration Review* 38 (January/February 1978), 7.

24. Walter L. Balk, *Improving Government Productivity: Some Policy Perspectives* (Beverly Hills, California: Sage Publications, 1975).

25. Quoted in "Performance Measurement Bill Passes Senate," *PA Times* 15 (1 November 1992), 4.

26. Michael R. Dulworth and Robert C. Taylor, "Assessing and Improving Organizational Productivity," in Joseph S. Wholey, Kathryn E. Newcomer and Associates, *Improving Government Performance: Evaluation Strategies for Strengthening Public Agencies and Programs* (San Francisco: Jossey-Bass, 1989):143–161.

27. Osborne and Gaebler, *Reinventing Government,* 145.

28. See, for example, John Greiner, "Motivating Improved Productivity: Three Promising Approaches," *Public Management* 61 (October 1979):2–5; and Robert E. Quinn, "Productivity and the Process of Organizational Improvement: Why We Cannot Talk to Each Other," *Public Administration Review* 38 (January/February 1978):41–45.

29. Greiner, "Motivating Improved Productivity," 4.

30. Anna C. Goldoff and David C. Tatage, "Joint Productivity Committees: Lessons of Recent Initiatives," *Public Administration Review* 38 (March/April 1978):184–186.

31. Jerome M. Rosow, "Human Dignity in the Public-Sector Workplace, *Public Personnel Management* 8 (January/February 1979), 8.

32. Richard E. Walton, "Quality of Working Life: What Is It?" *Sloan Management Review* 15 (Fall 1973):11–21.

33. Rosow, "Human Dignity in the Public-Sector Workplace," 13.

34. Frank M. Gryna, Jr., *Quality Circles: A Team Approach to Problem Solving* (New York: AMACOM, 1981).

35. Osborne and Gaebler, *Reinventing Government,* 143.

36. W. Edwards Deming, *Out of the Crisis* (Cambridge, Massachusetts: Massachusetts Institute of Technology, 1986).

Part 5

Supportive Workplace Relations

CHAPTERS:
13 *Personnel Policies and Employee Relations*
14 *Collective Bargaining and Labor Relations*

Analysis in Part 4 focused on the management of human performance. A related and equally important subject—the subject of Part 5—is the maintenance of supportive workplace relations. These two concerns are interdependent. Without constructive and mutually advantageous relations among employees, and between labor and management, superior human performance cannot be expected nor sustained.

Chapter 13 examines how personnel policies and benefits can create a supportive work environment and a dedicated workforce. Workplace rules clarify expectations, create order, and allow for the fair treatment of employees. Flexible policies and benefits help employees satisfy their personal needs and balance work and family responsibilities. Assuming that they are designed and implemented with care, they can do much to increase employee commitment and safeguard morale.

Chapter 14 examines collective bargaining and labor relations. The introduction of collective bargaining in the 1960s created a new set of concerns for public managers. Depending on the degree of skill with which it is handled, collective bargaining can either escalate tensions between labor and management or provide a constructive means of resolving differences and addressing mutual concerns.

Linking HRM Tasks and Outcomes: A Performance Model

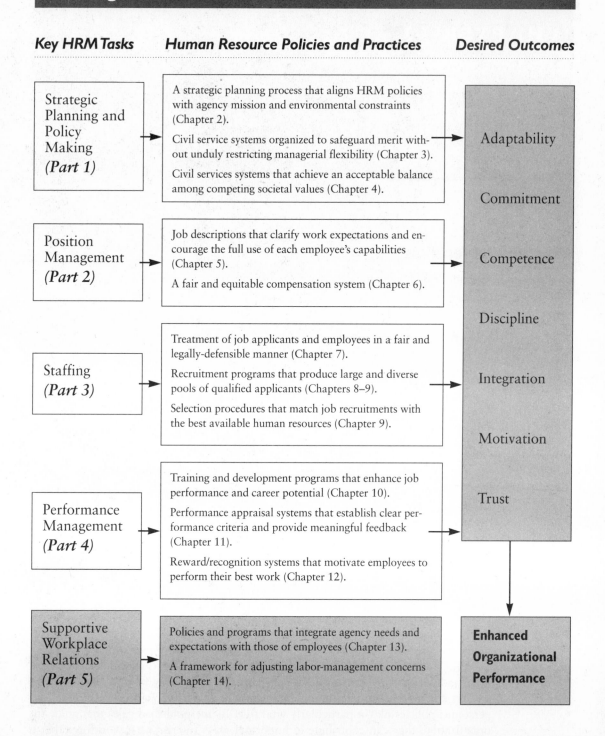

Key HRM Tasks	Human Resource Policies and Practices	Desired Outcomes

Strategic Planning and Policy Making (Part 1)

A strategic planning process that aligns HRM policies with agency mission and environmental constraints (Chapter 2).

Civil service systems organized to safeguard merit without unduly restricting managerial flexibility (Chapter 3).

Civil services systems that achieve an acceptable balance among competing societal values (Chapter 4).

Position Management (Part 2)

Job descriptions that clarify work expectations and encourage the full use of each employee's capabilities (Chapter 5).

A fair and equitable compensation system (Chapter 6).

Staffing (Part 3)

Treatment of job applicants and employees in a fair and legally-defensible manner (Chapter 7).

Recruitment programs that produce large and diverse pools of qualified applicants (Chapters 8–9).

Selection procedures that match job recruitments with the best available human resources (Chapter 9).

Performance Management (Part 4)

Training and development programs that enhance job performance and career potential (Chapter 10).

Performance appraisal systems that establish clear performance criteria and provide meaningful feedback (Chapter 11).

Reward/recognition systems that motivate employees to perform their best work (Chapter 12).

Supportive Workplace Relations (Part 5)

Policies and programs that integrate agency needs and expectations with those of employees (Chapter 13).

A framework for adjusting labor-management concerns (Chapter 14).

Desired Outcomes:

Adaptability

Commitment

Competence

Discipline

Integration

Motivation

Trust

Enhanced Organizational Performance

Personnel Policies and Employee Relations

Learning Objectives

After mastering the materials contained in this chapter, you will be able to:

1. Explain why it is important to take a strategic approach to policy development.
2. Distinguish between personnel policy manuals and employee handbooks as tools for improving employee relations.
3. Develop policies and programs designed to achieve specific organizational objectives.
4. Apply the principles of progressive discipline and just cause in a broad range of disciplinary situations.
5. Explain how flexible policies and benefit plans can help employees balance their personal and work responsibilities.

The human resource function exists, above all else, to foster positive employee relations. An organization may possess the latest equipment, the newest facilities, the largest budgets, and an impressive array of personnel tools, but without the cooperation and goodwill of its workers it will inevitably fail to accomplish stated objectives. In fact, the origins of the modern personnel department can be traced not only to the public sector's adoption of civil service reforms, but also to the private sector's search for better employee relations. Industrial managers in the early 1900s began to realize that high productivity and low turnover depended on the cooperation and goodwill of their workers, and that these in turn depended upon management's willingness to provide employment security, fair treatment, and opportunities for self-improvement. Recognition of this fact led organizations in the public and private sectors alike to establish personnel departments staffed by specialists in employee relations.

Positive employee relations are not achieved through good intentions alone. Human resource systems, personnel policies, and the day-to-day practices of managers all play critical roles in determining the quality of employee relations.[1] Among these, personnel policies play a particularly vital role. As the published rules that guide the organization, they can contribute in important ways to creating a workforce that is highly motivated and strongly committed to the organization and its goals. This chapter describes a broad range of personnel policies, assesses their potential for improving employee relations, and identifies key issues that persons designing such policies may wish to consider. A central theme is the desirability of replacing a rigid, paternalistic approach to employee relations with a flexible approach deliberately designed to empower employees, develop their talents, and respond to their unique needs and preferences.

The Role of Policy in Organizational Life

Organizational policies serve both as guides to action and symbols of management's intentions. As guides to action, they communicate to organizational members how strategic objectives are to be achieved. Through policy guidance, thousands of daily decisions are made more easily and quickly and in ways that promote organizational objectives. Policies, for example, provide the necessary machinery and decision criteria for handling transactions such as hiring, firing, training, and disciplining. They also communicate how employee rights are to be protected and what benefits are available to workers. Finally, they help protect the organization from legal risk by restricting the behaviors of organizational members to those that are legally defensible. In many civil service systems policy guidance is provided through two overlapping bodies of rules and policies—those generated by merit boards under a specific grant of statutory authority and those established by the director of personnel under his or her delegated authority as an administrator.

As guides to action, policies must achieve an appropriate balance between firmness and flexibility so that employees can exercise judgments on their own without being shackled by rigid, procedural rules. Policies should communicate desired principles rather than prescribe narrow rules. Doing so, however, is not always feasible. Safety rules and disciplinary procedures, for example, typically require firm and rather detailed policies, not only to prevent injuries and to safeguard employee rights, but also to protect the organization from legal risk. Risk management often requires adding an element of rigidity to policies beyond what is otherwise needed or desired.

Policies also serve as important symbols of management's intentions. They provide opportunities for management to communicate its commitment to certain values and philosophies. For example, if management is truly committed to creating a safe and healthy work environment, treating employees fairly, developing human resources, and assisting employees in balancing their obligations to work and family, then it must make certain that these commitments are clearly reflected in its policies and actions. Success in this regard will determine whether employee loyalty and confidence is built or destroyed.

This chapter does not attempt to review all categories of personnel policies. It does, however, review those that play particularly important roles in shaping and improving employee relations.

A Strategic Approach to Policy Development

Although most organizations understand the importance of taking deliberate steps to develop a highly motivated and committed workforce, they do not always know where to begin. Simply borrowing personnel policies and programs from other jurisdictions without regard to their relevance will not produce the desired results. Nor will writing policies without a clear sense of purpose. To be fully effective, an employee relations program should be developed in conjunction with the organization's strategic planning process. The task of the employee relations staff is to assist management in developing a "human resources plan" indicating the degree of commitment the organization is willing to make to developing employee relations, the specific objectives it wishes to achieve (e.g., reduced turnover, greater job satisfaction), and the motivational strategies it will adopt.

The task of defining strategic objectives begins with analysis of what the organization hopes to achieve from its employee relations program. Generally speaking, organizations seek to attract and retain loyal workers, ensure dependable work performance, keep interpersonal frictions to a minimum, and elicit special qualities such as enthusiasm, creativity, and a willingness to innovate. But each organization must decide for itself how these goals are to be achieved, and it must do so within the context of its unique needs and circumstances. First, discussion of strategic objectives must take into account the amount of resources available for employee relations programs. Comprehensive wellness and employee assistance programs, for example, may be consistent with the organization's strategic goals but may cost more than the organization is able to afford. Second, strategic objectives must be developed with distinct organizational problems in mind. For example, if absenteeism is not a serious problem, then it makes little sense to develop elaborate absenteeism control systems. Finally, strategic objectives must take into account the needs, preferences, lifestyles, and values of the contemporary workforce. Today's workers have a wide range of personal obligations to fulfill, including raising families, commuting, continuing their education, caring for elders, and running important errands during work hours. Values are also shifting. Some employees, for example, are insisting on work that is meaningful and challenging, and others are placing a higher value on recreation and leisure time. If flexibility is not built into personnel policies, employees may conclude that the organization is unconcerned with their needs and may become increasingly alienated as a result.

Consideration must also be given to *how* strategic objectives are to be achieved. They may be achieved, for example, by directing and controlling employees, rewarding them, or liberating and empowering them. The recent literatures on organizational excellence and workforce diversity emphasize the importance of empowering employees and responding to their individual needs and preferences. Jamieson and O'Mara suggest a "flex-management" approach for organizations wishing to move in this direction. This approach is composed of four distinct strategies: (1) careful matching of people to jobs; (2) individualizing rewards for performance; (3) informing and involving people more; and (4) making polices flexible enough to satisfy the needs and preferences of diverse groups of employees.[2] Flexibility is the key to this approach. It rejects the use of traditional personnel policies that tightly monitor work hours, time off, employee behavior, disciplinary processes, and work rules.

There are, of course, many other strategies that may be employed. Regardless of which of these are ultimately chosen, it is important to identify clear linkages between the objectives to be achieved, the strategies for achieving them, and the policies ultimately adopted. It is also important for each policy or program to be designed and implemented as part of a larger, well-integrated strategy for achieving organizational objectives. A 1992 report by the U.S. General Accounting Office, for example, found that although many federal agencies had adopted policies to assist employees in meshing their family and work responsibilities, they were not being implemented in a truly coordinated or strategic fashion, and policy goals were not being achieved effectively as a result.[3]

The following examples illustrate how to link personnel policies to specific organizational objectives and human resource strategies:

Policy	Organizational Objectives	Human Resource Strategy
Flextime	Reduce absenteeism Reduce turnover Increase commitment Increase job satisfaction	Increase flexibility in work scheduling, thereby empowering employees to satisfy their personal needs in regards to commuting, running errands, child care, etc.
Paid personal leave	Reduce absenteeism Reduce turnover Increase commitment	Allow paid leave so that employees can enjoy job and financial security while attending to personal problems or needs.

The purpose of conducting strategic analysis is to ensure that personnel policies are designed to achieve desired results. The best policies are those that are tailored to the needs and goals of the organization and are consistent with the requirements of state and federal law. Once they are written, they must be reviewed periodically to make sure that they continue to perform their intended functions. Policies that are not reevaluated and modified to fit changing organizational requirements can undermine employee morale and impair productivity.[4] The process of adding or modifying personnel policies normally involves forwarding recommendations from the employee relations staff or personnel director to the relevant policy-making body. At that point they often fall victim to legal, budgetary, or political constraints irrespective of their strategic value.

Policy Manuals and Employee Handbooks

Personnel policies cannot achieve their intended purposes unless everyone is aware of them. Policy manuals and employee handbooks are the primary vehicles for communicating policies to organizational members. A policy manual contains written policies in unedited form as established by those in authority. Its primary purpose is to inform managers and supervisors of personnel policies and to instruct them in how they are to be implemented. It functions both as a guide to managers and supervisors in executing their duties and as a means of ensuring fair and consistent treatment of employees. The purpose of the employee handbook, by contrast, is to communicate policies to employees generally. It summarizes policies in a brief, readable format and is typically distributed to employees when they first enter the organization. The goal of the handbook is to give employees the information they need to understand their rights, obligations, and benefits as expressed in policy. Although the policy manual and employee handbook should be consistent in their contents, they are not simply two versions of the same document. The manual contains formal policies and performs an instructional function for managers, and the handbook summarizes policies and performs an informational function for all employees.

The employee handbook is an important management tool for several reasons.[5] First, it provides an excellent opportunity for the employer to enhance its image, and ultimately each employee's loyalty and commitment, by explicitly stating the organization's values and highlighting favorable benefits and working conditions. An employer may use the handbook, for example, to convey that it is a model employer, one that is committed to developing its human resources and offering more than other organizations by way of employee benefits. To the extent that it is successful in this regard the handbook can help attract applicants to the organization, encourage them to remain with it, and increase commitment to it.

Second, the employee handbook can be a vehicle for transmitting and reinforcing the values that the employer hopes will shape the organizational culture. Handbooks often begin with a history of the organization, its place in the larger governmental structure, and a discussion of management values or principles. The latter may include, for example, a discussion of the importance attached to honesty, openness, and team effort. Handbooks may also signal the employer's intent to create and maintain a safe, well-ordered, and rewarding work environment. In short, the handbook provides one of the few places where information is brought together so that employees can see the ultimate purpose of their efforts and the values to which the employer is committed.

Third, the employee handbook can perform a control function by communicating workplace rules and setting parameters on what defines acceptable behavior. It may include, for example, the rules governing day-to-day conduct and the disciplinary procedures and sanctions that will follow from their violation. However, rules of conduct, although important to communicate, should constitute a relatively small part of the handbook. It is better to emphasize the benefits to be had from working together in an orderly and cooperative fashion than to create the perception that the handbook is essentially a rule book.

Finally, the employee handbook can be used to inform employees of their procedural rights in disciplinary situations and how disputes of all kinds may be resolved. It provides an opportunity for the employer to communicate a commitment to treating employees fairly and reducing frictions between them. The employee handbook often serves as the equivalent of a union contract in a nonunion setting by assuring employees of procedural due process. Because courts in several states have shown a willingness to enforce statements found in handbooks as implied contractual obligations, employers must take care to include only those rights and procedures that it is prepared to abide by. For example, if the handbook states that a probationary employee becomes a "permanent employee" after six months, and that permanent employees cannot be dismissed except after a showing of just cause, then the employer must act accordingly if it wishes to avoid a lawsuit. Employees should also be apprised of all subsequent policy changes. Disclaimers are sometimes added to the handbook at the insistence of the legal staff reserving the employer's right to repeal, modify, or amend policies at any time.

Exhibit 13.1 presents an overview of policies often covered in policy manuals and employee handbooks. Although the list is far from comprehensive, it does indicate the scope of what is typically covered and provides an introduction to some of the policies discussed later in this chapter.

Rules Governing Employee Conduct

Perhaps nothing is more harmful to employee morale than lack of order and discipline in the workplace. To guard against this eventuality, organizations establish rules governing personal conduct. Rules help create order, maintain discipline, and facilitate efficient agency operations by structuring relations between its members. Assuming that the rules are accepted as legitimate and enforced fairly, employees can trust that their rights will be respected, that hard work and loyalty will be rewarded, and that poor work and insubordination will not be tolerated. Employees usually understand the value of working within boundaries set by sensible rules. This can be reinforced by encouraging employee involvement in the rule-making process. If employees are allowed to participate in making the rules, they are more likely to view them as internal norms rather than as external controls.

Exhibit 13.2 presents a sample policy on employee conduct. Other, more specialized policies may cover subjects such as smoking, substance abuse, and sexual harassment.

Exhibit 13.2, with its rather long list of dos and don'ts, illustrates a fundamental dilemma that all policy developers confront. Rules of personal conduct are essential to the maintenance of order and the protection of people, property, and operational efficiency. Indeed, rules of the kind presented in Exhibit 13.2 provide the basis for disciplining employees on those occasions when sanctions are clearly warranted. However, an employee handbook containing long lists of dos and don'ts has the appearance of an old-style military procedures manual, reflecting distrust of employees and a desire for maximum conformity. If rules are added each time a new threat to the common good occurs, employees may become overly rule conscious and perceive them as external controls rather than as legitimate expressions of group norms. Long lists of rules may also rob employees of the flexibility they need to carry out work tasks effectively. Finally, they may create serious obstacles for agencies attempting to transform themselves from rule-driven to mission-driven organizations. The difficult task for policy makers is to find an acceptable balance in the number of rules included in written policy and the relative degree of firmness and flexibility reflected in their   language.

Employee Discipline

Ironically, maintaining discipline in the positive sense sometimes requires meting out discipline in the negative sense. The morale and productivity of a work unit can be greatly undermined if a few employees are allowed to violate work rules, disobey supervisors, refuse to cooperate with co-workers, miss work on a regular basis, or fail to perform their jobs dependably and competently. Although disciplinary systems are often viewed as punitive tools for controlling employee behavior, they actually play an

EXHIBIT 13.1

Major Categories of Personnel Policies

I. Employee Conduct
  A. Workplace Rules
  B. Disciplinary Action
  C. Grievance Procedures
  D. Political Activities
  E. Smoking
  F. Substance Abuse
  G. Sexual Harassment
  H. Employee Safety

II. Employment Policies
  A. Hours of Work/Scheduling
  B. Nepotism
  C. EEO/Nondiscrimination
  D. Probationary Period
  E. Selection Procedures
  F. Layoffs and Recalls

III. Leaves
  A. Personal/Family Leave
  B. Jury/Court Leave
  C. Leave Without Pay
  D. Sick Leave
  E. Vacation Leave

IV. Pay Policies
  A. Paydays and Payroll Periods
  B. Overtime and Compensation Time

V. Employee Benefits
  A. Payroll Deductions
  B. Deferred Compensation
  C. Life Insurance
  D. Medical, Dental, Optical Benefits
  E. Retirement Benefits
  F. Employee Assistance Program
  G. Child Care Assistance
  H. Wellness Program
  I. Holidays and Vacations
  J. Employee Development

EXHIBIT 13.2

SAMPLE POLICY ON EMPLOYEE CONDUCT

Purpose

To outline specific areas that may result in employee discipline.

Statement of Policy

It shall be the duty of employees to maintain high standards of cooperation, efficiency, and integrity in their work with the City. If an employee's conduct falls below standard, he or she may be subject to disciplinary action.

Some general things for which an employee may be disciplined include, but are not limited to:

1. Reporting to work under the influence of intoxicants or nonprescription/illegal drugs, or using such substances while on City property

2. Failure to follow the orders of one's supervisor(s)

3. Being absent from work without permission or failure to report to the supervisor or Department Head when one is absent

4. Being habitually absent or tardy for any reason

5. Failure to perform assigned work in an efficient or effective manner

6. Being wasteful of material, property, or working time

7. Inability to get along with fellow employees so that the work being done is hindered and not up to required levels

8. Failure to observe property security procedures

9. Conduct on the job that violates the common decency or morality of the community

10. Commission of a felony or gross misdemeanor

11. Violating safety rules and regulations

12. Speaking critically or making derogatory or false accusations so as to discredit other employees or supervisors

13. Removal of City money, merchandise, or property, including property in custody of the City, without permission

14. Lying to supervisors in connection with your job

15. Dishonesty, including intentionally giving false information, intentionally falsifying records, or making false statements when applying for employment

16. Being on City premises during nonworking hours without permission

17. Divulging or misusing confidential information, including removal from City premises, without proper authorization, any employee lists, records, designs, drawings, or confidential information of any kind

18. Accepting fees, gifts, or other valuable items in the performance of the employee's official duties for the City

---

EXHIBIT 13.2 *(continued)*

19. Inability or unwillingness to perform the assigned job
20. Falsification of time records for payroll
21. Abuse of sick leave privileges by reporting sick when not sick or obtaining sick leave pay falsely or under false pretenses
22. The use of profanity or abusive language toward a fellow employee or member of the general public while performing official duties as a City employee . . .

Source: Don Morrison, ed., The Local Government Institute, *Model Personnel Policies and Procedures*, Tacoma, Washington, 1993.

---

important role in maintaining positive employee relations. If administered fairly, predictably, and consistently by well-trained supervisors, disciplinary systems can be constructive tools for enhancing productivity and safeguarding morale.

Although the importance of disciplining employees may seem obvious, many supervisors are reluctant to impose sanctions on their subordinates and often postpone taking corrective action until their patience is totally exhausted. Redeker describes the typical chain of events as follows:

> *As a rule, supervisors dislike disciplining employees. It places them in direct conflict with a subordinate, with the risk that this conflict will somehow make it more difficult in the future for the supervisor to deal with the employee. The supervisor, fearing employee hostility or the breach of a relationship, puts off disciplining the employee for minor infractions and, then, overreacts when the employee goes too far. The result is a major confrontation, and the employee can reasonably argue that there has not been adequate notice that his or her behavior was errant.*[6]

Although the supervisor's reluctance to discipline subordinates is understandable, it is nonetheless the supervisor's duty to take corrective action when employees fail to fulfill their basic responsibilities as workers. Avoidance only reduces organizational effectiveness, undermines morale in the work unit, and causes additional problems, both practical and legal. Research indicates that carefully administered discipline can have a positive impact on worker behavior and productivity. O'Reilly and Weitz found, for example, that supervisors who applied sanctions frequently received higher unit performance ratings from top management than supervisors who applied sanctions less frequently.[7] Disciplinary actions taken by supervisors apparently serve as a warning to marginal employees to improve performance levels and abide by organizational rules. In short, the effectiveness of an organization's disciplinary system depends in no small measure on supervisors who are well trained and willing to apply discipline when the actions of employees clearly warrant it.

Disciplinary action is typically taken in two kinds of situations: when workplace rules are broken and when work performance is below standard. A violation of any of the rules listed in Exhibit 13.2, for example, may lead to disciplinary action, but because violations vary greatly in terms of degree, potential consequences, and frequency of occurrence, supervisors must determine in each instance what sanctions, if any, are appropriate. Guidance is sometimes provided in law or organizational policy. For example, theft and serious acts of insubordination or assault are often cited as grounds for immediate dismissal. Less serious offenses are typically handled through a system of progressive discipline. Whether the offense is judged to be a minor or a major one, it is important to investigate the facts at issue to ensure that the disciplinary action taken is well supported by the available evidence.

A different kind of calculus is usually required in situations involving poor work performance. The focus of the investigation shifts from the facts surrounding the violation of a rule to the underlying causes of identified performance problems. Traditional forms of discipline produce little improvement in such cases unless poor work performance is the result of deliberate and willful decisions by the employee. If the latter is the case, and counseling produces no improvement in work performance, then the imposition of sanctions is an appropriate response. If, however, the employee lacks the ability to perform job duties competently, or personal problems seemingly outside of the employee's control are the cause of poor performance, then the appropriate response may be training, reassignment, efforts to address the employee's personal problems, or outright dismissal.

Progressive Discipline

Progressive discipline is a system of increasingly harsher penalties for repeated misconduct or continued poor work performance that is willful in nature. Its underlying philosophy is to correct employee behavior using principles of behavior modification rather than to punish them simply for the sake of retribution. By giving problem employees every opportunity to change their behaviors, progressive discipline also enables supervisors to stand before an arbitrator or judge and argue that the employee's repeated refusals to adhere to established standards justified the employee's termination.

Progressive discipline policies outline a series of disciplinary steps that supervisors are to follow. The first step in situations involving minor offenses is to issue an oral warning. At this step the supervisor reiterates the organization's rules of conduct or performance expectations, specifies why the warning is being made, discusses causes of and solutions to the problem, and makes clear that subsequent occurrences may result in sanctions. Where appropriate, constructive counseling should precede the oral warning because informal resolution of the matter becomes more difficult once disciplinary action is initiated. Corrective counseling refers to informal efforts to resolve misconduct or performance problems by investigating the causes and using counseling, coaching, and training techniques to correct them. The wise supervisor views the violation of a rule or performance problem as an opportunity to counsel and train rather than to punish. If corrective counseling proves unsuccessful, an oral warning may then be issued.

Although the first warning is oral, the supervisor should record the date and substance of the discussion in a daily logbook so that subsequent disciplinary decisions can be more easily defended. The following is an example of informal documentation:

Employee's Name: James Swanson

Date: 11/16/93

Topic Discussed: Tardiness

Comments: Informed Jim that I had observed him coming to work 10 to 15 minutes late on recent occasions. Explained that attendance policies must be adhered to strictly because the public depends on us. Jim said he occasionally has trouble with traffic after dropping his children off at the daycare center but will try to leave the house earlier.

A written warning or reprimand is issued to an employee when an offense is so serious that it initially warrants more than an oral warning or when lesser offenses are not corrected with an oral warning. The written warning, which is shown to the employee and then placed in his or her personnel file, should include the following: a statement of the problem, including specific rules or standards violated, the number of times the violation has occurred, and the dates; references to earlier disciplinary actions, including counseling sessions that have a bearing on the present disciplinary action; a specific statement of the solution expected; a statement of the period in which the solution is to be demonstrated; and notice that additional discipline may be warranted if the problem is not corrected, including termination. The supervisor should again attempt to determine if there are underlying problems and offer to work with the employee in overcoming them. The seriousness of the situation also may be emphasized by asking the employee to read and sign the written statement before it goes into the personnel file. The letter of warning or reprimand should be drafted carefully, working from the assumption that every disciplinary action will be grieved. Exhibit 13.3 provides an example of a written warning.

The next step is often a disciplinary suspension without pay. It is imposed when the offense is so serious that it initially warrants a more severe disciplinary action than a written warning, or when lesser violations are not corrected with other disciplinary procedures. Because the purpose is to get the employee's attention, a short-term suspension is generally sufficient. An employee may also be placed on suspension without pay while awaiting the outcome of an investigation or trial when the nature of the charge threatens to impair the employee's effectiveness on the job or indicates the possibility of harm to others.

The final step is termination. An employee may be discharged when other discipline has failed or when the offense is so serious that immediate dismissal is warranted. It makes little sense to discharge an employee the first time a minor performance problem, rule violation, or act of insubordination occurs. Dismissals are costly both in human terms and in terms of the expenses incurred in recruiting, selecting, and training new employees. The great virtue of progressive discipline is that human and organizational costs need not be incurred until there is every reason to conclude that improved conduct or performance cannot be expected in the future.

EXHIBIT 13.3

EXAMPLE OF A WRITTEN WARNING

Date: 11/17/94

To: Wally Jones, Bus Driver

From: Bill Frederickson, Supervisor

The School District's policy on school bus safety clearly states that buses are not to be left running and unattended while children are loading. When I observed your bus unattended on September 30, I reiterated the policy to you and we discussed the serious harm that might occur from leaving a running bus unattended.

As we discussed this morning, I found your bus unattended again yesterday afternoon. Because of the potentially serious consequences of violating bus safety policy, you must ensure that this does not occur again. I have every expectation that you will do so because you have been a good employee. However, this memo should be considered a written warning. If there are any further violations of bus safety policy, you will be subject to further disciplinary action up to and including termination.

_____

Signature of Employee and Date

I acknowledge that I have received a copy of this document and have had an opportunity to discuss it with my supervisor.

Affirmative Discipline

Another type of discipline, sometimes called affirmative, constructive, or positive discipline, shifts the focus from the supervisor's decision to impose discipline to the employee's willingness to remain a member of the "employment family." Critics of progressive discipline argue that it rests on an illogical premise: that to get employees to perform progressively better you have to treat them progressively worse.[8] Rather than imposing a series of sanctions on employees, affirmative discipline provides a series of opportunities for the employee to reaffirm his or her commitment to the organization. Failure to make the necessary commitment is ultimately treated as a voluntary quit. Affirmative discipline involves a series of discussions, first oral and later written, about the employee's responsibilities, followed by an agreement to correct problems and maintain established standards. If further problems surface, the employee is given a one-day, paid "decision-making leave" and asked to return the next day with a decision to either resolve identified problems or resign. If the employee chooses to make the necessary commitment, then an action plan is drafted. Violation of the plan results in termination.

Advocates of affirmative discipline argue that it is less punitive and paternalistic than progressive discipline and is better suited for use with white-collar employees.[9] The affirmative approach is premised on clarifying work expectations and allowing employees to take responsibility for their own actions. In the final analysis, however, each organization must determine for itself which system of discipline fits best with its strategic goals and its beliefs about how people should be treated.

Due Process and Just Cause

Demonstrating respect for each employee's due process rights is an essential prerequisite for an effective employee relations program. The principle of *due process* states that no one shall be deprived of something of value, such as a job, a higher position, or a paycheck, except as the result of a process that is fair and just. Due process rights, which over the years have been codified in statute law and merit system rules, typically include the following: the right to a written statement of the charges, an opportunity to rebut the charges, the right to a decision based on a full and fair investigation of the facts, and the right to appeal any disciplinary action.

The concept of *just cause* combines respect for due process with the additional requirement that management must have a legitimate, job-related reason for the disciplinary action. The provision "no employee shall be disciplined or discharged except for just cause" is contained in nearly all collective bargaining agreements. Just cause provisions are also found in many disciplinary policies or merit system rules written for nonunion public employees.

Just cause exists if a "reasonable person," considering all relevant facts, would find sufficient justification in the employee's conduct to warrant the disciplinary action. In practice, however, what is "reasonable" is often left for an arbitrator or judge to decide. Fortunately, existing case law offers some guidance to supervisors and managers wishing to act in good faith. When the concept of due process is combined with the concept that management must articulate a legitimate, job-related reason for its actions, certain helpful principles emerge. Adolph M. Koven and Susan L. Smith, relying on principles developed by labor arbitrators, offer the following seven tests for determining whether just cause exists:[10]

1. *NOTICE: "Did the Employer give to the employee forewarning or foreknowledge of the possible or probable consequences of the employee's disciplinary conduct?"*

2. *REASONABLE RULE OR ORDER: "Was the Employer's rules or managerial order reasonably related to (a) the orderly, efficient, and safe operation of the Employer's business, and (b) the performance that the Employer might properly expect of the employee?"*

3. *INVESTIGATION: "Did the Employer, before administering the discipline to an employee, make an effort to discover whether the employee did in fact violate or disobey a rule or order of management?"*

4. *FAIR INVESTIGATION: "Was the Employer's investigation conducted fairly and objectively?"*

5. PROOF: *"At the investigation, did the 'judge' obtain substantial evidence or proof that the employee was guilty as charged?"*

6. EQUAL TREATMENT: *"Has the Employer applied its rules, orders and penalties even-handedly and without discrimination to all employees?"*

7. PENALTY: *"Was the degree of discipline administered by the Employer in a particular case reasonably related to (a) the seriousness of the employee's proven offense, and (b) the record of the employee in his service with the Employer?"*

The Importance of Documentation and Due Process

One of the more enduring beliefs in our political culture is that public employees are so secure in their jobs that it is virtually impossible to remove them from office. President Carter reinforced this perception when lobbying on behalf of his 1978 civil service reforms. Carter noted that only 226 of 2,800,000 civilian employees had been fired for incompetence in 1977, strongly implying that the numbers should have been much higher. The popular press reinforces this belief with alarming stories about government employees who violate rules routinely, absent themselves from work regularly, or clearly lack the necessary competence to perform job duties. These same employees, according to media accounts, are never sanctioned or are reinstated with backpay by an arbitrator or judge.

It is certainly true that public employees enjoy many substantive and procedural rights and that efforts to dismiss the truly incompetent or problem employee can be an arduous, costly, and time-consuming process. It is also true that many merit system rules originally created to protect employees from arbitrary or politically motivated treatment have long outlived their usefulness. Nonetheless, procedural protections and obsolete merit system rules are only partly to blame. In those instances when management decisions are overturned by a judge or arbitrator, responsibility often rests with the failure of supervisors to document each rule violation or observed performance problem and to follow up with counseling and discipline in an appropriate manner. Arbitrators and judges are reluctant to interfere with managerial discretion when progressive disciplinary procedures have been followed and due process requirements observed. Although admittedly difficult and time consuming, documenting problems and observing due process requirements are fundamental supervisory responsibilities. Providing supervisors with better training and holding them accountable for performing their documenting and disciplining duties produce far better results than tolerating problem employees and placing the blame on the merit system.

Absenteeism Control Programs

Absenteeism is a special concern for organizations because it disrupts agency operations, reduces productivity, and undermines the morale of those employees who must fill in for absent workers. Because absenteeism arises from many causes, no single policy or approach can eliminate it. A disciplinary approach, for example, is only effective when the employee lacks the motivation to attend work. If the cause of an absence is largely beyond the control of the worker, such as illness, child care problems, or transportation difficulties, then punitive actions have little effect. In short, an absenteeism control program, to be effective, must address the many causes of absenteeism in an integrated and comprehensive fashion.

An integrated, comprehensive approach, according to John Schappi, involves the simultaneous pursuit of preventive, corrective, and disciplinary measures.[11] Preventive measures are those that attempt to alleviate the most common causes of absenteeism. They include policies that allow employees to balance work and family obligations, promote job safety, and encourage healthy lifestyles. Corrective measures seek to encourage attendance by training supervisors how to counsel absence-prone employees and by providing rewards for those who attend regularly. Finally, disciplinary measures impose increasingly stiffer penalties on employees who are consistently absent. They are aimed at the chronic abuser who misses a few days here and there on a regular basis, particularly on Mondays and Fridays. The following is an example of a discipline-based absenteeism control policy:

- Two unexcused absences in a three-month period—verbal reprimand.
- One additional unexcused absence in the following six months—written reprimand.
- One additional unexcused absence in the following six months—five-day suspension.
- One additional unexcused absence in the following six months—discharge.

If an employee is able to attend work but deliberately chooses not to despite counseling efforts, then use of an absenteeism control policy such as this may be warranted. Such policies, however, have the following disadvantages: they provide employees a "right" to a certain number of unexcused absences before discipline begins; they are likely to be resented as unduly paternalistic, especially by technical and professional employees; and they are effective only when supervisors are willing to document absences and impose required reprimands and sanctions.

At some point the discharge of an employee who is excessively absent may be necessary regardless of the reasons for the absences. Operational efficiency requires the regular attendance of employees, and management ultimately has the right to dismiss those who cannot or will not perform their work duties dependably. The decision to discharge, however, is fraught with difficulties and subject to reversal by arbitrators and judges. One difficulty is lack of an absolute standard for defining excessive absenteeism. One approach is to establish a figure that is two or three times the average absenteeism rate. This may result in a policy that anything over three absences in one month or 12 in a year will be deemed excessive. Arbitrators, however, seldom feel constrained by rigid standards of this kind, preferring instead to look at such factors as the total amount of time absent, whether absences are frequent and intermittent or single extended absences, the employee's previous work record and number of years of service, and the prospects for an improved attendance record in the future. A second difficulty involves cases in which employees are absent for extended periods because of illness or injury. Often it is difficult to find replacements who are willing to work on a temporary basis, and management cannot be expected to hold a position vacant for an indefinite period. The Americans with Disabilities Act requires employers to provide "reasonable accommodation" for such workers by allowing disability leaves or finding other duties for them to perform. However, if it appears that there is little probability of the worker being able to return to work within a few months, then an employer is usually justified in terminating the worker's employment.

The employee relations staff can provide policy tools for controlling absenteeism, but it is the responsibility of supervisors and managers to communicate the importance of job attendance, discuss with employees the reasons for their absences, agree on corrective actions, and document all absences. Line officers can also assist in reducing absenteeism through efforts to improve job satisfaction, including job enrichment, career development, and various forms of employee involvement.

Employee Assistance Programs

Employee assistance programs (EAPs) provide counseling services designed to assist the troubled employee in particular. A "troubled employee" is one whose work performance and relationships with fellow employees have deteriorated because of drug or alcohol addiction, emotional stress, or mental illness. As many as 20 percent of employees in any given workplace may be defined as "troubled." Their presence is often disruptive and their higher absenteeism and turnover rates further reduce the work unit's productivity. The purpose of employee assistance programs is to identify and assist individuals in need of help before their health and work performance begins to deteriorate. These programs evolved out of the alcoholism treatment programs of the 1940s, which were based on the concept of "constructive confrontation."[12] Supervisors trained in this technique confront employees with evidence of deteriorating job performance and encourage them to seek assistance. By combining an implied threat of discharge with a sincere offer of assistance, supervisors can often succeed in getting employees to accept ownership of their problems. Although today's employee assistance programs continue to use constructive confrontation to help those with addictions to alcohol or drugs, they also assist employees in coping with a broad range of personal difficulties, including marital conflict, financial difficulties, and emotional or mental problems.

Employee assistance programs are now a standard feature in most public workplaces. A study by Klingner, O'Neill, and Sabet found that 86 percent of national agencies, state governments, and the 100 largest cities are using EAPs to combat problems such as drug and alcohol abuse.[13] EAPs are organized in a variety of ways, ranging from programs that simply refer employees to appropriate service agencies in the local community to in-house programs staffed by professional counselors and medical personnel. EAPs at both ends of this spectrum generally refer employees to outside agencies for alcohol and drug treatment programs. Employees may refer themselves to the EAP or they may be referred by supervisors who believe personal problems are affecting their work performance. Great care must be taken in either case to protect employee confidentiality or employees will be unwilling to seek assistance. The credibility of the employee assistance program may also be undermined by asking it to test employees for drugs.[14]

Considerable evidence now supports the claim that EAPs are cost-effective means of increasing employee morale and productivity. If counseling can resolve personal problems before they become debilitating, then the need for more extensive inpatient care at a later date can be greatly reduced. Savings also occur because it is less costly to rehabilitate current workers than to recruit and train new ones. In addition, by helping to restore otherwise valuable and productive employees to health, the employer can underscore its commitment to its human resources. EAPs should not, however, be viewed as a panacea. Evidence regarding their cost-effectiveness is seldom based on rigorous program evaluations. Although EAPs can be valuable components of an employee relations program, their effectiveness requires counselors who are highly competent and supervisors who are trained to recognize deteriorating job performance and willing to refer employees needing assistance.

Wellness Programs

Employee assistance programs provide services to the relatively narrow segment of the employee population experiencing problems such as substance abuse and emotional illness. Wellness programs, by contrast, are designed to promote the general health and fitness of all employees. Most illness-related absences result from potentially controllable problems such as smoking, high cholesterol, hypertension, and obesity. Wellness programs aim at maintaining the health of employees so that medical problems are less likely to occur. Specific activities include smoking cessation, weight reduction, blood pressure screening and monitoring, cholesterol testing, nutrition classes, stress management, and physical fitness programs. By reducing the risk of illness and accidents, and by increasing general employee fitness, organizations often can increase productivity and employee morale while reducing absenteeism and medical insurance costs.

Employers usually contract with local hospitals, clinics, and nonprofit agencies to provide wellness services to employees. Fitness programs are often established by obtaining discounts at local health clubs. Despite considerable evidence that wellness programs can produce positive results, employers are often reluctant to adopt them because the benefits of improved health may not be apparent for years. Another major concern is that only about 12 percent of employees typically participate in wellness programs, and they tend to be those who are already inclined to pursue healthy lifestyles. Inducing participation by those who need wellness programs the most can be very difficult. Finally, executive officers often lack the authority to establish wellness programs or cannot convince legislative bodies to provide the necessary resources. For example, state agencies in Texas received the necessary authorization from the Texas State Employee Health Fitness and Education Act of 1983—but with the stipulation that no new funds were to be authorized and no new fitness facilities built.[15]

Balancing Personal and Work Responsibilities

The changing character of the workforce described in the *Workforce 2000* report is focusing attention on how to assist employees in fulfilling their responsibilities to themselves, their families, and their work—all at the same time. Finding ways to narrow the gap between employee needs and the ability of traditional policies to meet them has become one of the most important tasks of the 1990s. There is growing recognition that employee loyalty, as well as the organization's ability to recruit and retain qualified job applicants, is contingent on the employer's willingness to help workers achieve personal goals. This in turn has led to the realization that isolated policies and programs, however well intended, have little impact. What is required is a comprehensive and integrated set of personnel policies and programs linked to a continuous process of strategic planning. The key to success in this regard is flexibility—flexibility in leave policies, nepotism policies, employee benefits, and work scheduling. Each of these is discussed below in the context of how they can help employees integrate their personal and work-related responsibilities.

Leave Policies

Leaves of absence allow employees to take time off from work, either on a paid or unpaid basis, without fear of losing their jobs. This not only allows employees to fulfill personal obligations but also serves the interests of the employer. From a strategic perspective, policy makers hope that the benefits derived from leave policies will increase each employee's commitment to the organization and provide a competitive advantage in recruiting and retaining the best available job applicants.

Emergency and Sick Leave Policies Most organizations allow paid leaves of absence for personal emergencies such as illness or a death in the family. Sick leave policies typically allow 8 to 12 days off per year at full pay for those employees who have completed their probationary periods. These policies represent an important benefit to employees because they provide security against lost income for episodes of illness and injury that are largely beyond their control.

Unfortunately, sick leave benefits are subject to abuse. A few employees will inevitably make a habit of calling in sick, particularly on Mondays and Fridays, when they are not in fact ill. One means of reducing sick leave abuse is to establish a "buy-back" option that pays employees at an hourly rate for all or part of their unused sick leave, either at the end of the year or at retirement. A second approach, which is also used extensively in the public sector, is to allow employees to contribute one or more sick days per year to a mutual aid fund that can be drawn on by any employee who has already exhausted his or her personal sick leave benefits. Employees may see this as a form of personal insurance as well as a way of helping needy co-workers. As a result, they may be willing to contribute sick days to a common fund rather than use them for reasons other than illness or injury.

A third approach is to eliminate sick leave benefits entirely, replacing them with personal leave days that may be used for any purpose. These are sometimes jokingly referred to as "mental health days" because everyone feels the need for a day off from time to time. This approach empowers employees to administer their own individualized program of leave benefits. Because it is a "no-fault" system, it also has the advantage of eliminating the need to police sick leave abusers. Although employees are still required to provide advance notice of their absences, there is no requirement that employees bring notes from their doctors, nor any investigations to determine if employees are truly home sick. Advocates of this approach argue that it eliminates the distrust and resentment caused when employees are questioned about their absences, and it eliminates the confusion created when supervisors must distinguish between excused and unexcused absences. Research indicates that organizations adopting all-purpose leave policies have experienced reduced absenteeism, better job scheduling, and improved employee morale.[16] However, because policies of this kind guarantee employees a greater number of paid absences, legislative bodies may not find the promised improvements in morale and scheduling worth the higher costs.

Family/Personal Leave Most employers also allow employees a certain number of days off each year to attend to personal needs, usually on an unpaid basis. Personal leaves are used for such purposes as recovering from an extended illness or injury, seeking treatment for alcoholism or drug addiction, obtaining additional education, and having a baby. Because many employers preferred to discharge women who became pregnant rather than grant a leave of absence, Congress enacted the Pregnancy Discrimination Act of 1978, requiring employers with disability leave policies to treat pregnancy and childbirth as they would any other disability. This established the right of female employees to be absent from work for the period allowed under existing disability leave policies, but it did not establish a right to additional maternity leave. Although some employers voluntarily allowed maternity leaves for the period after childbirth as well as during pregnancy and delivery, many did not. Concerned about the growing number of single parents and working mothers in the labor force, and the difficult choices they are often asked to make between job security and parenting, Congress imposed additional requirements in 1993. The Family and Medical Leave Act requires employers with 50 or more employees to allow up to 12 weeks of unpaid leave during any 12-month period for all employees who have been employed for at least one year, male and female alike. Leaves must be allowed for such purposes as childbirth and child care, care of a new child by adoption or foster care, care of a spouse, child, or parent with a serious health condition, and recovery of the employee from a serious health condition. Whether the employee receives pay for any portion of such leaves is left to the employer to decide. To assist employees in fulfilling their family and work responsibilities, many public employers offer leave benefits that go beyond the minimum requirements set by the Family and Medical Leave Act.

Military and Jury Duty Leave Federal law requires employers to grant employees leaves of absence to serve in the military and perform jury duty. Employers are required, for example, to reinstate veterans without loss of seniority who have served less than four years, are honorably discharged, and notify their employers within 90 days of discharge of their desire to return to their former positions. Full-time and part-time employees required to attend initial training or subsequent summer training in the National Guard or Reserves must also be granted leaves of absence.[17] Although these do not have to be compensated leaves, some employers voluntarily choose to pay employees their regular salary or to pay the difference between military or jury duty pay and their regular salary.

Nepotism Policies

Nepotism policies prohibit relatives and spouses from being employed in the same organization, the same office, or in a supervisor-employee relationship. A survey of governments in the Midwest found that one-third of public employers restricted relatives and married couples from working in the same office, and three-fifths prohibited supervisor-employee relationships between family members or spouses.[18] Nepotism policies in the public sector are established for two reasons: to protect the merit principle by preventing the appointment of employees on the basis of family connection rather than competence, and to avoid the potentially disruptive effects that may occur when married couples are allowed to work together. The latter rests on the widespread belief that married couples will fight on the job, form coalitions to advance their own interests, and in other ways undermine organizational productivity and morale.[19]

Nepotism policies are now under attack because they adversely affect the employment opportunities of dual-career couples. If an employer is prohibited from hiring both spouses, then one spouse (most often the woman) may have to choose between marriage and career. Those who favor abolishing nepotism polices argue that in white-collar occupations, such as those commonly found in the public sector, professional norms of conduct make it possible for married couples to supervise one another and to work in close quarters without the traditional problems of favoritism and marital discord.[20] Nepotism rules have been challenged in court, but in most instances they have been upheld.

Fringe Benefits and Cafeteria Plans

Employee benefit packages were designed for a society in which men worked and women stayed at home. Society has changed dramatically since the 1950s, but benefit packages have been slow to reflect these changes. The past three decades have seen significant increases in the number of women entering the labor force, the number of single-parent families, and the number of dual-income families. The traditional family composed of a father who serves as breadwinner, a mother, and children has declined from 75 percent of all families in this country in 1950 to only 10 percent in 1988.[21] Similarly, in 1960 only 18.6 percent of married women with a spouse present and children younger than 6 years of age were in the civilian labor force. By 1990, nearly 60 percent of such women were in the labor force.[22] As a result, many families no longer have a caregiver at home during working hours, and many of today's working parents must struggle to balance their obligations to work and family. Sick leave policies often prohibit the use of sick leave to care for a child or parent who is ill, and assistance with finding and paying for child care is often unavailable. In addition, medical benefits frequently are of little value to employees because they duplicate those received under the benefit plans of their spouses.

Given these demographic changes, the ability of organizations to recruit and retain the best workers and maintain employee commitment may depend increasingly on personnel benefits that help reconcile the diverse needs of employees. One way that benefit packages can assist the modern worker is to expand the range of benefits available. Child care assistance, for example, is one of the newest additions to benefit packages. Responsibility to family is consistently cited as one of the leading causes of absenteeism. According to one study, children who are sick, babysitters who are ill, school holidays, and transportation problems cause parents to miss an average of 5.4 days per year.[23] To help employees with their parental responsibilities, a growing number of employers are providing child care assistance. Among public employers, for example, 26.4 percent are now offering a child-care benefit of some kind, compared with 10.1 percent in the private sector.[24] Several state governments, including California, Illinois, Iowa, Massachusetts, Michigan, New Jersey, New York and Wisconsin, have established at least one on-site child care center. In 1991 the state of New York had 50 on-site child care centers serving more than 3,000 children.[25] New York provides rent-free space and maintenance within state buildings, whereas each center is run by a nonprofit corporation. Local governments are creating on-site centers as well. The County of Los Angeles, for example, found that its program "positively impacted recruitment and retention of critical employees, shortened maternity leaves and fostered employee loyalty."[26] Another type of child care assistance is direct financial aid. Programs of this kind involve arranging discounts for employees at local child care centers, providing employees with vouchers that are honored at local centers, or simply paying employees a monthly subsidy. A third type of assistance takes the form of an information and referral service that keeps employees informed about local child care options. Sick child care and elder care are two additional forms of assistance that are sometimes added to benefit packages.

A second way that benefit packages can be adapted to meet the needs of the modern worker is to establish cafeteria benefit plans. Under the typical cafeteria plan, each employee receives a standard benefit package, including medical, life, and disability insurance. Each employee is then allowed to choose additional benefits from among a menu of options, including extra vacation, life insurance for dependents, financial assistance, additional disability benefits, child care assistance, and optical/dental benefits not covered by the standard package. Single and married employees can choose the benefits that are most advantageous to them, thereby eliminating inequities created when all employees must accept the same standardized benefit plan.

Alternative Work Schedules

Adopting alternative work schedules is yet another way to accommodate the needs and wants of today's employees. Proponents argue that increased job satisfaction and employee commitment can be achieved by simply tinkering with the standard five-day, 40-hour workweek. Types of alternative work schedules include compressed work weeks, part-time work, job sharing, and flextime.

The *compressed work week* alternative allows employees to work the equivalent of a full week in less than five days by, for example, working four 10-hour days. This allows employees to spend additional time pursuing leisure activities or attending to personal responsibilities. However, because most public agencies are obligated to provide services to the public on a five-day-per-week basis, compressed work weeks are practical only where there is sufficient staff to maintain adequate service levels throughout the week.

Creating more *part-time jobs* is another work scheduling alternative. A part-time job is one in which the incumbent works less than 35 hours a week. By purposefully creating and advertising part-time jobs, employers can attract qualified workers who wish to devote more time to their families or to other personal needs. Part-time employees often receive the same benefits as full-time workers, except that benefits such as sick leave and vacations are prorated. A program established by New York state government allows employees to voluntarily reduce the number of hours they work. They are also allowed to return to a full-time schedule at the start of any pay period.[27] The Federal Employee Part-time Career Employment Act of 1978 sought to encourage federal agencies to establish more opportunities for part-time workers, but the number of such workers has remained relatively constant at just over two percent.[28]

Job sharing is a specific kind of part-time work. It entails creating two half-time jobs out of one full-time position. Job sharers may perform all job tasks jointly or divide tasks between them according to their skills and expertise. They may choose to work a half day each or to work full days on an alternating basis. As with other forms of part-time work, job sharing creates employment opportunities for persons wishing to commit more time to their families or other personal interests. Although a successful job sharing arrangement can increase job satisfaction and productivity, compatibility between the sharers is a critical prerequisite. According to a government report, employers must also "assure that the jobs being shared are amenable to this type of arrangement, recognize that splitting benefits may increase administrative requirements, and be prepared to deal with complications in performance evaluations that may result from overlapping duties."[29] These inherent difficulties limit the use of job sharing arrangements. In 1991, for example, only 775 workers were participating in the federal government's job sharing program.

Under *flextime* arrangements, employees work a full day but are free to choose their starting and quitting times within specified parameters. Among the various types of alternative work schedules, flextime is the easiest to implement and the one that is used most extensively in the public sector. The concept originated in Germany in the 1960s and was introduced in the United States in the 1970s. In most flextime systems there is a core period, possibly 9:00 A.M. to 11:00 A.M. and 1:00 P.M. to 3:00 P.M., during which all employees are expected to be at their jobs. "Flexible bands" are established around these core hours so that employees may choose when to arrive at and depart from work. Some policies ask employees to choose a schedule that they will work on a regular basis, and others simply require employees to put in a full day's work within the established parameters.

Flextime allows employees to accommodate a broad range of personal needs, such as avoiding traffic congestion, running errands, visiting the doctor, dropping children off at schools or daycare facilities, and continuing their education. With such flexibility, employees have less reason to take days off or arrive late for work. Employees also may feel a greater commitment to an organization that allows them an increased measure of personal autonomy. A review of the research literature provides considerable evidence that flextime arrangements can decrease absenteeism, increase job satisfaction, and increase organizational commitment.[30] Research also indicates that if flextime does not always increase job productivity, neither does it harm it. Flextime may not be appropriate, however, where employees require close supervision or where employees must be highly accessible to the public or other agency personnel. Despite these limitations, flextime remains a relatively cost-free means of accommodating both the personal needs of employees and operational needs of the organization.

Balancing Employee Rights and Agency Needs

An important goal of employee relations policies is to minimize friction with and between employees. Although this is never easy to do, it is especially difficult in areas involving individual rights, such as smoking, substance abuse, and polygraph testing. Crafting policies in these areas requires balancing the rights of employees with the needs of the employer. Often the rights of different groups of employees, such as smokers and nonsmokers, must be balanced as well. Policies that fail to strike an acceptable balance may adversely affect employee trust and morale and increase the risk of lawsuits. For these reasons caution is needed when attempting to regulate employee behavior, whether on or off the job. Although no policy will please everyone, purposefully designing policies so that they balance legitimate organizational needs with recognized employee rights is essential to maintaining positive employee relations.

Elements of an Effective Employee Relations Program

The goal of employee relations programs is to create and sustain a supportive work environment and a highly dedicated workforce. This is accomplished, in theory at least, by developing personnel policies with strategic objectives in mind and implementing them in an integrated fashion. Before closing this chapter, it is worth reviewing some of the elements of an effective employee relations program:

1. *Personal conduct policies that are designed and implemented to promote positive discipline in each work unit.*

2. *Disciplinary policies that guarantee due process and encourage proper conduct and improved work performance.*

3. *Employee assistance programs that help workers cope with personal problems and restore otherwise productive workers to health.*

4. *Flexible leave policies that assist employees in accommodating their personal obligations.*

5. *Flexible employee benefit plans and alternative work schedules that increase employee commitment by accommodating a diverse range of individual needs.*

6. *Policies regulating personal behavior (e.g., smoking and drug use) that balance legitimate organizational interests with individual rights.*

Identifying these elements is the easy part. Marshaling the necessary resources and implementing policies in a truly integrated fashion remains one of human resource management's greatest challenges.

■ **CASE 13.1**   Balancing Agency and Employee Needs

A county social services agency that provides home care services to elderly homebound clients recently hired a new licensed practical nurse, Rachel White, on the strength of her excellent recommendations. Although White seemed to lack confidence in her abilities, she nonetheless was performing well during her probationary period.

While still on probationary status, White stabbed her boyfriend during a weekend domestic dispute. She was arrested, charged with deliberate attempted homicide, and jailed. Concerned about her job, the distraught White called the agency director from jail to apprise him of the situation. She was subsequently released on her own recognizance, but not before the media had carried news of the stabbing and arrest.

White's attorney contacted the agency and asked that she be allowed to return to work pending the outcome of the trial. The Director chose instead to place her on leave without pay until the matter could be investigated further. His primary concerns were the safety of the agency's vulnerable clients and the potential impact of negative publicity. Subsequent investigation disclosed these facts:

1. White's attorney did not believe that she was dangerous and claimed that returning to work was essential to her emotional and financial well-being.
2. The agency's attorney believed that if White were allowed to return to work and subsequently harmed a client the agency could be sued for knowingly placing a potentially dangerous employee in a home.
3. Referring agencies expressed concern but did not say they would discontinue referrals if White returned to work.
4. The psychiatrist who examined White did not believe she was a threat to others. He viewed it as an isolated incident steeped in domestic discord.
5. Because of high demand for its services, the agency could not keep the position open for an indefinite period.

After considering these facts, the Director decided that client needs must come before employee needs and that the appropriate course of action was to discharge White.

1. What employee needs and agency needs are revealed in this case?
2. Because White's guilt had not yet been established in court, should she have been allowed to return to work or remain on leave without pay until after the trial?
3. Is the fact that White was still on probationary status relevant to the discharge decision?
4. If the clients had been less vulnerable, would a different decision have been more appropriate?

■ **CASE 13.2** The Case of the Troubled Employee

You are a manager in the state's Department of Labor and Industry. An employee you hired a few months ago as an accountant has begun to develop occasional attendance problems and the quality of his work has begun to slip. His immediate supervisor has not taken any steps to correct the problem because she was told by other employees that the employee was having marital problems.

Absenteeism and tardiness have now become a regular occurrence and you have occasionally smelled alcohol in the employee's work area. A part-time employee has been asked to work full-time to pick up the slack. She is now demanding overtime pay for everything beyond her usual 20 hours per week commitment.

One day the accountant comes to work with a letter from his doctor saying that he is under extreme stress because of a pending divorce. He asks for leave without pay for one month to "straighten things out."

1. What human resource management issues are raised in this case?
2. What laws, rules, or policies may need to be consulted to address the problems involved?
3. Does this situation seem to call for discipline, employee assistance, or some combination of the two? How will you respond to the request for a leave of absence?
4. Are there other actions you should have taken earlier or should take now?

Notes

1. David Jamieson and Julie O'Mara, *Managing Workforce 2000: Gaining the Diversity Advantage* (San Francisco: Jossey-Bass, 1991).

2. Jamieson and O'Mara, *Managing Workforce 2000*, 38–40.

3. U. S. General Accounting Office, *The Changing Workforce: Comparison of Federal and Nonfederal Work/Family Programs and Approaches* (GAO/GGD-92-84, April 1992).

4. Edwin A. Locke and Gary P. Latham, *Goal-setting: A Motivational Technique that Works!* (Englewood Cliffs, New Jersey: Prentice-Hall, 1984), 73.

5. John D. Coombe, "Employee Handbooks: Asset or Liability?" *Employee Relations Law Journal* 12 (Summer 1986):4–17.

6. James R. Redeker, *Discipline: Policies and Procedures* (Washington, D.C.: Bureau of National Affairs, 1983), 34.

7. Charles A. O'Reilly and Barton A. Weitz, "Managing Marginal Employees: The Use of Warnings and Dismissals," *Administrative Management Quarterly* 25 (September 1980):467–484.

8. Redeker, *Discipline*, 33.

9. John V. Schappi, *Improving Job Attendance* (Washington, D.C.: Bureau of National Affairs, 1988), 226–228.

10. Adolph M. Koven and Susan L. Smith, *Just Cause: The Seven Tests* (San Francisco: Coloracre Publications, 1985), 10.

11. Schappi, *Improving Job Attendance*.

12. Arthur T. Johnson and Nancy O'Neill, "Employee Assistance Programs and the Troubled Employee in the Public Sector Workplace," *Review of Public Personnel Administration* 9 (Summer 1989):68.

13. Donald E. Klingner, Nancy G. O'Neill, and Mohamed Gamal Sabet, "Drug Testing in Public Agencies: Public Policy Issues and Managerial Responses," *Review of Public Personnel Administration* 10 (Fall 1989):3.

14. Ibid., 68.

15. Nell H. Gottlieb, Linda E. Lloyd, and Jean N. Bounds, "The Adoption of Health Promotion Programs by State Agencies," *Public Personnel Management* 16 (Fall 1987):235–242.

16. B. H. Harvey, J. A. Schultze, and J. F. Rogers, "Rewarding Employees for Not Using Sick Leave," *Personnel Administrator* 28 (May 1983):55–59.

17. 38 U.S.C. 2021–2026.

18. Christine M. Reed, "Anti-Nepotism Rules and Dual Career Couples: Policy Questions for Public Personnel Administrators," *Public Personnel Management* 17 (Summer 1988):223–230.

19. Christine M. Reed and Linda J. Cohen, "Anti-Nepotism Rules: The Legal Rights of Married Co-Workers," *Public Personnel Management* (19 (Spring 1989):37–44.

20. Reed, "Anti-Nepotism Rules and Dual Career Couples."

21. Edward L. Suntrup, "Child-Care Delivery Systems in the Government Sector," *Review of Public Personnel Administration* 10 (Fall 1989):48.

22. U.S. General Accounting Office, *The Changing Workforce*, 10.

23. Cited in Schappi, *Improving Job Attendance*, 46.

24. Suntrup, "Child Care Delivery Systems," 50.

25. U.S. General Accounting Office, *The Changing Workforce*, 35.

26. "Lessons We Have Learned," *IPMA News* (July 1992):17.

27. U.S. General Accounting Office, *The Changing Workforce*, 24.

28. Ibid., 77.

29. U.S. General Accounting Office, *The Changing Workforce*, 25.

30. Jon L. Pierce, John W. Newstrom, Randall B. Dunham, and Alison E. Barber, *Alternative Work Schedules* (Boston: Allyn and Bacon, 1989). See also Arthur L. Finkle, "Flexitime in Government," *Public Personnel Management* 8 (May/June 1979):152–155; and Simcha Ronen and Sophia B. Primps, "The Impact of Flexitime on Performance and Attitudes in 25 Public Agencies," *Public Personnel Management* 9(no. 3 1980):201–207.

CHAPTER 14

Collective Bargaining and Labor Relations

Learning Objectives

After mastering the materials contained in this chapter, you will be able to:

1. Describe the historical origins of collective bargaining in the public sector.
2. Assess the applicability of the NLRA model to the public sector.
3. Provide examples of what occurs in each of the five stages of the collective bargaining process.
4. Prepare a strategy for successful labor negotiations.
5. Design grievance procedures for union and non-union employees.
6. Evaluate the future of labor relations in light of the problems facing governments today.

The scope of human resource management changes over time—sometimes as the result of deliberate planning and sometimes as the result of factors that are largely unanticipated. Beginning in the 1960s government agencies were asked to perform a role for which they were unprepared—that of labor relations. This was the result of executive orders, state laws, and municipal ordinances that allowed public employees to organize for the purpose of collective bargaining. After decades of pressing for higher wages and better working conditions by lobbying legislative bodies, many public employees suddenly found themselves able to collectively bargain in much the same way that private sector employees had for more than 30 years.

Ironically, collective bargaining has matured and gained acceptance in the public sector just as a growing number of critics are asserting that there are better ways of achieving constructive labor relations. In their view, collective bargaining draws an arbitrary line between "labor" and "management," creates an adversarial relationship between them, and impedes the search for better forms of cooperation.[1] This argument, developed more fully toward the end of the chapter, is one that managers must be prepared to evaluate. For the present, collective bargaining remains a well-established feature of human resource management—one that must be evaluated on its own terms. This chapter reviews the history of the labor movement in the public sector, describes the processes of organizing, bargaining, and resolving labor conflicts, and evaluates the future of labor relations in the public sector.

As in other areas of human resource management, labor relations comes complete with its own special language. Exhibit 14.1 provides a glossary of key terms.

Origins of Collective Bargaining in the Public Sector

The industrial revolution that dawned in England in the mid–eighteenth century created a new class of employee. Neither a domestic servant nor an apprentice craftsman, the new industrial employee worked a specified number of hours in exchange for an agreed-on wage and then returned home. Employment law gradually changed to reflect the altered character of the employment relationship. Under the new contract-based law, and in stark contrast to the earlier master-servant law, the employer retained full sovereignty in the workplace while owing no obligation to the worker beyond the payment of wages for labor.

English common law traditions greatly influenced American employment law. With the legal system legitimating the employer's right to unilaterally determine wages, terms, and conditions of employment, employees faced a long, uphill struggle to establish their right to organize and bargain collectively. Courts in the early 1800s, for example, often viewed unions as "criminal conspiracies in restraint of trade." Although a Massachusetts court invalidated the restraint of trade doctrine in 1842, unions continued to be suppressed through the use of such "union-busting" tactics as lockouts, blacklisting of union organizers, harassment of union sympathizers, injunctions, and outright violence.

As management became more "professionalized" in the period after the Civil War, counterorganization seemed the only available option for employees hoping to promote their common interests. Despite many setbacks, the American Federal of Labor (AFL) succeeded in organizing skilled workers and combining local unions into a powerful national organization after its formation in 1886. The Knights of Labor, and later the Congress of Industrial Organizations (CIO), succeeded in doing the same for unskilled and semiskilled industrial workers. As a result of the increased power of organized labor, strikes became common occurrences in the early 1900s. Recognizing that industrial peace was in the nation's best interest, Congress finally intervened in 1935 by passing the National Labor Relations Act (also known as the Wagner Act). This act established the right of employees in the private sector to organize and collectively bargain with their employers. Although many of the causes of labor unrest would remain unaddressed, the NLRA succeeded in establishing a framework for bringing the two sides together for purposes of bilateral negotiations.

Labor organizations were formed among skilled workers in the federal naval shipyards in the 1820s and among postal workers in the 1860s. For the most part, however, little union organizing took place in the public sector until the late 1800s and early 1900s. Unable to collectively bargain, the more aggressive unions lobbied congress for shorter work weeks, higher wages, and better working conditions. Displeased with the aggressiveness with which postal workers pressed their demands, President Theodore Roosevelt issued a gag order in 1902 forbidding federal employees from lobbying on their own behalf. When pressure from the postal workers con-

EXHIBIT 14.1

KEY TERMS IN LABOR RELATIONS

Arbitration A method of resolving labor disputes by employing a neutral third party, an arbitrator, to review the facts and make a decision that is binding on both parties. *Interest arbitration* occurs when an arbitrator is asked to intervene in contract negotiations to resolve impasses. *Grievance arbitration* occurs during the life of a contract when an employee files a grievance alleging that his or her rights under the contract have been violated.

Agency Shop A type of union security arrangement that requires employees who choose not to join a union to pay an amount equivalent to union dues as a condition of employment. These contributions are intended to defray the costs of collective bargaining and grievance handling.

Bargaining Unit A group of employees recognized as appropriate for representation by a labor organization for the purpose of collective bargaining.

Certification/Decertification Election An election, usually required by law, in which members of the bargaining unit certify or decertify a particular union as their exclusive bargaining agent.

Collective Bargaining Bilateral negotiations between labor and management teams over wages, terms, and conditions of employment. It results in an agreement specifying each side's respective rights and obligations.

Closed Shop A type of union security arrangement that requires prospective employees to join a union before they can be considered for employment. It is prohibited by the Taft-Hartley Act of 1947 but is practiced unofficially in rare instances.

Factfinding A method of resolving impasses in labor negotiations by employing a neutral third party, a factfinder, to assist the parties in reaching an agreement. The factfinder holds a hearing, investigates the disputed issues, and submits a set of nonbinding recommendations for settlement.

Mediation A method of resolving disputes in labor negotiations by employing a neutral third party, a mediator, to assist the parties in reaching an agreement by keeping them talking and encouraging them to move toward common ground.

Meet and Confer Discussions An alternative to collective bargaining in which labor and management representatives meet periodically to seek agreement on matters of mutual concern, frequently resulting in a nonbinding memorandum of understanding. To protect their sovereign authority, some states only authorize negotiations of this kind.

National Labor Relations Act (NLRA) of 1935 Also called the Wagner Act, the NLRA guarantees to private sector employees the right to organize and collectively bargain with employers. Although it does not apply to public employees, its framework has been adopted with some modifications by a majority of states to extend collective bargaining rights to public employees.

Public Employee Relations Boards (PERBs) A generic name for those administrative agencies charged with determining bargaining units, supervising certification elections, and ruling on unfair labor practices. For example, the federal PERB is the Federal Labor Relations Authority (FLRA).

EXHIBIT 14.1 *(continued)*

Right-to-Work Law A law that prohibits requiring union membership or financial contributions as conditions of employment. This, in effect, prohibits union shop and agency shop arrangements and mandates what is called the "open shop." Twenty states have enacted such laws. Federal employees are also guaranteed an open shop.

Union Shop A union security arrangement that requires employees to become union members after they are hired and to maintain membership as a condition of employment. Only five states allow this as an option for public employees.

Unfair Labor Practices Activities by a labor union or an employer that are judged to be contrary to the intent of laws regulating collective bargaining. Failure to bargain in good faith, for example, is an unfair labor practice, and whether it has occurred is usually determined by a public employee relations board.

---

tinued unabated, Congress responded in 1912 by passing the Lloyd-LaFollette Act, guaranteeing to federal employees the right to organize and lobby on matters of concern.

In the years following passage of the Lloyd-LaFollette Act, national labor organizations emerged to unite the various local unions. The National Federation of Federal Employees (NFFE) was formed in 1917, followed in the early 1930s by the American Federation of Government Employees (AFGE) and the National Association of Government Employees (NAGE). At the state and local level teachers, police, and firefighters also began organizing during the late 1800s, primarily as mutual benefit societies to provide insurance and pension benefits to their members. Other government workers began to organize as well, leading to the formation of the American Federation of State, County, and Municipal Employees (AFSCME) in 1936.

The NLRA, as noted above, does not apply to public employees. The more aggressive labor organizations used their right to lobby government to press for better wages and working conditions, but without the right to collectively bargain there was little else they could do to represent employee interests. This remained the situation until the 1950s, when a few governments began bargaining with their employees voluntarily. By the mid-1950s, for example, both Philadelphia and New York City were routinely negotiating labor agreements.[2] In 1959 Wisconsin became the first state to enact a statute authorizing collective bargaining for municipal employees. Beyond these few exceptions, however, little collective bargaining took place in the public sector prior to the 1960s.

The breakthrough for public sector unions came in 1962 when President Kennedy issued executive order 10988 establishing the right of federal employees to collectively bargain. Although it was a conservative policy—greatly limiting the scope of bargaining and prohibiting strikes—it nonetheless caused a rapid increase in union memberships and triggered the extension of similar rights to state and municipal employees. As a point of comparison, union membership among private sector employees peaked in 1954 at 38 percent of the nonagricultural work force and steadily declined thereafter to its current level of approximately 15 percent.[3] In the public sector, by contrast, membership in labor organizations grew at an unprecedented rate during the same period. Today 37 percent of the federal civilian workforce and 45.3 percent of state and local government employees belong to labor organizations.[4] Because employees usually are not required to belong to a union to be covered by a labor agreement, the percentage of employees actually represented by labor organizations is much higher.

The Legal Context of Labor Relations

Collective bargaining in the public sector takes place within a legal framework that restricts which employee groups may participate in bargaining, the scope of bargaining, and the means by which disputes are settled. This section describes the basic model created by the National Labor Relations Act, analyzes how that model has been modified for use in the public sector, and summarizes the variety of statutes currently governing labor relations in the public sector.

The NLRA Model

With the number of work stoppages increasing in the early 1930s Congress felt compelled to intervene to restore industrial peace. The NLRA represented a conservative, pragmatic response. Rather than authorizing government to impose labor settlements, a course of action adopted by other nations, Congress chose to create a framework within which the two parties could bargain with each other and secure their own settlement, hopefully without violence. The key underlying assumption was that successful bilateral bargaining requires the two parties to be more or less equal in terms of economic power. Creating the necessary balance of power could only be achieved by establishing an organization of workers alongside that of the corporation. In short, after years of protecting corporations and discouraging the formation of unions, Congress decided that industrial peace could only be secured by protecting the right of employees to organize, bargain, and strike.

The NLRA, as amended by the Labor Management Relations Act of 1947 (also called the Taft-Hartley Act), established a model that later influenced labor legislation in the public sector. For this reason the defining characteristics of this model are worth reviewing:

1. *Statutory protection of the right to organize, collectively bargain, and strike.*

2. *Statutory separation of labor and management (the right to organize and bargain extends only to nonsupervisory employees).*

3. *Statutory specification of unfair labor practices.*

4. *Identification of an administrative body to determine appropriate bargaining units, certify exclusive bargaining agents for each unit, and adjudicate complaints of unfair labor practices.*

5. *Subsequent negotiation and ratification of a labor agreement establishing mutual rights and obligations.*

The NLRA, in effect, seeks to guarantee a fair contest between two powerful combatants in determining wages and terms and conditions of employment. It encourages them to do battle on a field that has been somewhat leveled by government, according to rules and procedures established by government, and with disputes over the rules adjudicated by government. It authorizes government to act in the role of protector, while the outcomes are left to the combatants to determine, constrained only by the regulatory framework and economic realities. With both sides standing to lose if the business becomes noncompetitive, strong incentives exist to negotiate an agreement without resorting to the strike.

Modification of the NLRA Model

Before the 1960s few people believed that the NLRA model was applicable to the public sector. In the first place, the employer was the government itself. Critics argued that the equality of bargaining power on which the NLRA model was premised could not be realized in the public sector because one of the parties at the bargaining table had established the rules of the game in a way that favored the interests of management over those of labor.

Second, according to critics, collective bargaining violates the sovereignty doctrine that states that the sovereignty entrusted by the people to their elected officials cannot be lawfully delegated to others. To allow policy decisions regarding wages and terms and conditions of employment to be made by labor representatives and appointed officials, according to this argument, constitutes an illegal delegation of the people's sovereign power. (In practice, of course, government agencies frequently enter into contracts of all kinds without legislative approval, and the courts, with a few exceptions, have not found collective bargaining to constitute an illegal delegation of power).

Third, the NLRA model is not applicable to the public sector, according to critics, because it is not reasonable to allow public employees the right to strike. The Wellington-Winter thesis states that strikes in the public sector cause serious disruptions in the delivery of critical services, place intense pressure on public officials to settle disputes, and thus give public unions too much power relative to other groups wanting a share of available resources.[5] In addition, because many government services are difficult or impossible to secure through private means—such as police, fire, and educational services—the public interest is easily held hostage to union demands. The Boston police strike of 1919 is often cited as an example. Subject to poor working conditions and desiring the right to organize and affiliate with the AFL, the Boston police walked off the job on September 9, 1919. Boston was quickly gripped by lawlessness and mob rule. Declaring that "there is no right to strike against the public safety by anybody, anywhere, anytime," Governor Coolidge called out the state guard, discharged the striking police, and restored order. For years thereafter this incident would be used by critics as a reminder of what could happen if public employees were given the right to strike.

Concerns raised by critics in the pre-1960 period were not without merit. As a result, most policy makers agreed that before laws could be enacted authorizing collective bargaining in the public sector, modifications would have to be made to the NLRA model. Analysis of the laws subsequently adopted by federal and state governments reveals three basic modifications. First, the right to strike is denied either by law or in practice to federal employees and to employees in all but 12 states. Even among the latter states, the number of groups that can strike and the circumstances under which they are allowed to strike are often severely restricted. Second, in the absence of the right to strike, alternative dispute resolution procedures are mandated by many labor relations laws. To discourage illegal strikes, for example, binding arbitration is specified as a mandatory or optional means of settling contract disputes in nearly all states with labor relations legislation. Finally, in deference to the sovereignty doctrine, labor laws often restrict the scope of bargaining and require legislative approval of the financial aspects of labor agreements. In a few states, policy makers refused to authorize collective bargaining at all, permitting instead a "meet and confer" approach in which labor and management representatives negotiate issues of mutual concern without any legal obligation on the part of management to sign a memorandum of agreement.

Whether a modified version of the NLRA framework provides an effective vehicle for representing the interests of labor remains a matter of considerable debate. There are some who continue to argue that the inherent incompatibility of the NLRA model with public sector realities frequently places public labor relations in a state of crisis.

Labor Relations Statutes

Although the NLRA defines national labor relations policy for private and nonprofit organizations, Congress has not, despite many opportunities, enacted comparable legislation for public employees. As a result, labor relations policies and practices vary considerably from state to state. State legislatures faced two fundamental issues as they debated the adoption of labor legislation: should public employees be allowed to join labor organizations and, if so, should they be allowed to bargain collectively? A few states answered the first question in the negative, enacting legislation that prohibited union involvement. The courts, however, subsequently found such prohibitions to be unconstitutional. In *Atkins v. City of Charlotte,* for example, a U.S. District Court invalidated a North Carolina state law that prohibited government employees from joining labor organizations on the grounds that it violated their First and Fourteenth Amendment rights.[6]

A majority of states responded to the second issue by authorizing collective bargaining for at least some categories of public employees. Because the courts have recognized no constitutional right to collectively bargain, each state is free to authorize it, prohibit it, or enact no legislation addressing it at all. Where collective bargaining for a particular group of employees is neither authorized nor prohibited under state law, local ordinances may authorize it, or it may be entered into voluntarily by both parties. State legislation, according to Richard C. Kearney, "ranges from a single comprehensive statute providing coverage for all public employees in Iowa, to coverage of only fire fighters in Wyoming, to the total prohibition of collective bargaining in North Carolina."[7] Today, 42 states extend bargaining rights to at least one group of public workers. Of these, 28 states have enacted comprehensive legislation covering all major employee groups. In most instances these laws have adopted the modified NLRA model discussed above. As shown in Exhibit 14.2, a few states found it more prudent to authorize "meet and confer" negotiations rather than collective bargaining.

The federal labor relations system developed incrementally during the 1960s and 1970s as the result of a series of executive orders. Collective bargaining rights were not guaranteed by law until Congress enacted the Civil Service Reform Act of 1978. Although Title VII of the Reform Act did not alter the existing system significantly, by grounding it in statute law the system became less vulnerable to the whims of each new president. Title VII applies to all nonsupervisory employees except members of the armed services and foreign service and employees of the GAO, FBI, CIA, NSA, TVA, and U.S. Postal Service. Employees of the Postal Service and TVA are authorized to bargain under separate pieces of legislation, whereas employees of the other agencies exempted from coverage enjoy no collective bargaining rights.

The Labor Relations Function

The primary purpose of the labor relations function is to successfully negotiate labor agreements and maintain positive labor-management relations. As in other areas of human resource management, this function is performed jointly by many different people. Assuming that a state has created a public employees relations board (PERB) or similar administrative agency, and assuming that the particular government is large enough to have a central labor relations staff, the constellation of actors involved in collective bargaining will be similar to that shown in Exhibit 14.3. PERBs are typically charged with determining appropriate bargaining units, supervising elections of bargaining agents, ruling on unfair labor practices and disputes over what is negotiable, and assisting with impasse resolution.

When a labor agreement is about to expire, bargaining teams for each side meet around the "bargaining table" to negotiate a new contract. Management bargaining teams, typically three to four people, vary in their composition according to the size and level of government. In larger jurisdictions the director of labor relations generally serves as chief negotiator and is assisted by unit supervisors and personnel officers. In other jurisdictions, the chief negotiator may be a special assistant to the executive, finance officer, attorney, or contracted labor specialist. Labor's bargaining team is typically composed of a representative from the local union office who generally serves as chief negotiator, union stewards, and other employee representatives from the bargaining unit.

When state legislatures began authorizing collective bargaining in the 1960s, most governments were not prepared—either organizationally or in terms of staff expertise—to perform the mandated labor relations function. Unfamiliar with the specifics of collective bargaining, public organizations had to acquire labor relations expertise and determine who was to be responsible for negotiating contracts. Establishing a central labor relations staff was not a realistic option for small governments. The latter had little choice but to give responsibility for labor relations to already overburdened personnel officers, budget officers, or executive assistants.

EXHIBIT 14.2

STATE BARGAINING LEGISLATION, 1992

State	State	Local	Police	Fire-fighters	K–12 Teachers
Alabama	—	—	—	Y	—
Alaska	X	X	X	X	X
Arizona	—	—	—	—	—
Arkansas	—	—	—	—	—
California	Y	Y[b]	Y[b]	Y[b]	X
Colorado	—	—	—	—	—
Connecticut	X	X	X	X	X
Delaware	X	X[b]	X	X	X
Florida	X	X[b]	X	X	X
Georgia	—	—	—	Y	—
Hawaii	X	X	X	X	X
Idaho	—	—	—	X	X
Illinois	X	X	X	X	X
Indiana	—	—	—	—	X/Y
Iowa	X	X	X	X	X
Kansas	Y	Y[b]	Y[b]	Y[b]	X
Kentucky	—	—	X	X	—
Louisiana	—	—	—	—	—
Maine	X	X	X	X	X
Maryland	—	X[b]	—	—	X
Massachusetts	X	X	X	X	X
Michigan	Y[a]	X	X	X	X
Minnesota	X/Y	X/Y	X/Y	X/Y	X/Y
Mississippi	—	—	—	—	—
Missouri	Y	Y	—	Y	—
Montana	X	X	X	X	X/Y
Nebraska	X	X	X	X	Y
Nevada	—	X	X	X	X
New Hampshire	X	X	X	X	X
New Jersey	X	X	X	X	X
New Mexico	X	X	X	X	X
New York	X	X[b]	X	X	X
North Carolina	—	—	—	—	—
North Dakota	Y[c]	X[c]	Y[c]	Y[c]	X
Ohio	X	X	X	X	X

EXHIBIT 14.2 *(continued)*

State	State	Local	Police	Fire-fighters	K–12 Teachers
Oklahoma	—	X	X	X	X
Oregon	X	X[b]	X	X	X
Pennsylvania	X/Y	X/Y	X	X	X/Y
Rhode Island	X	X	X	X	X
South Carolina	—	—	—	—	—
South Dakota	X	X	X	X	X
Tennessee	—	—	—	—	X
Texas	—	—	X[b]	X[b]	—
Utah	—	—	—	—	—
Vermont	X	X	X	X	X
Virginia	—	—	—	—	—
Washington	X	X	X	X	X
West Virginia	Y[d]	Y[d]	Y[d]	Y[d]	Y[d]
Wisconsin	X	X	X	X	X
Wyoming	—	—	—	X	—

X: collective bargaining provisions;
Y: meet and confer provisions;
X/Y: collective bargaining on some issues; meet and confer on other issues.

[a]Negotiations may be established under civil service regulations.
[b]Local option permitted.
[c]Meet and confer established by attorney general opinion.

Source: Richard C. Kearney, *Labor Relations in the Public Sector,* (New York: Marcel Dekker, 1992), 70–71.

Larger governments, by contrast, were able to centralize the labor relations function so that labor agreements could be coordinated by a single set of actors employing a common and consistent strategy.[8] The virtues of a centralized approach remain equally valid today. First, elected officials, concerned about delegating their authority over a process that could greatly affect governmental budgets, are provided a means of ensuring budgetary control and political accountability. Second, inequities in wages, benefits, and working conditions that tend to develop when each agency is allowed to bargain with its own employees can be avoided through a centrally coordinated labor strategy. Third, whipsawing, a practice in which employees in one unit use concessions gained by other units to win similar concessions, can be greatly reduced through a centrally coordinated strategy. Finally, negotiating labor agreements demands professional skills, specialized knowledge, immediate access to budgetary

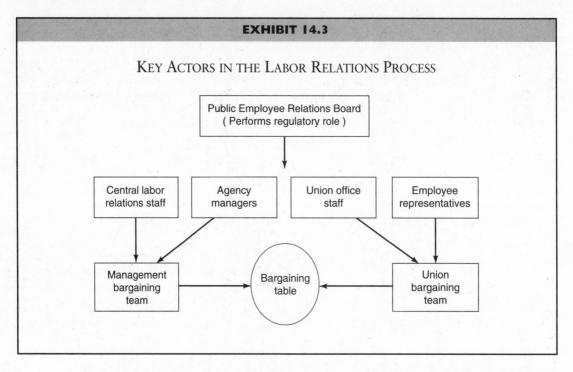

EXHIBIT 14.3

KEY ACTORS IN THE LABOR RELATIONS PROCESS

data, and large amounts of time and effort. A central staff composed of labor relations specialists brings together in one place the required information and expertise. Given these advantages, most large governments have created a central labor relations staff, housed either within the central personnel office or as a separate staff unit.

From the perspective of management's chief labor negotiator, government fragmentation places numerous constraints on his or her ability to pursue a coordinated and unified labor strategy. The chief negotiator must learn to work within the parameters set by legislative bodies because they usually must ratify the financial aspects of the labor agreement. In addition, civil service commissions and merit protection boards insist that bargaining decisions not intrude on their policy prerogatives. Finally, agencies with their own taxing authority or elected administrators may attempt to pursue a labor strategy at odds with that defined by the central labor relations staff. All of these examples are part of the reality of applying the NLRA model to fragmented governmental systems in which outcomes are driven more by politics than by competitive marketplace forces.

The Collective Bargaining Process

In the absence of national labor legislation covering public employees, there is no single collective bargaining process that can be described and analyzed. In fact, there are more than 100 state laws defining a mind-boggling number of rules for organizing employees and negotiating labor agreements. Nonetheless, for the federal government and those states that have adopted the modified NLRA model, it is possible to describe the collective bargaining process in general terms. It involves (1) determining appropriate bargaining units, (2) certifying one union as the exclusive bargaining agent, (3) negotiating a collective bargaining agreement, (4) pursuing authorized impasse resolution procedures if no agreement is reached, and (5) resolving conflicts that may arise during the life of the agreement. The first two stages represent the *organizational phase*. They occur only when a unit is first organized for purposes of collective bargaining (although a new bargaining agent may be elected from time to time). The third and fourth stages constitute the *negotiation phase*. They take place on a regular schedule, depending on whether the life of the contract is one, two, or three years. The final stage represents the *contract administration phase*. During this phase both parties implement the labor agreement and resolve grievances and disputes arising under it.

Stage One: Determining Appropriate Bargaining Units

A bargaining unit is a group of employees recognized as appropriate for representation by a labor organization for purposes of collective bargaining. Governments that are heavily organized must bargain with many different units. Among state governments, for example, there are more than one thousand bargaining units, with the number in each state ranging from none to well over 100. There are more than four thousand bargaining units in the federal government.

Before a union can be elected to represent employees, someone must determine which employees should constitute the bargaining unit. The process for doing so is generally set forth in state law or administrative rules. In practice, the process usually begins when a union attempts to organize a particular group of employees. When enough employees "show an interest" in being represented (a procedure to be explained further), the union petitions the public employee relations board or other designated entity to accept its view of which positions are to be included in the bargaining unit. An example of a petition form is presented in Exhibit 14.4. Management is then notified of the petition and given an opportunity to challenge the union's proposal. If the differences are minor, the board may attempt to resolve them informally. If they are serious, boards in most states are authorized to investigate and make a determination. Disputes are typically of two kinds: first, whether specific positions do or do not belong in the unit; and, second, whether groups of employees should be combined together as proposed by the union.

Determining appropriate units is not as easy as it might first appear. A unit may be composed of all nonsupervisory employees in an agency regardless of the nature of the work performed, or separate units may be established according to distinct occupational groups. As an example of the latter, clerical workers might be grouped into a single unit regardless of which agency they work for. The most often cited criterion for unit determination is "community of interest." This means that those in the unit should share similar kinds of skills, working conditions, and wage and benefit packages to ensure a community of interest at the bargaining table. Nonetheless, it is not always easy to determine whether "community of interest" is best served by grouping employees by agency, occupation, or both.

Another unit determination issue relates to size. From the union's perspective, large units are more difficult to organize and control, but when cohesiveness is high they can exert considerable bargaining power. Shared interests, however, are generally

EXHIBIT 14.4

EXAMPLE OF A UNIT DETERMINATION AND ELECTION PETITION

State Public Employees Relations Board

Petition for New Unit Determination and Election

Instructions: Submit an original and five copies of this petition to the State Public Employees Relations Board. If more space is required, attach additional sheets.

1. Name of Petitioner:
2. Address and Telephone of Petitioner:

3. Name of Public Employer:
4. Address and Telephone of Employer:

5. Description of the unit to be determined specifying inclusions and exclusions. Use correct job titles whenever possible.

   Inclusions:

   Exclusions:

5a. Approximate number of employees in the proposed unit:
5b. Is the petition accompanied by 30 percent proof-of-interest?   Yes _____ No _____

6. Name, Address and Affiliation of any labor organizations who claim to represent the employees in the proposed unit. (If NONE, write NONE.)

7. Expiration dates and brief description of any contracts covering any employees in the proposed unit.

8. Briefly state any known disagreement between the employer and the petitioner as to the nature and scope of the proposed unit. (If NONE, write NONE.)

9. Any other relevant facts:

Date: _____
By:_____

easier to define and pursue in smaller units. Management tends to prefer large, comprehensive units simply for the sake of administrative convenience. A system composed of large units reduces the number of contracts that must be negotiated and opportunities for whipsawing. The Massachusetts legislature, for example, chose to create ten statewide units, grouped not by department but by occupational field.[9] Also indicative of the trend toward fewer, larger units, the Civil Service Reform Act of 1978 made it easier to consolidate existing units in the federal government.

Yet another unit determination issue is whether supervisors should be excluded from collective bargaining, included in bargaining units with other employees, or included only in separate bargaining units created just for them. The issue does not arise in the private sector because supervisors are excluded from collective bargaining by the Taft-Hartley Act of 1947. Because there is no comparable law in the public sector, each state has had to decide the issue for itself. Some labor experts argue that there is less reason in the public sector to exclude supervisors because their economic interests are closer to the rank and file than to agency administrators, and the scope of their authority over subordinates is less than in the private sector. Others, however, continue to argue that their ability to maintain workplace discipline and carry out management policies will be undermined if they are grouped with nonsupervisory employees for bargaining purposes. A common policy response has been a compromise in which supervisors are allowed to collectively bargain but only as members of separate bargaining units. Eleven states exclude supervisors from bargaining, six more exclude certain classes of supervisors, 18 permit supervisors to bargain as members of separate units, and 22 appear to allow mixed units although in practice supervisors are often grouped in separate units.[10] In the federal sector, all persons exercising independent judgment in hiring, directing, rewarding, or disciplining employees are excluded.

Stage Two: Certifying an Exclusive Bargaining Agent

"Exclusive recognition" means that one union has been authorized to act as the sole representative of a particular bargaining unit. This practice is beneficial to both sides. The union is assured that management must deal with it alone concerning labor issues, and management is freed from having to cope with conflicting demands from multiple union representatives. Once elected, the exclusive bargaining agent is obligated to represent all members of the bargaining unit, whether or not they are union members, both at the bargaining table and in processing grievances. This is called the "duty of fair representation."

In those states without enabling legislation the process for union certification must be worked out by mutual consent. In most states, however, the certification process is outlined in labor relations statutes. Before an election is held to certify a particular union, employees normally must provide evidence that they want to organize for purposes of collective bargaining. This "showing of interest" may be accomplished by signing cards authorizing the employer to deduct union dues from their paychecks, or by signing cards that simply indicate their desire to be represented by a particular union. An example of an authorization card is presented in Exhibit 14.5. Although requirements contained in state law vary considerably, the most common practice is to require 30 percent of employees to "show interest." It is also common for other unions to have their names placed on the ballot by submitting authorization

---

EXHIBIT 14.5

SAMPLE AUTHORIZATION CARD

Representation Authorization
National Federation of Teachers

I hereby designate the National Federation of Teachers as the exclusive representative in collective bargaining for my welfare in wages, hours, fringe benefits, and other working conditions. This authorization will remain in effect until such time as it is revoked, in writing, by me.

Name (Printed) _____   Employer _____

Address _____   Position _____

Home Phone _____   Office Phone _____

Signature _____ Date _____

---

cards signed by at least ten percent of unit members. This "intervention" by another union typically occurs after the first union has secured approval for the proposed bargaining unit and a notice of election has been posted. An on-site or mail election is then arranged in which employees may choose between one or more unions. They are also given the option of voting for "no representative." In most states a union must receive a majority of the votes cast to be certified as the exclusive bargaining agent, although in a few states an absolute majority of those in the unit is required. If no choice receives a majority, a run-off election is generally arranged, usually between the top two vote-getters, or between the union with the most votes and the "no representation" option. Barring serious improprieties, the winning union will be certified as the exclusive bargaining agent. To give the union time to negotiate a contract and get established on a firm footing, "election bars" typically prohibit new elections for at least one year.

What employees choose to do, they can also undo. If members of the bargaining unit decide they no longer wish to be represented by a particular union, they can decertify the union in much the same manner as they certified it. Thirty percent, for example, may be required by law to show support for a decertification election, and a majority vote may be necessary for decertification to occur. Although it is relatively rare, decertification elections have occurred in the public sector. Unions are sometimes punished, for example, for being too willing to make concessions during periods of fiscal retrenchment. The process is often helped along by a rival union that wishes to become the next bargaining agent. Once an agent is decertified, a rival union may petition for a new election. In very rare circumstances, a public employee relations board may also decertify a union for violations of law. Such was the case when air traffic controllers, represented by the Professional Air Traffic Controllers Organization (PATCO), launched an illegal strike on August 3, 1981. President Reagan authorized the firing of 11,500 controllers who walked off the job (another one thousand had returned to work) and the Department of Labor asked the Federal Labor Relations Authority to decertify the union. PATCO was forced to file for bankruptcy when the FLRA complied with the decertification request.

Management must take great care during the certification campaign not to interfere with, restrain, or coerce employees who are exercising their legal right to organize. For example, threatening to sanction employees who are pro-union, or "bribing" employees with last-minute increases in benefits, are likely to be deemed unfair labor practices in most states. This can be a frustrating time for management, especially when the union is making outrageous claims or promises. In most cases management may rebut untrue claims and may describe current policies and management views regarding the advantages and disadvantages of union recognition, but the tenor of it words and actions will be scrutinized for any hint of coercion or interference. Management must also take care to remain neutral as regards rival unions. Finally, management usually must allow organizing efforts to take place at work within limits set by law and administrative rules. Solicitation by union representatives and employee organizers, for example, is normally allowed only during coffee breaks, lunch breaks, and before and after work. In the final analysis, if management wishes to avoid union recognition, the time to act is well before organizing efforts begin. Proactive steps may include addressing morale problems, implementing progressive employee relations programs, developing grievance procedures, and continuously soliciting the views of employees.

Stage Three: Negotiating the Labor Agreement

A collective bargaining agreement is negotiated when a unit is first organized and every year or two thereafter. Issues relevant to bargaining may be classified as mandatory, permitted, and prohibited. As examples, bargaining is often *mandatory* regarding wages, hours, and conditions of employment, *permitted* regarding grievance procedures and union security arrangements, and *prohibited* regarding specific management rights. As explained above, the scope of bargaining is usually narrower in the public sector because policy makers have been unwilling to accept the NLRA model without modifications. The scope of bargaining enjoyed by federal employees, for example, is extremely narrow. The Civil Service Reform Act prohibits bargaining over matters pertaining to an agency's mission, budget, organization, number of employees, internal security arrangements, and management's right to hire, assign, direct, lay off, retain, suspend, remove, demote, and discipline employees. Nor can employees bargain over matters determined under other federal statutes, such as wages, benefits, holidays, and leaves of absence. In short, the scope of bargaining for most federal employees is effectively limited to the effects of technology on employees, methods and means by which work is performed, and working conditions not covered by other statutory requirements. The scope of bargaining is less narrow under state law. States normally allow bargaining over wages, terms, and conditions of employment, but often within parameters set by strong management rights provisions.

Collective bargaining agreements range in length from 20 to more than 100 pages. The trend today is toward longer, more detailed agreements. Although contract language varies greatly from one agreement to the next, the following subjects are typically covered:

1. union recognition and rights
2. management rights
3. union security arrangements
4. grievance procedures
5. disciplinary procedures
6. compensation rates
7. hours of work and overtime
8. benefits: vacations, holidays, leaves, insurance
9. health and safety provisions
10. job security/seniority provisions
11. contract expiration date

Among these, union security is particularly important to the ability of a union to represent employees effectively. A financially secure union is more powerful politically and better able to fulfill its responsibilities on a sustained basis. The type of security arrangement written into the labor agreement plays a large role in determining a union's financial health. Whenever possible, unions attempt to negotiate a *union shop* arrangement, which requires everyone in the bargaining unit to be a dues-paying member of the union. Only five states, however, permit union shops. The worst arrangement from the union's perspective is the *open shop*. In an open shop the union must represent all employees in the bargaining unit without being able to require them to be members or to pay fees. At least 20 states and the federal government require an open shop. This creates a significant "free rider" problem for unions because employees can obtain virtually all of the benefits of union membership, including costly legal representation, without joining the union or paying dues. For example, according to Marick F. Masters and Robert Atkin, the American Federation of Government Employees represents some 700,000 federal employees, only 177,000 of whom are dues-paying members.[11] A union in this position can raise its dues, but it risks losing yet more members in doing so.

A security arrangement that offers a balance between freedom of association for employees and financial security for unions is the *agency shop*. Under an agency shop arrangement, an employee is not required to join the union but is required to pay a fee equivalent to union dues to underwrite the costs of his or her representation. Nineteen states specifically permit agency shop arrangements. The Supreme Court has ruled that it is constitutional as long as the union does not require individuals to support through their service fees an ideological or political cause with which they disagree (*Abood v. Detroit Board of Education,* 431 U.S. 209, 1977). At least two states responded to the Court's decision by setting service fees at 85 percent of full union dues.[12] Some states also allow religious objectors to contribute an equivalent amount to charity. In the final analysis, agency shop is a compromise that many public agencies are willing to accept, despite misgivings, because of its stabilizing effects. Weaker, less financially secure unions sometimes resort to making outrageous demands in an effort to rally employees behind them.[13]

The process by which issues such as union security are negotiated is a complex one. To capture the essence of this process, Richard C. Kearney has reduced its many elements to 11 basic steps. These are presented in Exhibit 14.6.

EXHIBIT 14.6

Eleven Steps in Collective Bargaining

1. Establish a bargaining committee and a negotiating team, including a chief spokesperson.
2. Analyze the experience under the previous contract (if any). Department heads and supervisors are asked to determine problem areas from management's perspective and offer advice on the next contract. Both parties study the grievance records under the old contract, including arbitration awards, and consider the motives, strategies, and views of their counterparts on the opposite team. The union committee solicits and screens demands from the membership.
3. Analyze wage and benefit data, especially comparable information from similar jurisdictions and occupational groups. Conduct a wage and fringe benefit survey if necessary. Respond to the other party's requests for data. Union reviews employer's financial data.
4. Analyze recent developments and relevant agreements in other jurisdictions for personnel policy-related changes. Both parties confidentially prioritize their demands and prepare justifications for them. Arrange prenegotiation conferences to establish the rules of the game and set schedules. Include preliminary discussions on acceptable data and facts to be used during negotiations.
5. Make formal representations, present written proposals and demands.
6. Set bargaining agenda, including which issues should be considered first. Attempt to resolve simple, noncontroversial matters first to create a cooperative environment. Consider dividing controversial issues into those that are primarily economic in their implications and those that are not, and whether to take up issues as a package or break them down into smaller decision units.
7. Arrange negotiating sessions. These normally should be held during regular working hours for short (one to three hours) periods. They should be held at a "neutral" location at the workplace or elsewhere. Provide for separate and private caucus rooms. Minutes of each meeting should be maintained by neutral secretary and kept by each party as well.
8. Conduct negotiations. Hold caucuses to exchange reactions of members of the bargaining team, reconsider tactics and strategy, and check with superiors for guidance and direction.
9. Execute written agreement.
10. Ratification of the agreement by union membership and legislative branch.

....

Source: Richard C. Kearney, *Labor Relations in the Public Sector* (New York: Marcel Dekker, 1992), 135–136.

In practice the bargaining process is much more dynamic than these 11 steps imply. Successful bargaining requires a relationship built on trust and a willingness to pursue common interests without resorting to threats and personal attacks. Success in this regard depends on such factors as the history of bargaining between the two parties, the political and economic climate, the constellation of personalities around the table, and the degree of training and experience possessed by participants. Bargaining often proceeds much like a poker game in which each side plays its cards close to the vest, maintains a "poker face," holds bargaining chips in reserve, bluffs in an effort to explore the other side's commitment to certain issues, and assigns someone to watch the other side for reactions.

When it is time to renegotiate an existing contract, spokespersons for each team will read their respective "demands," i.e., those changes they wish to make in the existing document. Neither side can safely assume that provisions won in previous bargaining sessions are automatically retained. Concession bargaining, for example, is the term used when management feels compelled during periods of fiscal stress to ask the union to give back gains, particularly economic benefits, that had been negotiated under previous contracts. Unions may be offered a choice between making concessions and accepting layoffs—a choice that puts the union leadership in a very difficult spot.

In most instances agreement on new contract language is reached without significant conflict because the participants have a mature working relationship, accept the realities of power, and recognize that agreement is necessary for continued organizational functioning. According to Arnold M. Zack, both parties share an interest in peacefully concluding their negotiations:

> *The labor-management relationship is like a marriage in that preservation of the partnership is usually considered to be more important to both than a victory for either in their immediate dispute. Indeed, a true victory for one party is bound to produce resentment in the other party and lead to an uncomfortable contract life. On the one side, the employer recognizes that continuation of the enterprise requires employees; that it has invested time and money in training its present employees; and that productivity will be enhanced if the employees are satisfied with their benefits and persuaded that their wages, hours, and working conditions are reasonable and equitable. On the other side, the employees recognize that continuation of their employment is dependent upon . . . their willingness to provide the requisite services.*[14]

These shared interests notwithstanding, peaceful settlements do not always occur. When the two parties are unable to make further progress in resolving disputed issues, a fourth stage in the bargaining process becomes necessary.

Stage Four: Resolving Impasses

Negotiators occasionally find that they cannot resolve their differences—either because all communications have broken down or because an impasse has been reached on specific issues. An impasse occurs when one side demands more than the other side is willing to give, thereby making settlement impossible. The strike, which is the mechanism used in the private sector to resolve impasses, is generally not available in the public sector. When strikes began occurring with increasing frequency in the 1950s among teachers and other local government employees, most state legislatures responded by prohibiting strikes and mandating severe penalties for those who violated the law. When these punitive laws proved ineffective, lawmakers began exploring alternative ways of resolving impasses. The typical policy response, as outlined in New York's Taylor Law, was to require binding interest arbitration when agreements could not be reached through mediation or factfinding. As shown in Exhibit 14.7, 36

EXHIBIT 14.7

STATE LEGISLATION ON DISPUTE RESOLUTION PROCEDURES FOR STATE AND LOCAL EMPLOYEES, 1991

State	Mediation	Fact-finding	Arbitration (conventional)	Arbitration (final-offer)
Alabama				
Alaska	X		X	
Arizona				
Arkansas				
California	X	X		
Colorado				
Connecticut	X	X		X
Delaware	X	X	X	X
Florida	X	X		
Georgia	X			
Hawaii	X	X	X	X
Idaho	X	X		
Illinois	X	X	X	X
Indiana	X	X	X	
Iowa	X	X	X	X
Kansas	X	X		
Kentucky	X	X		
Louisiana				
Maine	X	X	X	
Maryland	X	X		
Massachusetts	X	X	X	X
Michigan	X	X	X	X
Minnesota	X		X	X
Mississippi				
Missouri				

states authorize mediation, 33 states authorize factfinding, and 30 states authorize arbitration as alternative impasse resolution procedures.

The underlying strategy adopted by a majority of states was to regulate that which could not be effectively outlawed by substituting mediation, factfinding, and arbitration techniques for the strike. Although this strategy has not ended illegal strikes, it has greatly curtailed their use. Even among the 12 states that allow some public employees to strike, mediation and factfinding are often required before employees are allowed to walk off the job. For example, in Pennsylvania, where strikes are permitted among employees other than police and firefighters, negotiators must go to mediation if no agreement is reached well in advance of the budget submission

EXHIBIT 14.7 *(continued)*

State	Mediation	Fact-finding	Arbitration (conventional)	Arbitration (final-offer)
Montana	X	X	X	X
Nebraska	X	X	X	
Nevada	X	X	X	X
New Hampshire	X	X	X	
New Jersey	X	X	X	X
New Mexico	X	X	X	
New York	X	X	X	
North Carolina				
North Dakota	X	X		X
Ohio	X	X	X	X
Oklahoma		X	X	
Oregon	X	X	X	
Pennsylvania	X	X	X	
Rhode Island	X	X	X	
South Carolina				
South Dakota	X	X		
Tennessee	X	X	X	
Texas	X		X	
Utah				
Vermont	X	X	X	X
Virginia				
Washington	X	X	X	
West Virginia				
Wisconsin	X	X	X	X
Wyoming			X	

Source: Richard C. Kearney, *Labor Relations in the Public Sector* (New York: Marcel Dekker, 1992), 322–323.

date. If mediation does not produce an agreement within a specified time, the Public Labor Relations Board may appoint a factfinding panel, which will conduct a hearing and make a public report. If its recommendations are not acceptable to both sides, the union may choose to arbitrate or strike.

Efforts to break an impasse normally begins with mediation. *Mediation* is a method of resolving disputes by employing a neutral third party, a mediator, to assist the parties in reaching an agreement by keeping them talking and encouraging them to move toward common ground. Mediators may shuttle back and forth between the two parties delivering offers and counteroffers, or they may bring the two sides together and simply mediate discussions. Although mediators may make suggestions intended to persuade negotiators to come to a voluntary agreement, their role does not include dictating or engineering results. They are there to make sure communications do not fail and to provide appropriate nudges.

Sometimes state law or the labor agreement will specify a certain date before contract expiration at which the parties must begin mediation. More frequently, the mediation process begins when the two parties acknowledge that they need assistance in resolving disputes and request the services of a mediator. A majority of states now provide mediation services to deadlocked parties, often providing mediators free of charge. In states where mediation services are not available, the Federal Mediation and Conciliation Service will provide a mediator free of charge.

Although well-trained mediators can provide valuable assistance during negotiations, they cannot compel a favorable result. Despite the mediator's best efforts, voluntary agreement is not likely to occur when impasse results from the employer's inability to pay, the parties have a history of deadlocking, or the parties face strong pressures from elected officials and union members to hold out for better terms. When a mediator believes nothing will be gained from further mediation, he or she may recommend factfinding. Factfinding is often required by law before the two parties may resort to binding arbitration or a strike. *Factfinding* is a method of resolving impasses by employing a neutral third party, a factfinder, to assist the parties in reaching an agreement. The factfinder holds a hearing, investigates the disputed issues, and submits a report containing nonbinding recommendations for settling disputed issues. Factfinders are typically obtained in the same way as mediators. If the designated state agency does not have staff members available to perform these roles, it will prepare and mail to the parties a list of qualified individuals who can serve as either mediators or factfinders. Each party then strikes a name from the list alternately until only a single name remains. Factfinding can be very expensive, and for this reason it is common for the costs to be shared between the labor relations agency and the two parties.

Unlike a mediator, the factfinder performs the role of investigator and judge. The factfinder's task is to uncover key facts, state them in a disinterested manner, and offer recommendations that are fair and reasonable—all with the hope that rational persuasion, along with public pressure, will induce the parties to accept them voluntarily. But because factfinding involves the relatively few, stubborn cases that have not been resolved at earlier stages, its success rate is relatively low. It is required nonetheless by a majority of states in the hope that the parties to a dispute will opt for voluntary compliance rather than take their chances with binding arbitration.

Interest arbitration (which is not to be confused with grievance arbitration as defined later in this chapter) is a method of resolving labor disputes by employing a neutral third party, an arbitrator, to review the facts and make decisions that are binding on both parties. The process is similar to factfinding except that a settlement is imposed on the parties by the arbitrator after the hearing. Although arbitrators do not have to go through a lengthy training process or pass a battery of qualifying tests, they will not last long as arbitrators if they are perceived as biased toward one party or the other, or if their decisions are not viewed as consistent with the evidence. Nor can they survive by avoiding tough issues and making concessions to both sides. Arbitrators are obtained in the same way as mediators and factfinders. Private agencies such as the American Arbitration Association also keep rosters of available arbitrators to help the parties in their selection process. The American Arbitration Association typically provides a list of names, asks each party to rank order 12 of them, and then certifies the person who is the highest mutual choice.

Because strikes are widely prohibited in the public sector, binding arbitration usually represents the mechanism of last resort for resolving impasses. A majority of states now require binding arbitration for some categories of employees when voluntary mechanisms such as mediation and factfinding have failed to produce a settlement. In most states arbitration awards may be reviewed by the courts only if there is evidence of fraud or legal error, or if the arbitrator has clearly violated his or her authority. An alternative form of arbitration, sometimes called final-offer arbitration, requires the arbitrator to choose between the last best offers made by each side, either on an issue-by-issue basis or as an entire package. In contrast to conventional arbitration, the arbitrator is given no opportunity to fashion a remedy that gives a little to each side. The fact that compromise is not one of the arbitrator's options is intended to reduce the attractiveness of arbitration as a means of settling disputes. The hope is that the parties will try harder to reach an agreement earlier in the bargaining process rather than risk losing in arbitration.

Labor is normally at a disadvantage in collective bargaining without the right to strike. This disadvantage is partially eliminated through the use of binding arbitration because both sides theoretically have an equal chance of prevailing. Evidence suggests that arbitration has played a key role in reducing the number of strikes, whether legal or illegal. Nonetheless, binding arbitration remains highly controversial for several reasons. First, it runs contrary to the concept of voluntary, bilateral bargaining because contractual provisions are ultimately imposed on the parties by an outsider. Its continued use can only be justified on the grounds that it serves the public interest better than allowing strikes. Second, critics argue that arbitration involves illegal delegation of important policy-making powers to a person who is neither an elected nor an appointed government official. Although most legal challenges to binding interest arbitration have failed, more than one-third of state governments have placed restrictions on delegated authority by specifying factors that arbitrators must consider when making awards. These may include the welfare of the public, the ability of the government to pay, and the cost of living. Finally, many critics argue that arbitration has a chilling effect on collective bargaining. A chilling effect occurs, according to this argument, when either party believes it will prevail in arbitration. That party will not engage in genuine bargaining during negotiation, mediation, and factfinding, choosing instead to hold out for all it can get during arbitration. It may calculate that even if the arbitrator "splits the difference" between two sets of offers, the results will still represent a net gain. If a strategy of superficial bargaining proves successful, a narcotic effect may also occur. The parties may, for example, learn to bargain superficially and to accept mediation and factfinding only as a means of getting to binding arbitration. Although there is some evidence supporting the existence of chilling and narcotic effects, the fact remains that the vast majority of contracts are successfully negotiated without the use of arbitration.[15] In addition, chilling or narcotic effects may be reduced by instituting final-offer arbitration in which "splitting the difference" is precluded.

Although mediation, factfinding, and arbitration are the methods of impasse resolution used most frequently in the public sector, other techniques are also used. Med-arb, for example, is a method used for some municipal employees in Wisconsin. Under med-arb, the neutral third party begins by mediating the dispute. If no settlement is reached, he or she will then arbitrate on the basis of each party's final offer. The goal of this method is to create incentives for the two parties to settle the dispute voluntarily during mediation rather than risk a decision that could greatly favor the other party. It is a promising approach that may work well if there are enough individuals available who are trained in both mediation and arbitration.

The strategy of substituting some combination of mediation, factfinding, and arbitration for the strike may be illustrated by using the federal government as an example. If the bargaining teams in a federal agency believe that they might benefit from third-party assistance, they may select a mediator together or either party may request a mediator from the Federal Mediation and Conciliation Service (FMCS). The FMCS is an independent federal agency created in 1913 to help settle labor disputes in the private sector. It is now authorized to assist federal, state, and local agencies as well. The Civil Service Reform Act requires that when the mediator determines that attempts at a settlement are fruitless he or she must notify both parties, either of whom may then request the services of the Federal Services Impasse Panel (FSIP). The FSIP is a factfinding agency within the Federal Labor Relations Authority that provides assistance in resolving labor disputes, such as mediation and factfinding, if they are not first resolved by the FMCS or other third-party mediation. Deadlocked parties may go to binding arbitration if their procedures are approved by the FSIP. Alternatively, the FSIP can order further negotiations, with or without mediation or factfinding assistance. If voluntary settlement does not occur, the FSIP can hold a hearing and impose its own settlement on the parties. Use of the strike is not a legal option.

Stage Five: Administering the Labor Contract

The process of labor-management relations does not end with ratification of a new labor agreement. Both parties must continuously administer it by faithfully acting in accordance with its terms. Unfortunately, disputes inevitably arise regarding how it is to be interpreted and whether the rights of employees have been violated. The primary means of resolving such disputes is found in the grievance procedures that virtually all labor agreements contain. They provide an orderly system for adjudicating disputes and maintaining harmonious labor relations.

Grievance procedures lie at the very heart of the labor-relations process. From labor's perspective they represent the primary means of keeping the exercise of managerial discretion within acceptable bounds. Labor also views the right to grieve management actions as an essential aspect of workplace democracy. From management's perspective they perform organizational functions that are critically important to employee morale, work productivity, and avoidance of legal risk. First, morale and productivity is likely to be higher (and turnover lower) where employees trust that their grievances will be adjusted fairly and equitably. Second, grievance procedures provide a safety valve by allowing employees to release the personal frustrations that inevitably develop at work. Third, they provide due process guarantees that, if strictly adhered to by management, help protect the organization from risk of lawsuits and economic penalties. Finally, they provide valuable opportunities for management to discover and remove the causes of employee discontent.

A grievance is any type of complaint by an employee or union against an employer alleging a violation of the labor agreement. What constitutes legitimate grievances is rarely defined, but they must involve matters within the scope of the collective bargaining agreement. The following examples, obtained from actual cases that went to arbitration, illustrate the broad range of issues they may involve. Note that the first two examples involve grievances filed by the union to protect its own prerogatives, while the remaining examples involve grievances filed by the union on behalf of individual employees.

> *Union Rights.* Did a state Department of Health improperly deny use of a conference room to the union's County Executive Board for an after-hours meeting? (97 LA 310, 1991)
>
> *Unit Membership.* Was a newly created accounting clerk position in the Treasurer's Office of a local board of education properly excluded from the bargaining unit as a "confidential employee"? (97 LA 465, 1991)
>
> *Disciplinary Suspension.* Was a ten-day suspension an appropriate disciplinary action for a Therapeutic Program Worker who nodded off while on duty as sole caretaker for eight mentally retarded resident patients? (97 LA 1206, 1991).
>
> *Disciplinary Discharge.* Did the management of a city road shop have just cause for discharging a heavy equipment operator who operated a snow plow with a blood alcohol level three times the legal limit? (97 LA 564, 1991).
>
> *Promotion.* Did a local school district act appropriately in denying promotion to an employee who was less qualified but possessed more seniority than the individual who was promoted? (97 LA 1118, 1991).
>
> *Layoff.* Did a local government improperly lay off a part-time assistant in the Zoning Department on the grounds that the position had to be eliminated for financial reasons when the employee was subsequently rehired as secretary performing the same duties but with a loss of seniority? (97 LA 612, 1991)
>
> *Working Conditions.* Did a city police department improperly ban smoking in a new 911 communications center to protect sensitive equipment? (97 LA 768, 1991)

Grievance procedures normally outline a series of steps to be taken by the parties involved within specified time limits. The first step is usually to communicate the complaint to the immediate supervisor with the hope that it can be resolved informally. If this fails, a second step typically requires filing a formal, written complaint and forwarding it to the next higher management level. If the complaint is not resolved to the employee's satisfaction, the final step in roughly 80 percent of public sector labor agreements is to take the matter to binding arbitration. Establishing such procedures is a mandatory item for bargaining in most states.

Grievance arbitration is not to be confused with interest arbitration as described earlier in the chapter. In grievance arbitration, an arbitrator (or three-person panel) conducts a hearing to become as informed as possible about the relevant issues and facts. After each side has stipulated the disputed issues, the arbitrator listens to witnesses, examines relevant exhibits, and asks appropriate questions. The arbitrator subsequently makes "an award" that is binding on both parties and sometimes offers a written opinion supporting it. Although the remedial powers of arbitrators are broad, their decisions are checked by common sense, precedents set by other arbitrators, basic legal principles, and the terms of the contract itself. An arbitrator's award normally cannot be overturned by the courts unless it is clearly inconsistent with the language of the labor agreement or public law.

Nowhere is trust and mutual good faith more important than in the handling of grievances. Protracted grievances can be highly costly in terms of both money and morale. For this reason, management should take certain steps to enhance the system's integrity. First, supervisors should be well trained in human relations skills and taught the importance of treating employees fairly, responding to complaints promptly, and resolving them informally whenever possible. Second, ensuring that union stewards are well trained is equally important. The union's duty of fair representation compels it to represent all employees in the bargaining unit when grievances arise. However, assisting an employee with a frivolous or clearly unwarranted grievance undermines the credibility of the entire grievance process. A well-trained steward will know how to resolve such matters outside of the formal grievance process without violating the duty of fair representation. Supervisors should also be taught to work closely and cooperatively with union stewards. One study found that union stewards are less likely to file formal grievances when their management counterparts are viewed as accommodative, when employees do not hold an antagonistic attitude toward management, and when participants engage in informal dispute resolution activities.[16] Finally, it is important to observe all due process rights when handling grievances so that employees are treated fairly and management decisions are not overturned by an arbitrator. In *NLRB v. Weingarten,* the Supreme Court confirmed that employees have the right to have a union representative present before submitting to an investigatory interview.[17] This right, which extends to public as well as private sector employees, is not triggered unless the employee reasonably believes that the investigation may result in disciplinary action and he or she requests union representation before discussing the facts of the matter with management. The latter has an affirmative duty to inform employees of their Weingarten rights.

Grievance Procedures for Non-Union Employees

Precisely because grievance systems are so essential to maintaining harmonious labor relations, most agencies establish them whether or not their employees are represented by a union. Grievance procedures for nonunion employees tend to differ from those established for organized employees in two ways. First, they are outlined in personnel policies and administrative rules rather than in collective bargaining agreements. This means that decisions regarding what is just in any given situation must be determined in accordance with recognized principles of fairness and due process rather than on careful scrutiny of contractual language. Second, binding arbitration is seldom employed as the last step in the appeals process. Instead, the final determination is generally made by the agency head or a merit system review board. Binding arbitration is not used because the employer would have to pay the costs of arbitration, thereby undermining all semblance of impartiality.

Where formal merit systems exist, grievances involving disciplinary actions and prohibited personnel practices are appealed through a series of steps culminating in a decision by a merit system agency or civil service board. By contrast, less formal options are available to governments without merit systems or to governments desiring more flexible procedures outside of the merit system for handling certain categories of complaints. Grievable issues are of four basic kinds: discrimination charges, disciplinary actions, violations of personnel rules, and general complaints of perceived injustice. Grievances of the first two kinds are usually processed through formal merit system procedures to ensure a higher level of due process, whereas the latter two are often processed through more informal grievance systems. For example, a study of grievance policies in 22 agencies in the Southwest found eight that used in-house appeals systems to process disciplinary actions and 11 that used such systems to process charges of discrimination.[18] The remaining agencies used more formal systems with stronger due process guarantees for grievances involving disciplinary actions and discrimination.

Most agencies with in-house grievance systems use multiple-step procedures, sometimes combined with peer review. As shown in Exhibit 14.8, the typical system establishes a series of steps through which appeals are reviewed by successively higher levels of management. The process ends with an appeal to the agency head who makes the final determination. In systems with peer review, a panel composed of an equal number of employee representatives and management appointees considers the evidence and makes a determination that is rarely overturned by the agency head. Whether or not peer review is involved, grievance procedures typically encourage prompt and informal resolution of complaints, set time limits for processing grievances, allow a fellow employee to be present at each step, and allow employees to go directly to the personnel officer rather than to the supervisor if the complaint is confidential or if the employee fears reprisal.[19] Advice regarding the design of grievance procedures for nonunion employees is presented in Exhibit 14.9.

Grievance Procedures in the Federal Sector

Pursuing a grievance can be highly confusing because of the bewildering array of overlapping appeals processes that may exist. There may be a procedure for all employees outlined in personnel policies or administrative rules, and another procedure for organized employees outlined in the collective bargaining agreement. Organized employees with both options available to them normally elect to follow the one defined in the labor agreement. But there may also be additional appeals processes, often defined in law, for such purposes as pursuing a charge of discrimination, an adverse action, or a prohibited personnel practice. The federal government provides an example of a complex system of this kind.

For organized employees, grievances other than those involving discrimination and serious disciplinary actions end in binding arbitration, although awards are reviewable by the Federal Labor Relations Authority (FLRA). For grievances involving charges of discrimination, by contrast, organized employees may follow the negoti-

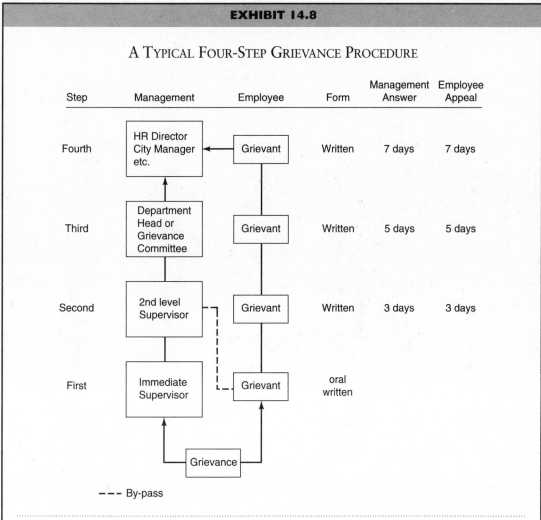

EXHIBIT 14.8

A TYPICAL FOUR-STEP GRIEVANCE PROCEDURE

Step	Management	Employee	Form	Management Answer	Employee Appeal
Fourth	HR Director City Manager etc.	Grievant	Written	7 days	7 days
Third	Department Head or Grievance Committee	Grievant	Written	5 days	5 days
Second	2nd level Supervisor	Grievant	Written	3 days	3 days
First	Immediate Supervisor	Grievant	oral written		
	Grievance				

– – – By-pass

From George W. Bohlander, "Public Sector Independent Grievance Systems: Methods and Procedures," *Public Personnel Management* 18 (Fall 1989), 347.

ated grievance procedure, including binding arbitration and subsequent appeals to the FLRA and the Equal Employment Opportunity Commission (EEOC), or appeal to the EEOC directly. Finally, for decisions involving serious disciplinary actions, such as suspensions of more than ten days, employees may use their negotiated grievance procedures with a subsequent appeal to the Merit System Protection Board (MSPB), or appeal to the MSPB directly. It is a complex system composed of overlapping appeals processes, and knowing how to proceed in any given instance is not always easy.

EXHIBIT 14.9

DESIGNING THE GRIEVANCE PROCEDURE

- Employees at all levels in the organization should be involved in the design of the grievances system. They can provide facts and feelings of which HR professionals and other managers may not be aware. Involvement will increase understanding of, trust in, and commitment to the grievance program.
- The right to file a grievance and be free from retaliation should be stated as part of the grievance policy and be widely advertised to employees.
- The issues which may be grieved, filing and reply times, and employee representation should be clearly identified.
- The procedure should specify management's intent to assist the grievant to identify and obtain relevant information.
- The grievance system should be designed with 3 or 4 review steps: (a) the grievant's immediate supervisor, (b) the supervisor's immediate supervisor, (c) department head, and (d) the senior manager in the agency. A grievance committee can be used to hear testimony and make recommendations to senior agency managers.
- Members of the HR department, except if a chair of a grievance committee, should be prepared to advise both the grievant and managers as cases arise. The HR department should monitor the grievance process to assure that it is properly conducted. Accurate grievance records should be kept.
- A grievance should be presented orally to the supervisor at step 1. The grievance can be presented in writing at the first step but no later than step 2. The written grievance should include a brief description of the issue and the requested remedy. All management response should be in writing.
- At all grievance steps, both parties should be permitted to present appropriate witnesses and documentation.

Source: George W. Bohlander, "Public Sector Independent Grievance Systems: Methods and Procedures," *Public Personnel Management* 18 (Fall 1989), 352.

The Impact of Collective Bargaining

During the 1950s and 1960s when collective bargaining rights were first being extended to public employees, critics expressed several concerns about potential adverse impacts. First, critics feared that public unions would prove sufficiently powerful to drive up wages and benefits in a highly labor-intensive sector of the economy. However, a review of the literature by Timothy Loney suggests that collective bargaining has not led to significantly higher aggregate pay and benefits.[20] Wages for all public employees have gone up significantly but not much more for unionized than non-unionized employees. Second, critics feared that binding arbitration would cause government costs to increase because arbitrators would give unions much of what they demanded. Most research, however, has not found this to be the case. Salaries for teachers, for example, were not found to be significantly higher when awarded through arbitration than through negotiated settlements. Third, some critics argued that arbitrators would substitute their judgment for elected officials in disputes involving policy issues. Evidence suggests that this has not occurred because management rights provisions tend to limit bargaining on policy matters. Exceptions include police and teachers. They were found to be more successful than other employee groups in shaping policy issues. Finally, some critics argued that collective bargaining would adversely affect government operations through work stoppages and protective work rules. On this subject Loney found the evidence to be mixed and inconclusive. In the final analysis, the dire consequences predicted by those who resisted the rise of public sector bargaining have not materialized.

The Future of Unions and Labor Relations

Public sector unions experienced a decline in memberships during the 1980s, and the political and economic climate of the 1990s has been no more hospitable. The economy continues to grow at only a modest rate, and governments at all levels continue to struggle with fiscal crises. In this environment political leaders are reluctant to raise taxes or approve costly wage and benefit packages. Taxpayers are less willing to support services with higher tax burdens and more likely to demand greater government efficiency through privatization. Wage freezes, layoffs, and concession bargaining have become commonplace as a result. Public opinion polls also continue to disclose little public confidence in unions as societal institutions; they are widely viewed as self-serving and ineffective. In short, unions will find it difficult to maintain their financial viability and succeed in pressing traditional labor demands in the current context of slow economic growth, continuing fiscal crisis, and declining memberships.

To make matters worse, the problems facing unions are not limited to those posed by an adverse political and economic environment. A more fundamental issue is whether union structures and the collective bargaining process remain effective vehicles for representing the interests of employees and advancing the larger interests of the organization. Unions have contributed in important ways to promoting workplace democracy, protecting employee rights, and improving wages and working conditions. But the ability of unions to retain their relevance in the twenty-first century is far from certain.

Several factors point to the growing obsolescence of unions as currently constituted. First, the traditional NLRA framework encourages a legalistic, reactive, and often adversarial approach to labor-management relations. This restricts the ability of organizations to make rapid and appropriate responses to the serious problems confronting them. Although unions have succeeded in reducing the arbitrary and capricious treatment of employees by extending the rule of law to labor-management relations, their focus on protecting contractual rights often causes them to neglect the larger problems confronting management and employees alike—such as the effects of retrenchments, rule-bound systems, technological obsolescence, and the needs of a changing workforce. In addition, the ponderous process of negotiations restricts the ability of either side, and both sides together, to respond easily and quickly to the wide range of organizational concerns that arise on a daily basis. Formal rights and rules, while facilitating uniformity of treatment, further reduce flexibility and efficiency. Mass actions such as the strike are too heavy-handed and slow to be useful in resolving immediate organizational problems. It is not surprising, therefore, that unions are being viewed increasingly as impediments rather than contributors to the capacity of organizations to respond appropriately to changing environmental conditions.

Second, the relevance of unions for public employees will remain in doubt as long as they cling to attitudes and strategies developed in the industrial settings of the nineteenth century. The technical and professional workers who constitute the bulk of union members in the public sector are much less accepting than other workers of mass actions, seniority and protective work rules, and adversarial confrontations. Solidarity is difficult to maintain among educated and independent-minded employees whose interests lie somewhere between those of labor and management. In addition, public opinion polls indicate that technical and professional employees are more likely to value meaningful and satisfying work, opportunities to develop their potentials, and greater involvement in policy decisions. These workers may not find a measure of due process in an overall context of managerial domination acceptable. In short, unions have to rethink their strategies and goals if they are to demonstrate their relevance to white-collar public employees.

Third, the employee rights movement and the resulting statutory and judicial constraints on managerial prerogatives have undercut the traditional role of the union as protector of employee rights. Wrongful discharge rulings by the courts and enactment of occupational health and safety, civil rights, and family leave legislation provide the sorts of protections once offered only through collective bargaining and union vigilance. To remain relevant unions have to identify new and broader roles in the workplace.

Fourth, unions must respond to the needs of a changing workforce by aggressively negotiating the kinds of benefit packages and development programs that today's workers need the most. Accommodating the needs of a more socially diverse workforce requires moving beyond the traditional focus on wages and working conditions to push for such things as child care assistance, remedial education, and flexible employee benefit plans. Without such a shift in emphasis, unions cannot hope to establish their relevance to the immigrants, ethnic and racial minorities, and working mothers now entering the workforce in greater numbers.

Finally, unions may have to rethink their organizational structures and ways of doing business if they are to avoid being bypassed by changes taking place in many of today's organizations. The competition from abroad faced by corporations and the semipermanent state of fiscal crisis faced by governments are causing organizations in the private and public sectors alike to explore new forms of labor-management cooperation. The increasing number of Quality of Worklife programs, Labor-Management Committees, and Total Quality Management experiments are heralding very real changes in management thinking and operation. Hoping to increase employee commitment and obtain quality improvements, federal agencies and many agencies at the state and local level are adopting cooperative, team-based, and problem-solving approaches to labor-management relations. In addition to strengthening guarantees of job security and fair treatment, these programs often encourage greater employee participation in decision making through the use of semi-autonomous work teams and problem-solving tasks forces. The latter appear to be particularly relevant to such subjects as job redesign, training and development, absenteeism, quality control, workplace safety, and adaptation to technological change.[21] These experiments in labor-management cooperation reject the crude and arbitrary distinction between supervisory and nonsupervisory personnel that has shaped traditional labor-management relations. Unless unions are prepared to participate in developing and implementing these programs they may find themselves replaced by new forms of employee associations.[22]

The foregoing discussion does not lead inevitably to the conclusion that unions are obsolete or that adversarialism has no place in labor-management relations. Some form of employee organization will still be needed for articulating the concerns of workers, adjusting grievances, and producing a motivated workforce. But unions may have to redefine their structures, goals, and ways of doing business. Alternatives to the NLRA framework should be explored that do not reduce matters of mutual concern to a contest between two powerful antagonists. Mechanism should be explored that allow employees to constantly negotiate over a broad range of problems affecting them as employees and affecting the agency's ability to serve the public effectively. In short, the search should continue for better ways to build agreement and foster harmonious labor relations.

■ CASE 14.1   An Unfair Labor Practice?

Linda Garcia is a data entry operator in the state's Department of Revenue. Linda values personal growth and is anxious to develop new skills and advance to more responsible positions within the Department. She also believes employees should organize to pursue their collective interests. She and several co-workers have been soliciting signatures on a petition asking for a union representation election. One day the Bureau Chief calls Linda into his office and informs her that a data entry supervisor position will soon be vacant. He also states that while he has always viewed Linda to be a person with supervisory potential, applicants for the vacant position must be able to "view things from a true manager's perspective." Linda continues to collect signatures, but the union loses in the subsequent election. Two months after the meeting with the Bureau Chief, Linda applies for the data entry supervisor position. She does not receive an interview.

1. Does the Union have grounds to file an unfair labor practice? What factors are likely to be considered in determining whether one has occurred?
2. If an unfair labor practice has occurred, when did it occur?
3. Examine the actions of both Linda Garcia and the Bureau Chief. In your view, should either or both have acted differently?

▲ **EXERCISE 14.1**   The Case of the Intoxicated Snow Plow Operator

Arbitrators will overturn disciplinary decisions if they find that management did not have just cause for its actions. This exercise requires you to put yourself in the shoes of the arbitrator. Using the seven tests of just cause outlined in Chapter 13 as your guide, consider the following facts and render your decision.

The Facts (Although the names have been changed, the following facts are based on actual testimony at an arbitration hearing.) Joe Reynolds had worked as a heavy equipment operator for the City Public Works Department for 24 years. On February 24, 1990, he reported for work at 8:00 A.M. and was sent out on his regular snow removal route. Approximately 15 or 30 minutes later Assistant Superintendent Wilson called Reynolds by radio and told him to proceed to Section 5. Wilson became suspicious when Reynolds slurred his speech and seemed confused about where Section 5 was located. Wilson testified at the hearing that he and the Department Superintendent subsequently caught up with Reynolds a block from the garage. (Reynolds testified that this incident never occurred). Wilson asked Reynolds if he had been drinking and whether he was okay. He also offered to drive him home. Reynolds responded that he had not been drinking and that he was fine. Wilson then instructed him to proceed to Section 5. As Wilson was leaving, Reynolds "floored" the truck, swerved into the southbound lane of traffic and then back to the northbound lane erratically. Wilson ordered him back to the garage by radio and asked for a policeman to meet him back at the garage. Reynolds returned to the garage, where a police officer arrested him when he could not stand on one leg successfully. At the police station Reynolds was given a breathalyzer test which showed a blood alcohol concentration of .27, nearly three times the legal limit. Reynolds was discharged three days later for operating a snowplow under the influence of alcohol. It was his first such offense. Although a state law had apparently been broken, there was no City policy requiring discharge for working while under the influence of alcohol.

At the hearing Reynolds admitted that he had been drinking at a card party the night before but denied the above incident had occurred. He also argued that other employees, including managers, had come to work intoxicated and had never been disciplined. He could not, however, provide firm evidence that others had actually operated vehicles while intoxicated. At the time of the hearing Reynolds had completed a rehabilitation program and was occasionally attending Alcoholics Anonymous meetings.

1. Did the City forewarn Reynolds of the consequences of operating equipment under the influence of alcohol? (Test #1)
2. Did the City adequately investigate the facts before deciding that a policy or rule had been violated? (Test #3) Did the City have substantial proof of guilt? (Test #5)
3. Had the City applied its rules and penalties even-handedly to all employees in similar circumstances? (Test #6)
4. Was the degree of discipline reasonably related to the seriousness of the offense and the record of the employee in his service with the City? (Test #7)
5. Do you find that the City had just cause to discharge Wilson?

If *Labor Arbitration Reports* is available to you, you may wish to check your decision and analysis against that of the arbitrator (97 LA 564).

Notes

1. Charles C. Heckscher, *The New Unionism: Employee Involvement in the Changing Corporation* (New York: Basic Books, 1988); and Karl E. Klare, "The Labor-Management Cooperation Debate: A Workplace Democracy Perspective," *Harvard Civil Rights-Civil Liberties Law Review* 23 (Winter 1988):39–83.

2. Michael T. Leibig and Wendy L. Kahn, *Public Employee Organizing and the Law* (Washington, D.C.: Bureau of National Affairs, 1987), 23–24.

3. Heckscher, *The New Unionism*, 3, note 1.

4. Richard C. Kearney, *Labor Relations in the Public Sector* (New York: Marcel Dekker, 1992), 21, 27.

5. Harry Wellington and Ralph K. Winter, Jr., *The Unions and the Cities* (Washington, D.C.: Brookings Institution, 1971).

6. 296 F. Supp. 1068 (1969).

7. Kearney, *Labor Relations,* 67.

8. John F. Burton, Jr., "Local Government Bargaining and Management Structure," in David Lewin et al., eds., *Public Sector Labor Relations: Analysis and Readings* (Sun Lakes, Arizona: Thomas Horton and Daughters, 1981).

9. Kearney, *Labor Relations,* 109.

10. Joel M. Douglas, "Collective Bargaining and Public Sector Supervisors: A Trend Toward Exclusion?", *Public Administration Review* 47 (November/December 1987):485–497.

11. Marick F. Masters and Robert Atkin, "Bargaining Representation and Union Membership in the Federal Sector: A Free Rider's Paradise," *Public Personnel Management* 18 (Fall 1989):311–323.

12. Kearney, *Labor Relations,* 88.

13. R. Douglas Collins, "Agency Shop in Public Employment, *Public Personnel Management* 15 (Summer 1986):176.

14. Arnold M. Zack, *Public Sector Mediation* (Washington, D.C.: Bureau of National Affairs, 1985), 2–3.

15. Kearney, *Labor Relations,* 343–346.

16. Michael J. Duane, "To Grieve or Not to Grieve: Why 'Reduce it to Writing'?" *Public Personnel Management* 20 (Spring 1991):83–90.

17. 95 S.Ct. 959 (1975).

18. George W. Bohlander, "Public Sector Independent Grievance Systems: Methods and Procedures," *Public Personnel Management* 18 (Fall 1989):339–354.

19. Ibid.

20. Timothy Loney, "Public Sector Labor Relations Research: The First Generation," *Public Personnel Management* 18 (Summer 1989):162–175.

21. Kearney, *Labor Relations,* 419.

22. This theme is developed by Heckscher, *The New Unionism*.

Acknowledgments

Pages 4–5: Excerpt from Benton G. Moeller, "What Ever Happened to the Federal Personnel System?" *Public Personnel Management* 11 (Spring 1982), 6. Published by the International Personnel Management Association.

Page 33: Exhibit 2.3 from Eugene B. McGregor, Jr., *Strategic Management of Human Knowledge, Skills, and Abilities: Workforce Decision-Making in the Postindustrial Era* (San Francisco: Jossey-Bass, 1991).

Page 83: Exhibit 5.3 from Ronald A. Ash, "Job Elements for Task Clusters: Arguments for Using Multi-Methodological Approaches to Job Analysis and a Demonstration of their Utility," *Public Personnel Management* 11 (Spring 1982). Published by the International Personnel Management Association.

Page 88: Exhibit 5.5 modified and reproduced by special permission of the publisher, Consulting Psychologists Press, Inc., Palo Alto, CA 94303. From *Position Analysis Questionnaire* by E. J. McCormick, P. R. Jeanneret and R. C. Mecham. Copyright 1969 by Purdue Research Foundation. All rights reserved. Further reproduction is prohibited without the Publisher's written consent.

Page 122: Exhibit 6.8 from Helen Remick, "The Comparable Worth Controversy," *Public Personnel Management* 10 (Winter 1981), 378. Published by the International Personnel Management Association.

Page 194: Exhibit 9.3 adapted from Debra D. Burrington, "A Review of State Government Employment Application Forms for Suspect Inquiries," *Public Personnel Management* 11 (Spring 1982), 82. Published by the International Personnel Management Association.

Page 229: Exhibit 10.3 from Glenn R. Herbert and Dennis Doverspike, "Performance Appraisal in the Training Needs Analysis Process: A Review and Critique," *Public Personnel Management* 19 (Fall 1990), 254. Published by the International Personnel Management Association.

Page 249: Excerpt reprinted by permission of *Harvard Business Review* from "An Uneasy Look at Performance Appraisal" by Douglas McGregor (September/October 1972). Copyright 1972 by the President and Fellows of Harvard College; all rights reserved.

Pages 250–251: Exhibit 11.2 from Jack Engelhard, "The Company Man," *The New York Times*, February 6, 1982, 23. Copyright © 1982 by The New York Times Company. Reprinted by permission.

Page 254: Exhibit 11.4 adapted from Craig Eric Schneier and Richard W. Beatty, "Integrating Behaviorally-based and Effectiveness-based Methods" *Personnel Administrator* 24 (July 1979): 68. Reprinted with the permission of *HRMagazine* (formerly Personnel Administrator), published by the Society for Human Resource Management, Alexandria, VA.

Page 256: Exhibit 11.5 from Stephen J. Carroll and Craig E. Schneier, *Performance Appraisal and Review Systems* (Glenview, IL: Scott, Foresman, 1982), p. 104.

Page 257: Exhibit 11.6 from Gary P. Latham and Kenneth N. Wexley, *Increasing Productivity Through Performance Appraisal* (Table 3.7), © 1981 by Addison-Wesley Publishing Company, Inc. Reprinted by permission of the publisher.

Page 258: Exhibit 11.7 from Gary P. Latham and Kenneth N. Wexley, *Increasing Productivity Through Performance Appraisal* (pp. 227–231), © 1981 by Addison-Wesley Publishing Company, Inc. Reprinted by permission of the publisher.

Page 260: Exhibit 11.8 from Stephen J. Carroll and Craig E. Schneier, *Performance Appraisal and Review Systems* (Glenview, IL: Scott, Foresman, 1982), 140.

Pages 264–265: Exhibit 11.10 from Norman R. F. Maier, "Three Types of Appraisal Interviews," *Personnel* 34 (March/April 1958): 39.

Page 279: Exhibit 12.1 reprinted by permission of *Harvard Business Review* from "One More Time: How Do You Motivate Your Employees?" by Frederick Herzberg (HBR Classic, Sept./Oct. 1987). Copyright © 1987 by the President and Fellows of Harvard College; all rights reserved.

Page 284: Excerpt from C. Y. Wu, "Refining Concepts of Performance in Development Effectiveness, Profitability and Productivity." Article originally appeared in the *Philippine Journal of Public Administration*, Volume XVII (3) (July 1973): 287–311.

Pages 307–308: Exhibit 13.2 from Don Morrison, ed., The Local Government Institute, *Model Personnel Policies and Procedures,* Tacoma, Washington, 1993.

Pages 334–335: Exhibit 14.2 from Richard C. Kearney, *Labor Relations in the Public Sector* (New York: Marcel Dekker, 1992), 70–71. Reprinted by courtesy of Marcel Dekker, Inc.

Pages 345–346: Exhibit 14.7 from Richard C. Kearney, *Labor Relations in the Public Sector* (New York: Marcel Dekker, 1992), 322–323. Reprinted by courtesy of Marcel Dekker, Inc.

Page 353: Exhibit 14.8 George W. Bohlander, "Public Sector Independent Grievance Systems: Methods and Procedures," *Public Personnel Management* 18 (Fall 1989), 347. Published by the International Personnel Management Association.

Page 354: Exhibit 14.9 George W. Bohlander, "Public Sector Independent Grievance Systems: Methods and Procedures," *Public Personnel Management* 18 (Fall 1989), 352. Published by the International Personnel Management Association.

Index